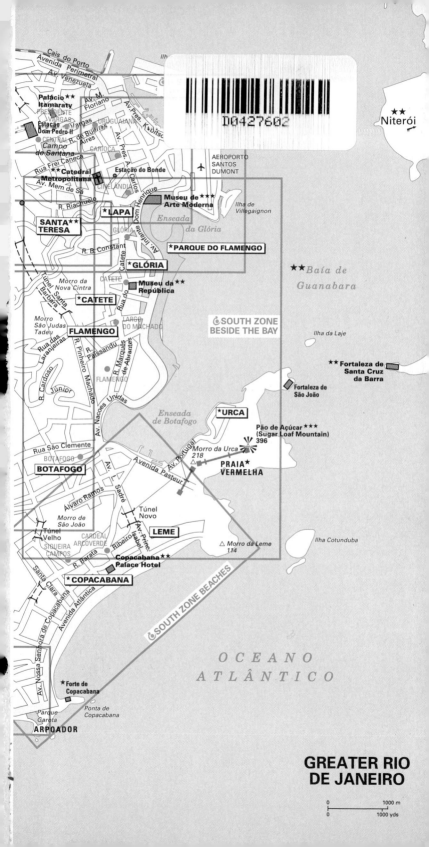

GREATER RIO DE JANEIRO

D0427602

★★ Niterói

Cais do Porto
Avenida Perimetral
Av. Venezuela

Palácio ★★ Itamaraty
Estação Dom Pedro II
Campo de Santana
Rua Frei Caneca
★★ Catedral Metropolitana
Av. Mem. de Sá
R. Riachuelo

SANTA ★★ TERESA
★ LAPA

Estação do Bonde
CINELÂNDIA

Museu de ★★★ Arte Moderna
Ilha de Villegaignon

Enseada da Glória

GLÓRIA
★ PARQUE DO FLAMENGO

R. B. Constant
★ GLÓRIA
CATETE
★ CATETE

Morro da Nova Cintra
Túnel Santa Bárbara

Museu da ★★ República

Morro São Judas Tadeu
FLAMENGO
LARGO DO MACHADO

Rua das Laranjeiras
R. Pinheiro Machado
R. Paissandu
R. Marquês de Abrantes
FLAMENGO

Av. Nações Unidas

★★ Baía de Guanabara

Ilha de Laje

★★ Fortaleza de Santa Cruz da Barra

Fortaleza de São João

AEROPORTO SANTOS DUMONT

SOUTH ZONE BESIDE THE BAY

Enseada de Botafogo

Rua São Clemente
BOTAFOGO

Álvaro Ramos
Sadré

★ URCA

Av. Portugal
Av. Pasteur
Morro da Urca 218
PRAIA ★ VERMELHA

Pão de Açúcar ★★★ (Sugar Loaf Mountain) 396

Túnel Novo
Morro de São João
Túnel Velho
CARDEAL ARCOVERDE
SIQUEIRA CAMPOS
R. Barata
LEME

△ Morro da Leme 114

Ilha Cotunduba

Copacabana ★★ Palace Hotel
★ COPACABANA

Santa Clara
Av. Nossa Senhora de Copacabana
Avenida Atlântica

SOUTH ZONE BEACHES

OCEANO ATLÂNTICO

★ Forte de Copacabana
Parque Garota
ARPOADOR
Ponta de Copacabana

0   1000 m
0   1000 yds

RIO DE JANEIRO

Pão de Açúcar, ©Brasil2/iStockphoto.com

General Manager   Cynthia C. Ochterbeck

THE GREEN GUIDE TO RIO DE JANEIRO

Editor	Rachel Mills
Principal Writers	Françoise Klingen, John Malathronas, Sue Chester, Jane Egginton, Huw Hennessy
Contributors	Carlos-Eduardo Pinho, Milly Salem, Norma Tait, Linda Lee

With a special thanks to the government of the state of Rio de Janeiro:
Governo do Estado do Rio de Janeiro, Secretaria de Turismo Esporte e Lazer do Estado do Rio de Janeiro, Empresa de Turismo do Estado do Rio de Janeiro – TURISRIO.

Production Manager	Natasha G. George
Cartography	GeoNova Publishing, Inc. Thierry Lemasson
Photo Editor	Yoshimi Kanazawa
Layout & Design	Natasha G. George, Rachel Mills
Cover Design	Laurent Muller and Ute Weber
Contact Us	The Green Guide Michelin Maps and Guides One Parkway South Greenville, SC 29615, USA www.michelintravel.com
	Michelin Maps and Guides Hannay House 39 Clarendon Road Watford, Herts WD17 1JA, UK ℰ01923 205240 www.ViaMichelin.com travelpubsales@uk.michelin.com
Special Sales	For information regarding bulk sales, customized editions and premium sales, please contact our Customer Service Departments:

USA	1-800-432-6277
UK	01923 205240
Canada	1-800-361-8236

Note to the Reader
While every effort is made to ensure that all information printed in this guide is correct and up-to-date, Michelin Apa Publications Ltd. accepts no liability for any direct, indirect or consequential losses howsoever caused so far as such can be excluded by law.

One Team…
A Commitment to Quality

There's just one reason our team is dedicated to producing quality travel publications—you, our reader.

Throughout our guides we offer **practical information**, **touring tips** and **suggestions** for finding the best places for a break.

Michelin driving tours help you hit the highlights and quickly absorb the best of the region. Our descriptive **walking tours** make you your own guide, armed with directions, maps and expert information.

We scout out the attractions, classify them with **star ratings**, and describe in detail what you will find when you visit them.

Michelin maps featured throughout the guide offer vibrant, detailed and easy-to-follow outlines of everything from close-up museum plans to international maps.

Places to stay and eat are always a big part of travel, so we research **hotels and restaurants** that we think convey the essence of the destination and arrange them by geographic area and price. We walk you through the best shopping districts and point you towards the host of entertainment and recreation possibilities available.

We **test**, **retest**, **check and recheck** to make sure that our guidebooks are truly just that: a personalised guide to help you make the most of your visit. And if you still want a speaking guide, we list local tour guides who will lead you on all the boat, bus, guided, historical, culinary, and other tours you shouldn't miss.

In short, we remove the guesswork involved with travel. After all, we want you to enjoy exploring with Michelin as much as we do.

The Michelin Green Guide Team

PLANNING YOUR TRIP

©Antonio Lacerda/UPPA/Photoshot

WELCOME TO RIO DE JANEIRO

CONTENTS

DISCOVERING RIO DE JANEIRO

TurisRio

YOUR STAY IN RIO DE JANEIRO

HOW TO USE THIS GUIDE

PLANNING YOUR TRIP

The blue-tabbed PLANNING YOUR TRIP section at the front of the guide gives you **ideas for your trip** and **practical information** to help you organize it. You'll find tours, a host of breaks in the great outdoors, a calendar of events, information on sightseeing, kids' activities, currency, useful words and phrases, and more.

INTRODUCTION

The orange-tabbed INTRODUCTION section explores **Nature** from the climate to the National and State Parks. The **History** section spans from before the colonization of Brazil through to Independence from Portugal and today's Republic. The **Art and Culture** section covers architecture, art, literature, music and Carnival, while the **Country Today** delves into modern Rio de Janeiro.

DISCOVERING

The green-tabbed DISCOVERING section features Rio de Janeiro's Principal Sights, arranged by region, featuring the most interesting local **Sights**, **Walking Tours**, nearby **Excursions**, and detailed **DrivingTours**.

🖹 Contact information, ⊷ admission charges, ⊕ hours of operation, and a host of other **visitor information** is given wherever possible. Admission prices shown are for a single adult, unless otherwise indicated.

STAR RATINGS★★★

Michelin has given star ratings for more than 100 years. If you're pressed for time, we recommend you visit the ★★★, or ★★ sights first:

★★★   Highly recommended
★★   Recommended
★   Interesting

Sidebars

Throughout the guide you will find peach-colored text boxes (like this one), with lively anecdotes, detailed history, and background information.

Address Books – Where to Stay, Eat and more...

WHERE TO STAY

We've made a selection of hotels and arranged them within the districts by price (🅖 *to fit all budgets, see the Legend on the cover flap for an explanation of the price categories*). For the most part, we've selected accommodations based on their unique regional quality, their regional feel, as it were. Wherever you want to go in Rio de Janeiro, you will be able to find a hotel nearby.
🅖 *See Where to Stay at the back of the guide for full reviews.*

WHERE TO EAT

We thought you'd like to know Rio de Janeiro's popular eating spots. So, we selected restaurants that capture the regional experience—those that have a unique regional flavor (🅖 *see the Legend on the cover flap for an explanation of the price categories*). We're not rating the quality of the food per se; as we did with the hotels, we selected restaurants for different districts and categorised them by price to appeal to all wallets.
🅖 *See Where to Eat at the back of the guide for full reviews.*

MAPS

- Rio de Janeiro **City map** with Principal Sights highlighted.
- **District maps** with the Principal Sights highlighted alongside recommended tour routes.

All maps in this guide are oriented north, unless otherwise indicated by a directional arrow. The term "Local Map" refers to a map within the chapter or Tourism Region. A complete list of the maps

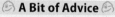

A Bit of Advice

Green advice boxes found in this guide contain practical tips and handy information relevant to the sight in the Discovering section.

found in the guide appears at the back of this book, along with a comprehensive index and list of restaurants and accommodations.
See the map Legend at the back of the guide for an explanation of map symbols.

ORIENT PANELS

Vital statistics are given for each principal sight in the DISCOVERING section:

- **Information**: Tourist Office/Sight contact details.
- **Orient Yourself:** Geographic location of the sight with reference to surrounding boroughs, towns and roads.
- **Parking:** Where to park.
- **Don't Miss:** Unmissable things to do.
- **Organizing Your Time:** Tips on organising your stay; what to see first, how long to spend there, crowd avoidance, market days and more.
- **Especially for Kids:** Sights of particular interest to children.
- **Also See:** Nearby PRINCIPAL SIGHTS featured elsewhere in the guide.

SYMBOLS

Kids	Interesting for Children	&#9855;	Wheelchair Accessible
	Also See		Tours
	Tourist Information	P	On-site Parking
	Hours of Operation	▶	Directions
	Periods of Closure	✗	On-site eating Facilities
	Closed to the Public		A Bit of Advice
	Entry Fees		Warning
	Credit Cards not Accepted		

Contact – Addresses, phone numbers, opening hours and prices published in this guide are accurate at the time of press. We welcome corrections and suggestions that may assist us in preparing the next edition. Please send your comments to:

UK
Michelin Maps and Guides
Hannay House
39 Clarendon Road
Watford, Herts WD17 1JA
travelpubsales@uk.michelin.com
www.michelin.co.uk

USA
Michelin Maps and Guides
Editorial Department
P.O. Box 19001
Greenville,
SC 29602-9001
www.michelintravel.com

Parade of Beija-Flor Samba School in
the Carnival
©Antonio Lacerda/UPPA/Photoshot

MICHELIN DRIVING TOURS

Unless you're intent on driving, a good option is to hire a car and driver through a travel agency. Most have English-speaking drivers who will recommend the best and safest places to stop for photos or a bite to eat.

INLAND: PETRÓPOLIS AND TERESÓPOLIS

Rio de Janeiro to Teresópolis: 78mi/125km; approximately 2hrs.

▶ *Leave Rio by Linha Vermelho. Once past the airport, turn right onto BR-040/116. The road merges with Rod. Washington Luiz, which is a partial toll road. Then follow signs to the center of town.*

The imperial city of **Petrópolis** (*see p 208*) can be visited as a day-trip from Rio. Along the way there are spectacular views of **Parque Nacional da Serra dos Órgãos** (*see p 87*) and the winding mountain roads have lay-bys to pull over in and take photographs of the dramatic scenery. If you have time, and if the weather is good, venture a little further to Itaipava and from there, take the twisting highway to **Teresópolis**. Visit the Parque Nacional da Serra dos Órgãos to view upclose its impressive peaks.

▶ *The drive back to Rio takes a spectacular route through the center of the park.*

COSTA VERDE (GREEN COAST)

Rio de Janeiro to Paraty: 151mi/244km; approximately 4hrs.

😊 A Bit of Advice 😊

The distances shown on **road signs** are based on the outer limits of town, not the city center, which can add considerable time to your journey, particularly for larger cities.

Local Drives

Very few tourists drive in the Rio city center. Taxis are readily available and very reasonably priced and public transport is cheap and efficient. For a local driving route and stops along the way see the following section of Discovering Rio de Janeiro:

WEST ZONE BEACHES

The *Costa Verde*, west of Rio, is one of the most scenic routes in Brazil. It features lush mountain forests running down to sandy beaches, with picturesque colonial villages in sheltered bays. En-route to the historic site of **Paraty** (*see p 204*), you pass pristine offshore islands, including island paradise **Ilha Grande** (*see p 200*).

▶ *For the scenic, though longer coastal route, head north out of Rio along Av. Brasil, joining the BR-101. Continue along this road, passing Angra dos Reis about halfway. Note that the winding road into Paraty has no streetlights, so should not be attempted at night.*

COSTA DO SOL (SUN COAST)

Rio de Janeiro to Búzios: 104mi/167km; approximately 3hrs.

▶ *Leave Rio via the bridge to Niteroi and drive east on BR-101. At Rio Bonito take the exit right onto RJ124. This well-paved road continues eastward, becoming the RJ106, skirts the top of one of the largest lakes in Brazil, the Lagoa de Araruama, and runs north of Cabo Frio.*

East of Rio along the scenic *Costa do Sol* are stunning beaches with clear sparkling water. When you reach the Cabo Frio headland there are a clutch of small but lively beach resorts: Arraial do Cabo, Cabo Frio, and stylish **Búzios** (*see p 196*).

WHEN AND WHERE TO GO

Reveillon, City's New Year's Eve party—fireworks over Praia de Copacabana

©Joseph Luoman/iStockphoto.com

When to Go

Rio de Janeiro lies on the South Atlantic Coast just above the Tropic of Capricorn, an area that enjoys warm tropical temperatures the whole year round. The tropical climate also means that rainfall can occur at any time too. If you want to avoid the crowds and the hottest, most humid weather, the best times to visit the city are from April to June (equivalent to northern hemisphere fall), and between August and October (equivalent to northern hemisphere spring). Temperatures during these periods average around 77°F/25°C during the day, and a more comfortable 59°F/15°C at night.

The peak summer holiday season runs from mid-December to the end of February, when it is hottest and most humid by day and night. Daytime temperatures can reach 104°F/40°C, only falling to about 68°F/20°C at night. Heavy rain showers often burst over the city at the end of the day, but the skies usually clear by nightfall. This is also the busiest time of year, when most Brazilians flock to Rio for their holidays, particularly during NEw Year and Carnival (which is usually mid- or late February). Flights, internal transport, and hotels are heavily booked in advance, the most popular beaches and restaurants are packed, and the price of accommodation rises by up to 30 percent.

Wintertime, between May and September, sees clearer skies, and cooler but drier days. It is a good idea to bring an extra layer of clothing to wear in the cool evenings and early mornings. Be aware too, that if you visit at this time of year, although you will have more space on the beaches the city's normally lively atmosphere becomes more muted.

Month	Temp	Humidity	Rainfall
January	26°C	High	4.9in/125mm
February	26°C	High	4.8in/122mm
March	25°C	Medium	5.1in/130mm
April	24°C	Medium	4.2in/107mm
May	22°C	Medium	3.1in/79mm
June	21°C	Mild	2in/53mm
July	20°C	Mild	1.6in/41mm
August	21°C	Mild	1.7in/43mm
September	21°C	Mild	2.6in/66mm
October	22°C	Medium	3.1in/79mm
November	23°C	Medium	4.1in/104mm
December	25°C	Medium	5.4in/137mm

Where to Go

Rio de Janeiro is first and foremost an enormous playground for lovers of the great outdoors, with its superb beaches and offshore islands; stunning granite peaks looming out of steamy tropical forests, as well as lush parks and gardens decorated with colonial statuary.

Immerse yourself in Rio's beach culture on one of the golden sandy beaches. Scattered from Leme in the east to Grumari in the west, you will find Copacabana, Ipanema, Leblon, São Conrado, Barra da Tijuca, Recreio dos Bandeirantes, Macumba and Prainha, each with its own appeal and special character.

On a clear day, the first-time visitor's priority should be heading up one of its many mountains. Viewing the city of Rio from natural landmarks Sugar Loaf and Corcovado allows you to work out the lay of the land and soak up the vistas of this curvaceous city. There is, however, much more to Rio than meets the eye at first glance. As the nation's former capital, it is a city full of history, heritage, and rich cultural tradition. The architecture of the historic center offers modernist masterpieces including the Metropolitan Cathedral, alongside Eclectic gems such as the Municipal Theater and the grand old 19C mansions in Santa Teresa. Rio is a vibrant living city, whose population of around

five million is spread deep inland and crammed into its sprawling favelas. To find some of the most beautiful green open spaces in South America, follow the coastal road west from Rio and take a trip along the *Costa Verde* (Green Coast).

Suggested Itineraries

GETTING AN OVERVIEW OF RIO DE JANEIRO FROM ABOVE

Morning   Take the Cog railway up Corcovado to the Cristo Redentor statue★★★ to experience views over Rio (♿ *see p 134*).

Afternoon   Bohemian Santa Teresa★★ by vintage trolleybus★★ (♿ *see p 128*). Have lunch on the terrace of Espírito Santa (♿ *see p 236*) then visit Centro Cultural Parque das Ruínas★ (♿ *see p 129*) for stunning city views.

Evening   Walk Pista Cláudio Coutinho★ (♿ *see p 153*) on Morro do Urca, then take the cable car up Pão de Açúcar★★★ (♿ *see p 152*) to watch the evening sunset.

SPORTY RIO DE JANEIRO

Morning   Try your hand at hang gliding in São Conrado (♿ *see p 181*). Join the beach sports at Ipanema★★ (♿ *see p 162*).

Afternoon   Lunch at Garota da Ipanema (♿ *see p 163*) where the famous Bossa Nova song was composed. Tour the football mecca of Maracanã stadium★ (♿ *see p 120*), or better still get tickets for a match (♿ *see p 274*).

Evening   Watch a Samba School rehearsal (♿ *see p 106*) or a show at the Cidade do Samba (♿ *see p 106*).

Praia Vermelha with a view to Pão de Açúcar

R. Mills/Michelin

View from Parque da Cidade—Morro Dois Irmãos, Pão de Açúcar, and Corcovado in a single frame

Y. Kanazawa/Michelin

DOWNTOWN ART AND CULTURE

Morning Visit the Museu de Arte Moderna (MAM)★★★ (*see p 146*) set in Parque do Flamengo★ and then go on to Catedral Metropolitana ★★ (*see p 113*) or Mosteiro de São Bento★★★ (*see p103*).

Afternoon Lunch at Confeitaria Colombo (*see p 234*) in the historic center then stop by at Theatro Municipal★★★ (*see p 109*) for a tour or Centro Cultural Banco do Brasil★★ (*see p 103*) to see their world-classs temporary exhibits.

Evening Dinner and live music show in colorful Lapa★ (*see p 122*)

NATURAL AND TROPICAL RIO DE JANEIRO

Morning Hike Pico da Tijuca★ in the lush Parque Nacional da Tijuca★★★ (*see p 139*). Have a picnic lunch at Bom Retiro (*see p 141*).

Afternoon Visit the gorgeous Jardim Botânico★★★ (*see p 174*) and Parque Catacumba (*see p 171*).

NEARBY RIO DE JANEIRO

Morning Cross Guanabara Bay by ferry to visit Niemeyer's Museu de Arte Contemporanea★★ (*see p 192*).

Afternoon Hire a taxi and visit a couple of Niteroi's beaches along the coastal road. For lunch, drive to Zefiro (*see p 245*) which is in the Fortaleza de Santa Cruz da Barra★★ complex (*see p 193*). Afterward, take a guided tour of the historic fort and enjoy spectacular views across the bay.

Evening Keep the taxi for the return trip and detour to the Parque da Cidade (*see p 194*) for incredible sunset views★★★ from the hang gliding ramp at the highest point of the park.

Local Walking Tours

Listed below are the sights within the Discovering Rio de Janeiro section of the guide, where you can find local walking tours:

KNOW BEFORE YOU GO

Useful Websites

www.rio.rj.gov.br/riotur/en/
Official hub of RioTur, City of Rio de Janeiro Tourism Authority; lots of useful information, including accommodations listings, activities, highlights, and events calendar. There's also a snazzy interactive map.

www.riodejaneiro-turismo.com.br
Useful overview of the main tourist attractions, news, and events, hosted by RioTur.

www.carnivalspecial.com
All about the Rio Carnival, including online tickets to Sambódromo parades and other events, by Rio Carnival Services, a Miami-based travel company.

www.aescrj.com.br
Official site of the Rio de Janeiro Samba School Association *(in Portuguese only)*, with online booking for Carnival seats in the Sambódromo, with useful background information, including maps and details of all the samba schools.

www.rcvb.com.br
For both visitors and businesses, the official website of the Rio Convention and Visitors Bureau has useful information for planning your trip, including advance dates of the Carnival and other major events. Not easy to navigate, but worth the effort to dig out some handy tips.

www.brazilmax.com
Claiming to be the "Hip Guide to Brazil," BrazilMax offers an eclectic mix of information and tips, covering Rio and the whole of Brazil; from art and culture, to sport, ecology, and even political jokes. For those looking beyond the conventional tourist view.

www.riothisweek.com
Covering both Rio and São Paulo, this stylish online magazine covers live music, nightlife, culture, and the latest in trendy lifestyle tips.

www.gringo-rio.com
Chatty tips about what's on, activities, weather, and surf conditions, from unashamedly gringo expats.

www.ikoporan.org
If you're interested in doing volunteer work during your visit, Rio-based Iko Poran is an umbrella group which can link you up with a wide range of group and individual programs, in the city or throughout Brazil.

Tourist Offices

ABROAD

◆ **Australia**
Brazilian Consulate General
17/31 Market Street
Sydney
☏+61 2 9267 4414
pmenezes@brazilsydney.org

◆ **UK**
Brazilian Tourist Office
32 Green Street
London
W1K 7AT
☏+44 (0)20 7399 9000
tourism@brazil.org.uk

◆ **USA**
New York
☏+1 646 378 2126

Los Angeles
☏+1 310 341 8394

IN RIO DE JANEIRO

RioTur (*see Useful Websites above*) is the official tourism authority, and has various information kiosks around the city; free maps and useful leaflets are available and most staff speak English. At the International Airport, there are desks open daily 6am–midnight:

Terminal 1, International Arrivals, ✆21 3398 4077; Domestic Arrivals, ✆21 3398 3034. **Terminal 2**, International Arrivals, ✆21 3398 2245; Domestic Arrivals, ✆21 3398 2246. The information desk at the Rodoviária Novo Rio (**Central Bus Station**) is open daily, from 8am–8pm; ✆21 2263 4857/3213 1800.

In **Copacabana**, there is an information kiosk on Avenida Princesa Isabel, 183 *(the main road dissecting Copacabana and Leme)*; open Monday–Friday, 9am–6pm; ✆21 2541 7522/2542 8004/2542 8080.

There is also a **phone information service** in Portuguese and English, *Alô Rio*, which is open Monday–Friday, 9am–6pm; ✆21 2542 8080/2542 8004/0800 285 0555.

International Visitors

EMBASSIES & CONSULATES

Brazilian Embassies Overseas:

- **Australia**
  19 Forster Crescent, Yarralumla
  Canberra, ACT 2600
  GPO BOX 1540
  ACT 2601
  ✆+61 (2) 6273 2372
  brazilemb@brazil.org.au
  www.brazil.org.au

- **Canada**
  450 Wilbrod Street,
  Ottawa,
  Ontario,
  Canada, K1N 6M8
  ✆+1 613 237 1090/+1 613 755 5160
  mailbox@brasembottawa.org
  www.brasembottawa.org

- **UK**
  32 Green Street
  London
  W1K 7AT
  ✆+44 020 7399 9000
  info@brazil.org.uk
  www.brazil.org.uk

- **USA**
  3006 Massachusetts Avenue, NW
  Washington, DC
  20008-3634
  ✆+1 202 238 2805
  trade@brasilemb.org
  www.brasilemb.org

Consulates in Rio:
🕙*Most consulates are open Mon–Fri, 9am–noon, some also open in the afternoons; call first to check.*

- **Australia**
  Veirano e Advogados Associados
  Avenida Presidente Wilson 231
  Centro
  ✆21 3824 4624
  www.brazil.embassy.gov.au

- **Canada**
  Avenida Atlántica 1130, 5th floor
  Copacabana
  Atlântica Business Center
  Copacabana 22021-000
  ✆21 2543 3004
  rio@international.gc.ca

- **UK**
  British Consulate-General
  Praia do Flamengo 284, 2nd floor
  Flamengo
  ✆21 2555 9600
  brazil.consular@fco.gov.uk
  http://ukinbrazil.fco.gov.uk/en

- **USA**
  American Consulate-General
  Avenida Presidente Wilson 147
  Centro
  ✆21 3823 2000
  ircbsb@state.gov
  www.embaixadaamericana.org.br

Entry Requirements

PASSPORTS AND VISAS

On arrival, non-Brazilian visitors fill out an immigration form, part of which must be kept in your passport, to be shown on departure.
A visa is not required to enter Brazil as a tourist for passport holders from EU countries. Citizens of the US, Canada,

and Australia do need a visa; available from your nearest Brazilian diplomatic office (⌖ see addresses above). Visitors' passports must be valid for at least six months; a return ticket and proof of sufficient funds may be requested on arrival. Visitors may stay for up to 90 days, a period which is extendable at the discretion of the Federal Police, for a further 90 days. Tourists are not allowed to work in Brazil.

CUSTOMS REGULATIONS

In addition to clothes and personal items, visitors may bring in one of each of the following items: radio, CD player, laptop computer, movie camera and still camera. Visitors entering the country can also bring ½ gal/2 liters of alcohol and 400 cigarettes for personal use, but no dairy products.

Duty free—unlike many other countries, visitors can purchase duty-free goods on arrival in Brazil as well on departure. Only non-Brazilian currencies are accepted, or bank cards.

Facility for the disabled on Praia de Ipanema

Y. Kanazawa/Michelin

Health

Private health, dental care and pharmacies in Rio are of a high standard. Private medical care is expensive; visitors are strongly urged to take out medical insurance.

Inoculations

Rio de Janeiro is not in a malaria or yellow fever-risk area.

An international certificate of vaccination against yellow fever is compulsory, however, if you are planning to visit many other areas of Brazil, including the Amazon Basin and Pantanal regions. It is also compulsory if, within three months prior to your arrival in Brazil, you have visited affected areas of Africa and South America. For details, visit *www.MASTA.org*.

There are some mosquitoes in Rio, particularly prevalent during hot, wet weather. Dengue fever is a flu-like illness, carried by mosquitoes, which has had serious outbreaks in recent years. There is no vaccine, but you can protect yourself by using a good repellent and wearing long-sleeved shirts and trousers in mosquito areas. A polio vaccination is compulsory for children aged between three months and five years *(proof must be shown, such as the vaccination booklet or a letter from your GP)*.

Accessibility

Facilities for visitors with disabilities are scarce in Brazil, and in Rio are limited mostly to airports, shopping malls, and smarter hotels and restaurants. There are special elevators and platform ramps for wheelchair users on certain stations on the Metrô network. For details see *www.metrorio. com.br/acessibilidade.asp*.

Coop Taxi RJ offers a customized taxi service for people with reduced mobility; ☎ *21 3295 9606*.

GETTING THERE AND GETTING AROUND

By Plane

Rio de Janeiro is served by all the major international airlines with regular flights from North America, Europe, and the rest of the world. It has two major airports: **Galeão Antonio Carlos Jobim International Airport** serves all international and most internal destinations, while downtown **Santos Dumont Airport** is used mainly for a commuter service to and from São Paulo. Allow up to an hour to get to the international airport during rush-hour periods. Check-in procedures are thorough but can be slow; allow two hours for domestic departures, three hours for international flights.

An **international departure tax** of US$38 is usually included in your ticket but, if not, you must pay either in US$ or reais, before leaving the country.

ANTONIO CARLOS JOBIM INTERNATIONAL AIRPORT

Rio's main International Airport, formerly known as Galeão, is on Ilha do Governador, an island in Guanabara Bay, some 13mi/20km north of the city center (*21 3398 4526; www.infraero. gov.br*). It has two adjacent terminals, connected by a moving walkway: most flights use Terminal One, with the newer Terminal Two for other international and domestic flights. The airport has a RioTur information desk, bureaux de change (câmbio), ATMs, post office, left-lugage office, shops, restaurants, and cafes.

SANTOS DUMONT AIRPORT

Rio's domestic airport overlooks Guanabara Bay, a 10min walk east of Cinelândia Metrô station (*21 3814 7070; www.infraero.gov.br*). The scheduled flights from here are mainly hourly weekday commuter shuttles to São Paulo, with connections to other local and international departures.

AIRPORT TRANSFERS

From the international airport a good option is to buy a prepaid fare at the desk in the arrivals hall. Rates range from R$58 to Flamengo, and R$60 to R$67 to the beach hotels of Copacabana and Ipanema. Prepaid fares cost about 30 percent more than regular taxis, but you can relax and enjoy your first views of the city without worrying about the unpredictable cost. Minimum charge is R$3.60, and the journey to Copacabana, for instance, should cost about R$40.

There are also standard taxis to hire and a special hourly shuttlebus service, which goes to the city center, Santos Dumont Airport, and to the major hotels.

REGIONAL AIRLINES

Gol and Varig
(National—terminal one)
(International—terminal two)
International Airport
*0300 115 2121
www.voegol.com.br

Tam
(National and International—terminal two)
International Airport
*0800 570 5700
www.tam.com.br/

😊 A Bit of Advice 😊

Be aware of taxi scams targeted at newly arrived visitors; prices vary widely and some less than scrupulous drivers will take you on a scenic route, doubling the rate accordingly.

MAJOR AIRLINES

The following airlines use terminal one:

✈ **Aerolineas Argentinas**
International Airport
☎ 21 3398 3737
www.aerolineas.com.ar

✈ **Air France**
International Airport
☎ 21 3398 4526
www.airfrance.com

✈ **American Airlines**
Av. Pres. Wilson 165
Centro
☎ 21 3398 3259
www.aa.com

✈ **British Airways**
International Airport
☎ 21 3393 8944
www.britishairways.com

✈ **Continental Airlines**
Av. Atlântica 1702
Copacabana
☎ 21 2257 2105
www.continental.com

✈ **Iberia**
International Airport
☎ 21 3398 3168
www.iberia.com

✈ **Lufthansa**
Av. Nilo Pecanha 50
Centro
☎ 21 2219 3360
www.lufthansa.com

✈ **United Airlines**
Praca Floriano 55
Centro
☎ 21 2217 1950
www.united.com

By Ship

INTERNATIONAL CRUISES

Princess and Crystal Cruises include Rio within longer itineraries, visiting other South American destinations with sailings from New York or Miami. There are no regular "point to point" cruises from the UK or USA to Rio.

Cruise Lines
Princess
Richmond House
Terminus Terrace
Southampton
SO14 3PN, UK
☎ +44 845 3555 800

Crystal Cruises
2049 Century Park East
Suite 1400
Los Angeles
CA 90067, USA
☎ (toll-free) +1 888 722 0021/
+1 866 446 6625

CARGO SHIPS

The only way to go by water from the UK to Brazil is on a cargo ship via occasional sailings from Tilbury and Southampton. The transatlantic crossing takes up to two weeks and although cabins are comfortable, with some amenities, the long journey and high prices *(£1,500–£2,000 return)* rules out most travelers.

Cargo Shipping Agency
Strand Travel
357 Strand
London
WC2R 0HS, UK
☎ +44 020 7010 9290
www.strandtravel.co.uk

PORT

Cruise ships dock in the Pier Mauá terminal by Praça Mauá; a short walk to downtown for bus and subway services, but it is always safer to take a taxi, especially after dark as the area around Praça Mauá can be dangerous late at night. ☎ 21 2516 2618.

LOCAL FERRIES

Going across Guanabara Bay to Niteroi and the islands makes for a pleasant and picturesque excursion, and there are plenty of ferries, catamarans, and hydrofoils available. Ferries depart from the Estação das Barcas ferryport by Praça XV Novembro.

To **Niteroi**—*every 10–30min, daily 6am–11:30pm; R$2.50 one way; 20min journey.*

To **Ilha Paquetá**—*nine departures daily from 6am–11:30pm; Mon–Fri R$4.50 one way; Sat and Sun R$17 return; 70min journey.*

To **Cocotá, Ilha do Governador**—*10 departures Mon–Fri only, from 8:10am–7:50pm (plus 9pm on Fri); R$3.40 one way; 55min journey.*

To **Charitas**—*by catamaran: Mon–Fri only, every 15min from 6:50am–9pm; R$7/8 one way; 20min journey.*

By Train

Trains are only used by people of low income—they serve the suburbs and the Baixada Fluminense. They are not useful for most tourist destinations.

By Subway

&See also Metro Map page 22.
Rio's modern, air-conditioned subway system (Metrô) is small but efficient, clean and comfortable. It's the quickest way to travel from downtown to the main Zona Sul beach areas *(20min to Copacabana; no station as yet in Ipanema/Leblon—due to join network in 4 to 5 years).*
There are two lines: **Line 1** goes from Cantagalo, in Copacabana to Saens Peña in Tijuca district; **Line 2** from Estácio to Pavuna. The Metrô/Bus system links stations with other areas of the city.

Cantagalo Metrô station
Y. Kanazawa/Michelin

Trains run Monday to Saturday, 5am to midnight. On Sundays and public holidays the Metrô runs from 7am to 11pm. Extended timetable during New Year's and Carnival when trains run all night.

Metrô Rio
&0800 595 1111
www.metrorio.com.br

A single Metrô ticket costs R$2.30. Multiple tickets are available, but are no cheaper.

By Coach/Bus

City buses are cheap, plentiful, and go just about everywhere, with stops along all the main roads. You have to flag the bus down when it approaches the bus stop. The entrance is usually at the front and the exit at the rear. Have the correct money ready as you have to go through a turnstile to get inside. Buses are considered safe during the day, but beware of pickpockets during crowded rush-hours (avoid standing near the exit), and it is better to take a taxi by night, especially if you are carrying luggage or other valuables.

Rio Onibus
&(toll-free) 0800 5952000
http://www.rio.rj.gov.br/smtr

Single journeys cost R$2 to R$3.50.

Metrô Rio
Subway system

Bicicletário
Bycicle Parking

Horário de funcionamento / Subway schedule
Segunda a sábado: 5h a meia-noite / Monday to Saturday: 5AM to midnight
Domingos e feriados: 7h às 23h / Sundays and Holidays: 7AM to 11 PM

Tempo de viagem / Travel Time (aproximado):
Siqueira Campos - Cinelândia: 14'56   Estácio - Maracanã: 4'18"
Siqueira Campos - Saens Peña: 28'28"   Estácio - Pavuna: 32'27"

0800 595 1111
WWW.METRORIO.COM.BR

METRÔ RIO

LONG-DISTANCE BUSES

The main inter-city bus terminal is Novo Rio Rodoviaria, Av. Francisco Bicalho 1, Santo Cristo, in the old port area, near downtown (*021/3213-1800; www.novorio.com.br*). Buses from here travel across the entire state, including Petropólis, Paraty, and Buzios. For safety, it's advisable to take a taxi rather than walk to the terminal. Prepaid taxi vouchers are available at the booth next to the taxi stand.

By Car

Driving in Rio de Janeiro city is not recommended for the faint-hearted. Brazilians drive fast, and rarely use signals, or brakes. Traffic can be maddeningly congested; only wily taxi drivers know their way around the gridlock.
Unless you are on toll roads, driving at night outside the city is not recommended. Toll roads are becoming

increasingly popular around Brazil but they can be expensive.

Be very alert on inter-city highways: the traffic is fast, and often congested with long-distance heavyweight trucks. There is no legal requirement for truck drivers to make compulsory stops to rest; many therefore drive for long distances and accidents caused by tired drivers have been known to happen.

Beware of drivers braking suddenly to avoid being photographed by cameras at radar speed traps, and also beware the many speed bumps that are not always well marked and can be hard to spot.

Driving in Rio

CAR RENTAL

There are many car rental agencies; minimum age is 25, and you need a credit card and full driving licence (preferably international though foreign licences widely accepted by major companies). The police will accept foreign licences as long as you are in the country as a tourist (be prepared to prove this with the stamp and form in your passport (*see p 17*).

🚗 **Avis**
   Avenida Princesa Isabel, 350
   Copacabana 22011-010
   ✆ 21 2543 8481
   www.avis.com

🚗 **Europcar**
   Avenida Princesa Isabel, 245
   Copacabana
   ✆ 21 2275 0460
   www.europcar.com

🚗 **Localiza**
   Avenida das Américas, 679 Loja C
   Barra da Tijuca
   ✆ 21 2494 5762/2493 4477
   www.localiza.com.br

😊 **A Bit of Advice** 😊

There are roadside diners, called **lanchonetes**, on major roads around Brazil, where long-distance buses make regular stops. Meals here are good value, and they usually have a store and public restrooms.

GASOLINE OR ALCOHOL

Older cars run on just alcohol (ethanol), or just gasoline (petrol), whereas newer cars run on both. At the time of writing, a liter of gasoline costs approximately R$2.60 and alcohol is about 65 percent of this price.

All service stations have gasoline, but outside of main towns they might not have alcohol.

INSURANCE

Insurance is compulsory so make sure this is included in the price of your car rental. Be sure to check the car carefully for damage before you drive out of the garage; otherwise, you may be liable when you return it.

ROAD REGULATIONS

City center speed limit is 50mph/ 80kph, and 68mph/110kph on highways. Driving under the influence of alcohol is strictly prohibited; a recently introduced zero-tolerance law has been passed and the permitted limit is 0.2 grams of alcohol to a liter of blood. This means a beer or a glass of wine will take you over the legal limit. Always carry your passport and driving licence with you.

😊 **Tire Safety** 😊

Proper inflation is essential for the performance and longevity of the tire. Operating your tires underinflated can also result in a tire failure.

PARKING

Parking can be a problem, both finding a space and for the security of the car (leave no valuables visible inside); it's worth paying a little more for a hotel that has a secure garage.

IN CASE OF ACCIDENT

In emergencies dial the police on **190** or dial **193**, which is staffed by the local fire department. This service is in Portuguese only, but passers-by are likely to have cellphones and can phone on your behalf. When you hire a car, make sure that the car rental agency gives you a list of phone numbers to call in case of accidents.

By Taxi

Official taxis are yellow with a blue stripe along the side; meters are placed in the front window, with fares clearly displayed. (*Minimum fare 2009 pricing: R$4.30. Tarifa 1 applies Mon–Fri, 6am–9pm; Tarifa 2 is a higher charge all day Sun and 9pm–6am*). There are taxis which you can book and which give fixed fares. If you use a taxi lined up outside a hotel, the fixed fare is likely to be considerably higher.

Coop Taxi RJ
(Special service for people with reduced mobility, plus tours with interpreters; 24-hour assistance.)
℘ 21 3295 9606
http://especialcooptaxirj@ig.com.br

- **Coopatur Radiotaxi**
  ℘ 21 3885 1000/2573 1009

- **Cootramo**
  ℘ 21 3976 9944/3976 9945

- **RoyalCoop**
  ℘ 21 2548 5897

- **Transcoopass**
  ℘ 21 2590 6891

- **Transcootour**
  ℘ 21 2590 2300

By Bicycle

There are a number of cycle lanes and several bike rental companies in the beach areas. Cycling on the main roads is not recommended. For a scenic ride, the Lagoa Rodrigo de Freitas has a bike and running track around its perimeter; there are also special beachside paths along Copacabana, Ipanema, Leblon, Barra da Tijuca and Recreio dos Bandeirantes. Adventure companies run offroad excursions through mountainside trails (👁 see Outdoor Fun p 31).

BIKE RENTAL

Rental rates vary widely, as does the quality of bikes; from R$10–100 per day; R$30–160 per week.

Bike & Lazer
www.bikeelazer.com.br

Ipanema—Rua Visconde de Pirajá 135 loja B ℘ 21 2267 7778
Laranjeiras—Rua das Laranjeiras 58 loja A ℘ 21 2285 7941

Special Bike
www.specialbikebotafogo.com.br

Botafogo—Rua São João Batista, 28-A ℘ 21 2539 3980
Copacabana—Rua Barata Ribeiro, 458-D ℘ 21 2547 9551,
Ipanema—Rua Teixeira de Melo, 53 – Lojas J/K ℘ 21 2513 3951
Jardim Botanico—Rua Jardim Botânico, 719 – Loja 2 ℘ 21 2239 9700

Projeto Pedala Rio
The pedala project is a bike scheme where registered members can rent bikes from "stations" in the city. The stations hold 10 to 14 bicycles and are open from 6am to 10pm. To use the bikes, the rider must register online (*site is in Portuguese*) and pay a fee of R$10 for a day pass, R$30 for a week and R$350 for a year. Bank account details are stored as R$350 is charged to the account if the bike is not returned. *www.Mobilicidade.com.br.*

WHAT TO SEE AND DO

Sightseeing

If your time is limited, we have suggested itineraries in *Where to Go* (🕮 *see p 14*). The following is a wider selection of sights and activities.

ADMISSION TIMES

Major attractions, such as **Sugar Loaf** ★★★ (🕮 *see p 152*) and **Corcovado** ★★★ (🕮 *see p 134*) are open daily, although most museums and galleries are closed on Mondays. The **Metropolitan Cathedral** ★★ (🕮 *see p 113*) and major churches are open daily, but show respect for the congregation if you are visiting during a service.

BEACHES

Rio de Janeiro's beautiful beaches are the city's playgrounds, with **Copacabana Beach** ★★★ (🕮 *see p 159*) and **Ipanema Beach** ★★★ (🕮 *see p 162*) as world-famous icons. Early every morning in high season, tractors with rollers flatten down the sands ready for the coming crowds. They're a great social leveler for Cariocas, where everyone, rich and poor, dresses down in just a t-shirt and pair of Bermuda shorts for men, and *tanga* and *canga* (bikini and sarong) for women. The only sensible footwear is flip-flops: *havaianas*.

Each beach attracts different crowds with their own agenda: Copacabana is the best for beach soccer (particularly between Postos 4 & 5), but it is the beach, rather than the neighborhood that is the highlight; Ipanema remains the trendiest spot for Rio's beautiful set, and best for beach volleyball and futevôlei; **São Conrado** is the landing pad for hang gliders; and outlying **Barra da Tijuca** ★★, **Recreio dos Bandeirantes** ★, **Prainha** ★★ and **Grumari** ★ (🕮 *see west zone beaches*) are the best beaches for surfers. Joggers, cyclists, and body-beautiful keep-fit fanatics work out along the

😊 A Bit of Advice 😊

Although Rio de Janeiro's tanga bikinis may look virtually invisible, going topless or naked on public beaches is not socially acceptable. The only naturist beach, for men and women, is Abrico, tucked away at the far end of Grumari.

Não é permitida a prática de *topless*

Topless is not allowed

Y. Kanazawa/Michelin

pavements of all the main beaches. For families with young children, there are play-areas on and near some of the beaches (🕮 *see p 34*). Beaches closer to downtown, such as **Botafogo** and **Flamengo**, are popular with local residents, but unfortunately the water is too polluted now for safe swimming. All you need is a towel or a beach-mat and suncream; leave valuables in your hotel safe and don't even bother bringing a book; people-watching is much more fun. There are plenty of snack bars lining the oceanfront, selling cool, refreshing coconut milk; and vendors ply the beach offering ice-cream, hot dogs and all manner of snacks. Shady umbrellas are dotted along the sands and you can hire deck chairs for about R$4 a day. Being the Atlantic coast, the water is not that warm, and the surf can be

😊 A Bit of Advice 😊

Don't forget to drink lots of water and wear plenty of sunscreen!

high, so be wary of the dangerous undertow. There are *postos* (lifeguard posts) at intervals along the oceanfront, running from east to west, with Posto 1 on **Leme Beach**(*see p 158*) to Posto 12 at the far end of Leblon; they are manned all day and have freshwater showers for bathers.

On Sundays, one lane of the beachfront road is closed from Aterro do Flamengo all the way to Leblon, giving more space for strolling families, cyclists, skaters, and joggers.

MUSEUMS AND GALLERIES

With its rich cultural history and past prominence as the Brazilian capital, Rio is well served by many excellent museums and galleries; from major institutions such as the Modern Art Museum, to small specialist museums like the Casa do Pontal, with its superb collection of folk art. Many museums are housed in beautiful buildings, both modern and colonial, and some are set in lush grounds.

Best Major Collections
Museu de Arte Moderna (MAM)★★★
Housed in a Postmodern building designed by Alfonso Eduardo Reidy, this impressive collection has some 11,000 modern artworks by leading Brazilian artists; it also holds special

Museu de Arte Moderna

Y. Kanazawa/Michelin

exhibitions of design and photography. Set in landscaped grounds designed by Roberto Burle Marx.

Museu Nacional de Belas Artes★
The country's largest collection of Brazilian art, comprising some 20,000 pieces from the 17C to 20C; housed in the former home of the Brazilian Academy of Fine Arts. The museum also contains a few European and other foreign works.

Museu Histórico Nacional★
Rio's largest museum contains an absorbing portrayal of Brazilian history, from the pre-Columbian period to modern times. The National History Museum is based in an impressive colonial building that was the city's former arsenal.

Museu Internacional de Arte Naïf (MIAN)
One of the world's best collections of naïve art, with more than 8,000 pieces from Brazil and abroad brought together 40 years ago by French jewelry designer Lucien Finkelstein. Housed in a lovely old mansion set in landscaped gardens.

Museu da República★★
This historical museum, set in the beautifully restored Catete Palace, is best-known as the site where President Getúlio Vargas committed suicide in 1954. It has a fine collection of Republican artifacts and artworks, as well as an arthouse cinema, cafe, and bookstore.

Historic House Museums
Museu Imperial★★★
The Neo-classical Palácio Imperial de Petrópolis is the home of the most visited museum in Brazil. This palace was the summer residence for the imperial family and the rooms are faithfully preserved and beautifully presented.

Museu Villa-Lobos
A specialist collection relating to Latin America's greatest classical composer, who produced more than 1,000 works during the first half of the 20C, includ-

Parque Nacional da Tijuca

Y. Kanazawa/Michelin

ing his best-known piece, *Bachianas Brasileiras*. The museum contains a huge musical archive, as well as personal items, including his piano, photographs, and artworks.

Museu da Chácara do Ceu★★

A small but excellent collection of modern art, furniture, and artifacts, spaciously exhibited in a light and airy villa on a Santa Teresa hilltop; its shady grounds give great views of downtown and surrounding hillsides.

Specialist Museums
Museu da Casa do Pontal★★

This highly reputable folk art museum contains a large collection of some 8,000 pieces, with wooden and ceramic artifacts and tableaux, representing Brazilian life from the 1950s to the present day; it is set in large, ecologically conserved grounds.

Museu do Indio★

This museum, supported by Funai (the National Indian Foundation), is dedicated to Brazil's indigenous peoples; with an impressive collection of artifacts, documentation, and photographs of the 270 groups living in the country today. It also runs special exhibitions, seminars, and educational workshops.

PARKS AND GARDENS

If the beaches get too hot, Rio de Janeiro has acres of shady green spaces where you can take refuge; from intimate manicured lawns to vast expanses of tropical forest in its enveloping mountainsides.

Jardim Botânico★★★

The elegant and peaceful botanical gardens were established in the 19C to nurture imported species, with the Avenue of Palms its awe-inspiring centerpiece. Today, the Giant Amazon lily-ponds, fountains, orchids, and hummingbird garden make this one of Rio's top attractions, recognized by UNESCO as a World Biosphere Reserve.

Parque Nacional da Tijuca★★★

The city's lungs, this huge national park spreads around the city, encompassing major sights including Corcovado. Hundreds of trails criss-cross the park's forests, with summits such as Pico da Tijuca and Pedra da Gávea offering some of the best views of the whole city.

Sítio Roberto Burle Marx★★★

This enormous estate is a garden nursery of thousands of plants, both native and imported species. The former banana plantation also contains a 17C chapel, a reconstructed old coffee warehouse, and artworks displayed in the famous designer's original studio.

Parque do Flamengo★

The neat lawns and wide green open space of this park is often referred to as "Aterro" (landfill) as this splendid park was reclaimed from the ocean. Home to Museu de Arte Moderna, it is a lovely family-oriented place to relax and play sports.

Parque Ecológico Chico Mendes

A wildlife sanctuary named after the ecologist who was assassinated in 1988 because of his activism. Guided tours take visitors around the 222acre/90ha grounds, which are home to many birds and reptiles; there is also an observation tower and children's playground.

CHURCHES AND MONASTERIES

Rio de Janeiro has many superb historic churches and monasteries, most of which are concentrated around Centro, Lapa, and Santa Teresa.

Igreja da Candelária★

The opulent Candelária Church was made with marble from Verona and designed after Lisbon's Basilica. First built in 1775, the imposing twin-domed church was restored in 1898.

Igreja de Nossa Senhora da Glória do Outeiro★★

This gorgeous Baroque jewel stands on a leafy hilltop overlooking Gua-

Igreja de Nossa Senhora da Glória do Outeiro

Y. Kanazawa/Michelin

nabara Bay. Its 18C interior has an intricately carved wooden altar, with blue and white tiles lining the walls.

Igreja e Mosteiro de São Bento★★★

Founded in 1590, this is the oldest monastery–church in the city and also considered one of the loveliest in Brazil. The highlight of São Bento's Baroque interior is the Blessed Sacrament Chapel, a marvel of Rococo ornamentation.

Catedral Metropolitana★★

This striking modern church (1976), designed by Edgar de Oliveira da Fonseca in the form of a conical pyramid, is sometimes unkindly compared to an upturned bucket, but it stands proud among downtown's business towers and the Arcos de Lapa.

Igreja e Convento de Santo Antônio★

The church and monastery of Santo Antônio is the second-oldest convent in Rio, dating from 1726. One of its most important religious icons is its statue of Santo Antônio, which attracts Carioca devotees praying for a spouse.

Igreja da Ordem Terceira de São Francisco da Penitencia★★

This stunning Baroque church is accessed by the same entrance as Santo Antônio, beside Carioca Metrô station. Completed in 1736 it has an impressive gold interior and wood decoration.

VIEWS

With its intricate topography of curvaceous bays, granite domes, and lush jungle hillsides, Rio is a photogenic paradise. There are plenty of *mirantes* (lookout points), from where you are rewarded with superb panoramas of the city and its surrounds.

The spectacular panorama from **Corcovado**★★★ (see p 134) is best viewed in the morning before the air becomes hazy; if coming by road, stop en-route for breathtaking views from the **Dona Marta viewpoint**★★★ (*see p 139*), 1,115ft/340m above sea level. The city parks, forts and beaches of **Niterói**★★ (*see p 192*) offer great views looking back over Guanabara Bay, particularly of **Sugar Loaf**★★★ (*see p 152*) at sunset. The mountain itself also has amazing views over Rio's beaches and up to Corcovado.

There are various other viewpoints on the way up to **Tijuca National Park**★★★ (*see p 139*); the park's highest summits: Pico da Tijuca, Pico do Papagaio and Pedra da Gávea offer the most complete views of the city.

From the **Centro Cultural Parque das Ruínas**★ (*see p 129*) and other parts of **Santa Teresa**★★ (*see p 128*), there are beautiful views of downtown's modern skyline, as well as of Sugar Loaf and Corcovado. **Catacumba Park**(*see p 171*), a wooded park by Lagoa Rodrigo de Freitas, has a trail going up the Morro dos Cabritos and from the peak there are fantastic **views**★★ of Ipanema, Leblon, and Tijuca Forest.

TOURS

Art and Culture
Local experts take guided walking tours and excursions around the city, covering diverse themes including film, theatre, fine art, photography, fashion, history, and architecture.

- **Acadetur**
  ☎ 21 3113 1920

- **Iko Poran Community Tour**
  www.ikoporan.org
  ☎ 21 3852 2916

- **Lisa Rio Tours**
  www.lisariotours.com
  ☎ 21 2237 4615/9894 6867

- **Novos Rumos**
  ☎ 21 2247 7662

- **Roteiros Culturais**
  www.culturalrio.com.br
  ☎ 21 9911 3829

- **Solar de Santa Turismo**
  www.solardesanta.com
  ☎ 21 2221 2117

Culinary Tours
Matching the cultural melting pot of Rio's inhabitants, the city offers a fabulous array of cuisines from around the whole country. From the national classic *feijoada* to African-influenced seafood concoctions from the northeast; children's menus also provided. Private cooking courses are available, most lasting a couple of hours, at the end of which you get to eat your own gastronomic creation. From R$108 per person, including ingredients.

- **Cook Rio**
  www.cookrio.com

- **Curumim Eco Cultural Tours**
  www.curumim.tur.br
  ☎ 21 2217 7199 / 9999 4157

Favela Tours
There are more than 600 *favelas* or shantytowns in Rio, home to more than a million cariocas, twenty percent of the city's population. Despite the favelas' notoriety, most inhabitants lead peaceful, hardworking lives in difficult conditions. Organized tours offer a fascinating insight into the favelas; some include interaction with the residents in their schools and community workshops, from funk band gigs to martial arts classes. A visit is highly recommended but be sure to go with a recognized tour operator.

- **Favela Tours**
  www.favelatour.com.br
  ☎ 21 3322 2727

- **Mangueira**
  www.mangueira.com.br
  ☎ 21 3872 6786 / 3872 6787

- **Pousada Favelinha**
  www.favelinha.com

- **2 Bros Foundation**
  www.faveladodarocinha.com.br

Music

The official Carnival only lasts for five days a year, but luckily you can experience the exuberant atmosphere from as early as July, by visiting the city's 14 samba "schools" at their weekly rehearsals for the big event. These are open parties, rather than shows for spectators, and are great fun but heaving with people; some of the samba schools are in the favelas, so an organized tour might be safer and more relaxed.

Other specialist music tour guides take visitors to burgeoning alternative events, such as funk rhythm parties in the favelas.

◆ **Baile Funk Tour**
www.bealocal.com
℘ 21 9643 0366

◆ **Henrique Joriam**
www.agenteseveporai.com.br
℘ 21 2205 6048

◆ **Rio Carnival**
www.rio-carnival.net
℘ USA/Canada +1 877 559 0088;
UK +44 203 355 6343

One of Rio's newest sights for visitors is the **Cidade do Samba** (☀ see p 106), opened in 2005, which is a purpose-built compound in the re-emerging port district, and intended to be the new cultural home of Carnival. Each samba school has its own atelier here, where you can see the giant floats in construction; costumes are also on display and there are weekly shows in the build-up to the Carnival parade.

Soccer Tours

Maracanã★ stadium tours (☀ see p 121) take fans into the heart of what was once the world's biggest stadium: inside the changing rooms, showers, and an indoor warm-up pitch. Plus, there is a museum, store, and footprints in cement of the great Brazilian football stars through the ages, including Garrincha, Pele, Zico, and Roberto Dinamite.
Football matches (☀ see p 274) usually take place late afternoons; tour

agencies take groups from hotels in air-conditioned buses, avoiding the crush on the public buses and nearest Metrô station (Maracanã).

◆ **Be A Local**
www.bealocal.com
℘ 21 9643 0366

◆ **Henrique Joriam**
(☀ see Music tours)

◆ **Lisa Rio Tours**
(☀ see Art and Culture tours)

◆ **Maracanã Sports Complex**
www.suderj.rj.gov.br
℘ 21 2334 1705

◆ **Rio Sports Tour**
www.riosportstour.com

Taxi Tours

Travel agencies and licenced tour guides offer private tours of the city. Although more expensive than finding your own way around, they offer more flexibility and comfort; and local guides are available who speak most foreign languages and know all about their home town.
Contact RioTur for recommended agencies (℘ 21 2271 7000; www.riode janeiro-turismo.com.br).

Scenic Cruises and Ferries

Rio's winding bays and islands are best appreciated from the water and there is a range of boat excursions available, from a ferry ride to **Ilha Fiscal**★ (☀ see p 195), **Ilha de Paquetá** (☀ see p 195), or **Niterói**★★ (☀ see p 192) to cruises around the main highlights of **Guanabara Bay**★★ on board the English-built WWI tugboat Laurindo Pitta (contact Espaço Cultural da Marinha for information).
Further afield, chartered yachts sail along the Costa Verde to Angra dos Reis and Paraty; or along the Costa do Sol to Buzios, Arraial do Cabo, and Cabo Frio.

◆ **Espaço Cultural da Marinha**
℘ 21 2104 6992

- **Fantasia Turismo**
  www.fantasiatur.com.br
  𝄞 21 2548 6172

- **Marlin Yacht Charters**
  www.marlinyacht.com.br
  𝄞 21 2225 7434/9986 9678

- **Pink Fleet**
  www.pinkfleet.com.br
  𝄞 21 2555 4063

- **Praça XV Ferries**
  𝄞 0800 704 4113

- **Saveiros Tour**
  www.savelros.com.br
  𝄞 21 2225 6064/9448 7558

- **Tropical Cruises Brasil**
  www.tropicalcruises.com.br
  𝄞 21 99636172/2487 1687

Helicopter Tours

Aerial excursions are available with several companies; from six- to seven-minute flights around main city highlights for R$150 per person, to one-hour flights for R$875 per person covering the whole city as far as Barra da Tijuca and including Niterói.

- **Helisight**
  www.helisight.com.br
  𝄞 21 2511 2141/2542 7895

- **Heli-Rio**
  www.helirio.com.br
  𝄞 21 2437 9064/7065

Outdoor Fun

ADVENTURE SPORTS

Hang gliding, paragliding, diving, mountaineering, and abseiling are just some of the white-knuckle adventures on offer, making full use of Rio's magnificent natural setting. Specialist agencies registered with the relevant professional organizations are essential for these skilled activities, and there are several reputable operators in the city.

Hang Gliding, Paragliding, and Skydiving

Hang gliding and paragliding are very popular in Rio, with excellent winds and thermals over its forested hills and soft landings on its sandy beaches. The main center for hang gliding is **São Conrado** (ⓘ see p 181), with a take-off ramp on Pedra Bonita, high above Tijuca Forest *(up to R$240 per flight, including return transportation from hotel, plus R$10 for National Park and Hang Gliders' Association)*; both activities are also available in Parque da Cidade (ⓘ see p 194), **Niterói**. *(flights are cheaper from Niteroi).*

- **Delta Flight**
  www.deltaflight.com.br
  𝄞 21 3322 5750/9693 8800

- **Brazilian Hang Gliding and Parasailing Association**
  www.abvl.com.br/

- **Just Fly**
  www.justfly.com
  𝄞 21 9985 7540/9798 1804

- **Luciano Miranda** (Niterói)
  𝄞 21 9761 6113

For **sky-diving**, there are courses at Jacarepaguá Airport in Barra da Tijuca; contact Barra Jumping *𝄞 21 2258 0700/8112 4320; www.barrajumping. com.br*; and Rio Turismo Radical, *𝄞 21 8133 7787; www.rioturismoradical. com.br.*

Scuba Diving

The best dive sites, with the clearest waters and the most coral and wildlife, are on the Costa do sol, around Arraial do Cabo and Cabo Frio; as well as off Angra dos Reis and Ilha Grande on the Costa Verde. In Rio itself the best diving is in the Cagarras Islands (outside Guanabara Bay) where there are shipwreck sites.

- **Brazil Divers**
  𝄞 21 3717 5065/7843 3840
  www.brazildivers.com.br

- **Tridente**
  ✆21 7834 0804/2645 1705
  www.tridente.tur.br

- **Dive Point**
  www.divepoint.com.br
  ✆21 2239 5105/8816 5267

- **Traineira**
  www.traineira.com.br
  ✆21 7845 6033

WALKING AND HIKING

From the cultivated avenues of imperial palms in the **Botanical Gardens**★★★ (*see p 175*), to the waterfalls and tropical forests of the **Tijuca National Park**★★★ (*see p 139*), Rio de Janeiro is one of the greenest cities in the world. Specialist agencies with guides qualified in biology and photography take tours of the city's open spaces, from gentle walks lasting a couple of hours to more challenging all-day hikes.

- **Curumim Eco Cultural Tours**
  www.curumim.tur.br
  ✆21 2217 7199/9999 4157

- **Florestaventura**
  www.florestaventura.com
  ✆21 2556 9462/9256 9361

- **Indiana Jungle Tours**
  www.indianajungle.com.br
  ✆21 2484 2279/9298 3071

Mountaineering in the National Park of Serra dos Órgãos
©Michelle Gloria/TurisRio

- **Rio Hiking**
  www.riohiking.com.br
  ✆21 2552 9204/9721 0594

- **Trilharte**
  www.trilharte.com.br
  ✆21 2225 2426/2205 0654

CYCLING AND MOUNTAIN BIKING

Tours take groups of cyclists along the safe, oceanfront cycle-paths from **Ipanema**★★ to **Copacabana**★, and to the **Botanical Gardens**★★★. Or, for something more challenging, professional cyclists take training sessions in **Leblon** and **Lagoa**; plus road cycling and off-road mountain-biking excursions also available.

- **Pack Tours**
  www.packtours.com.br
  ✆21 5053 9810/3807 2146

- **Trilhas do Rio**
  www.trilhasdorio.com.br
  ✆21 2424 5455

GOLF

There are three golf clubs, all in the western suburbs: **São Conrado** has the Gávea Golf Club (✆21 3322 4141); and **Barra da Tijuca** has the Golden Green Golf Club (✆21 2434 0696) and Itanhanga Golf Club (✆21 2494 2507). Ask your hotel if it has an agreement for guests to play at these clubs; Itanhanga is the most exclusive, but Gávea does hold amateur and semi-professional tournaments. There is a nine-hole course at Banana Golf, in **Recreio** (✆21 3411 6110); it's more basic but open to all. The are also excellent golf clubs in **Búzios**★★ and on the Costa Verde.

MOUNTAINEERING AND ROCK CLIMBING

With its massive granite domes, Rio has masses of climbing opportunities with fantastic views at the summit. There are hundreds of routes up **Sugar Loaf**★★★, **Morro da Urca**, Corcovado★★★, and the high peaks in **Tijuca National Park**★★★. The major destination for mountaineering is outside the city of Rio in the National Parks of **Serra dos Órgãos**★★ and **Itatiaia**★★★ (*see p 87*). Specialist agencies and climbing clubs offer a range of climbs in the city and further afield to suit both hardened professionals and beginners in search of a challenge.

◆ **Centro Excursionista Brasileira (CEB)**
 21 2252 9844
 www.ceb.org.br

◆ **Crux Eco Adventure**
 21 9392 9203
 www.cruxecoaventura.com.br

OFF ROAD

Along the Costa do Sol, off-road jeeps and buggies take adventure tours of the lush forests and wild sand-dune beaches that dot the coast. These usually include a stop for lunch and a dip in the sea or a crystal-clear waterfall.

◆ **Hoca Tour**
 www.hocatour.com.br
 21 9322 0870/3472 7576

HORSEBACK RIDING

For a quiet escape on horseback, there are stables close to Barra da Tijuca and as far afield as Paraty that offer horse treks into the mountains, as well as local clubs that offer lessons and courses to both beginners and experienced riders.

◆ **Pousada Picinguaba**
 www.picinguaba.com
 21 3836 9105

◆ **Clube Marapendi**
 www.clubemarapendi.com.br
 21 3325 2440

◆ **Haras Horse Shoe**
 www.horseshoe.com.br
 21 2428 1023

TENNIS

There are some clubs with courts, such as the Rio Sports Center in **Barra da Tijuca** (*21 3325 6644, www.riosportscenter.com.br*) and Novo Rio Country Clube, in **Recreio** (*21 2490 1393/2490 7038, www.clubenovorio.com.br*).

There are also a few public courts near the Lake, and some of the larger hotels have courts available to the public, such as the Sheraton in **Barra da Tijuca** (*2529 1104/25291103*).

For more information, contact: **Confederação Brasileira de Tênis**, (*11 3325 0160, www.cbtenis.com.br*). **Federação de Tênis do Estado do Rio de Janeiro** (*21 3416 0924, www.fterj.com.br*).

WATER SPORTS

You can take part in just about every aquatic activity imaginable in Rio's waters; from swimming to scuba diving, and there are plenty of specialist operators available to satisfy all needs. The ocean is not warm, however, and beginners should be wary of the powerful undertow off most beaches.

Sailing
Regattas take place in **Guanabara Bay**★★ and on **Lagoa Rodrigo de Freitas**★; yachts from around the world are moored in the Marina da Glória (*see p 125*), which is the main base for sailing clubs. Some have yachts available for charter and run sailing courses:

◆ **Brasil Yacht Charter**
 www.sailing.com.br
 21 3154 9977

◆ **Clube Dos Caicaras**
 Lagoa
 21 2529 4800/2529 4823

◆ **Federação de Vela do Rio de Janeiro (FEVERJ)**
 www.feverj.org.br
 21 2533 0194

😊 A Bit of Advice 😊

Rio's oceans have unpredictable and powerful undertows and rip-tides; the best sign is to see if locals are swimming and, if they are, swim near to others, especially if you are not a strong swimmer.

Strong current hazard

Y. Kanazawa/Michelin

Surfing

Rio has some excellent conditions for surfers; the **west zone beaches** (🧭 *see p 178)* have the best waves: Ipanema, Arpoador, Barra, Macumba-Pontal, Prainha, and Grumari. Bodyboarding, kiteboarding, wakeboarding, para-sailing, and windsurfing are all catered for here too. There are many surfing and watersports companies:

♦ **Rico Surf**
www.ricosurf.globo.com
🕻 21 2438 1821/2438 4096

♦ **Surf Bus Beach Tours**
www.surfbus.com.br
🕻 21 2539 7555/8702 2837

For other recommended operators, contact:

♦ **Federação do Surf do Estado do Rio de Janeiro**
🕻 21 8891 0754/2490 0754
www.feserj.com.br.

Swimming

The smarter hotels have their own pool, often on the rooftop, which are great for cooling off and soaking up the view. If you are a strong swimmer and want to brave the ocean, the cleanest beaches are **Ipanema**★★★ (🧭 *see p 162)* and **Leblon**★★ (🧭 *see p 166)*—but be careful to swim only where the locals are.

Activities for Children

Throughout this guide, sights of particular interest to children are indicated with a Kids symbol. Cariocas love children and it is the norm for families to socialize together, at all hours of the day and night. There is even a national holiday for children, the Dia da Criança, on October 12, with special activities and entertainment around the city.

FAMILY FUN

Top attractions for children include:

Beaches—**Copacabana Beach**★★★ (🧭 *see p 159)* and **Ipanema Beach**★★★ (🧭 *see p 162)* are particularly child-friendly, with the Baixo Bebê play area at the far end of **Leblon Beach**★★ (🧭 *see p 166)*, as well as another playground on Praça Nossa Senhora da Paz, three blocks in from the beach, halfway along Ipanema.

Parks and Gardens—**Botanical Gardens**★★★ (🧭 *see p 174)*, with its towering Avenue of Palms, Giant Amazon lily ponds, and Hummingbird Garden should all delight young nature lovers. **Parque do Flamengo**★ (🧭 *see p 146)* is a family-friendly, green- and wide-open-space to visit. It has cycle and rollerblading tracks and on Sundays the tree-lined main roads through the park are closed to traffic.

Zoo—the **Jardim Zoológico** (🧭 *see p 121)* is great for young kids, with some 2,000 animals, including native and foreign species. There is a special petting area, as well as an adoption scheme for endangered animals such as the tiny tamarins.

Planetarium—Rio de Janeiro's **Planetário da Gávea** (*see p 172*) is an excellent place to learn about the constellations of the Southern Hemisphere for children and adults alike. This site includes the Universe Museum and state-of-the-art telescopes that children can use to gaze up at the nighttime stars.

Sugar Loaf and Corcovado—the views may impress older kids, but the ride up, on the cablecar to **Sugar Loaf** ★★★ (*see p 192*) and cog railway to **Corcovado**★★★ (*see p 134*) will be the main attractions for most children; plus the chance to spot wildlife on the trails around the parks.

Jeep Tours
Kids will love these convertible jeep tours in and around the city. Visits take in **Corcovado**★★★ (*see p 134*), **Guanabara Bay**★★ (*see p 192*), **Sugar Loaf** ★★★ (*see p 192*), **Tijuca National Park**★★★ (*see p 139*), the **Botanical Gardens**★★★ (*see p 174*)... The Jeeps collect you from your hotel in the morning and take you on the adventure of your choice. Guides speak several languages and the fleet includes 35 well maintained jeeps (*21 2108 5800; www.jeeptour. com.br*).

Books

Carnival under Fire. Ruy Castro. (Bloomsbury, 2004.) Witty, passionate, and acutely observed social history of Rio de Janeiro by one of the city's most highly respected writers.

Futebol. Alex Bellos. (Bloomsbury, 2002.) Authoritative and insightful account of why the "beautiful game" is the lifeblood to many Brazilians.

Brazil in F... Ameri... conder... Brazil: p... and eco... but a har...

Red Gold. John... 2004.) Hard... ...se of the decimation of Brazil's indigenous population by the earliest European colonizers.

Films

Rio, 40 Graus (Rio, 40 Degrees). (Dir. Nelson Pereira dos Santos, 1955.) A semi-documentary following a group of boys from a favela as they roam around the city: selling peanuts in Copacabana, going to a soccer game at Maracana, and meeting various characters en-route. A classic, which still packs a punch today. The debut of Nelson Pereira dos Santos, launching his career as one of Brazil's most important film directors.

Central do Brasil. (Dir. Walter Salles, 1998.) A touching but unsentimental tale of Dora, a teacher who writes letters for illiterate customers at Rio de Janeiro's main train station, joining up with Josué, a young boy in search of his lost father.

Cidade de Deus (City of God). (Dir. Fernando Meirelles, 2002.) A brutal, but compelling view of juvenile gang violence in Rio de Janeiro's favelas.

Favela Rising. (Dir. Matt Mochary and Jeff Zimbalist, 2006.) A more positive counterbalance to *City of God*, with Anderson Sa founding an Afro-reggae group as a means to escape from the drugs and violence of the favela where he was born.

ALENDAR OF EVENTS

nnual Events

Below is a selection of Rio de Janeiro's most popular annual events. The highlight of the year is the Carnival, for which you will need to book months in advance. For detailed information contact **RioTur** (☝ *see p 16*).

JANUARY
Jan 20
Festa de São Sebastião

Evening procession in honor of the patron saint of the city; from São Sebastião dos Capuchinhos in Tijuca to the Catedral Metropolitana. Festivities also include an umbanda festival at the Caboclo Monument in Santa Teresa, and a 6.2mi/10km road race from Flamengo to Botafogo. ☎*21 2240 2669*.

Jan–Feb
Rei da Praia

Volleyball tournament on Ipanema Beach, with the winning woman crowned Queen of the Beach, followed by the men's contest to crown the King.
www.reidapraia.com.br.
☎*21 2495 7426 / 3154 7944.*

FEBRUARY
Feb–Mar
Carnival (☝ *see p 82*)

Hailed as the "greatest party in the world", Rio's carnival overwhelms the city for four days and nights of spectacular samba-school parades in the Sambódromo, concerts, elegant balls, and street festivities.
www.rio-carnival.net
☎*21 271 7068 (RioTur)*

MARCH
Mar 1
Foundation of Rio de Janeiro

Church mass in São Sebastião dos Capuchinhos, marking the founding of Rio de Janeiro on March 1, 1565 by Estácio de Sá.

early Mar
Oi Vert Jam

Skateboarding competition and exhibition, Lagoa Rodrigo de Freitas.
www.rioskatejam.com.br/
☎*21 3478 7400*

Apr 23
Dia de São Jorge

Vigil for St George, leading figure in Afro-Brazilian tradition. Mass and procession at Igreja de São Jorge, Rua da Alfândega 382.

MAY–JUNE
Rio das Ostras Jazz and Blues Festival

Held in a beach resort 205mi/170km east of Rio, this is one of the best music festivals in Brazil, attracting top Brazilian and international artists.
www.riodasostrasjazzeblues.com.

JUNE
Festas Juninas

Festivities for major Catholic saints run all month; key days include 13th: Santo Antonio, 24th: São João, and 29th: São Pedro.

mid–late June
Rio Marathon

26mi/42km coastal route from Barra to Botafogo, plus half marathon and fun 6km run.
www.maratonadorio.com.br
☎*21 2223 2773/7840 7583*

JULY
early July
Portas Abertas

Open-studio art festival in hillside neighborhood of Santa Teresa, with painting, sculpture, and gastronomic events.
www.arco-iris.org.br
☎*21 2507 5352*

New Year in Rio de Janeiro

Reveillon, the city's New Year's Eve party, is second only to Carnival for its size, spectacle, and sheer exuberance. Rio's municipality hosts free parties all across town, with the biggest on Copacabana Beach. Up to five million people party all night and watch the sun come up over the ocean. Leading Brazilian and international rock stars perform on open-air stages on the sand and a dazzling fireworks display fills the night sky at midnight. The biggest crowds usually gather in front of Copacabana Palace Hotel, the grand old dame of Avenida Atlántica; but you can also get great views from any rooftop bar along the Avenida Atlántica.

AUGUST

First Sun

Brazilian Grand Prix

Top horseback race at the Jockey Club in Gávea (not the Formula One event, held in São Paulo).
21 3534 5000

Aug 15

Feast of the Assumption

Mass and procession from Glória Church overlooking the city center and bay, with foodstalls and events.

SEPTEMBER

Sept 7

Independence Day

Celebration of independence from Portugal, which Pedro I proclaimed on this day in 1822. Large military parade down Avenida Presidente Vargas, from Candelaria past Praça XI.

late Sept–early Oct

Festival do Rio

One of the most important film festivals in Latin America, with screenings across the city.
www.festivaldorio.com.br
21 2579 0352

OCTOBER

Every Sun (and 1st Sun in Nov)

Festa da Penha

One of Rio's most popular religious festivals, with lively celebrations in the northern suburb of Penha.

Oct 12

Festa de Nossa Senhora de Aparecida

National holiday for the patron saint of Brazil, plus Children's Day, with city-wide events for kids.

Oct

Parada do Orgulho Gay do Rio

Second in Brazil only to the Gay Pride Parade in São Paulo, this event celebrates sexual diversity with a huge street party on the south zone beaches.

NOVEMBER

Nov–Feb

Noites Cariocas

Summer festival of late-night weekend concerts at dockside Pier Mauá, north of Centro; lively party atmosphere.
http://oinoitescariocas.oi.com.br/
21 8871 0194/8883 0327

DECEMBER

Dec–Feb

Verão do Morro

Weekend pop and rock concerts from panoramic setting atop Sugar Loaf, featuring top Brazilian bands and DJs.
www.morrodaurca.com

Dec 31

Iemenja

Major Afro-Brazilian Candomble festival of the Goddess of the Sea; various beach locations.

Reveillon

The year ends with a bang at the city's New Year's Eve party.
(*See above.*)

BASIC INFORMATION

Business Hours

Banks—Mon–Fri 10am–4pm.
Offices—Mon–Fri 9am–6pm.
Shops—Shopping Malls open Mon–Sat 10am–10pm. The largest shopping centers also open on Sunday, from 3–9pm. Most other shops open Mon–Fri 9am–7pm, and Sat 9am–1pm.
Supermarkets—open Mon–Sat 8am–10pm; a few also open on Sundays or 24hrs.
Gas Stations—may open 24hrs, although not all of them do so.

Communications

NEWSPAPERS & MAGAZINES

The three bestselling daily newspapers in Rio are *O Globo (www.oglobo.com.br)*, *Extra (http://extra.globo.com)* and *O Dia (http://odia.terra.com.br)*. Weekend editions include a pull-out entertainment section, such as *O Globo's Rio Show (Friday)* and Veja's Sunday supplement, *Veja Rio*. Weekly national news magazines include *Epoca*, *Veja*, and *Isto é*. Foreign newspapers and magazines are widely available, either at newsstands or in larger hotels.

TELEPHONE

There are plenty of public phone boxes, known as *orelhões* (big ears) because of their curved plastic hood. They take cards *(cartões telefônicos)*, which you can buy from post offices and newsstands, but not coins.
You can dial direct to most countries in the world using the blue phone boxes (the yellow phone boxes will only allow you to call locally or within Brazil). Dial 00, then the long-distance operator code (21 for Embratel or 23 for Intelig) and then the country's own code followed by the area code (minus the zero) and the number.
To call Rio de Janeiro from abroad, first dial your home country's international access code, then 55 (the code for Brazil), then 21 (Rio's code), followed by the number.

Cellphones

You can use your cellphone in Rio but first check with your service provider because the coverage and the cost varies from one company to another, and from parts of Brazil to another; in general it is expensive and the service is outdated. Alternatively, Connect-Com offers a cellphone rental service, which costs about R$10 a day, plus the call charges (*℘21 2215 0002/9311 1112; www.connectcomrj.com.br*).

Newsstand in Centro

Y. Kanazawa/Michelin

INTERNET

There are many internet cafes, particularly in Copacabana, Ipanema, and other tourist areas. Charges range from about R$4–R$8 per hour. Hotels often provide internet access for guests too, sometimes with a wireless broadband connection in your room; service charges can be high, though, and connection speeds variable. Free Wi-Fi is available on the beachfront of Copacabana and Ipanema.

RADIO AND TV

Brazilian TV is dominated by Globo, one of the largest media networks in the world. Hotels usually show only Brazilian channels, although upscale hotels also have satellite, with US and European channels, including CNN and BBC Worldwide. After Globo, SBT is the next-most popular channel, which broadcasts a popular mix of game shows and live chat shows. Other channels include Bandeirantes, Record, Rede TV, and TVE.
There is a huge number of national and local radio stations, including Radio Globo, the biggest network. Radio broadcasts on FM, AM, and shortwave, as well as digitally on TV and the internet. Local stations are listed on Radio Station World *(http://radiostationworld.com)*; or check the BBC World Service *(www.bbc.co.uk/worldservice)* for its South America schedule.

Safety and Security

Rio de Janeiro has a bad reputation for crime and violence. It's arguable that some of this image is sensationalized in the media but, although tourists are rarely targeted, there are common-sense precautions you should take to avoid becoming a victim.

Discounts

If you plan to do a lot of sightseeing, the RioPass could save you some

Orelhões—public phone boxes

Y. Kanazawa/Michelin

money—it costs R$93.50 for seven days, which includes four of the city's main attractions, including Sugar Loaf and Corcovado *(www.riopass.com; ℰ21 2240 2359)*.

Electricity

Most places use 110V or 120V, some hotels also have 220V. Power points have twin sockets, and most will take either round- or flat-pinned plugs.

Emergencies

Emergency Hospitals

- ◆ **Lourenço Jorge**
  Av. Ayrton Senna 2000
  Barra da Tijuca
  ℰ21 3111 4680

- ◆ **Rocha Maia**
  Rua General Severiano 91
  Botafogo
  ℰ21 2295 2295

😊 A Bit of Advice 😊

Take photocopies of key pages from your passport, and note the numbers of your insurance policy, travelers' checks, visas, and credit cards. Keep one copy in a separate place from the originals and leave one copy at home.

- **Souza Aguiar**
  Praça da República 111
  Centro
  ✆ 21 3111 2629

- **Miguel Couto**
  Rua Mario Ribeiro 117
  Gávea
  ✆ 21 3111 3800/3111 3799

24-Hour Drugstore
- **Drogaria Pacheco**
  Av. N S Copacabana, 534/A, B
  Copacabana
  ✆ 21 3208 4600

Mail

Opening times of *correios* (post offices) vary, but most open Mon–Fri 9am–5pm, and until noon on Saturday. The postal service is usually reliable; allow at least a week for postcards and letters mailed in each direction. There are yellow postboxes on the street, but it's safer to use the post office. You can also buy stamps in newsstands and in larger hotels.

There are also express mail services, SEDEX, and Express Mail Service (EMS). For addresses of post office branches in Rio, visit *www.correios.com.br*.

Money

CURRENCY

The Brazilian currency is the **real** (R$) (plural, **reais**). There are 100 centavos to the real. Coins are 1, 5, 10, 25, and 50 centavos, and 1 real; notes come in denominations of 1 *(being phased out)*, 2, 5, 10, 20, 50, and 100 reais.

Currency Exchange

US dollars and Euros are the most widely accepted foreign currencies. There is little difference in exchange rates between banks and *câmbios* (bureaux de change). Câmbios give a slightly better rate, and banks charge commission for changing foreign currency. Câmbios are also open for longer hours, particularly at weekends. The official exchange rate is published daily in newspapers.

CREDIT CARDS

Major international credit cards are accepted in Brazil; the most popular are Mastercard, Visa, and then American Express. Credit card receipts will be priced in reais, although you will be billed in the currency of your own country, using the official exchange rate. Hotels will usually only let their own guests use their bank cards to withdraw reais.

ATMS

There are many ATMs outside banks at which international cards can be used, but check first with your bank that your card can be used overseas. It is advised to use an ATM inside a bank, and in daylight hours.

SAMPLE PRICES

Metrô/bus fare: R$2.40
Draught beer: $3
Large bottle of mineral water: R$2.50
Airmail stamp for postcard: $3
Taxi Copacabana to Centro/Lapa (daytime): R$20
Sugar Loaf cablecar: R$44
Corcovado cog railway: R$45

State Holidays (2010)

1 January	New Year's Day
12–17 February	Carnival *(4–8 March, 2011; 17–21 February, 2012)*
2 April	Good Friday
21 April	Tiradentes Day
23 April	St Georges Day

1 May	Labor Day
3 June	Corpus Christi
7 September	Independence Day
12 October	Our Lady of Aparecida/ Children's Day
2 November	All Souls' Day
15 November	Proclamation of the Republic Day
20 November	Black Consciousness Day
25 December	Christmas Day

Public toilet by Praia Vermelha

Y. Kanazawa/Michelin

Smoking

Smoking is not allowed on public transport in Rio; some restaurants and bars have non-smoking areas. In general, anti-smoking restrictions are not as rigorous as in Europe and the US.

Tipping

Unlike Europe and the US, tipping is not customary in Brazil. Most restaurants automatically add ten percent to the bill.

Time Zone

Rio de Janeiro is three hours behind GMT, two hours ahead of Eastern Standard Time, and five hours ahead of Western Pacific Time. Between November and February clocks go forward one hour, when it becomes only two hours behind GMT.

Toilets

Public toilets are rare in Rio; apart from at the airports, bus station and major tourist attractions. Your best bet is to use the nearest busy restaurant or shopping mall, which usually turn a blind eye to tourists in need.

USEFUL WORDS AND PHRASES

PRONOUNCIATION

d followed by *i* or *e* is pronounced *jee* as in *jeep*; i.e. *dia*. Similarly, *t* followed by *i* or *e* is pronounced *chee* as in *cheep*; i.e. *noite*.
An acute or ˆ accent over a vowel denotes stress, i.e. *farmácia* , or *Você*. *ão*, as in *Não* is pronounced *ow*, as in *cow*. *nh = ny*, as in *senhora*.

GREETINGS

Good morning	*Bom dia*
Good afternoon	*Boa tarde*
Good evening/night	*Boa noite*
Hello/Hi	*Oi*
Goodbye	*Adeus/Tchau*

INTRODUCTIONS

How are you?	*Tudo bem/bom?*
I am well	*Tudo bem*
Cool/fine/great	*Tá legal/Tá ótimo*
What is your name?	*Qual é seu nome?*
My name is	*O meu nome é*
Pleased to meet you	*Prazer*
I don't understand	*Não entendo*
Please	*Por favor*
Thank you	*Obrigada(m)/Obrigado(f)*
Yes	*Sim*
No	*Não*
Sorry	*Desculpe*
You	*Você*
(or, more polite: o senhor, a senhora)	
Me	*Eu (ay-oo)*
Us/We	*A gente*

QUESTIONS

When…?	*Quando?*
Where is…?	*Onde está/onde fica?*
How much is…?	*Quanto é?*
Why?	*Por que?*
How?	*Como?*
Who?	*Quem?*

BASICS / SHOPPING

Bank	*Banco*
Bathroom	*Banheiro*
Beach	*Praia*
Bureau de change	*Casa de câmbio*
Credit card	*Cartão de crédito*
Money	Dinheiro
Post Office	*Correio*
I want to buy…	*Quero comprar…*
Open	*Aberto*
Closed	*Fechado*

EATING AND DRINKING

Breakfast	*Café da manhã*
Lunch	*Almoço*
Dinner	*Jantar*
Without meat	*Sem carne*
Drink	*Bebida*
Water	*Água*
Mineral water (still/sparkling)	*Água mineral (sem/com gas)*
Beer	*Cerveja*
Wine	*Vinho*
Fruit juice	*Suco de fruta*
Milk	*Leite*
Tea	*Chá*
Coffee	*Café*
With/without sugar	*Com/sem açúcar*
Menu	*Cardápio*
Bill	*Conta*

EMERGENCY / HEALTH

Help!	*Socorro!*
Stop—thief!	*ladrão!*
Call the police/fire/Ambulance	*Chame a policia/bombeiros/ambulância*
Doctor	*Médico*
Emergency	*Emergência*
I feel ill	*Estou doente*
Please help	*Ajuda-me, por favor*
Fever	*Febre*
Diarrhoea	*Diarreia*
Head	*Cabeça*
Stomach	*Estômago (Barriga)*

Sanitary towels	*Absorventes higiênicos*
Tampons	*Absorventes internos*
Condoms	*Camisinhas/preservativos*

NUMBERS

1	*Uma/uma*
2	*Dois/duas*
3	*Três*
4	*Quatro*
5	*Cinco*
6	*Seis* (half-dozen = *meia*)
7	*Sete*
8	*Oito*
9	*Nove*
10	*Dez*
20	*Vinte*
30	*Trinta*
40	*Quarenta*
50	*Cinqüenta*
60	*Sessenta*
70	*Setenta*
80	*Oitenta*
90	*Noventa*
100	*Cem, Cento e…*
1,000	*Mil*

DAYS OF THE WEEK

Monday	*Segunda-feira*
Tuesday	*Terça-feira*
Wednesday	*Quarta-feira*
Thursday	*Quinta-feira*
Friday	*Sexta-feira*
Saturday	*Sábado*
Sunday	*Domingo*

TIME

Minute	*Minuto*
Hour	*Hora*
At one o'clock	*A uma hora*
At ten o'clock, etc	*As dez horas*
Half past…	*E meia*
Quarter past…	*E quinze*
Quarter to…	*Quinze para as…*
Late	*Tarde*
Early	*Cedo*

GETTING AROUND

Airport	*Aeroporto*
Bus station	*Rodoviaria*
Bus stop	*Ponto/Parada de ônibus*
Ticket	*Passagem/Bilhete*
Ticket Office	*Bilheteria*

CONVERSION TABLES

Weights and Measures

1 kilogram (kg) 6.35 kilograms 0.45 kilograms	2.2 pounds (lb) 14 pounds 16 ounces (oz)	2.2 pounds 1 stone (st) 16 ounces	*To convert kilograms to pounds, multiply by 2.2*
1 metric ton (tn)	1.1 tons	1.1 tons	
1 litre (l) 3.79 litres 4.55 litres	2.11 pints (pt) 1 gallon (gal) 1.20 gallon	1.76 pints 0.83 gallon 1 gallon	*To convert litres to gallons, multiply by 0.26 (US) or 0.22 (UK)*
1 hectare (ha) 1 sq. kilometre (km²)	2.47 acres 0.38 sq. miles (sq.mi.)	2.47 acres 0.38 sq. miles	*To convert hectares to acres, multiply by 2.4*
1 centimetre (cm) 1 metre (m)	0.39 inches (in) 3.28 feet (ft) or 39.37 inches or 1.09 yards (yd)	0.39 inches	*To convert metres to feet, multiply by 3.28; for kilometres to miles, multiply by 0.6*
1 kilometre (km)	0.62 miles (mi)	0.62 miles	

Clothing

Women	🇧🇷	🇺🇸	🇬🇧
	36	5	3½
	37	6	4½
Shoes	38	7	5½
	38½	7½	6
	39	8	6½
	40	9	7½
	41	10	8½
	36	6	8
	38	8	10
Dresses	40	10	12
& suits	42	12	14
	44	14	16
	46	16	18
	36	06	30
	38	08	32
Blouses &	40	10	34
sweaters	42	12	36
	44	14	38
	46	16	40

Men	🇧🇷	🇺🇸	🇬🇧
	40	7½	7
	41	8½	8
	42	9½	9
Shoes	43	10½	10
	44	11½	11
	45	12½	12
	46	13½	13
	46	36	36
	48	38	38
Suits	50	40	40
	52	42	42
	54	44	44
	56	46	48
	37	14½	14½
	38	15	15
Shirts	39	15½	15½
	40	15¾	15¾
	41	16	16
	42	16½	16½

Sizes often vary depending on the designer. These equivalents are given for guidance only.

Speed

KPH	10	30	50	70	80	90	100	110	120	130
MPH	6	19	31	43	50	56	62	68	75	81

Temperature

Celsius (°C)	0°	5°	10°	15°	20°	25°	30°	40°	60°	80°	100°
Fahrenheit (°F)	32°	41°	50°	59°	68°	77°	86°	104°	140°	176°	212°

To convert Celsius into Fahrenheit, multiply °C by 9, divide by 5, and add 32.
To convert Fahrenheit into Celsius, subtract 32 from °F, multiply by 5, and divide by 9.
NB: Conversion factors on this page are approximate.

Bondinho running on the Arcos da
Lapa to Santa Teresa
©Gräfenhain Günter/SIME/4Corners Images

RIO DE JANEIRO TODAY

Capital of Rio de Janeiro state, the city of Rio is a cosmopolitan metropolis full of joie de vivre; a huge Garden of Eden of awe-inspiring natural beauty with a mixture of forested, curvaceous hills and miles of sunlit beaches; and a cultural center with a history influenced by Europe, South America, and Africa alike.

Evolution of the City

The establishment of Rio de Janeiro by **Estácio de Sá** on 20 January 1565 was primarily a strategic act. The Bay of Guanabara was the best natural harbor between Bahia and the Rio de la Plata and, given the number of successful French incursions, the main preoccupation of successive Rio governors was defense. They built a fortified castle on the Morro do Castelo and the city grew around it, constrained by the undulating landscape and clinging to the fortress like a medieval town.

Although Rio de Janeiro went through three major makeover periods—once when it became the sole capital of Brazil after 1767, a second time with the arrival of the Portuguese royal family in 1808, and finally during the first part of Dom Pedro II's reign in the 1850s and 1860s —its colonial aspect did not significantly change until the beginning of the 20C. In 1902–1906 mayor **Pereira Passos** began to carry through the biggest urban transformation of the city. At the time, Rio de Janeiro had about 500,000

inhabitants, concentrated around the primitive nucleus of Morro do Castelo that had hardly changed in 300 years. Pereira Passos and his health secretary Oswaldo Cruz started a program of fumigation, slum clearance, and compulsory vaccination against smallpox (which was misinterpreted by the poor and led to prolonged riots in November 1904). Passos adopted the Haussmann model in fin-de-siècle Paris by opening up big boulevards: two great diagonal avenues, the Avenida Central (currently Avenida Rio Branco) and the Avenida Mem de Sá, cut through the colonial grid of the Centro; the Avenida Beira Mar ran parallel to the coastline and served as the basis for the development of the Zona Sul; and the magnificent Avenida Atlântica was inaugurated in 1906. Finally, in 1920, the Morro do Castelo was excavated, providing space for the reconstruction of the city center. The hill was used for landfill that joined the coast to the island of Villegaignon where the Santos Dumont Airport stands today.

In 1938, work began to relieve the congested city center. In order to link the North and South zones, and to ensure free movement of traffic, the tunnels that are now characteristic of the Rio road system, were constructed.

The designs were executed in two phases. The first was carried out under Enrique Dodsworth from 1942–1943, and consisted of the opening of the Avenida Presidente Vargas, the greatest artery of the city that still absorbs the bulk of the traffic between the center and the North Zone. The second phase was completed during the administration of the governor Carlos Lacerda (1960–1965) with the opening of two large tunnels that bind the North and South Zones: Santa Bárbara and Rebouças. The park of Flamengo, a masterpiece of urban design

Avenida Rio Branco in 1950s

© INTERFOTO Pressebildagentur/Alamy

by **Robert Burle Marx** (⏻ *see p 74*), was inaugurated in 1961, completing Rio's facelift.

The final growth of the city westward was conceived in the late sixties and early seventies by **Lúcio Costa**. This was a staged urbanization which, unlike previous attempts, sought to preserve the natural lagoons and the shape of the coast. It proposed the creation of urban nuclei throughout the long Avenida das Americas, separated from each other by large, open spaces. At the same time industrial zones were designed-in rather than be left to grow unchecked. Although it has not been strictly followed, this pilot plan has guided, in general, the urban middle-class expansion into Barra da Tijuca and Jacarepaguá.

Economy

After the Federal District and São Paulo, Rio de Janeiro state has the third-highest per capita income in Brazil, standing at US$13,500 per person and contributing 12 percent to the country's GDP. Roughly two-thirds of the economy is based around services. **Tourism** is the obvious cash generator, especially during Carnival when Rio de Janeiro welcomes around 400,000 foreign revelers for a week, but it is not its sole source of income.

The desirability of living in the city has turned it into a major financial, commercial, and media center, being among others the headquarters of **O Globo**, South America's biggest media conglomerate; **Petrobras**, the country's state oil monopoly; and **Vale do Rio Doce**, Brazil's largest energy and mining company. It is one of the world's major textile manufacturing centers with many US and European houses outsourcing their clothing production to Petrópolis, Nova Friburgo, or Valença; and with its many institutes, colleges, and universities, Rio de Janeiro is Brazil's second-largest research center, corresponding to 17 percent of the country's research output.

Surprisingly for a state that accumulated its wealth from coffee, it owes only just over one percent of its GDP to agriculture: around 30 percent of Rio de Janeiro's income today comes from the industry sector. The state is the second-most industrialized in Brazil after São Paulo, with the country's largest petrochemical complex at Macaé, north of Rio de Janeiro; South America's largest steelworks in Volta Redonda; and shipbuilding works in the south that account for 90 percent of Brazil's naval output. Finally, ever since the 18C, the city of Rio de Janeiro has been prominent in the trade and manufacture of jewels, precious rocks, and metals stemming from the interior of Minas Gerais; one can still trace this tradition to the modern jewelry shops of Copacabana and Ipanema.

Rio de Janeiro has had a long connection with sports, having been the host of the PanAmerican Games in 2007. In 2009 the economy was strong enough to see Rio de Janeiro selected as one of the final four possible hosts for the 2016 Olympic Games. The city is also expected to host Brazil's 2014 FIFA World Cup.

Government

Rio de Janeiro was the sole capital of the Portuguese colony of Brazil from 1763 onward and the capital of independent Brazil from 1822 to 1960. In 1892 it formed the city-state of Guanabara. In 1976 the surrounding state of Rio de Janeiro was merged with the state of Guanabara for administrative purposes, forming today's state of Rio de Janeiro with the city itself as its capital.

Brazil's federal state system resembles closely that of the USA. The state of Rio de Janeiro is administered by a directly elected governor for four years; it sends three senators to the Federal Senate in Brasília, as well as 46 federal deputies to the House of Representatives. The current governor, **Sérgio de Oliveira Cabral Santos Filho**, is keen to emulate the "zero tolerance" crime policies of former New York City mayor Rudolph Giuliani.

The city of Rio de Janeiro is governed by a mayor who serves a four-year term. The term of the current mayor, **Eduardo da Costa Paes**, ends in December 2012.

State and country flags

The state flag is composed of four blue and white squares with a coat of arms in the middle. In the foreground flies an eagle, symbol of Brazil's royal family, over the Serra dos Orgãos. The outer part of the coat of arms has a branch of sugarcane on the left and coffee on the right—the crops that provided for its wealth. The date on the coat of arms: 9 April 1892, is that of the first constitution of the state. In the stars of the Brazilian flag, Rio de Janeiro is represented by the Beta Star (Mimosa) of the Southern Cross.

People and Population

The population of Rio de Janeiro state is 15.4 million of which 6.1 million live within the greater metropolitan area of Rio de Janeiro (estimated 2007), the second largest in Brazil after São Paulo. The population increase varies between 0.8 and 1.4 percent per annum, much of it due to immigration from Europe, mainly from Portugal, and from the northeast of Brazil. Yet all of them are affectionately called "Cariocas."

THE "CARIOCA"

The appellation "Carioca" indicates not only a person who was born in the city, but also, more inclusively, those who have adopted Rio de Janeiro as their home. Its origin is still being debated, but the prevalent consensus is that the word is of Tupi origin and means the "white house," an allusion to the first dwellings of the Portuguese. Some writers even pinpoint which white house it refers to: an old hovel left behind in 1503 on Flamengo beach by Gonçalo Coelho.

The typical characteristics of the Cariocas are their warm natures, their extrovert temperaments, and their disarming spontaneity. Like all Brazilians they are very demonstrative, using physical contact through embracing or kissing, not only within the family but also in greetings between friends. They are immensely proud of Rio de Janeiro and its beauty. The rapport with their bodies is very different from that of Western Europeans and North Americans. No one is scandalized when a woman appears on the beach in the tightest pair of shorts or a "dental floss" tanga swimsuit and no one bats an eyelid or even notices the groups of youths who walk around bare-chested and barefoot.

Dress is also informal. Men would only wear a tie to work in some offices in the city center: jeans and T-shirts are the norm in most places. Bermuda shorts are common for men and women, and the universal footwear is sandals or flip-flops, even at night. Due to the heat, cleanliness and personal hygiene are of great importance—this is the land, after all, where European sailors learned

Palácio Guanabara—Seat of the Rio de Janeiro state government

Y. Kanazawa/Michelin

Copacabana Beach Sidewalk

I. MacIntyre/Michelin

to have baths in order not to offend the native peoples.

Cariocas are a blend of three main races: the native Indians, Europeans, especially the Portuguese, and black Africans who arrived as slaves for the exploitation of sugar in the 17C, gold in the 18C, and coffee in the 19C. Every race contributed to the constitution of the Cariocas, be it through their physical features, the elements of their cultures, the language, the cooking, the religion, or their general attitude.

INDIGENOUS POPULATION

The original Amerindians who lived on the coast of Rio de Janeiro were the Tupi. Extensive ethnographic material comes from the Franciscan friar André Thevet and the Calvinist priest Jean de Léry who lived among them in the 1550s. We know that they moved about "as naked as they came out of the womb," and that they were extremely hospitable to these strangers who were considered allies. Unfortunately the native Indians disappear from history around the beginning of the 17C, having been decimated by the Portuguese in combat, or through imported diseases against which they had no immunity. What survives from the Tupinambá, however, are the local toponyms: from the Bay of Guanabara ("Bay That Looks Like the Sea") to the

beach of Ipanema ("Bad Water," i.e. not good for fishing because of the surf) and the national park of Tijuca ("Marsh"), the places the Amerindians named so long ago still define contemporary Rio de Janeiro.

AFRICAN ANCESTRY

About four million slaves reached Brazil over the 300-odd years of the slave trade. Aside from influencing the language—many Brazilian children's terms are of African origin—their religious traditions, which amalgamated with Christianity, created today's syncretic religions of Candomblé and, especially in Rio de Janeiro, Umbanda. The slaves also brought with them their cooking —a heavy influence in traditional cuisine—their dances, and their strongly percussive music which mutated into samba and today dominates the city's airwaves.

During the late 20C the immense contribution the African and mixed-race population has made to the life and culture of Rio de Janeiro has been recognized and celebrated as something that makes the city unique and special.

EUROPEANS

The Portuguese were the victors against the Indians and the French. As such it comes as no surprise that it is their culture that prevailed: their Christian Catholic religion; their Portuguese language, albeit mixed with Tupi and African terms; and their art which was founded on European principles. In the state of Rio de Janeiro other European groups are also prevalent, such as the Finns in Penedo and the Germans in the mountain region of Petrópolis and Freiburg.

The racial breakdown in the metropolitan area (2000 census) is 53 percent white, 35 percent mixed race *(pardo)*, 10.5 percent black, and of the rest only 0.3 percent identify as indigenous.

It is worth noting, though, that this racial predominance is a fairly recent phenomenon. By 1600 Rio de Janeiro had a population of some 2,000 souls (with almost no European women), by 1700 it had reached 10,000, and by 1800 the city numbered close to 45,000 people composed mostly of African slaves and free citizens of mixed heritage. It was only through a late 19C and early 20C immigration strategy to attract Europeans to work in the city—and the country—that the current proportions came about.

Urban landscape

Every visitor will immediately notice the huge social differences found within the city's landscape. The usual problems associated with economically challenged neighborhoods exist here. Government programs are improving the services and the basic infrastructure for the approximately two million people living in the poorest neighborhoods and slums. The majority of the residents of the favelas are hardworking and law-abiding citizens; the areas should however, only be visited by organized tours (see p29).

Religion

For the second-largest city in the most populous Catholic country in the world, Rio de Janeiro is surprisingly religiously diverse: in the 2000 census only 54 percent identified as Roman Catholic. The historically prevalent religion in whose name the country was colonized has long been in retreat. Equally surprising is the percentage that identify as atheist (16.7 percent), a proportion twice as large as in the rest of Brazil.

Evangelical churches have been growing fast in the last two decades. Twenty-two percent of Cariocas belong to one

Favela Rocinha, with a view to the upmarket condominiums of São Conrado and Pedra da Gávea

©Joseph Luoman/iStockphoto.com

Candomblé believers carry a boat in honor of Yemanjá on Copacabana beach

©Marcelo Sayao/epa/Corbis

of the many variations of evangelical churches established in the city with a large majority (14 percent) favoring the Pentecostal variety.

Finally, around 5 percent believe in one of the African religions such as Candomblé and Umbanda, or belong to one of the minor spirit churches—whose congregation believe in immortality of the soul and reincarnation and have no relation with the African religions.

Both Candomblé and Umbanda are characterized by a syncretism of Christianity and African beliefs whereby Catholic saints and their images are fused with deities of the African continent, called *orixás*, such as Xangô, the god of thunder and lightning; Oxóssi, the god of forests; Ogum, the god of war; Yemanjá the goddess of the sea; and Exu, the devil. Although these African religions have been persecuted down to recent times, not only did they survive, but they are also responsible for Rio's second most spectacular participatory festival after Carnival. On the night of 31 December, it seems that the whole population of the city descends on Copacabana Beach to launch candlelit paper boats into the sea in honor of *Yemanjá* (see p 161).

Food and Drink

The cosmopolitan character of Rio cuisine is evident in the great variety of dishes from all over Brazil that are served in thousands of restaurants in the city. You can easily find *moquecas* (fish stews) and *vatapás* (mash made out of bread, shrimp, coconut milk, and palm oil), traditional dishes of the north and the northeast with African and Indian ingredients and seasonings, *churrascos* (barbecues) typical of the south of the country, and *cozidos* (stews) of Portuguese and Spanish influence. As becomes the frenetic pace of a big city, however, quick meals are also popular, usually accompanied by tropical fruit juices or soft drinks, eaten standing at the counters of *lanchonetes*, snack-bars that have multiplied at least as quickly as the big international fast food franchises.

churrasco

Porcão

51

Feijoada

©Andy Caulfield/Tips Images

The *feijoada* is the most characteristic dish of Rio de Janeiro. It is traditionally eaten on Saturdays; a distant echo of the times when a pig was slaughtered on the plantations. The cheap cuts were left for the slaves who cooked them in a black bean stew. Today, the *feijoada* still contains cuts that range from cutlets, sausages, and belly to trotters and even ears, cooked in a stew with oil, garlic, onion, and bay leaves. The indispensable accompaniment is white rice, *couve* (sautéed collard greens) with crackling, and *farofa* (manioc flour cooked golden in butter) with some drops of appetizing pepper sauce. Similar to the *feijoada*, the *cozido* is a Carioca institution: a large pot with different kinds of meats (beef, chicken, pork, and sausage) and vegetables (pumpkins, carrots, squash, potatoes, tomatoes, green beans, and onions) is allowed to cook very slowly for up to eight hours, the various ingredients being added at set intervals depending on cooking time.

Plates of Portuguese origin are common in Rio de Janeiro, location of the Lisbon court after 1808. As a first course one may try *caldo verde*, a soup made with greens, *paio* (a type of dried pork sausage), and potatoes. As dessert, one can sample several sweet dishes of Portuguese origin. Some have a base of egg yolk (quindim de côco), as well as fruit compote. Tropical fruit (pineapple, mango, watermelon, for example) and even European fruit acclimatized to Brazil are enjoyed as dessert.

Because of the climate, Cariocas are not as tempted by wine. Beer rules—and the locals like their beer icy cold: you will often see them carry bottles and cans in foam coverings so that the heat does not warm up their drink as they sit back and enjoy it. You can ask for beer in two ways: as *chopp,* when you get it on tap and as a *cerveja,* when you get a bottle or a can.

Caipirinha, the archetypal Brazilian cocktail, consists of white rum *(cachaça)*, sugar, and mashed limes mixed over crushed ice. Its popularity has led to a variety of combinations made with different spirits such as vodka and saki and also cocktails called *batidas* which are mixtures of fruit juices, *cachaça*, and sugar. There is an enormous range of flavors: passion fruit, coconut, *caju* (which is not the nut but the green, bitter cashew fruit), peach, banana, and pineapple to name but a few.

Caipirinhas

©Pascal Dewulf/Fotolia.com

HISTORY

Rio de Janeiro is the jewel in the Bay of Guanabara, which has featured strongly in Brazil's exploration long before the establishment of the city itself. It has witnessed battles between the Portuguese, the French and the local Amerindians; lived through the exploitation cycles of brazilwood, gold and coffee; and has ended up as the cultural capital of Brazil and South America in a long and eventful history spanning over 500 years.

Prehistory

Scientists broadly agree that South America was the last great continental mass to be populated by wandering tribes from Asia through the Bering Strait, around 13–15,000 years ago, although some artifacts have been found in Brazil's Serra da Capivara and controversially carbon-dated to a much earlier time. Unlike in the cooler Andes, the climate and the environment did not lend itself to the viable development of a complex civilization, with the jungle relentless in covering up any possible tracks of cultural complexity. To this day, nothing has been unearthed around Rio de Janeiro that points to the existence of any ancient sophisticated civilization; the earliest pottery fragments date from AD 1000.

When, during the course of the 16C, the Europeans started colonizing Brazil and South America, they called the inhabitants "Indians" without regard. Yet, at the time, more than 400 ethnic groups existed in Brazil alone who differentiated themselves from each other through language, traditions, and institutions. Each tribe congregated in villages that, in turn, formed independent polities. In general, the Amerindians engaged in hunting, fishing (without metal hooks), agriculture, and fruit collecting. They were also in a state of perpetual war, with raids against neighboring tribes aimed at catching prisoners who were, in some tribes, consumed in acts of ritual cannibalism. There were no distinct social classes, and although individual ownership of huts and tools was customary, the land, the rivers, and all natural resources belonged collectively to the polity. Interestingly, some tribal groups,

most notably the Guarani, believed in the existence of a Supreme Being, a Creator of all things.

More frequent, however, was the worship of mythical heroes who had taught a particular group the rites and rules of survival. Any artistic manifestations were confined to dances, chants, rock paintings, body paintings, and the production of utensils for transport, storage, and warfare, such as dugouts, baskets and pots, as well as clubs and arrows. The standard and the preferred medium—stone, clay, wood, or straw— varied widely from tribe to tribe.

Currently about 200 tribal ethnic groups exist in Brazil, conscious of their kinship, their traditions, and their past history, although most have lost many of their original characteristics and have been assimilated.

Altogether their population amounts to about 300,000, of whom 155,000 are speakers of Amerindian languages. An estimated two dozen tribes are still uncontacted.

Discovery and Conflict (1500–1568)

The "discovery" of Brazil is attributed to **Pedro Álvares Cabral**, who led an expedition to the Indies but was blown-off course and ended up landing near present Porto Seguro in Bahia.

There are maps, however, that suggest that the Spanish had already landed upon the South American continent, and there are some who believe that Cabral's discovery was not accidental, but that he was on a secret mission. Cabral named the country Ilha de Vera Cruz, because he falsely believed that

Rio de Janeiro's Original Inhabitants

At the time of the arrival of the Portuguese, most of the aboriginal tribal groupings that occupied the Brazilian coast were part of the Tupi-Guarani linguistic family. In the present state of Rio de Janeiro, they lived in a large band between Cabo Frío and Angra Dos Reis. In this area there were two main rival factions that spoke the Tupi-Guarini language; the Tupinambás (or Tamoios) and the Temiminós (or Maracajás). From the same linguistic group, there were the Tupiniquins in the North coast and the Guararapes in the Valley of the Paraíba do Sul. Also part of this linguistic group were the Goitacás, in the area near the present town of Campos and the Guaianás further south near today's Paraty. Those that didn't speak Tupi-Guarani were called Tapuias by the Portuguese. The Temiminós were readily Christianized and, as they were the mortal enemies of the Tamoios, they willingly allied themselves with the Portuguese. It was thus the Goitacás, and most importantly the Tamoios, who offered the greatest resistance to the Portuguese incursions, suffering relentless persecution until they were wiped out.

he had come ashore on an island rather than an entire continent.

The first expedition to explore and exploit the recently discovered lands was dispatched under the command of Caspar de Lemos. His most illustrious passenger was the Italian navigator Amérigo Vespucci, whose letters back to Lorenzo de' Medici gave an account of his trip that identified the whole continent with his name. As was the custom at the time, the places were baptized according to the religious calendar. Such examples include the Cabo de São Tomé (Cape St Thomas) which he reached on December 21 1501, and the Angra dos Reis ("Cove of the Kings," in this case, the Magi) which he reached on January 6 1502. Rio de Janeiro itself (River of January), where the expedition passed on New Year's Day 1502, was a misnomer, because the narrowness of Guanabara Bay (approx 1km/0.6mi) fooled the Portuguese into thinking they had encountered the mouth of a wide river. Unlike the Island of Vera Cruz, though, the erroneous name stuck. As late as 1570, at a festival in Coimbra, three river figures representing the Ganges, the Nile, and the "River of January" paid their respects to Portuguese King Sebastião.

The expedition reported back that the shores of the new country were full of brazilwood trees *(Caesalpinia echinata)* from which a precious red dye could be extracted and which eventually gave its name to the colony. The exploitation of brazilwood was immediately declared a monopoly of the Portuguese crown, but it was impossible to police and it attracted adventurers of other nationalities, mainly French corsairs. In fact, it was the French, not the Portuguese, who first colonized the coast of Rio de Janeiro, where great forests of this tree species existed.

The history of the next 70-odd years is one of a struggle between the Portuguese and the French for possession of the land and control of the brazilwood trade. The Portuguese eventually emerged victorious, predominantly because Portugal's interest in the new country was far greater than France's.

Brazilwood in Jardim Botânico

Y. Kanazawa/Michelin

Carta do Brasil (1519) by Lopo Homem-Reinéis, depicting the exploitation of brazilwood

April 22 1500—"Discovery" of Brazil by Pedro Álvares Cabral.

1501–1502—First Brazil expedition and accidental discovery of Guanabara Bay, named Rio de Janeiro.

1503— The Portuguese crown sends a second expedition to explore the territory of Brazil, under the command of Gonçalo Coelho. One division reaches Rio de Janeiro and another division, under the command of Amérigo Vespucci, anchors near Cabo Frío for five months where he builds a fortified storehouse.

1503–1504—Arrival in Rio de Janeiro of Binot Paulmier de Gonneville, the first French explorer in Brazil, who succeeds in breaking the Portuguese brazilwood monopoly. When he returns to France, he alleges to have discovered a new "Austral Land." Centuries later this declaration was used by the French to lay claim to the continent of Australia.

1516–1519 and 1525–1528— Because of the continuous harvesting of brazilwood by the French, the Portuguese crown organizes two military expeditions under the command of Cristóvão Jacques. In July 1527 he succeeds in fighting off the French in the first of many naval battles between the two powers over the control of the brazilwood trade.

December 1519—During their circumnavigation of the globe, Magellan and his sailors spend two weeks replenishing their strength in Guanabara Bay, which they describe as "paradise."

1532— The Portuguese King João III organizes the first colonizing expedition, commanded by Martim Alfonso de Souza. He introduces the cultivation of the sugar cane with an *engenho* (sugar plantation) in São Vicente close to the present port of Santos, on the coast of São Paulo. On the beach of today's Flamengo in Rio de

Janeiro, he constructs what some authors describe as an engenho but others as a simple warehouse.

1534–1536—King João III tries to promote the Brazil trade and stimulate settlement by dividing the coast of Brazil into 14 *hereditary captaincies* (strips of land from coast to interior that are guarded and exploited by the captain and their heirs) in return for a ten percent tax levied on the colony's products. Rio de Janeiro falls partly under the captaincy of São Vicente donated to Martim Afonso de Souza, and partly under the captaincy of São Tomé, given to Pero de Góis.

1547— Six hundred colonists and six sugar factories are already working in the captaincy of São Vicente.

1548— Although the hereditary captaincies will survive into the 18C, only two prosper: those of São Vicente and Pernambuco in the northeast. The inability to police the colonists and the general lack of success of the captaincy system leads to the creation of the state of Brazil under the jurisdiction of the Kingdom of Portugal and the Algarve.

1549— The first governor, Tomé de Sousa, arrives in Bahia and founds Salvador, the first capital of Brazil.

1555— Following the lead of the Portuguese crown, Huguenot leader Admiral Gaspar de Coligny sends the French adventurer Nicolas Durand de Villegaignon to Brazil with the objective of establishing the colony of Antarctic France. Villegaignon arrives with two ships and 600 settlers and founds Fort Coligny, the first Protestant outpost in the New World, on a small fortified island in the Bay of Guanabara. Today the island bears Villegaignon's name and houses the Brazilian Naval Academy of Rio de Janeiro.

1559— Villegaignon departs for France, sickened by the religious discord among his compatriots. He never returns.

March 1560—A fleet commanded by the third Governor of Brazil, Mém de Sá, drives the French out of Fort Coligny, but they remain on the mainland, aided and abetted by the Tamoio Indians, who are hostile to the Portuguese.

September 14 1563—The Jesuit priests Manuel da Nóbrega and José de Anchieta succeed in pacifying a branch of the Tamoio near today's Paraty, through the signing of the Peace Treaty of Iperoig with their leader Cunhambebé. This first ever treaty between native Americans and Europeans splits the anti-Portuguese resistance and makes possible an attack on the French.

January 20 1565—The Portuguese finally set up a settlement in the Bay of Guanabara: Captain Estácio de Sá, a nephew of Mém de Sá, establishes the military fort of São Sebastião do Rio de Janeiro in today's Urca district. Estácio's memory lingers on in the Rio suburb that bears his name.

January 1567—After two years of bloody fighting, the French and the Tupinambá in Rio de Janeiro are comprehensively defeated by the Portuguese and their Temiminó allies in two major battles. On January 20, Captain Estácio de Sá is killed by a poisoned arrow in the battle of Uruçu-mirim (around

Lithography depicting a sugar refining mill from A Colourful and Historic Journey to Brazil (19C) by Jean-Baptiste Debret

The Slave Trade

By 1550, the Portuguese policy was clear: protect the new colonies against foreign encroachment and establish *engenhos* (sugar plantations) to take advantage of the explosion in sugar prices that took place around that time. Indeed, the population of Lusoamerica exploded twenty-fold from around 6,500 people in 1546–48 to 150,000 by the end of the 16C. At first, Indian slaves were employed in the engenhos, but the Indians were unused to hard labor and had no immunity to imported European diseases. The Portuguese looked to the nearest continental mass with a surplus of humanity: the stretch of Africa between the Gulf of Guinea and Angola where they had established trading posts.

By the third quarter of the 16C, the transatlantic slave trade was in full swing. Historians have estimated that, just from the port of Luanda, slave exports doubled from some 2,600 a year during the period stretching from 1575 to 1587 to over 5,000 from 1587 to 1591.

Around 50 percent of those transported died en route and the back-breaking work involved in the engenhos ensured that the average young male slave was expected only to live seven years in captivity, which means that the demand for slaves was constant. The Africans sent to Brazil belonged to different tribal groups: in the 16C they arrived primarily from Senegal and the Gambia; in the 17C mostly from Angola and the Congo; in the 18C from Benin. Upon arrival they were split to prevent any actions of solidarity and to force them to communicate in Portuguese. Altogether, about 40 percent of all slaves who came to the Americas would end up in Brazil, an estimated minimum of 3.65 million souls—more than half of them arriving after 1800 to support the coffee boom.

After centuries of the trade, slavery in Brazil had become very institutionalized and deeply rooted in the population's psyche. Its abolition took place on May 13, 1888 with the passing of the Golden Law (see p 61). After a long and protracted legislative battle, slavery in Brazil ended, making it the last country in the western hemisphere to outlaw the practice.

today's suburbs of Glória and Flamengo), while in the north his uncle attacks their positions in Paranapecu (present Ilha do Governador).

March 1567—Mém de Sá moves his nephew's settlement further north, by the Morro do Descanso (Hill of Rest, at the present center of Rio de Janeiro) which becomes the nucleus of the future metropolis. A citadel is built on top of the hill, along with other religious and administrative buildings, which accounts for its later name, Morro do Castelo (Castle Hill), which was destroyed in 1922.

Colonization (1568–1808)

THE SUGAR CYCLE (1568–1693)

Between 1600 and 1650, more than 90 percent of Brazil's earnings were based on sugar exports while the brazilwood trade, much less profitable, declined. Rio de Janeiro remained, however, the most strategic port between Salvador and the Rio de la Plata and it kept growing, eventually eclipsing São Vicente: by 1583 there were only three engenhos in Rio de Janeiro compared with over 100 in Bahia and Pernambuco; by 1629 sixty such plantations were operating.

Yet, while the engenhos were flourishing in the New World, it was events in the Old World that determined the fate of the Portuguese colonies. The young **King Dom Sebastião** was lost in battle in an expedition against the Moors in Morocco. He left no direct heirs and for the following 60 years Brazil was ruled by a union of the Iberian crowns of Portugal and Spain, under the Spanish sovereign Philip II.

As a consequence, the borders between the Spanish and Portuguese colonies in South America were temporarily suspended and European power struggles spread to the continent. There were no more incursions by the French, who were allied to the Spanish, but these were replaced by invasions by the Dutch, the mortal enemies of the Spanish Crown. More successful than the French, the Dutch obtained a firm foothold in Brazil and governed the northeast for 30-odd years. Despite such success, they also eventually withdrew when their attention was diverted as they engaged in a protracted war against Britain.

The 1640 restoration of the Portuguese monarchy under the Braganças eventually brought Brazil back under Portuguese control, but the focus remained in the northeast where the cultivation of sugar was still highly lucrative, until the discovery of gold in the south. Although the first and second governors of Brazil under the Braganças (Jorge and then Vasco Mascarehnas) received the title of Viceroy, it was not until 1714 that the vice-royalty of Brazil was officially established.

1568— Mém de Sá donates the lands on the opposite side of Guanabara Bay to Chief Araribóia of the Temiminó to thank him for his help against the French. Christianized, he adopts the name of his godfather Martim Afonso, the lord of São Vicente, and founds the settlement of São Lourenço dos Índios (the present city of Niterói).

1572— King Sebastião, in whose honor the original settlement in Rio de Janeiro was named, divides Brazil into two administrative regions: North and South. The government of the North is headquartered in Salvador, and the government of the South in Rio de Janeiro.

1575— The governor of Rio de Janeiro, Antonio Salema, organizes an expedition to combat the remaining French who are still clinging on to Cabo Frío with the help of the Tamoios. He expels the French and massacres their Indian allies. He also constructs an engenho for the king himself close to the lagoon of Rodrigo de Freitas with money from the royal coffers.

1578— The government of the colony is again reunified, with Salvador as its capital, to reflect its increasing importance in the sugar trade.

1578— Disappearance of King Sebastião at the Alcácer-Kibir battle.

1580— Union of the Iberian Crowns under Philip II.

1584— Philip II closes all Spanish and Portuguese ports to the Dutch, who are in revolt against his rule.

March 1599—Dutch navigator and buccaneer Olivier Van Noort lands surreptitiously under Sugar Loaf Mountain and makes an attempt to sack Rio de Janeiro, but he is driven back. He goes on to become the first Dutchman to circumnavigate the globe.

1624–1627—The Dutch invade Salvador, Bahia.

1630–1654—The Dutch invade and occupy Recife and Olinda, in Pernambuco. Between 1637 and 1644 the Dutch count and prince João Maurício de Nassau-Siegen manages Companhia das Índias Ocidentais no Brasil in Brazil.

1640— Proclamation of the Duke of Bragança as King João IV of Portugal and of the Union of the Iberian Crowns.

THE GOLD CYCLE (1693–1808)

There are many claims as to who the first man to discover gold in Brazil was, but the current consensus favors Antônio Rodrigues de Arzão. In 1693, he mined an ounce of the precious metal in the Itaverava hills, in the present state of Minas Gerais. This was a momentous event not just for the history of Brazil,

Alferes Joaquim José da Silva Xavier, the Tiradentes (1940) by J. W. Rodrigues

Museu Histórico Nacional

but also for the city of Rio de Janeiro which became the main shipping port for the extracted gold. At its peak (1735–1754) exports averaged 14–15 tons per year.

Rio's new-found wealth once again attracted the interests of the French. In 1710, a squadron comprising six ships and 1,200 men under admiral **Jean François Duclerc** tried to take Rio de Janeiro by force, but was comprehensively defeated.

Duclerc was taken prisoner and mysteriously assassinated. Louis XIV was furious and vowed revenge: the next year French Admiral René Duguay-Trouin, sailing with 17 ships, 600 cannons, and 6,000 men, succeeded in capturing a heavily fortified and well-defended Rio de Janeiro after an 11-day battle. He freed the French prisoners from Duclerc's expedition, held the Portuguese governor Castro Morais to ransom, and extracted a heavy penalty in gold. It was the biggest naval victory of the French in Brazil, but was of no lasting consequence: this was a plundering expedition; the dream of Antarctic France had faded.

Passeio Público today

RioTur

Inevitably, in 1763, the government of Brazil was unified and transferred to Rio de Janeiro, which became the new capital of Brazil. This represented a fundamental shift of the economic center of gravity from the north to the south of the country which has not been reversed since.

Stirred by the US revolution and by French illuminist ideas, several notables from Minas Gerais organized a conspiracy, known in Brazil as the Inconfidência Mineira, with the aim of declaring the independence of Brazil. In 1789, they are betrayed, apprehended, and exiled, apart from their leader, a dentist called **Joaquim José da Silva Xavier**. In 1792, he is hanged publicly in Rio de Janeiro from a gallows erected in what today is Praça Tiradentes, a square named after his nickname: Toothpuller.

Much of the gold went to finance the arts: this was the time of Brazilian Baroque, as rich lay fraternities competed with each other by commissioning lavishly decorated churches, mainly in Minais Gerais, Bahia, and Rio de Janeiro. Viceroy Dom Luís de Vasconcelos e Souza commissioned the first public works in Rio, including the **Passeio Público** (see p 124), the first public park in the Americas, which resulted from the draining of a fetid lagoon. Yet, although the town continued to expand, it still remained a colonial backwater until the Napoleonic wars caused the Portuguese court to take refuge in the city.

1693— Antonio Rodrigues de Arzão discovers gold in Minas Gerais.

1704–1705—Opening of the Caminho Novo, by Garcia Rodrigues Paes, a route that snakes Serra do Mar from the gold mines of Minas Gerais down to the ports of Paraty, Angra dos Reis, and Rio de Janeiro.

1710— Admiral Jean François Duclerc tries to capture Rio de Janeiro, but fails.

September 21 1711—French Admiral René Duguay-Trouin captures Rio de Janeiro and leaves after extracting ransom money.

1714— Establishment of the Vice Royalty of Brazil.

1727— Coffee seeds are smuggled from French Guyana into Brazil by Francisco de Melo Palheta.

1763— Rio de Janeiro becomes the capital of Brazil.

1770— João Alberto de Castelo Branco, a former appeals court judge, starts the cultivation of coffee in Rio de Janeiro. The first seedlings sprout in a garden in the current Rua Evaristo da Veiga beside the Teatro Municipal.

1785— Prohibition by Portuguese Queen Maria I of the establishment of any manufacturing industry in Brazil. This decree, occurring during a point when the mines were being depleted, leads to widespread discontent in the colony.

1789— The Inconfidência Mineira (Minas Conspiracy) is discovered and its leaders imprisoned.

1792— Tiradentes is hanged in Rio de Janeiro.

Independence and Monarchy (1808–1889)

Once again, events in Europe decisively influenced the history of Brazil. Napoleon's Iberian invasion and subsequent peninsular wars forced the Portuguese royal family and court to flee to their transatlantic colony and to transfer the seat of government to Rio de Janeiro. In all, 15,000 courtesans, aristocrats, and administrators fled to Rio at a time when the city numbered around 45,000 locals, mostly slaves. This was the first and only time in history when a colonial town become the capital of a European state; as such, Rio de Janeiro was elevated in status and its nouveau-riche elites gained much prestige with the dishing out of titles such as Count, Viscount, or Duke. The Regent—and after Maria the Mad's death in 1816, King—João VI inaugurated many of today's city landmarks, such as the **Botanical Gardens** (♿ see p 175) and instituted such public institutions as a central bank and a royal press. The prohibition on manufacturing industry was revoked and trade with Brazil was opened to all friendly nations with Portugal's prime ally, Great Britain, receiving particularly favorable customs terms.

In 1816, João VI invited a group of French artists to Brazil in order to establish an Academy of Fine Arts. Its most famous

Portrait of João VI and Carlota Joaquina (19C) by Manuel Dias de Oliveira

Museu Histórico Nacional

members were the painter **Jean-Baptiste Debret** (1768–1848), who depicted the city, its costumes, and characters from 1816 to 1831, when he left Brazil, and architect **Grandgean de Montigny**, who introduced Neo-classical architecture and whose main work is Casa França-Brasil.

Although the Napoleonic Wars ended in 1815, João VI only reluctantly left Brazil for Portugal six years later. He left behind as Regent his elder son Pedro who had come of age in the colony. When the Portuguese deputies in Lisbon tried to restore the previous state of affairs, he

Long Road to Abolition

1831 Under pressure from Great Britain, all slaves entering Brazil are declared free and the importation of slaves is prohibited. However, the authorities only pay lip service to the law and turn a blind eye to the trade: in the 1830s and 1840s the average number of imported slaves is still 35,000 per annum.

1850 The slave trade is finally abolished; Brazilian ships are prohibited to carry African slaves under penalty of heavy fines.

1864–1869 Paraguayan War, dubbed Dom Pedro's War. Slaves are promised emancipation and they fight as volunteers alongside poorer soldiers, creating a camaraderie that lasts after the war ends.

1871 Passing of the Law of the Free Womb, freeing children born of slave mothers.

1885 Passing of the Law of the Sexagenarians, freeing the slaves who are more than 60 years old.

May 13 1888 Passing of the Golden Law, by Princess Isabel, Dom Pedro's daughter and Regent, while he is on a trip abroad. This is the law that finally and fully emancipates the 700,000 slaves left in the country.

Dom Pedro II

©Corbis

declared Brazil's independence at Ipiranga on September 7, 1822. He ruled in Rio de Janeiro as Pedro I, but faced resistance from his government assembly when he tried to propose an absolutist constitution. However, he also departed in 1831 to claim the throne of Portugal when it became vacant. He, in turn, left power to his five-year old son, Pedro II. After a period of Regency Pedro II was coronated at the age of 15. His 50-year reign defined 19C imperial Brazil. After brazilwood and gold it was now coffee cultivation in and around the capital, especially in the Valley of Paraíba, that enriched the elites and underlined the city's importance.

1808— The Portuguese royal family and Court flee Lisbon for Brazil.

1809— Establishment of the Botanical Gardens in Rio de Janeiro.

1810— Creation of the Royal Library (now National Library) *see p 111.*

1815— Elevation of the status of Brazil to that of an equal partner with Portugal under the United Kingdom of Brazil, Portugal, and the Algarve—with the capital in Rio de Janeiro.

1816— Death of Maria the Mad, and elevation of her son to King João VI.

1821— João VI returns to Portugal to assume the throne, leaving his son Dom Pedro in Brazil.

September 7 1822—Dom Pedro proclaims the independence of Brazil, declaring "Independência ou Morte"! (Independence or death!). He becomes Dom Pedro I of Império do Brasil.

April 7 1831—Dom Pedro I abdicates in favor of his son Dom Pedro de Alcântara, still only five years old.

1840— After a decade's regency, Dom Pedro II ascends to the throne, at the age of only 15.

1840–1870—The golden age of coffee cultivation in the Valley of Paraíba around Rio de Janeiro.

1844— Protectionist customs tariffs, favorable to industrialization in Brazil, are established by minister Alves Branco.

1854— Inauguration of the first Brazilian railroad, connecting Guanabara Bay to the auriferous mountain ranges of the interior.

1861–1868—Establishment and reforestation of the Tijuca massif, establishing what would later become the Tijuca National Park (*see p 139*).

1888— Abolition of slavery.

The Old Republic (1889–1930)

Discontent started when Pedro II led Brazil to the war against Paraguay (1864–1870), which had disastrous results from a political and economic perspective. The emancipation of the slaves in 1888 was deeply unpopular amongst the land-owning aristocracy. As a result, the economic elite, along with the army, felt empowered enough to depose the king and declare a republic.

The first president was Marshal Deodoro da Fonseca, followed by the much-feared Marshal Floriano Vieira Peixoto, who consolidated the republic by repressing dissent.

The Old Republic, as it was called, was nicknamed a democracy of *café com leite* (coffee with milk) because, with few exceptions, the presidency and the government posts were bound together with the coffee-producing oligarchies of São Paulo and the cattle-owning landocracy of Minas Gerais, while Rio de Janeiro's upper classes provided the bulk of the bureaucracy in the capital.

The republic was not universally loved. In the south, the states of Santa Catarina and Rio Grande do Sul tried unsuccessfuly to rebel. The navy mutinied in Rio de Janeiro itself and bombed the capital from the sea, but its defiance was doomed as the army controlled the land. In 1896–97, there was an uprising of a semi-religious mass cult of landless peasants and recently emancipated slaves in Canudos in the interior of the state of Bahia. It required five campaigns and a large force to put it down, and its consequences were long-lasting and unexpected.

Culturally, the uprising provided Brazilian literature with one of its biggest and best known epics, *Os Sertões* by Euclides da Cunha. Linguistically, it created one of Brazil's internationally known expres-

Manoel Deodoro da Fonseca (c.1895)

Library of Congress

sions: the poor soldiers who fought in the Canudos revolt were granted a hill in Rio de Janeiro to settle on; they named it "favela"—after "Morro da Favela" a hill covered in favela plants where they had decamped by Canudos—a word that eventually became a byword for the ramshackle Rio shantytowns.

November 15 1889—Proclamation of the republic under the presidency of Manoel Deodoro da Fonseca
1891— First republican constitution of Brazil.

Brazilian flags over Praia de Ipanema

R. Mills/Michelin

The Flag of Brazil

The army in Brazil was deeply inspired by the—today outmoded—positivist philosophy, which had many adherents in the late 19C. Its founder and main proponent was August Comte (1798–1857) who believed in a secular, industrial society governed by reason and logic. The positivist motto was eventually drawn on the flag of Brazil: *Ordem e Progreso* (order and progress) where on today's flag it can be read on the central white banner. The green is said to represent the forests of Brazil; the yellow its gold; and the blue is the sky of Rio de Janeiro on the night of November 15, 1889 (the day of the proclamation of the Republic)—each star representing one of the Brazilian states.

1893–94—Mutiny of the Navy in Rio.

1896–1897—Canudos revolt.

1914— World War I interrupts European imports and encourages the expansion of local industrial activities. Brazil enters the war on the side of the Allies on October 27 1917 and captures 46 German ships that were anchored in Brazilian ports.

1929— Crisis in the New York stock exchange and crash of coffee prices destabilizes the Brazilian economy and the *café com leite* politics.

From Dictatorship to Democracy to Dictatorship again

Concerned by the post-1929 crash collapse in coffee prices, a military coup put an end to the Old Republic and its domination by the coffee and cattle-breeding oligarchies. Concerned by the post-1929 crash collapse in coffee prices, a military coup put an end to the Old Republic and its domination by the coffee and cattle-raising oligarchies. In 1930 **Getúlio Vargas** (1883–1954), with the support of several states and the army, took over the command of the provisional government, dispersed Congress, suspended the Constitution of 1891, appointed interveners to replace elected governors in the states and decreed that no act from the provisional government could be contested by the Judiciary, until order was reinstated.

The Constitutionalist Revolution (sometimes known as the Paulista War) erupted in São Paulo in 1932 with the aim of pressuring Vargas into creating a new Constitution. The uprising was quelled, but a constituent assembly was convened and a new Constitution promulgated in 1934. However, under threat of political revolution, Vargas revoked that Constitution and enacted another, establishing the authoritarian Estado Novo (New State), that lasted from 1937 to 1945, with strong government intervention in the economy.

After sustained US pressure, Brazil entered World War II on the side of the Allies, and fought alongside them, most notably in Italy, but when the war was over the prevailing anti-dictatorship mood brought the Estado Novo to an end and elections were called. Vargas created a party and put himself to the vote, but lost. Still, he kept his contacts and made a remarkable comeback in 1951 when he won comprehensively with a populist, left-wing program. When in power though, things turned sour, a hostile press, a collapse in coffee prices, and a balance of payments

©Bettmann/Corbis

General Getúlio Vargas (center), then the head of the military junta in a railway coach arriving at Rio de Janeiro to take charge of the new government on November 19, 1930

crisis tipped Vargas over the edge. One of his close associates tried to assassinate Carlos Lacerda, one of the governments most vituperative newspaper critics. Lacerda was only wounded, but his bodyguard was killed. Vargas was implicated, though he denied the accusations, and his dramatic reaction still divides Brazilians. On 24 August 1954 he shot himself in Rio de Janeiro's **Catete Palace** (◔ see p 149) leaving behind a dramatic suicide note that touched a chord with an emotional nation.

This dénouement absolved him of every fault and turned him into a labor legend in the eyes of many of his compatriots. Vargas' Vice President, João Café Filho, continued to govern until 1956, when Juscelino Kubitschek, a centrist politician, won the elections with a positive vision of the future. His strategy of rapid industrialization and the building of a new capital, Brasília, in an arid region of the center-west caused a balance of payments crisis. He financed it by printing money against the advice of orthodox economists and took a stand by refusing the help of the IMF. This strategy was popular at home, but it created an "institutional" inflation in the economy: in 1955 inflation stood at 11.7 percent; by 1964 it had risen to 89.9 percent. Still, within four years, the new capital was ready to accept the legislative chambers and on 21 April 1960, the anniversary of Tiradentes' death, the capital was officially transferred from Rio de Janeiro to Brasília.

Matters came to a head with the presidency of João Goulart, who came to power after Kubitschek's successor Jânio Quadros resigned within nine months. Goulart was a Vargas protégé and was responsible for raising the minimum wage by 100 percent, thus infuriating the elites. His alleged ties with the banned Communist Party were unacceptable to the army, and they deposed him on April 1, 1964, plunging Brazil into the longest and harshest dictatorship in its existence. Indeed, after 1968, the strict censorship caused many politicians, journalists, filmmakers, musicians, and intellectuals to leave for Europe. The military dictatorship lasted 21 long years.

Heads of the military dictatorship 1964–1985

1964–1967	Marshal Humberto de Alencar Castelo Branco
1967–1969	Marshal Arthur da Costa e Silva
1969–1974	General Emílio Garrastazu Médici
1974–1979	General Ernesto Geisel
1979–1985	General João Baptista de Oliveira Figueiredo

This was a time of a crisis of confidence for Rio de Janeiro, which had lost its capital status and in 1976 its state status when the city was merged with the surrounding state of Rio de Janeiro: of the 21 daily newspapers circulating in 1960, only seven still remained in 1980, while all 15 weekly magazines closed. Businesses left the city center and despite a short economic boom—between 1968 and 1973 Brazil's economy recorded a 14 percent annual growth—Rio de Janeiro was a city under great economic strain.

1930—	Revolution of 1930 and rise of Getúlio Vargas.
1931—	The Christ the Redeemer statue on Corcovado is inaugurated.
1943—	Brazil enters World War II and fights in Italy alongside the Allies.
1946–1951—	Eurico Gaspar Dutra wins the first democratic elections for 20 years.
1951–1954—	Ex-dictator Getúlio Vargas returns to power constitutionally.
1954—	Getúlio Vargas commits suicide.
1956–1961—	President Juscelino Kubitschek de Oliveira wins the elections, promising to build Brasília.
April 21 1960—	(Tiradentes Day) Transfer of the capital from Rio de Janeiro to Brasília. Rio de Janeiro becomes the city-state of Guanabara.

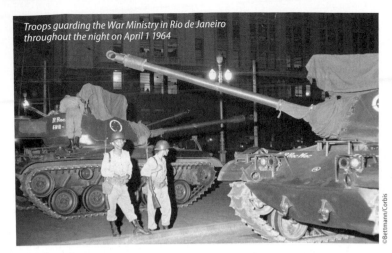

Troops guarding the War Ministry in Rio de Janeiro throughout the night on April 1 1964

©Bettmann/Corbis

1961— The left-wing president Jânio Quadros is elected, but soon resigns.

1961–1964— João Belchior Marques Goulart inherits the presidency, but is deposed by a military coup because of his left-wing credentials.

1960s–1970s— Opening of the tunnels to Zona Sul (South Zone) and middle-class flight to Copacabana, Ipanema and, later, Barra, shifting the population to the south of Rio de Janeiro.

1974— Oil discovery in the Bacia de Campos, 50mi/80km from the coast of Rio de Janeiro, re-energizes the state.

1975— Fusion of the States of Guanabara and of Rio de Janeiro, with a common capital in Rio de Janeiro.

The New Republic

Brazil's rising external debt, a rampant inflation that reached 235 percent in 1985, a balance of payments crisis, plus international pressure forced the military to step down, call elections, and transfer power to an indirectly elected president. He was Tancredo Neves, who on his day of inauguration was stricken with stomach pains and had to be admitted to hospital. He died there after seven operations and the mantle passed to his vice-president, José Sarney. Like many before him, Sarney tried to stabilize the currency and reign in the galloping inflation (1,783 percent by 1989), but failed.

Fernando Collor de Melo, a Carioca politician with a power-base in the northeast, became the first directly elected president of Brazil in the New Republic, inheriting an inflation of nearly 100 percent a month. Despite several dramatic measures such as reducing the

Oil rig at Bacia de Campos

©Gustavo Gilabert/Corbis Saba

federal budget, freezing savings and prices, sacking public employees, and privatizing industries, inflation continued its upward rise. His critics accused him of bypassing Congress and shunning public debate and he made many political enemies. Accused of corruption, he became the target of a congressional investigation and was successfully impeached at the end of 1992.

His vice-president, Itamar Franco, came to power and he appointed Fernando Henrique Cardoso as finance minister. Cardoso tackled inflation head-on, and produced a complex plan, the focus of which was the introduction in 1994 of a new currency, the Real.

Amazingly, Cardoso succeeded: he reigned in inflation. When Itamar Franco resigned, he put himself forward as candidate and was elected president for two terms, the maximum under Brazil's 1988 constitution. His reform program brought much-needed stability and foreign investment.

The 2002 election brought to power an ex-union leader, **Luiz Inácio** (Lula) **da Silva**, who became Brazil's first president from the Worker's Party. Despite some concerns in the international community, Lula has been successful in pushing forward Brazil's industry and commerce along with a domestic social program to eliminate hunger. In 2006, he too, gained a second term.

Lula

©Riccardo Antimiani/EIDON/UPPA/Photoshot

1985— Indirect election of president Tancredo Neves who dies before resuming his office.

1985–1990—Presidency of José Sarney.

1988— The latest Brazilian constitution institutes universal suffrage: this is the first time that voting is extended to the illiterate masses.

1990–1992—Fernando Collor de Mello is the first directly elected President. Corruption scandals result in his impeachment.

1992–1995—Vice-president Itamar Augusto Franco inherits the presidency.

1994— Fernando Henrique Cardoso, an economist and technocrat by nature, succeeds in capping inflation by introducing a new currency, the Real.

1995–2002—Presidency of Fernando Henrique Cardoso over two terms.

2002— Luiz Inácio (Lula) da Silva from the Worker's Party wins the October election in the second round with 60 percent of the vote.

2006— President Lula wins a second term.

The Success of "Plan Real"

Year	Annual Inflation Rate %
1994	929
1995	22
1996	11
1997	4

ART AND CULTURE

"Tupi or not Tupi, that is the question," poet Oswald de Andrade famously asked, and this bilingual ironic wordplay demonstrates the existential dilemma of Brazil's artists, torn between their African, Amerindian, and European roots. Capitalizing on their cultural diversity, Rio's artists have made a significant impact in shaping Brazil's heritage—noteworthy Rio de Janeiro highlights being the Baroque churches and Modernist buildings, world-class literature, and a wide range of remarkable music.

Architecture

COLONIAL ARCHITECTURE

The early colonial architecture has not survived Rio de Janeiro's various facelifts. One building that survived these transformations because of its royal connections and thus provides the best illustration of early colonial architecture in Rio de Janeiro is the **Paço Imperial**. This was built in 1743 by the Portuguese architect **José Fernandes Pinto Alpoim** (1700–1765) for Rio's governor Gomes Freire de Andrade. After 1767 it was used by the viceroys of Brazil and later, temporarily, by the royal family as the imperial palace.

It is mostly in the **coffee plantations** in the valley of the Rio Paraíba (*see p 212*) that visitors can find examples of the so-called colonial architecture, in fact an adaptation of the urban architecture to the rural environment. Even so, by the time the houses were erected the coffee barons had largely abandoned the traditional style of the

17C and 18C sugar *engenhos*, which consisted mainly of large, sober, plain bungalows. The plan of the coffee farms was organized in the form of a square: the *casa-grande*, residence of the proprietor; an open yard for the drying of the beans; warehouses where coffee was stored; and finally, the *senzala*, the slave quarters. Although ample and grand, the houses were rather crude due to lack of proper materials and specialist manpower. They were built quickly by slaves practicing half-timbered "pau-a-pique" techniques using stones and adobe walls based on wooden frames. The facades, the doors, and the windows tended to the Neo-classical style, which was in vogue at the time, while the interior decoration consisted of imported wallpaper and large paintings with themes of classical antiquity. It is typical of 18C rural architecture that can still be encountered in the gold mining towns of Minas Geráis: two levels, with the top floor dominated by large ornamented windows and balconies with railings, inner courtyards, thick wooden doors

Colonial: Paço Imperial

H. Choimet/Michelin

and ceilings. What identified the Paço Imperial as a weighty building is the central three-story marble baroque portal that towers over the surroundings and, one imagines, the rest of the 19C city.

BAROQUE AND ROCOCO

These styles appeared much later than in Europe and of all the forms of artistic manifestation, it was in religious art and architecture that Baroque and especially Rococo found their most profound expression. This is hardly surprising: since Baroque had been affirmed as the religious art of the Counter-Reformation as a backlash against Protestant purity, it was through the Catholic church that it was introduced in Brazil in places where there were enough faithful to justify the expense: first in the northeast (Bahia and Pernambuco) and later in Rio de Janeiro and Minas Geráis.

There are three distinct stages of evolution of Baroque in Brazil. Originally (1549–1640) the anonymous artisans looked to reproduce the European standards and prescriptions without, however, using proper materials. The results were poor imitations with little artistic merit; therefore, any interest in the buildings and artifacts tends to be purely historical. The second phase can be placed between the Bragança Restoration (1640), and the move of the capital of Brazil to Rio de Janeiro (1763). This corresponds to the belated evolution of Mannerist style and the introduction of Baroque. The discovery of gold and the ensuing riches brought many Portuguese artists to Brazil, thus raising the quality and creative standards. Finally, from the second half of the 18C until the arrival of the **French Mission** in 1816, the wealth generated by the gold reached its apex. As lay fraternities—the "third orders"—competed with each other in extravagance, this period also coincides with the pinnacle of Brazilian Rococo that manifested itself in several distinct styles.

Baroque: Igreja Nossa Senhora da Glória do Outeiro

H. Choimet/Michelin

The architectural model adopted by the **Company of Jesus** was based on simple and austere lines. The general plan included a rectangular patio, which was surrounded by the church itself, the college, the workshops, and the Jesuit residences. The aim was the education and instruction of the natives: there was ample space in front, the *terreiro*, which became the origin of many squares in the country. The church that epitomizes this style in the state of Rio de Janeiro is that of **São Pedro d'Aldeia**: a single nave without pillars serves as a large congregation room with plenty of light, good acoustics, and an altar visible from every angle.

The **Franciscans** built large monasteries surrounded by covered galleries but, as the orders became richer, they built adjoining churches. One such case in point is Rio's **Church of São Francisco da Penitência** by the convent of Santo Antônio—despite the members' wealth, the whole complex maintains the ascetic character of the monastical brotherhood.

The constructions of the Jesuits and the Franciscans were stern and simple, whereas the **Carmelite** and the **Benedictine** orders built churches heavily laden with gold decorations, appealing as much to the emotions of the faithful as displaying the ostentatiousness of their paymasters. Indeed, the later Rococo structures are distinctly different from anything found in Portugal, having been built by second-generation artisans born and bred in Brazil who were isolated from the trends in Europe. The masterpiece of Carioca Baroque is the **Monastery of São Bento**, established 1617 and steadily extended and enriched over 200 years—whose rather plain, Mannerist exterior hides an opulent, heavily gilded, three-nave interior creating, as it is said, "a forest of gold." The later Rococo jewels are the church of **Nossa Senhora da Glória do Outeiro** (1739) with its unusual entrance under a tower galley and, even more so, the two Carmelite churches: **Nossa Senhora da Ordem Terceira do Monte do Carmo** (1770) and the nearby recently-restored **Nossa Senhora do Carmo da Antiga Sé** (1761) with its remarkable silver altar, which served as Rio's cathedral until the inauguration of the modernist **Cathedral of São Sebastião** in 1976.

NEO-CLASSICISM

Unlike previous movements, Neo-classicism appeared in Brazil at the same time as in Europe, with the arrival of the **French Mission** brought to Brazil by João VI in 1816, possibly the single most influential artistic incident in Brazil's history. Afterward, under Emperor Pedro II, Neo-classicism acquired a patron with the depth of cultural appreciation and clout any architectural tendency requires in order to fully flourish. It was adopted as Rio de Janeiro's main urban style: the building footprints grew, favoring the monumental; the roof tiles disappeared from view; the facades acquired a symmetry with rows of windows around a characteristically triangular portico with Doric, Tuscan, or Ionic columns on the ground floor while Corinthian ones were favored for the upper levels.

The **Casa França-Brasil** was the first Neo-classical building in Rio de Janeiro. Built in 1819 by **Auguste Henri Victor Grandjean de Montigny**, its influence was immense and can be readily seen in the buildings that followed: the old Pedro II Hospice, currently the **Federal University of Rio de Janeiro**, in Botafogo; the house of the Marquesa de Santos, currently Museu do Primeiro Reinado, in São Cristóvão; the **Catete Palace**, Brazil's presidential lodgings from 1894 to 1960; and the **Imperial Palace** in Petrópolis, which is the best illustration of Neo-classicism outside the city of Rio de Janeiro itself, and also some stately homes in the Coffee Valley follow this style.

Some elements of 18C architecture continued to be used in some houses and one can sometimes see typically Colonial half-timbered "pau-a-pique" walls and sloping tiled roofs, next to typically Neo-classical Doric columns. The Rua do Comércio in the city of Paraty is an excellent demonstration of this mixture of two styles.

ECLECTICISM

Eclecticism started to express itself in Rio de Janeiro toward the last quarter of the 19C until well into the beginning of the 20C. One of its characteristics was the juxtaposition of multiple styles on the same building with the predominant being either Italianate Renaissance, Gothic Revival, Neo-classical, or French Empire, which was particularly influential in the public domain. The graceful **Museu Nacional de Belas Artes** and the **Theatro Municipal** provide the standards of this latter style whose essential elements were mansard roofs, round arches, Corinthian pillars, and the alternation of linear and circular facades.

Neo-Classicism: Museu Imperial, Petrópolis

H. Choimet/Michelin

Eclecticism: Theatro Municipal

Sadly a combination of modernist dogma and a lack of concern with the preservation of the monuments have conspired to flatten some of the best instances of Carioca Eclecticism such as the Monroe Palace at Praça Floriano—seat of the Senate until its move to Brasília—which was built in 1904–1906 and demolished after a long resistance campaign in 1976. Thankfully there are still some beautiful examples of this style in Rio de Janeiro, at **Palacio Laranjeiras** at Parque Guinle, and—some say the best example—the glamorous **Copacabana Palace Hotel** (1923), whose stylish façade, based on the Hotel Carlton in Cannes, brings a touch of French *fin-de-siécle* design to Rio's most famous beach.

Private villas adopted varied European regional styles, according to the taste of their proprietors. They traveled to Europe—especially to the sanatoriums of Switzerland for health reasons—and admired the wooden chalets that were particularly suited to Rio's climate, as well as the rustic dwellings of France and the Florentine or Venetian *palazzos*. As a result, more or less faithful reproductions appeared in the vicinity of Rio de Janeiro, especially in the city of Petrópolis, where visitors can stroll through whole streets of Alpine chalets

Neo-Gothic: Palacete da Ilha Fiscal

Art Deco: Edifício Biarritz

with Neo-classical porticoes, giving a rather colorful "folly" character to these constructions.

The bright green **Palacete da Ilha Fiscal**, on the eponymous island of the Bay of Guanabara, is a superb example. Designed by Adolfo José Del Vecchio as a neo-Gothic chateau on the express orders of Pedro II so that "it matches the Serra do Mar views" behind it, this was the last great building built by slave labor and was inaugurated in April 1889, only months before the monarchy itself collapsed in Brazil.

Eclecticism ruled in Rio de Janeiro absolutely until the middle of the 1920s when it was partly replaced by its more avant-garde versions of Art Nouveau, with its decorative preference for flora, movement, and iron railings, and by Art Deco, with its more stylized curves, leaded glass, and ziggurats. The most famous Art Deco monument in Rio de Janeiro—maybe in the world—is, of course, the **Cristo Redentor** statue (1931) on Corcovado.

After the orgy of reconstruction in the 1960s and 1970s, it is a miracle that any Art Nouveau or Art Deco houses have survived. They can found in Urca on Rua Urbano Santos 26 and in Copacabana on the Ruas Ronald de Carvalho e Viveiros de Castro. Beautiful examples also shelter in the suburb of Flamengo, in Castelinho do Flamengo at 158 Flamengo Beach, now **Cultural Center Oduvaldo Vianna Filho**, built in 1916–1918 by the Italian architect Gino Copede; the **Edifício Seabra** at 88 Flamengo Beach, Rio's first apartment block built in 1910 by Italian architect Mario Vodret, also nicknamed "The Carioca Dakota," because of its resemblance to the Dakota Building

1930's: Copacabana Palace

Contemporary: Museu de Arte Contemporânea, Niterói

H. Choimet/Michelin

in New York; and the **Edifício Biarritz**, the best known Art Deco Rio landmark at 268 Flamengo Beach, designed in the early 1940s by French architect Henri Sajous who also built the startling Igreja da Santíssima Trinidade at Rua Senador Vergueiro (1938). The **Casa de Arte e Cultura Julieta da Serpa** built in 1920, is a highlight which should be seen illuminated at night to fully appreciate its French style.

MODERNISM

Ironically, as the French Mission defined Neo-classical public architecture and the Swiss chalets influenced buildings in the private sphere, it was French–Swiss architect, **Le Corbusier** (1887–1965), who spawned the biggest artistic revolution that occurred in Brazil in the 20C.

In 1936 a group of young architects under **Lúcio Costa** (1902–1998) was given the task of designing the new headquarters of the Ministry of Education and Health.

The resulting **Capanema Palace** exemplified a new architecture characterized by the employment of metallic structures, the front "wall of glass," and the just-discovered reinforced concrete. In the same year Le Corbusier came to Rio de Janeiro for a series of lectures based on his functionalist theories that would fire up Brazil's architectural minds. From that point on Modernist architecture became an expression of the national culture, looking to interpret Le Corbusier's principles in a Brazilian accent, adopting the futuristic as a sign of the country's forward progress.

Le Corbusier's most illustrious pupil was **Oscar Niemeyer** (b. 1907), one of the biggest Modernist names in 20C architecture, whose curvilinear concrete creations reveal his unique blend of Brazilian baroque with the modernist imagination. Carioca born and bred, he graduated from the Escola Nacional de Belas Artes in 1934 and worked with Lúcio Costa from 1937 to 1943. Extremely prolific, by the 1970s he had completed 600 projects on four continents including the United Nations building in New York (with Le Corbusier), the French Communist Party's HQ in Paris, and most major buildings in Brasília.

Although the Modernist dream was realized in Brasília, there are many examples of Modernism in Rio de Janeiro, other than the all-important Capanema Palace, such as the **Airport Santos Dumont** (1937) by Milton and Marcelo Roberto, the **Museu de Arte Moderna** by Affonso Eduardo Reidy, the pyramidal **Catedral Metropolitana** (1976) by Edgar Fonseca, and the extraordinary **Museum of Contemporary Art** in Niterói (1996) designed by Niemeyer himself.

Currently, the new, and as yet not open to the public, **Cidade da Música** in Barra da Tijuca (2008), designed by Moroccan-born architect **Christian de Portzamparc**—a building on stilts looming over a garden landscaped by award-winning Brazilian architect **Fernando Chacel**—appears to be inheriting the crown of the most original modernist structure this side of Brasília.

Sítio Burle Marx

Y. Kanazawa/Michelin

Landscape Architecture

Landscaping does not come up often in the examination of a country's creative output unless that country is Brazil, the birthplace of **Roberto Burle Marx** (1909–1994) who is considered the greatest 20C tropical landscape designer.

Born in São Paulo, he moved with his parents to Rio de Janeiro when he was four. He then studied painting in Berlin, Germany, where he discovered the beauty of his homeland's flora in that city's Botanical Gardens. He returned to Brazil in 1930 and graduated from the Escola Nacional de Belas Artes. At only 29, he created the memorable Capanema Palace gardens in 1938 and went on to draw up plans for the open spaces and common grounds of several public buildings using exuberant exotic foliage.

His work in Rio de Janeiro includes the **Instituto Moreira Salles** (1950)— where he also designed its striking blue tiles—the **Museu da Chácara do Céu** in Santa Teresa (1972), and the landscaping of the **Museu de Arte Moderna**. Still, the Burle Marx compositions a casual visitor is most likely to encounter are the stylized black-and-white **wave mosaics** on the sidewalks of Copacabana Beach, based on a traditional Portuguese design, and his biggest commission, the open, welcoming **Parque do Flamengo** (1961).

Burle Marx's first love had always been horticulture. In 1949 he bought a 90acre/36.5ha old plantation in the suburb of Guaratiba where he cultivated rare tropical plants. In 1985 he donated his estate to the federal government, which has now transformed it into **Sítio Burle Marx**, one of Rio's most beautiful sites.

Sculpture

Until the mid-18C sculpture in Brazil meant one of two things: the decorative engraving for the altars, side chapels, and the sacristies of the churches or "talha," the carving of the often wooden and occasionally terra-cotta figures of saints and angels.

Most of the early statues from that period have been created by anony-

São Paulo Week Of Modern Art

If the arrival of the French Mission was the event that kick-started much of Brazilian art, the Week of Modern Art (11–18 February 1922) in São Paulo was a veritable earthquake. In that short space of time artists from all over the country were brought together and a new Brazilian consciousness was adopted, one that reflected upon the history and embraced the full range of cultural influences of the country. This occasion represented the first collective gesture of rupture with the old values of the previous century and the dawn of an autochthonous art movement.

A direct consequence of this was the birth of the Colonial Revival style that adapted elements of Portuguese architecture of the 17C and 18C using modern designs. In Rio de Janeiro this can be best seen in the Casa do Trem, which became part of the Museu Histórico Nacional after the building was remodeled for the exposition on the centenary of the Independence of Brazil in 1922.

Mestre Valentim

The most important late 18C sculptor in Rio de Janeiro was Valentim da Fonseca e Silva known to Cariocas as Mestre Valentim (c. 1740–1813). He was the major executor of the public works during the administration of Viceroy Dom Luís de Vasconcelos e Souza (1779–1790) and his chief commission was the construction of the *Passeio Público*, the first urban park in the Americas. In this he was aided by the best contemporary Carioca artists such as painter Leandro Joaquim and decorators Francisco dos Santos Xavier and Francisco Xavier Cardoso de Almeida.

The sculptures of Mestre Valentim contain traces of rococo with Neo-classical and romantic undertones. They can be seen as carvings and sacred images in many Rio churches, such as Nossa Senhora da Conceição e Boa Morte, São Pedro dos Clérigos and Santa Cruz dos Militares. His most impressive work, however, are his gold carvings in Nossa Senhora do Monte do Carmo's Novitiate Chapel. He also built two elaborate fountains, the Chafariz do Carmo, popularly called Chafariz do Mestre Valentim, currently situated in Praça XV, and the Chafariz das Saracuras which now adorns Praça General Osório at Ipanema. His bust in the *Passeio Público* was unveiled in 1913.

mous artists, but in the **Monastery of São Bento** one can find samples of the outstanding carver of the period, Portuguese monk **Domingos da Conceição** (1643–1718), whose powerful and realistic pieces foreshadowed what was to come. Although he designed and sculpted part of the nave and the first chapel, his masterpieces are the immense statues of São Bento, Santa Escolástica, and Our Lady of Montserrat to whom the church is dedicated.

In the next decade **Manuel** and **Francisco Xavier de Brito** introduced the Baroque carving of Lisbon to Brazil. Their 1726 work for the Rio church of **São Francisco da Penitência** in the carved jacaranda altar, around the doors, or in the choir defined what would be termed the "Brito style"—elaborate oval or circular medallions framing angels and puttos—which would eventually dominate Brazilian religious interiors.

The most significant artist of the end of the 18C was **Mestre Valentim da Fonseca e Silva** (c. 1740-1813) (◐ *see sidebar above*).

Another important Carioca sculptor is **Rodolfo Bernardelli** (1852–1931), one of the best representatives of Eclectic decorative sculpture in Rio de Janeiro. Having studied in Italy, he developed a taste for Classicism, expressed in lines of geometric severity. His sculptures, generally in bronze, were adopted in the public buildings of the time and can be best seen in the **Teatro Municipal** and in Rio's **Biblioteca Nacional**.

Modernism in Rio de Janeiro also had its greats, through **Celso Antônio Silveira de Menezes** (1896–1984) and **Bruno Giorgi** (1905–1993) who both participated in that seminal work, the Capanema Palace. Celso's *Reclining Girl* in unpolished granite adorns its gardens and his *Maternity* stands in front of number 242 Botafogo Beach. Bruno Giorgi is better known for his monumental work in Brasília, but he was also commissioned to execute the *Monument to Brazilian Youth* in 1947, again in the gardens of the Capanema Palace.

Painting

Like the contemporary woodcarvers, the first Renaissance painters who arrived in Brazil in the 16C and 17C were mostly monks who worked anonymously in the larger towns of the richer northeast, decorating churches from copies of European templates. One of the first famous Brazilian names was **Ricardo do Pilar** (1630–1702) who worked in the **Monastery of São Bento**. He was influenced by Dutch Baroque painting that arrived in Brazil during the occupation of Pernambuco, via painters such as **Albert Eckhout** (1610–1665) and **Frans Post** (1612–1680); Post concentrated on drawing Brazilian landscapes

A Colorful and Historic Journey to Brazil (1839) by Jean-Baptiste Debret

©AISA/World Illustrated/Photoshot

while Eckhout produced still lifes and native portraits.

In the Baroque and Rococo periods of the 18C much of the painting involved church frescoes and illusionist *trompe l'oeil* ceilings by artists like **Caetano da Costa Coelho**, whose definitive identity was only established in the 1940s; **José Joaquim da Rocha** (1737–1807) who worked mostly in the northeast; and the best regarded, **Manuel da Costa Ataíde** (1762–1830), who was based in Minas Geráis.

The arrival of the French Mission brought to Rio de Janeiro highly influential painters such as **Nicolas-Antoine Taunay** (1755–1830) and **Jean-Baptiste Debret** (1768–1848), both versed in the Neoclassical European ideal. In their series of paintings of 19C Brazilian life they developed a distinct Brazilian romanticism, idealizing the figure of the native Indian. In the academy they founded local painters studied, such as Debret's pupil **Manuel de Araújo Porto-Alegre** (1806–1879), the first Brazilian caricaturist, and **João Zeferino da Costa** (1840–1916) whose most important works are the murals of Nossa Senhora de Candelâria. Independence and the Age of Empire fashioned a Romantic –Nationalist monumental school of painting that achieved its apogee with **Victor Meirelles** (1832–1903) through his paintings of the Paraguayan War, *Battle of Guararapes* (1879) and the *Naval Battle of Riachuelo* (1883).

In the same artistic vein, other significant painters include Rodolfo Amoedo (1857–1941) whose works can be admired at the Municipal Theater, the National Library or the Pedro Ernesto Palace; Pedro Américo (1843–1905), whose pieces are exhibited at the National Museum of Fine Arts; Eliseu D'Angelo Visconti (1866–1944), who did the interior decoration of the Municipal Theater; and Antonio da Silva Parreiras (1860–1937), considered one of the best Brazilian landscape painters—he has a museum entirely dedicated to his works in Niterói.

The São Paulo Week of Modern Art, in 1922 (see sidebar p 74), revealed the emergence of a new breed of artists such as Anita Malfatti (1889–1964), Tarsilla do Amaral (1886–1973), Lasar Segall (1891–1957) and Emiliano Di Cavalcanti (1897–1976). From the 1920s onward, manifestos and reactive trends appear every decade in the Rio de Janeiro–São Paulo axis.

The list is long and impressive: groups of interest include the Bernardelli nucleus of 1931 where artists such as **Milton da Costa** (1915–1988), **Yoshiya Takaoka** (1909–1978), and **José Pancetti** (1904–1958) found their voice with landscapes of the then still-idyllic Rio suburbs; Neoconcretism (or Op-art) based around the Frente group in the late 1950s, influenced by black-and-white cinema with painters such as **Ivan Serpa** (1923–1973), **Franz Weissman** (1911–2005), **Lygia Clark** (1920–1988), **Amilcar de Castro**

The Cinema Novo

In 1955 the film *Rio, 40 degrees* by **Nelson Pereira dos Santos**, was a landmark production, the precursor of a new, low-budget directorial style, influenced by the post-war Italian Neo-realism which functioned outside the studio system. In 1963 the Cinema Novo (New Cinema), whose motto was encapsulated in the phrase "a camera in the hand and an idea in the head," reached its maturity with *Vidas Secas* by the same director. Some films and directors reached international audiences, especially the award-winning **Glauber Rocha** (1939–1981), with his films *Black God, White Devil* (1964) and *Antônio das Mortes* (1969) which won him the award for Best Director at the Cannes Film Festival.

(1920–2002), **Lygia Pape** (1927–2004) **Hélio Oiticica** (1937–1980); abstract art in the 1960s, conceptual art in the 1970s, performance art in the 1980s and, finally, Post-modernism and Deconstruction in the 1990s.

Cinema and Television

Brazilian cinema was born in Rio de Janeiro, where as early as July 8, 1896 the first projection in Brazil took place. A year later the first movie theater was established in the Rua do Ouvidor. The city was the star of the first film shot in the country in 1898 by Alfonso Segreto who filmed the landscape of the Bay of Guanabara, and it is still an important inspiration for Brazil's film-makers. From the 1940s until the mid-1960s, the Hollywood studio system prevailed in Brazil and their productions marked out Rio de Janeiro as the cinema hub of the country. In particular, the output of the Atlântida studios—films called *chanchadas*—enjoyed great popular success, being a mixture of comedies, romances, and musicals. Still, the best-known Brazilian film from that early period is *Black Orpheus* by French director Marcel Camus which was shot in Rio de Janeiro and won Best Film in Cannes in 1959. It is based on the play *Orfeu da Conceição* by Vinícius de Moraes, which itself is an adaptation of the Greek legend of Orpheus and Eurydice set during the Rio Carnival. In 1954, landmark film *Rio 40 graus (Rio 100 Degrees F.)*, directed by Nelson Pereira dos Santos, spurred the Cinema Novo movement ("a camera in the hand and an idea in the head"), a wave of

Brazilian neorealist cinema influenced by Italian moviemakers, addressing national issues such as class, race and poverty in the name of political conscience. One of the most important among these low-cost productions is internationally-acclaimed Glauber Rocha's *Deus e o Diabo na Terra do Sol* (Black,God, White Devil, 1964).

Brazilian cinema suffered from the dictatorship of the 1960s and 1970s and only resurfaced internationally with the docu-drama *Pixote* (1981) by the Argentinean Hector Babenco who used real street kids to illustrate the life in the urban jungles of Rio de Janeiro and São Paulo.

Although it took some time for Brazilian directors to find their proper voice after the return of democracy, Brazilian cinema currently enjoys a renaissance, kicked off by the Oscar-nominated *Central do Brasil* (1998), a film that catapulted director **Walter Salles** into the A-list of Hollywood players.

City of God
O2 Filmes

Yet, the Brazilian film that most visitors in Rio de Janeiro will have seen—and may be apprehensive because of—is *City of God* (2002) by **Fernando Meirelles**. Its raw, shocking, and casual brutality has spawned a whole genre of violent films such as the TV series *City of Men* (2002–2005) also by Meirelles and the films *Man of the Year* (2002) by José Henrique Fonseca, *Carandiru* (2003) by Hector Babenco, as well as *Bus 174* (2002) and *Tropa de Elite* (2007) by José Padilha. The biggest media sensation, however, has been the international success of the Brazilian *telenovelas* produced mainly by the Globo Television network. These are soap operas with a storyline that is serialized only for a limited period but whose transmission floods television screens six days a week. The first telenovela, *2-5499 Engaged* by Dulce Santucci, was launched as far back as 1963 and, like all early attempts, it was overtly melodramatic and similar to the radio soaps of the 1950s. In November 1968, the modern phase of telenovelas was launched with *Beto Rockfeller*. This soap opera had a spirited, colloquial dialog, a central romance, a climactic ending, and a highly localized ambience, elements that have defined the genre ever since. Brazilian telenovelas have to date been exported to more than 125 countries, have served to draw tourists to particular regions they have featured and, more importantly, have brought new audiences to classic Brazilian authors whose works they adapted.

Carmen Miranda

©Photoshot

Music

For centuries, the types of music of the main racial groups in Brazil remained separate and unconnected. Indian aboriginal music was largely repetitive, long, and monotonous; it was chanted during ritual festivals and ceremonial dances. It was straightforward for the proselytizing Jesuits to refocus their Indian converts to Christian hymn-singing; in fact the Tupi and Guarani were very susceptible and had a good ear for choral music.

On the other hand, the music of the black slaves, highly rhythmic and percussive, was sung in the plantations and in the clandestine Afro-Brazilian religious services, whereas the folk music of the European colonists was characterized by nostalgia, expressing the homesickness of the Portuguese faced with the challenges of the new lands.

Classical music was one of the passions of the Braganças and, with the coming of the Portuguese royal family to Brazil, its development was sponsored heavily. The Carioca cleric **Jose Mauricio Nunes Garcia** (1767–1830), influenced by Mozart, Bach, Handel, and Haydn—although he never left the city—became music master of the Royal Chapel and produced several distinguished works such as a Te Deum, a requiem and oratorios like *The Beheading of John the Baptist, Santa Cecília* and *Nossa Senhora do Carmo*. One of his alumni was another Carioca, **Francisco Manoel da Silva** (1795–1865) who composed the Brazilian national anthem in 1831.

After the 1840s Brazilian classical music remained attached to Italian opera and produced at least one talented composer, **Carlos Gomes** (1836–1896), who was sent by Dom Pedro II to study in Italy where he was influenced decisively by Verdi and Ponchielli. His best-known opera *The Guarani*, with a libretto based on the book by Jose de Alencar, was staged in 1870 in Milan's La Scala.

The bridge between classical and popular music in Brazil occurred with *choro*, a largely instrumental music that emerged in Rio de Janeiro in the 1860s and 1870s. It has been dubbed "Brazilian jazz," although it preceded the genre by several decades.

The main composer of choro and other popular music works was *Chiguinha Gonzaga* (1847–1935), a classically trained piano teacher, who was much admired at the time in music and theater circles. She made history in 1899, when she was asked to write the first Carnival marching song specially commissioned for the event, the composition *Ô abre alas* ("Let me get through").

The next milestone of the evolution of Brazilian popular music was 1917, with the appearance of the first recorded samba song, *Pelo Telephone* ("On the Phone"), credited to Donga and Mauro de Almeida. Originally the word "samba" meant a group of friends having a party, but by 1920 it had become specific to the music performed during Carnival. The city of Rio de Janeiro soon became the capital of samba and the main springboard of its composers and interpreters: **José Barbosa Da Silva** or **Sinhô** (1888–1930); **Ernesto Joaquim Maria dos Santos** or **Donga** (1889–1974); **Américo Jacomino or Canhoto** (1889–1928); **Angenor de Oliveira** or **Cartola** (1908–1980); as well as choro musicians such as **Alfredo da Rocha Vianna Filho** or **Pixinguinha** (1898–1973) and **Jacob do Bandolim** (1918–1969).

Although born in Portugal, the person who promoted Rio de Janeiro and samba around the world was **Carmen Miranda** (1909–1955) with her kooky Carnival costumes and flamboyant hats. Dubbed "The Brazilian Bombshell," she appeared in 14 Hollywood films between 1940 and 1953 that shaped the sometimes one-dimensional party image of Rio de Janeiro which prevails today.

In the late 1950s, another Carioca musical format enjoyed international success: it was bossa nova, a moody, intimate song style with complex jazz-influenced harmonies and lyrics celebrating life in Rio de Janeiro. It was launched with the album *Canção do Amor Demais* by the singer Elizete Cardoso in 1958. This album saw the collaboration of the two masters of the genre: **Vinícius de Moraes** (1913–1980) and **Antônio Carlos Jobim** (1927–1994). They later co-wrote *Girl of Ipanema* (Music: Jobim,

Antônio Carlos Jobim
©William Meyer/Alamy

lyrics: de Moraes) which became a bestselling song and won a Grammy award in 1965.

In the second half of the 1960s other movements from São Paulo and Bahia took over. Brazilian music embraced rock and pop with the *tropicalismo* movement and artists such as Caetano Veloso, Gilberto Gil, Maria Bethânia, Gal Costa, and Rita Lee among others. Eventually it mutated into the unobtrusive and homogeneous **MPB** (Música Popular Brasileira), the equivalent of AOR in the US, which has dominated the airwaves since the 1980s. The keyword was fusion: even traditional samba mixed with rock and funk influences, typified by the music of Jorge Ben Jor, or diversified and merged with "Nordestino" styles such as *pagode* typified by Zeca Pagodinho and Jorge Aragão.

Yet, since the mid-1990s, the traditionalists have gained ground. While a branch of samba represented by musicians such as Martinho da Vila and Paulinho da Viola remained true to its roots and still identified with the Carioca spirit, a new generation has been re-discovering the delights of choro—largely forgotten since the advent of bossa nova—with young groups such as Regional Carioca, Trio Madeira Brasil, and Tira a Poeira. In 2000 the birth of Pixinguinha (23 April) was declared the National Day of Choro, when this 130-year-old most Brazilian of rhythms is celebrated countrywide.

Arguably, the greatest contemporary Carioca music artist is the internationally acclaimed **Chico Buarque**. A multi-talented individual (musician, composer, poet, and author), he composed bossa nova pieces in the 1960s when he started writing protest songs and theater pieces during Brazil's dictatorship. His work was heavily censored and he had to seek refuge in exile, becoming one of the most vociferous critics of the military regime; but he returned to Brazil after the amnesty.

Theater

Early Brazilian theater was used for the catechism of the natives; the Jesuit José de Anchieta wrote the first Brazilian plays to that effect. Although European plays were staged in Bahia and Minas Geráis in the 17C, Rio de Janeiro has been the stage for most of the history of the Brazilian theater after the arrival of the Portuguese royal family, especially after the inauguration of the Teatro Real de São João in 1813, later **Teatro João Caetano**. Today the city has about 30 theaters located mostly in the Centro and the Zona Sul, while the grand Teatro Municipal in the center is dedicated exclusively to opera, ballet, and classical music.

The early 19C saw the emergence of the comic genius of the writer **Luís Carlos Martins Pena** (1815–1848) whose farces were dubbed *comédia de costumes* while the end of the 19C and the beginning of the 20C were periods marked by the strong influence of French revues. Tiradentes Square became the epicenter of this theatrical form with celebrated authors such as **Arthur Azevedo** (1855–1908) and his main partner **Moreira Sampaio** (1851–1905).

In 1938 **Paschoal Carlos Magno** founded the Teatro do Estudante, a Rio rep company formed by university students. In 1943 it witnessed the birth of modern Brazilian theater with the production of *The Bridal Dress* by **Nélson Rodrigues** (1912–1980), under the direction of the highly influential **Zbigniew Marian Ziembiński** (1908–1978). There followed two golden decades—until the advent of dictatorship. In the strict censorship that ensued, theater suffered

as much as cinema. Today films and soap operas seem to monopolize the work of thespians, theater having become a niche art form which mostly appeals to a middle-class audience. However, the old administrative capital is still the cultural capital of the country and remains the springboard to fame, the central platform to launch a national career.

Literature

The first description of Guanabara Bay was sent in a letter by Tomé de Souza at the end of 1552 describing the natural beauties of the land to the King of Portugal. More significant depositions were made by the Frenchman Jean de Léry who was there between 1557 and 1558 in his book *Journey to the Land of Brazil*, and by Pero de Magalhães Gandano with his *History of the Province of Santa Cruz* in 1576.

Once again it was the arrival of the Portuguese court in Rio de Janeiro in 1808 that stimulated literature in the city. The arrival of the press in the same year resulted in the establishment of magazines such as the *Rio de Janeiro Gazette* in 1808, the *Rio de Janeiro Courier* in 1822, and the *Journal of Commerce* in 1827. Thanks to them the fast transmission of new European literary trends suddenly became possible, directly influencing the intellectual life in the capital. One of the first to arrive with the court was British trader **John Luccock**, who wrote the first English book on Rio, *Notes on Rio De Janeiro and Southern Parts of Brazil*, based on his residence there from 1808 to 1818. It was published in 1820 and described the material conditions, the people, the mores, and the intellectual life of the city at the time.

It was in the middle of the 19C when the country's national literature started taking shape and the first wave it adopted was Romanticism which was in vogue in Europe at the time. There were many authors of this period who based their romances in Rio de Janeiro. One of the most illustrious was **Jose de Alencar** (1829–1877) who was born in Ceará but whose *Guarani* (1847) takes place in the Serra dos Órgãos near Teresópolis. His *Senhora*, published in 1875, is an urban romance full of spirited detail and comment about the social life of the capital.

The Carioca journalist and doctor **Joaquim Manoel de Macedo** (1820–1882), born in Itaboraí near Rio de Janeiro, wrote more than 40 romances, among which *A Moreninha* is considered his masterpiece. Many of his works had been published initially in periodicals and magazines, a common practice among the authors at the time. Macedo was also a great *flâneur* of Rio de Janeiro, as depicted in his *Stroll Through The City Of Rio de Janeiro* (1862–63) and *Memories of the Rua do Ouvidor* (1878).

Manuel Antonio de Almeida (1831–1861) published only one book *Memoirs of a Police Sergeant* (1853) in which he vividly portrayed the everyday life and the popular customs of Rio de Janeiro. With his simple and direct style, and his objective, non-judgmental vision of society, de Almeida is considered the father of Brazilian literary realism, a movement which followed his pioneering work.

Joaquim Maria Machado de Assis (1839–1908) is the most illustrious representative of Brazilian literature and one of the most-translated early Brazilian authors. Rio de Janeiro appears in almost all his books such as *Quincas Borba* (1891), *Dom Casmurro* (1900), and *Esaú and Jacó* (1904). His sardonic black humor, peculiar and attenuated, reads as very modern today and it was certainly rare in his hemmed-in, deferential era.

His intellectual heir is **Alfonso Enriques de Lima Barreto** (1881–1922) who portrayed the Carioca environments, customs, and traditions with fine irony and social satire in such books as *Memories of the Notary Isaías Caminha* (1909) and *Life and Death of M.J. Gonzaga de Sá* (1919). Lima Barreto and Machado de Assis influenced much of the output that subsequently sprang from Rio de Janeiro which usually took the form of a prose chronicle viewed irreverently, with humor and caustic irony.

These themes were followed by Carioca authors such as **Paulo Mendes Campos** (1922–1991), **Fernando Sabino** (1923–1994) and the cartoonist, humor-

©UPPA/Photoshot

Paulo Coelho

The best known Carioca author is Paulo Coelho (b. 1947) who started off as a rock lyricist, but after several trips to Europe including a pilgrimage to Santiago de Compostela began writing books with spectacular success: his *Alchemist* (1987) is maybe the best selling Brazilian book of all time. Today Coelho has sold more than 100 million books in over 150 countries worldwide.

ist, and playwright **Millôr Fernandes** (b. 1924).

In the 1940s, Brazilian literature saw the human subject and the conditions of its existence become the focus of many literary works. Authors such as **Clarice Lispector** (1920–1977), **Pedro Nava** (1903–1984) and his urban novels, or **João Guimarães Rosa** (1908–1967), whose vivid descriptions of the Minais Gerais outback provide great inspiration, dealt particularly well with existentialist issues.

Finally, among the great poets to be linked to Rio, **Manuel Bandeira** (1886–1968) added a transcendental dimension to the themes drawn from the ordinary on which he based his work. **Carlos Drumond de Andrade** (1902–1987) was most influential in the development of Brazilian modernist poetry. His everyday poems describe the plight of modern man in a world in crisis which still leaves space for hope, love, and tenderness.

Carnival!

One of the greatest parties on earth, the Rio de Janeiro Carnival is the looking-glass through which the world tends to judge the city and consequently, the whole of Brazil. Yet in Rio *Carnaval* is an umbrella concept that embraces many diverse events with one common denominator: the five-day period leading to Ash Wednesday.

Yes, the largest spectacle is the televised procession of the samba schools on Sunday and Monday in the Sambódromo. But there is also the *carnaval da rua*, the lively street parties where whole neighborhoods dance with abandon; the *blocos* or *bandas*, informal, although frequently massive, street marches behind a band—the best-known are Banda da Ipanema, banda do Bola Preta in Centro, and Suvaco do Cristo in Jardim Botânico, and the many masked balls and glitzy club nights with special appearances by international artists.

Originally inherited from the Portuguese *entrudo*—the practice of throwing water at people—it is as late as the 1920s that Rio de Janeiro's Carnival was adopted as a great popular holiday. Indeed, it was in 1928 that the first Escola de Samba was founded in the suburb of Mangueira. Other samba schools soon followed suit in different quarters of the city: these were not educational establishments, but associations which originally brought together neighbors and friends to assemble a float for Carnival but have now developed into multi-million dollar industries.

The *raison d'être* for the samba schools, that can count on between 3,000 and 5,000 full-time members, is the production of the allegorical floats, the fancy dress costumes, and the special effects to be used during the parade in the Sambódromo. The 20 biggest samba schools are part of Grupo Especial (Division A) whose parades fall on the Sunday and Monday of Carnival—the most popular nights—whereas Grupo de Acesso (Division B) schools appear on Friday and Saturday. The schools enter the Sambódromo through Avenida Presidente Vargas, at the Armação end, and finish the parade in the appositely named Praça da Apoteose (Apotheosis Square). They have exactly 90 minutes to cross 766yds/700m of the old Avenida Marquês de Sapucaí which now runs through the Sambódromo. They are in official competition, their appearance evaluated by juries with promotions and relegations between the divisions just as in sport. The rules of the parade, the Carnival theme, and the composition of the juries vary from year to year.

Imperatriz Leopoldinense Samba School performing at the Sambódromo

©Fernando Bizerra Jr/UPPA/Photoshot

Sambódromo

Designed by Oscar Niemayer, the "Sambadrome" is the home of Rio de Janeiro's spectacular Carnival. For that particular reason, this gigantic stadium has probably been visited by more people than any of the architect's other buildings. Before it opened in 1984, this was just a regular city street. Now its 766yd/700m length is lined on both sides with grandstand seats (concrete bleachers) and plush boxes together capable of holding 60,000 spectators. On Carnival competition nights—and even during the many practice runs that precede the main event—it is one of the most exciting places on earth. Samba schools, with their endless ranks of colorful costumed dancers and gigantic painted floats, make their way down the runway, singing along to samba anthems, and dancing to the thunderous rhythm of the *bateria*. When the dancers pass under the huge monumental "M" that spans the runway at the end of the stadium (called the Apotheosis Square), they are exhausted, but, hopeful that they have done enough to get the jury's approval and perhaps win the title.

Samba Parade

The distinct elements of a samba parade, in order of sequence:

Comissão de frente Until the 1970's, this opening group was formed by directors of the school, dressed formally, welcoming the public and opening the parade of their own school. Today, regulated with a maximum of 15 people, its function is to introduce the theme chosen by the school through elaborate costume and choreography.

Carro abre-alas The key allegorical float that opens the procession for a school. Often the symbol of the school (a lion, an eagle etc) or its coat of arms are represented.

Mestre-Sala and Porta-Bandeira Two persons who wave the standard of the school. The Porta-Bandeira normally carries the flag, protected and assisted by the Mestre-Sala.

Alas The internal marching divisions of the schools like the traditional— and obligatory—section of the Bahian women, guardians of the traditions of samba origins, which normally accommodates the section of the composers and musicians and the children's section.

Carros alegóricos Richly decorated, they are the spectacular floats that present a feature of the theme or plot.

Destaques Celebrities from the school or artistic world, who are integrated into the school, and take an important role in a float.

Passistas The best movers of the schools, the ones with "samba legs." They dance individually and provide an alternative focus to the marching masses. Women are scantily dressed while men run nimbly about with percussive instruments. Throughout the parade, they do exhibition dances in front of the cameras, disclosing the agility of their feet, the dexterity of their hands, and the shaking of their hips.

Bateria The heart and soul of the School, whose function is to keep the beat and provide support for the thousands of people who sing the samba-enredo. A battery is mostly percussive and has between 200 and 300 members.

Samba-enredo Especially composed every year according to the chosen theme of the school, and decided by an internal competition. It is performed by a *puxador* (singer), and a small group of musicians, accompanied by a sound float which keeps up with the school.

Diretores de harmonia Not really vocal directors, but floor managers who are responsible for the synchronization of the set, so that the parade does not suffer visual or aural "holes," namely delays between sections.

Carnavalesco The all-powerful creative director, normally an arts professional who conceives the overall spectacle.

NATURE

Visitors who expect an amorphous sprawl—standard for a city of several million—cannot but be astonished by the junglelike and exuberant vegetation of the undulating landscape that hugs the highway from the international airport to downtown. Rio de Janeiro's magic works immediately upon arrival, because the city is an integral part of its environment.

Landscape

The city of Rio de Janeiro is the capital of the eponymous state that comprises an area of 16.953sq mi/43,909sq km and a coastline of 153mi/246.2km in the southeast of Brazil. It borders the state of Espírito Santo in the north-northeast, São Paulo in the west, Minas Geráis in the northwest and is washed by the South Atlantic in the south and east.

The city itself measures 43.5mi/70km from east to west and 27.3mi/44km from north to south and has an area of 473sq mi/1,225sq km. Its terrain is remarkably diverse: the existence of high cliff-faces capriciously cut close to the seashore creates natural landmarks such as the hills of Sugar Loaf Mountain, Dois Irmãos, and Corcovado. The tropical forests, sandbanks, beaches, inland lagoons, and bays provide not only a continuously varying landscape but also a range of picturesque and photogenic backdrops to a city that easily deserves the epithet *"La ville merveilleuse,"* coined by French poet Jeanne Catulle-Mendes in 1912.

The city's surroundings are a reflection of the state's topography which is dominated by two main mountain ranges, the Serra do Mar and the Serra da Mantiqueira.

The Serra do Mar is one of the major mountain ranges of Brazil. It rises sharply along the Atlantic coast, extending over 621mi/1,000km from the state of Santa Catarina to the north of the state of Rio de Janeiro. Local names are given to sections of the Serra do Mar, such as Serra da Bocaina in the neighborhood of Paraty, Serra da Estrela by Petrópolis, and Serra dos Órgãos near the city of Teresópolis.

The Serra da Mantiqueira, more to the interior, is a separate mountain range which forms an imposing escarpment leading toward the central Brazilian plateau with peaks that regularly top 6,560ft/2,000m. It is centered in the massif of Itatiaia, whose summit of Agulhas Negras stands at 9,158.5ft/2,791.5m and forms the fifth-largest peak of Brazil.

Between the two mountain ranges runs the valley of Rio Paraíba that cuts through the state of Rio de Janeiro

View of the city from Pão de Açúcar—hills rise close to the seashore

F. Klingen/Michelin

Costa Verde—blue sea against the background of green mountains of tropical forests

F. Klingen/Michelin

southwest to northeast and passes through several towns and villages that are part of the historical and architectural itinerary of the Brazilian coffee cycle.

The coastline of Rio de Janeiro state also presents characteristics of great diversity and outstanding beauty, which have been exploited for touristic purposes. Three great bays dent the coast: the **Bay of Guanabara**, where the city of Rio de Janeiro is located; the Bay of Sepetiba farther west, separated from the sea by the extensive Marambaia sandbank; and that of **Ilha Grande** in the south, full of small, charming beaches encrusted within the cliffs of the Serra do Mar.

The **Costa do Sol** on the eastern side harbors countless beautiful beaches, especially around the peninsula of Cabo Frio where the chic resort of Búzios is located. Because of the presence of large bodies of water such as that of Araruama and Saquarema lagoons, the area is also dubbed the "Lake District," famed for its permanent blue skies and cool breezes.

The south coast, between the island of Itacuruçá and the city of Paraty, is called the **Costa Verde** with good reason: it looks like a tropical version of the glacial fiords, as the Serra do Mar dives abruptly into the Atlantic. This sudden encounter of cliff-faces that can easily reach 1,640ft/500m and the ocean

has created a multitude of jagged bays and a labyrinth of islands that meander their way close to the continent. There are approximately 300 islands, all within 3.1mi/5km from the coast, which used to shelter pirates and corsairs; something like 50 shipwrecks between Angra dos Reis and Ilha Grande are testimonies of 16C and 17C raids and battles. The beaches of Costa Verde are small and delicate, fashioning tranquil retreats that are often accessible only from the sea. The setting is particularly picturesque because of the strong contrast between the blue sea and the green mountains covered by thick tropical forests.

The Rio de Janeiro city landscape is a synthesis of the geological aspect of the state, a transition area between the open terrain of the Costa do Sol and the serrated scenery of Costa Verde. It combines the typical elements of both, such as inland lagoons like the heart-shaped **Lagoa Rodrigo de Freitas** with an area of 544acres/220ha, rocky outcrops that rise abruptly from the sea like **Sugar Loaf Mountain** and **Pedra da Gávea**, a maze of islands in the **Guanabara Bay**—the largest being Ilha do Governador with an area of 11.5sq mi/30sq km—and a gamut of beaches that range from the closed and sheltered (Praia Vermelha and Praia da Urca) to those with a strong surf (Ipanema, Leblon and Barra da Tijuca).

Climate

Because of its accentuated geological relief, the climate of Rio de Janeiro state is quite varied depending on altitude, vegetation, and proximity to the ocean. In the mountains the temperatures can be quite low in the winter. In the National Park of Itatiaia there is at least one month with an average low of 50°F/10°C, while during the summer the thermometer never crosses 86°F/30°C. In the interior valley of the Rio Paraíba, the climate is subtropical and temperate. The cities of **Petrópolis** and **Teresópolis** perched in the Serra do Mar have cooler temperatures and higher rainfall than the coast, which is why they were the preferred residences of the imperial family during the summer.

The coastal area is sunny, subject to high temperatures and plenty of wind, primarily on the north shore. The Costa do Sol (Sun Coast), as the name suggests, has lower rainfall, an abundance of sunshine, and slightly higher temperatures. The **Cabo Frio-Búzios** region is the area with the lowest precipitation, counting just 100 days of rain a year, with June and July being the driest months. Those factors combined with the constant winds favor sailing activities and explain the popularity of the area. On the other side of Rio, the sudden escarpment formed by the Serra do Mar acts as a barrier to the moist oceanic winds. As a result the Costa Verde (Green Coast), where the

Rain clouds gathering over the Costa Verde

Y. Kanazawa/Michelin

cities of Angra dos Reis and **Paraty** are situated, has the highest precipitation index in the state.

The climate in the city of Rio de Janeiro is generally very hot and humid, with a drier season during the months of June and July. Annual precipitation ranges between 47–111in/1,200–2,800mm; because of the tree cover, the areas of the **Tijuca National Park** and the **Botanical Gardens** have a higher than average humidity. The average annual temperature is 72°F/22°C, while daily averages in the summer between November and March can regularly top 95°F/35°C with frequent rainstorms in the afternoon.

Flora

Rio de Janeiro city and state lie completely within the Brazilian biome of *Mata Atlântica*, the **Atlantic Rain Forest**, whose biological significance can not be overestimated. Extending along the Atlantic coastline between the states of Rio Grande do Norte and Rio Grande do Sul and as far inland as the Iguaçu Falls, the Mata Atlântica is one of the top five biodiversity hotspots on Earth, rated above the Amazon. It contains seven distinct ecosystems with an estimated 20,000 plants species of which 8,000 are endemic.

This high species diversity of the Mata Atlântica is a function of its geological history, its location, and the extreme environmental variations of the biome. In short: significant climatic changes in the past, elevations that vary from sea-level to just under 9,834ft/3,000m—the highest on the eastern seaboard of the American continent—and the spanning of the tropic of Capricorn are the most important factors. Bordering the Atlantic is also enormously influential, because coastal rain forests are more abundant in terms of biodiversity than inland ones.

As one climbs higher, one travels through such ecosystems as mangroves and *restingas* (sandbanks) at sea-level; tropical rain forest up to 2,624ft/800m; deciduous and semi-deciduous seasonal rain forest up to 4,921ft/1,500m—char-

Itatiaia Massif, Parque Nacional do Itatiaia

©TurisRio

National and State Parks of Rio de Janeiro

Vestiges of the old Atlantic rain forest can be found in the various national and state parks around Rio de Janeiro. **Ilha Grande**★★★ *(see p 200)* is an Environmental Protection Area (22sq mi/56sq km) subdivided into a **State Park**, **Marine State Park**, and the **Biological Reserve of Praia do Sul**. On the coast around Paraty, the **Serra da Bocaina National Park** (379sq mi/981sq km), divided between the states of Rio de Janeiro and São Paulo, extends from sea-level all the way to the peak of Tira-Chapéu at 7,218ft/2,200m.

Further inland, the **National Park of Itatiaia**★★★ (116sq mi/300sq km), one of the most important parks in South America, is surrounded and extended by the Serra da Mantiqueira Environmental Protection Area (1,633sq mi/4,229sq km). The first and oldest National Park of the country, it was created in 1937 to serve as a research station for Rio's Botanical Gardens and is the only part of Rio de Janeiro state ever to get frost or snow. It is divided into a Lower *(best time to visit Oct–Feb)* and Upper zone *(best time to visit May–Aug)* and contains the most impressive part of the Mantiqueira mountain range, stretching between 2,677ft/816m and 9,144ft/2,787m in altitude. The Lower zone is dominated by rare virgin Atlantic Rain Forest, whereas the Upper zone is capped by uniquely-shaped rock formations and breathtaking mountain trails. Waterfalls, lakes and rivers dot the park. The flora and fauna is rich and varied, with over a hundred species of flora found nowhere else in Brazil. In particular, the variety of species of insects is huge, with more than 4,000 types of butterfly and 1,000 species of bees and wasps. Birdlife too is prolific. The park offers places to stay, or you can base yourself in the nearby town of Itatiaia *(see p 231)*. From Rio take the President Dutra Highway (BR-116) toward São Paulo and the main park entrance is 5mi/8km by paved road from Itatiaia. The visitor's center is here, open from 10am–4pm, entrance to park R$3.

More to the north lies the **National Park of Serra dos Órgãos**★★ (46sq mi/120sq km) with its remarkable mountain peak formations. Created in 1939, this vast area of lush tropical forest encompasses part of the municipalities of Petrópolis and Teresópolis and contains some of the best hiking and climbing in the whole of Brazil. Temperatures in winter can plummet to –5 in the higher altitudes. In the summer the warm air from the coast condenses on the mountains, causing abundant rainfall, almost always preceded by fog. *The main Teresópolis entrance has a visitor's center and is a good place to enter the park. Open from 8am–5pm (small entrance fee), with overnight camping possible if booked in advance.*

Finally on the northeastern coast there is a perfect stretch of a sandbank ecosystem in the **National Park of Jurubatiba** which is currently closed to the public while the infrastructure is being built.

Aerial view of Floresta da Tijuca

www.terrabrasil.org.br

In that context, the **Tijuca National Park** (12.7sq mi/33sq km), all of which lies within Rio de Janeiro city limits, is all the more remarkable for being there at all. The whole forest, which is divided by trails into four separate sectors, is replanted secondary native forest. It was the dream of **Emperor Pedro II** who recognized that unbridled monoculture was damaging the fragile Atlantic ecosystem of Rio de Janeiro and decided to reverse the process. The reforestation of Floresta da Tijuca started in 1862 and 100,000 seedlings of native trees were planted over 13 years. A second phase between 1874 and 1887 planted 30,000 more. This project was stopped in 1889 when the monarchy was overthrown and since then the area has remained almost untouched. Today the forest is almost indistinguishable from the nearby primary Mata Atlântica reserves.

acterized by a hot and humid summer and a dry winter, unlike tropical rain forests that have no dry seasons; and higher up still, the "altitude fields"—treeless expanses with scrub vegetation that look remarkably like the Andean Altiplano on the other side of the continent.

Sadly Brazil's "other" rain forest—as the Mata Atlântica has been dubbed—which for centuries reigned over the coast and rendered it impenetrable, has been almost completely obliterated. Today a mere six percent of its forest-cover is left, the result of five centuries of colonization, the clearing of the land for the sugar and coffee cultivation, and 20C urbanization.

The most common flora in Rio de Janeiro includes hardwoods such as the graceful pink-and-silver trumpet trees *(Tabebuia sp.)*; gigantic jequitibás such as *Cariniana legalis* and *Cariniana estrellensis*; sapucaias *(Lecythis ollaria)* that can live for thousands of years; angico trees *(Piptadenia sp.)*; asparagus ferns *(Asparagus setaceus)*; evergreen quebrachos *(Schinopsis sp.)*, and many epiphytes and creepers, such as orchids, lianas, mosses, lilies and begonias, 75 percent of which are endemic and count among them some well-known garden species such as *Begonia egregia*. In fact, it is not uncommon to find the odd wild orchid

Restinga da Marambaia—home to native birds

Y. Kanazawa/Michelin

Beija-flor, hummingbird in Parque Nacional da Tijuca

www.terrabrasil.org.br

A Paradise for Bird-watchers

The parks in and around Rio de Janeiro include some of the top bird-watching destinations of Brazil. Even a stroll in Rio's Botanical Gardens can be an exciting experience: one can spot **toucans**, **parakeets**, **woodpeckers**, and **tanagers** among others. There are seabirds, ranging from **cormorants** to **ospreys** in the coastal areas; the freshwater lagoons are populated with aquatic species such as **herons** and **grebes**; the rain forests teem with insect eaters like **antwrens**, **antshrikes**, and **flycatchers** as well as frugivores like **toucans** and **toucanets**; and the higher elevations are the realm of birds of prey like **eagles**, **kestrels**, **vultures**, **kites**, and **hawks**. Visitors are particularly enamored by the great variety of **hummingbirds** and many rural hotels and restaurants hang special bird-feeders on their verandas which act like magnets for these buzzing tiny birds.

There are over 180 endemic bird species in Brazil, around 100 of which can be found in Rio de Janeiro. Rare and endemic species include the hooded berry-eater (*Carpornis cucullatus*) and black-headed berry eater (*Carpornis melanocephalus*), the three-toed jacamar (*Jacamaralcyon tridactyla*), 15 species of tanagers such as the olive-green tanager (*Orthogonys chloricterus*) and cherry-throated tanager (*Nemosia rourei*), the star-throated antwren (*Myrmoterula gularis*) and unicolored antwren (*Myrmotherula unicolor*), the Itatiaia spinetail (*Schizoeaca moreirae*), the rufous-backed antvireo (*Dysithamnus xanthopterus*), the white-bibbed antbird (*Myrmeciza loricata*) and Rio de Janeiro antbird (*Cercomacra brasiliana*), the pin-tailed manakin (*Ilicura militaris*), the black-capped piprite (*Piprites pileatus*), the bay-chested warbling finch (*Poospiza thoracica*), and many species of cotingas like the black-and-gold cotinga (*Tijuca atra*) and the gray-winged cotinga (*Tijuca condita*).

or begonia sprouting on trees in the city of Rio de Janeiro, even in urban areas like Copacabana and Ipanema. Last, but not least, is the botanical family of bromeliads whose presence is associated with a healthy forest environment. Brazil has more than 1,000 species of bromeliads and colorful examples can be found on Rio's hillsides and in the public gardens of the city. There is also a wonderful collection at the **Jardim Botânico** (*see p 175*).

Fauna

The endemic animal biodiversity of the Mata Atlântica is as impressive as its flora. There are 94 reptile species, 73 mammals including 21 species of primates, 160 species of birds, and a staggering 282 species of amphibians. Most of these can be found in the parks around Rio de Janeiro, especially in Itatiaia and Serra dos Órgãos.

Rio's Marsupials

Because of the fame of their bigger cousins in Australia, visitors to Rio de Janeiro are surprised to hear that indigenous marsupials have lived in South America since the time of the dinosaurs; in fact the didelphids, better known as opossums, are the most ancient terrestrial mammals on the planet. The common opossum *Didelphis marsupialis* and the Gray Four-eyed Opossum, *Philander opossum* are easily found in forested areas all around Rio de Janeiro: they are as big as a small cat, measuring around 50–70cm including their tails. They are omnivorous, eating anything from worms, reptiles and eggs to fruit and corn. The female keeps her litter for approximately 90 days in her pouch, where the nipples are located; it is only when the young are fully weaned and leave the pouch that they start gaining weight. They are of particular interest to science, because of their undeveloped immune systems: they seem to co-exist, rather than fight parasites which can kill humans, such as the *trypanosomes* that cause Chagas disease.

The sad news, however, is that because of the devastating habitat loss—it is here that the largest cities of Brazil are situated and most of the population lives—the Atlantic rain forest also contains the most endangered species in Brazil. Out of the 202 Brazilian animal species that are officially endangered, 171 live in this biome, including six species of primates.

Many of the mammals that live in Brazil can be found in Rio de Janeiro. In the less trodden parts of Tijuca National Park one can find brown capuchin monkeys, crab-eating foxes, tapirs, giant otters, coatis, peccaries, armadillos, lesser anteaters, opossums, and sloths. Reptiles are rarely spotted but include constrictors such as boas, and also poisonous lanceheads and coral snakes. Further out in the parks of Itatiaia and Serra da Bocaina one can also find pumas, otters, tapirs, howler monkeys, marmosets, capybaras, and monkeys, such as the rarest primate in the world muriqui *(Brachyteles sp.)*, whose population decreased from several hundred thousand to just over 1,300, living in about 15 scattered protected areas.

Capuchin monkeys *(Cebus sp.)* can readily be seen on the trees around the National Parks' restaurants and hotels. They are the most common primate species in Brazil and are easily recognized from the black tuft of hair that resembles a Capuchin's cap. They are apparently very intelligent and are best-known in the West for providing the "organ grinder" monkeys of not so long ago.

Although jaguars do not live in Rio de Janeiro, mountain lions or pumas *(Puma concolor)* are not uncommon in the larger parks like Itatiaia. Like all cats they are solitary and tend to ambush their prey. Ocelots *(Leopardus pardalis)* are the wild felines a visitor is most likely to

Brown capuchin monkeys

©Michael Patrick O'Neill/NHPA/Photoshot

Ocelot

©Martin Wendler/NHPA/Photoshot

spot, because they tend to hunt during the day. There is no danger of mistaking them for jaguars, because they are only the size of a domestic cat. Unlike cats, however, they are not afraid to jump in the water: they are excellent swimmers and fish are a regular part of their diet. Another animal that a casual visitor might encounter is the lesser anteater *(Tamandua tetradactyla)*. This small, agile solitary mammal, only up to 33in/85cm long with a prehensile 16in/40cm tail has long had a relationship with man: Indians used to keep them as pets to keep their reservations free of ants and termites. Although cute and curious, it should be treated with respect: it has four sharp clawed digits.

Some species of armadillo can also easily be seen, like the six-banded *(Euphractus sexcinctus)* and three-banded *(Tolypeutes tricinctus)* armadillo. Like the anteaters they can be seen foraging for insects, as well as ants and termites, either licking the ground in front of them as they walk or destroying nests with their claws. The presence of both species in Tijuca National Park helps keep down the population of termites in the city.

The animals that have become most adapted to the presence of humans, to the extent that they will hang around trails and car parks to seek food, are the South American coatis *(Nasua nasua)*. They resemble their close relatives, the North American raccoons, being about the same size, with spotted eyes, gray backs, white bellies and bushy ringed tails.

They differ from raccoons in that their snouts are long and flexible and they permanently nuzzle the ground like pigs. They are omnivorous and often raid both trash cans and chicken coops in outlying communities.

Most other animals are nocturnal and well-camouflaged so the chance of seeing them is small, except maybe for tree sloths, the two-toed *(Choloepus sp.)* and the three-toed *(Bradypous sp.)* varieties that hang from branches all day long, only coming to the ground to defecate once a week. They move extremely sluggishly because they have a slow metabolism and body temperature, since their leaf-and-fruit diet is not nutritious enough for their size. Still, they belong to evolution's survivors: their ancestors appeared 35 million years ago and included the extinct, elephant-sized *Megatherium*.

Lesser Anteater

©AllCanadaPhotos/Photoshot

Praia de Ipanema and Morro Dois Irmãos in the background
©Cipriani Giordano/SIME/4Corners Images

HISTORIC CENTER AND SURROUNDS

Encompassing the areas known as Praça XV, Castelo, Cinelândia, Largo da Carioca, Praça Tiradentes and Lapa, Rio de Janeiro's original downtown is both the city's birthplace and its historic heart. Among its pleasant public squares and parks are splendid colonial churches and grand buildings and some of the best museums in the country. This is a center of entertainment too, with theaters, cinemas, and bars, as well as music venues and cultural centers that have breathed life back into the city's old neighborhoods. Here in Rio, cultural centers are not the preserve of the "chattering classes"—they are creative powerhouses, filled with musicians, artists, and dancers, constantly re-inventing traditional art forms.

Highlights

1 Tea in the elegant upstairs of **Confeiteria Colombo** (🕭 see p 112).

2 The startling inside of **Catedral Metropolitana** (🕭 see p 113).

3 Sunday morning mass at the dazzling **Igreja e Mosteiro de São Bento** (🕭 see p 103).

4 Nightlife underneath the arches at **Arcos da Lapa** (🕭 see p 122).

5 Exhibitions at the cultural center **Banco do Brasil** (🕭 see p 102).

Head for the Hills

Having successfully expelled the French in 1567, the Portuguese military abandoned the initial core of the city between Morro Cara de Cão and Sugar Loaf Mountain for the easier-to-defend Morro do Castelo. The hill was surrounded by low-lying lagoons, and besides this, it dominated the approaches to Guanabara Bay. From then until the 19C, the entire city of Rio did not extend beyond the boundaries of what is today called Centro (the "center").

The area comprised a meadow later to become Praça XV (🕭 see p 98) and the nearby hills, namely Morro do Castelo, Morro de Santo Antônio, Morro de São Bento, and Morro da Conceição.

Viceroys and Kings

Rio's importance grew when gold and diamonds were discovered in Minas Gerais, and new wealth brought urban improvements such as the Arcos da Lapa

Praça Floriano and Theatro Municipal

(⌖ see p 122), and buildings like the Palace of the Governors—today known as Paço Imperial (⌖ see p 100). In 1763, Rio became the capital of the colony and home of the viceroys, but urban development truly accelerated with the arrival of Prince Regent Dom João and 15,000 members of the Portuguese court in 1808.

Their arrival unleashed a new cycle of reforms. Heavily influenced by the Neo-classical movement that was promoted by the French Artistic Mission of 1816, notable buildings from this period include the Casa França-Brasil (⌖ see p 103) and the exquisite Palácio Itamaraty (⌖ see p 117).

Igreja de Nossa Senhora do Carmo da Antiga Sé

New Freedoms

With the end of the empire in 1889, the dominant Neo-classical style gave way to the exuberance of Eclecticism, perhaps best displayed in the Municipal Theater (⌖ see p 109), the headquarters of the Superior Electoral Board (⌖ see p 102), or the National Museum of Fine Arts (⌖ see p 110), among others.

The 20C saw successive modernization programs in the historic center. Much of its essential character disappeared in the name of grand schemes to "Parisianize" the city. The first of these (undertaken by Mayor Pereira Passos in 1903 and much-imitated by consecutive mayors) saw the creation of the Avenida Central (now Avenida Rio Branco) at the expense of many colonial buildings. In their place came the playground that was Cinelândia (⌖ see p 107).

Later on, with the creation of additional avenues and landfills, Rio's topography was considerably reengineered to expand its boundaries.

Avenida Presidente Vargas linked the historical core to the northern zone (Zona Norte). Then, the Aterro do Flamengo (or Parque do Flamengo) connected the old downtown to the South Zone (Zona Sul). More recently, Rio's historic center has enjoyed various initiatives regarding the revitalization of the area and the conservation of its architectural heritage.

Places of Worship

The historic center is studded with religious buildings, some of them dating from the earliest days of the colonial period. Many were created over several decades, such as the imposing church of Candelária (⌖ see p 105). A number of religious buildings were built on *morros* (hills), including the splendid São Bento Monastery, whose monks can enjoy panoramic views of Guanabara Bay, and the church and convent of Santo Antônio, in Largo da Carioca.

Moving with the Times

Some of Rio de Janeiro's museums and historic sights, especially in this part of town, are being restored and renovated. It is a good idea to brush up on your Portuguese and bring a dictionary with you

😊 A Bit of Advice 😊

Bear in the mind that most Rio churches are still thriving centers of worship, with loyal, local congregations; office workers stream in to say their prayers at lunchtime and after work, not just on Sundays. You are advised to show respect, not wear beach gear, and don't expect the level of information and facilities that you might find at a tourist attraction.

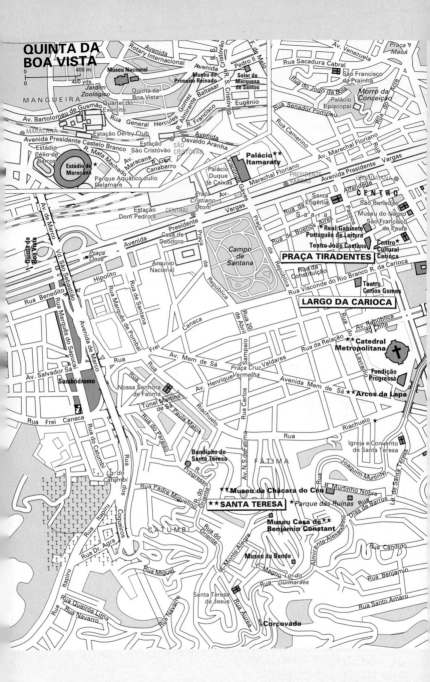

as you may not always find explanations in English. There is plenty to entertain, with a full program of theatrical and musical performances, but show some caution: the historic center is best visited during weekdays because once the banks and big firms close, the streets become almost deserted, and quite unsafe for visitors. If you plan ahead and avoid wandering around after dark, it is well worth trying to catch some evening entertainment in Lapa and Cinelândia.

HISTORIC CENTER AND SURROUNDS

0 — 400 m
0 — 400 yds

Labels on map:

Igreja e Mosteiro de São Bento ★★★
Ilha das Cobras
Ilha Fiscal
Ilha de Paquetá
Espaço Cultural da Marinha
Praça Dr. Ladário
Rua Visconde Inhaúma
Praça da Candelária
Casa França-Brasil ★
Centro Cultural Banco do Brasil ★★
Centro Cultural dos Correios
Igreja da Candelária
Praça Pio X
R. de Buenos Aires
Igreja da Santa Cruz dos Militares ★
Igreja de Nossa Senhora da Lapa dos Mercadores ★
Arco do Teles ★
Chafariz do Mestre Valentim
Estação das Barcas
★ PRAÇA XV DE NOVEMBRO
Paço Imperial ★★
Palácio Tiradentes ★
Praça Marechal Âncora
Av. Presidente Kubitschek
Museu Naval e Oceanográfico
Av. Alfredo Agache
Niterói ★★
★★ Baía de Guanabara
Avenida Nilo Peçanha
Praça do Expedicionário
★ Museu Histórico Nacional
★ Igreja de Nossa Senhora de Bonsucesso
CARIOCA
Av. Almirante Barroso
R. Mal. Aguinaldo
Santa Casa da Misericórdia
Santa Luzia
R. de Santa Luzia
Av. Gen.
Theatro Municipal ★★★
★ Museu Nacional de Belas Artes
R. Araujo Porto Alegre
Palácio Guanabara
Av. Churchill
Marechal Câmara
★ CASTELO
Av. Gen. Justo
AEROPORTO SANTOS DUMONT
Biblioteca Nacional
Santa Luzia
Academia Brasileira de Letras
Centro Cultural Justiça Federal
★ CINELÂNDIA
Praça Floriano
CINELÂNDIA
Av. Almirante Alves de Souza
Praça Itália
Trevo dos Estudantes
Praça Senador Salgado Filho
Rua do Passeio
Passeio Público
R. Teixeira de Freitas
Praça Deodoro
Rua Jardel
Jercolis
Museu de Arte Moderna ★★★
Av. Almirante Silvio de Noronha
Campus da Escola Naval
Ilha de Villegaignon
Praça Pistoia
Monumento aos Mortos da Segunda Guerra Mundial
★ LAPA
Praça Paris
Enseada da Glória
★ PARQUE DO FLAMENGO
★★ Baía de Guanabara
Mendes
GLÓRIA
Constant
Avenida Infante Dom Henrique
Marina da Glória
Igreja de ★★ Nossa Senhora da Glória do Outeiro
★ GLÓRIA
Museu da República
Flamengo

Historic Watering Holes

Botequims (traditional bars) are linked inextricably with the history and the culture of Rio de Janeiro. There is a more than generous sprinkling of them in the historic center, and a visit to one should not be missed. Cariocas are as proud of their charming botequims as they are of their beautiful beaches. Many of them have operated for more than a century, serving up the classic botequim fare of sandwiches, snacks, and ice cold *chopp*, the draft beer that came over with the royal family in 1808.

PRAÇA XV ★

Praça Quinze de Novembro is one of Rio de Janeiro's most famous squares, an enduring reminder of November 15, 1889—the day Brazil became a republic. Around Rio, it is known simply as Praça XV. One of the first plazas to be created in the city, the square and surrounds are at the very heart of the historic center, boasting a high concentration of splendid colonial churches, monuments and cultural centers. It is best explored on foot, following the route of the walking tour described here.

▶ **Orient Yourself:** Between Rua Primeiro de Março and Avenida Alfredo Agache, this area includes the square, the dock of Mercado Velho, the Estação das Barcas (the ferry port), and Praça Marechal Âncora (🕑 *see p 108*).

🙊 **Don't Miss:** Igreja de São Bento and particularly Mass held here on Sundays.

🕐 **Organizing Your Time:** Most of the museums and cultural centers are closed on Mondays, although many of the churches here do still open.

Kids **Especially for Kids:** Step on board a submarine from the 1970s and a World War II destroyer at the Espaço Cultural da Marinha.

A Bit of History

From Meadow to Main Square

An engraving of this area from 1580 shows a rustic building on the edge of a pristine beach, backed by expansive empty meadowlands. This lone church, the Ermida de Nossa Senhora do Ó, built for nobleman Manuel de Brito, was the genesis of Rio's famous square. In 1590, the church was given over to the Carmelite order. They soon outgrew the old building, and started work on their own convent in 1611, the **Convento do Carmo**. The area the convent overlooked became known as Praça do Carmo. The sea retreated, and this area grew in size, becoming the popular meeting place it is today. Emblem of justice and the totem of Rio's colonial city squares, a *polé* (pillory) was erected in the centre of the praça, which became known as Terreiro da Polé. In 1743, the Count of Bobadela built the Paço dos Governadores, a headquarters for the governor of the colony, a move that strengthened the square's place at the center of city life.

Praça XV and Paço Imperial on the left

Y. Kanazawa/Michelin

In the Name of Progress

In 1808, the Portuguese Prince Regent Dom João fled Lisbon to set up court in Rio de Janeiro. He needed a home for his mother, Queen Maria, a pious woman, prone to bouts of madness. While the prince took up residence in the governor's palace, he installed her in the Carmelite convent nearby. As a result, the convent's church became the royal chapel, and later, the city's first cathedral (*see p 104*). Various renovation works, including those that heralded the arrival of the royal family, altered many of the convent's original features. Today, a modern building housing offices of the Faculdade Cândido Mendes stands behind the convent's facade.

Inside the dome of the legislative chamber, Palácio Tiradentes

Y. Kanazawa/Michelin

Back to the Future

Throughout the 19C, the bustling plaza was a popular venue for big public events. It hosted float parades and fireworks displays; even bullfights and rodeos. Today, the city is attempting to resuscitate the area by restoring the old buildings and staging music and dance festivals in the square.

Walking Tour

▷ *1.5km/1hr. Begin at Palácio Tiradentes.*

Palácio Tiradentes★
Rua Primeiro de Março. ◷*Open Mon–Sat 10am–5pm, Sun noon–5pm.* ⏥*Free Admission.* ☏*21 2588 1411. Guided tours Mon–Fri.* ☏*21 2588 1251. Permanent and temporary exhibits can be seen without a guided tour.*
Built between 1922 and 1926, the Tiradentes Palace was erected on the spot where independence hero **Joaquim José da Silva Xavier** (1748–1792) was imprisoned. This soldier had also worked as a merchant and a dentist—hence his nickname **Tiradentes** (tooth-puller). His hometown was named after him and the day of his death is celebrated as a national holiday.
In front of the palace, the centerpiece of the sweeping plaza is a statue of Tiradentes by Francisco de Andrade. The independence martyr is symboli-

cally portrayed by the artist as a long-haired, long-bearded messianic figure epitomizing selflessness.
The palace was built in grand, Eclectic style, with strong neo-greek influences and a profusion of architectonical details and themes in keeping with the aspirational ideas of the republic. Its monumental **central dome** *(guided tour only)* is a re-creation of the Rio skyscape on the night of 1889 when the republic was proclaimed. Former home of the Brazilian national Congress when Rio was still the nation's capital city, the building today houses the legislative assembly of the state of Rio de Janeiro .

▷ *Turn right at Rua Primeiro de Março, then right again onto Praça XV.*

Panteão de Osório
Praça XV.
This monument was erected by popular subscription in honor of **Marshal Manuel Luís Osório** (1808–1879), Marquis of Herval, for his military prowess during the **Paraguayan War** (1864–1870). The equestrian statue was commissioned in 1887 from sculptor Rodolfo Bernardelli (1852–1931), and forged in Paris with the bronze of the enemy cannons taken during the war. In 1892 the embalmed body of Osório was transported to a crypt in this monument. The inauguration of the Pantheon took place in 1894, with great ceremony.
The pedestal, made of Alpine granite has two bas-reliefs in bronze: the first

shows the battle of Tuiuti and the second, the attack at Paso de la Patria.

Chafariz do Mestre Valentim
Praça XV.
The building of this fountain, also known as Chafariz da Pirâmide (the Fountain of the Pyramid), was supervised by **Mestre Valentim**, according to a 1780 design by engineer Marechal Jacques Funck. It is comprised of a squat square tower topped by a pyramid, which once displayed the Portuguese arms in marble, but was substituted in 1842 for an armillary sphere topped by the imperial crown in bronze.

Columns stand proud at the four corners. At the front is a door and an inscription. On the other sides, enormous shells once received the water that collected in tanks just below but, unfortunately, the fountain is no longer functioning.

Below the fountain, recent excavations led to the restoration of the old *cais* (wharves), revealing the outline of the area as it was at the end of the 18C, bounded by the sea.

Paço Imperial★★
Largo do Paço, Praça XV. ⏱Open Tue–Sun noon–6pm. ⊚$R2. ✕ ☎21 2533 4407. (Atrium Restaurant; ☎21 2220 0193; www.restauranteatrium.com.br).
This is the most important example of public colonial architecture still standing in Rio de Janeiro today. Built in 1743, to serve as headquarters and residence

for the Governor of Rio, the building also housed the Royal Mint.

With the arrival of the Portuguese royal family in 1808, it became the royal palace and, after the proclamation of independence in 1822, the Paço Imperial (Imperial Palace). However, the building did not serve this function for long. The royals found it uncomfortable and moved to Quinta da Boa Vista (⏱ *see p 121*), which became the official residence of the monarchs until 1889. The palace was only used for festivals, ceremonies, and official receptions and the proclamation of the republic (1889) led to its decline.

Many important events took place in the building: the **Dia do Fico** is the name given to January 9, 1822, when the Prince Regent proclaimed his intention of staying in Brazil to the gathered crowds. This decision flew in the face of the parliament of Lisbon which wanted to maintain Brazil's surbordinate status as a colony, and thus unleashed the process of independence.

On May 13, 1888, after having signed the **Golden Law** (Lei Áurea) which abolished slavery in Brazil, Princess Isabel stood at a window of the palace to proclaim the end of the practice.

A careful process of restoration was carried out between 1982 and 1985, returning the building to its original character, without trying to conceal the renovations that had been made over the years. It has been successfully transformed into a multi-cultural space dedicated to the arts. It offers first-class permanent as well as temporary exhibits, a movie theater, a library, a cafeteria and restaurant, a CD–DVD store, and a colorful patio area. On the first level, don't miss the **Sala dos Arqueiros**, a large room of Eclectic style, with delicate decorative works, an exquisite skylight, picturesque balcony, and the **maquete** (model) of the center of the city, by architects Antônio José de Oliveira and Fernando Cosmeli.

Courtyard, Paço Imperial

Y. Kanazawa/Michelin

▶ *Cross the square, with Guanabara Bay to your right. Walk toward the Arco do Teles, the arch that connects two buildings across a narrow lane.*

Arco do Teles and Travessa do Comércio★★

Off Praça XV. ✗

The width of this arch and the street it crosses reveal the claustrophobic dimensions of old Rio de Janeiro, built like a Portuguese city with tall, thick-walled houses crowded together and facing each other across narrow stone-paved alleys.

In 1790, the Arco do Teles was almost destroyed by a ferocious fire, but it survived and still forms the entrance to the narrow street of Travessa do Comércio. The narrow alley boasts a set of three colonial *sobrados* (multi-story buildings), with unique facades, built by Brigadier José Fernandes Pinto Alpoim and commissioned by the Teles de Menezes family, after whom the arch is named.

Today, the street is pedestrianized, and is an enchanting throwback to Rio de Janeiro in days gone by, even though some of the old buildings (numbers 8, 10, 12, and 16) are little more than facades concealing modern interiors. The street itself is filled with *sobrados*, charming wrought-iron balconies and old-fashioned lamp posts. There is also a number of enticing little bars and restaurants, where locals congregate after work (*see Entertainment p 248*).

▸ *Walk along Travessa do Comércio, until you reach Rua do Ouvidor.*

Igreja de Nossa Senhora da Lapa dos Mercadores★

Rua do Ouvidor 35. ⓒ*Open Mon–Fri 8am–2pm.* ⬭*Free Admission.* ☏*21 2509 2339.*

In 1747 wealthy traders who wanted a place to worship created the Brotherhood of Our Lady of Lapa Merchants. The brotherhood built this church—a delicate baroque jewel—though it has since undergone several renovations. The most major of these was between 1869 and 1872, when the facade was re-built and the bell tower and carved interior were completed. Neo-classical elements were added to the original Baroque features. High up on the gable studs are images of Saint Felix and Saint João da Mata. Above the three arched entranceways are windows with marble

Travessa do Comércio

©Ricardo De Mattos/Michelin

surrounds and the two side widows are topped by niches containing statues of Saint Bernardo and Saint Adriano.

In the center is a **medallion** from worked marble, representing the coronation of the Virgin. Found during excavations of the courtyard, it is believed to have belonged to the Ordem Terceira de São Francisco da Penitência (*see p 115*), who occupied the neighboring property. Buried by devotees in the 18C, to hide it from corsair attacks on the city, the medallion was forgotten and only found after the purchase of the property by the brotherhood, during the 19C remodeling.

In 1893, the bell tower was destroyed by a stray shell from the battleship *Aqui-*

Igreja de Nossa Senhora da Lapa dos Mercadores

Y. Kanazawa/Michelin

Centro Cultural do Banco do Brasil

Y. Kanazawa/Michelin

dabã during the revolt of the navy. The statue that adorned the tower, symbolizing faith, fell to the ground but escaped almost intact. The tower was immediately re-built, and the old bells, which were reinstated, are today the oldest in the city. The brotherhood continues to preserve the shell that damaged the structure, and the statue is displayed in a niche within the sacristy.

▶ *Stay on Rua do Ouvidor, and walk toward the main road Rua Primeiro de Março. Turn right to number 36.*

Igreja da Santa Cruz dos Militares★

Rua Primeiro de Março 36. ◷*Open Mon–Fri 8am–4pm, Sat–Sun 8am–noon.* ⊛*Free Admission.* ✆*21 2509 3878.*

At one time on this spot, a small seafront fort built to defend the Bay of Guanabara stood here, called the Fort of the Holy Cross. In 1623 the dilapidated building was given by Governor Martim de Sá to the soldiers of the Rio garrison.

Over the next five years, the soldiers built a small church here which they used for military funerals (burial within churches was only prohibited in 1850). However, when construction was complete, squabbles began over who should run the church, and the soldiers were excluded until 1780, by which time it was once again a ruin. They started over,

under the supervision of Brigadier José Custódio de Sá, and the new church in marble and granite was completed in 1811. It was consecrated in the presence of the Prince Regent, recently arrived from Portugal. A magnificent **organ** dating from 1934 and painstakingly restored in 2007 is used in recitals, which are performed by musicians from around the world.

The facade mimics the church of Gesù of Rome, with its four niches, twin volutes rising in a flourish to the gable end, twelve pilasters, and statues of the Evangelists, marking a late influence of the Jesuitical Roman style in Brazil.

▶ *Continue along Rua Primeiro de Março, until you reach number 42.*

Centro Cultural da Justiça Eleitoral

Rua Primeiro de Março 42. ◷*Open Wed–Sun noon–7pm.* ⊛*Free Admission.* ✆*21 2253 7566.*

Housed in the headquarters of the Superior Electoral Board, a fine example of Rio Eclectic style (1896), this new cultural center offers a wide variety of activities: art exhibits, an Electoral museum, an area dedicated to recitals and other artistic events, and reading rooms as well as a documentation center.

▶ *Continue along Rua Primeiro de Março to number 66.*

Centro Cultural do Banco do Brasil (CCBB)★★

Rua Primeiro de Março 66. ◷*Open Tue–Sun noon–8pm.* ⊜*Free Admission (event charges vary).* ✕ ✆*21 2285 6350. www.bb.com.br/cultura.*

The CCBB is owned by Banco do Brasil, which had its headquarters here from 1926 until 1960, when it moved to the new capital, Brasília. Banco do Brasil was founded by **Prince Regent Dom João** upon his arrival in Rio from Portugal in 1808, and is still one of the country's major financial institutions. Inaugurated in 1906, this late 19C building housed a trade association and a public stock exchange before being acquired by the bank in 1923. Since 1989 it has served as a cultural center.

Upon entering the facility, visitors are bathed in light from the atrium's stained-glass cupola. The CCBB offers a quality agenda of cultural events ranging from the fine arts to theater, cinema and music. Expect a wide selection of well-known temporary exhibitions (retrospectives, contemporary art, etc.), along with a permanent display on Brazilian currency. Most of the events take place on the lower floors, with the clever use of the bank vaults as rooms for exhibiting works of art. The fourth floor is given over to the bank's own museum and historical archives. The center's library, on the fifth floor, is open to the public and contains over 100,000 volumes, including rare periodicals. The CCBB also hosts a broad spectrum of films, plays, and concerts on site.

▷ *Casa França-Brasil is very close by. Turn right onto Visconde de Itaboraí, to number 78.*

Casa França-Brasil★

Rua Visconde de Itaboraí 78. ◷*Open Tue–Sun 10am–8pm.* ⊜*Free Admission.* ✕ ✆*21 2253 5366. www.fcfb.rj.gov.br.*

The France-Brazil House owes its existence to the French Artistic Mission of 1816. This group of artists and architects came to Rio de Janeiro at the request of Dom João, who had just ascended to the Portuguese throne. A leading light in the mission was the architect Grandjean de Montigny, who designed the building in the Neo-classical style but with touches of the Brazilian Baroque—take a peek at the roof, for instance, with its picturesque garrets and eaves.

In its early days, the building housed customs offices, later bank archives, and then a court, but it suffered from many ill-advised renovations. In 1983, it was agreed to restore the building and create a cultural center focusing on the cultural ties between France and Brazil. The result revealed the Neo-classical lines of the original architecture, creating a large central space with smaller side galleries.

The cultural center's agenda draws on the links between France and Brazil, with exhibits and events on a variety of themes: painting, sculpture, photography, literature, theater, and music.

▷ *End of Walking Tour.*

Additional Sights

Igreja e Mosteiro de São Bento★★★

Rua Dom Gerardo 68. ◷*Open Mon–Fri 7am–noon, 2pm–6pm; Sat from 7:15am, Sun from 8:15am.* ◷*Monastery currently closed for restoration; church still accessible.* ⊜ *Free Admission.* ✆*21 2291 7122. www.osb.org.br.*

A few blocks away from Praça XV, atop a steep hill *(accessed by foot or by elevator)* stands this Benedictine church and monastery. The ancient Benedictine Order came to Rio de Janeiro from Bahia in the early 17C, and its devotees were among the first inhabitants of the city. Their church here was inaugurated in 1641 and its frontispiece was completed in 1669.

Viewed from the peaceful outdoor patio, the church seems unassuming enough, but the interior is nothing short of dazzling. Of particular note are intricate wood carvings designed by the skilled artist and monk, Domingos da Conceição Silva and 14 panels by German monk **Friar Ricardo do Pilar** (1630–1641), one of Brazil's most gifted colonial painters. The chapel was one of the first works by **Mestre Inácio Ferreira Pinto** (1765–1828), who later

Dazzling interior of Igreja de São Bento

Y. Kanazawa/Michelin

worked on the royal chapel. On Sundays at 10am a solemn mass is held in the church, followed by Gregorian chants from the monks. Even if you are not religious, try to visit at this time as it is a very moving experience—but get there early as this is a very popular event, and space is limited.

Igreja de Nossa Senhora do Carmo da Antiga Sé★★

Rua Primeiro de Março (no number). ⓞ*Open Mon–Fri 8am–6pm.* ⬭*Free Admission.* ℘*21 2242 7766.*
This church began life as the chapel of the former Convento do Carmo (ⓒ*see p 98*). Built in 1761, the full name is often shortened to 'Antiga Sé' (old cathedral) because it was Rio de Janeiro's cathedral from 1808 until 1976. During the 19C it also served as the **royal chapel**, then the imperial chapel. During the reign of Pedro I, the facade was re-built in Neoclassical style.
A statue of the Virgin Mary crowns the tower; in front lies the image of the patron saint of Rio de Janeiro, São Sebastião. The interior is lavishly decorated in Rococo-style gilt woodwork. Of rare delicacy, it dates back to 1785 and is attributed to **Mestre Inácio Ferreira Pinto**. The triumphal arch is particularly beautiful. A number of galleries are decorated with paintings by colonial artist **José Leandro Carvalho** (1788–1834). The church has seven altars, the main

one in shining silver. In the sacristy is an evocative image of Christ on the Cross and a marble font decorated with colorful mosaics.
The church was the scene of important historical events such as the consecration of King João VI of Portugal in 1816, the marriage of his son Dom Pedro to Princess Leopoldina of Austria, Napoleon's sister-in-law. The remains of **Pedro Álvares Cabral**, Portuguese navigator and the first European to reach Brazil, are said to be held in the church's crypt. Vestiges of the original church were recently unearthed and open to the public.

Igreja da Ordem Terceira de Nossa Senhora do Monte do Carmo★

Rua Primeiro de Março (no number). ⓞ*Open Mon–Fri 8am–3:30pm.* ⬭*Free Admission.* ℘*21 2242 4828.*
Only separated from the old cathedral by a passage, this church (1770) boasts an elegant Baroque façade entirely made of granite and framed by two bell towers partially adorned with *azulejos*. Other notable features include a striking 18C marble portal imported from Lisbon, adorned with a medallion featuring the Virgin Mary, and a delicate rococo interior decoration by the artist Luís da Fonseca Rosa and his disciple, Valentim da Fonseca e Silva, known as Mestre Valentim.

Note the finely crafted candlesticks throughout the church and the exquisite main altar, all in silver. Valentim decorated the **novitiate chapel** with particularly beautiful rococo-style carvings (1772–1773).

Igreja da Candelária★

Praça Pio X. ◷*Open Mon–Fri 8am–4pm, Sat–Sun 8am–noon.*
✆*Free Admission.* ☏*21 2233 2324.*
Standing 210ft/64m high, this church is one of the largest and most luxurious in Rio de Janeiro, albeit not the quietest because of traffic noise from the encircling road. In the early 1700s, Spaniards aboard a vessel called the *Candelária* promised that they would build a church dedicated to our Lady of Candelária to repay the Lord's mercy should they manage to escape the severe storm in which they were caught. In 1775, work on replacing the original building began, a project that would continue in piecemeal fashion until the completion of the dome in 1877.
One of Rio's landmarks, the **dome**★—part of a beautiful golden ceiling above the altar—was a gargantuan task to accomplish. A total of 1,422 pieces of *Lioz* limestone were cut and polished in Lisbon, and shipped here to be assembled in place.
The eight statues by **José Cesário de Sales** that adorn the dome also made the journey from Portugal. They represent the four Evangelists Matthew, Mark, Luke, and John, and Religion, Faith, Hope, and Charity. A beautiful bronze door in Louis XV style by **Teixeira Lopes** should also be noted.

Centro Cultural dos Correios

Rua Visconde de Itaboraí 20.
◷*Open Tue–Sun noon–7pm.*
✆*Free Admission.* ✕☏*21 2253 1580.*
www.correios.com.br.
The Post Office Cultural Center has been part of the Rio art scene since 1993. There are ten exhibition rooms, an art gallery for small shows, a 200-seat theater, and a large open-air patio used for events. The center promotes traditional arts as well as cinema, video, dance, and music. The building itself dates from the early 20C, and was once

Igreja da Candelária

Y. Kanazawa/Michelin

the post office headquarters. The original semi-enclosed **elevator**, restored to its former glory, is a rarity in the city and is used daily by visitors.

Espaço Cultural da Marinha 🧒

Av. Alfredo Agache (no number).
◷*Open Tue–Sun noon–5pm.* ✆*R$10, R$5 children under 12.* ☏*21 2233 9125.*
www.mar.mil.br/.
Despite its name, the Naval Cultural Center, located on the old customs dock, is actually a small maritime museum. Within is the restored *Galeota Dom João VI*—a ship given to King Dom João in 1818.
Made from the finest Brazilian wood, with a simple covered cabin, it is decorated with several carved figures, includ-

CARNIVAL TIME

Cidade do Samba

Rua Rivadávia Correa 60, Gamboa. Open Tue–Sat 10am–5pm. R$10. ✆21 2213 2503/2213 2546.

Opened in 2005, "Samba City" is one of Rio de Janeiro's newest sights for visitors. The purpose-built compound in the revitalized port district is intended to be the new cultural home of Carnival (☞*see Entertainment p 254*). Each samba school has its own warehouse here, where you can see the giant floats being constructed, carnival costumes being made, and musicians rehearsing throughout the day. The run-up to Carnival (*Nov–Feb*) is a particularly busy period. Each Thursday at 7pm, visitors may have the unique opportunity to watch a mini version of Brazil's major event (*R$150, R$75 concessions, buffet included*).

Moored at the dock, the torpedo-boat *Bauru*, which ran World War II anti-submarine patrols, is now a walk-on museum, as is the *Riachuelo*, a 328yd-/300m-long British-built submarine. From the pier, visitors may take a boat across to **Ilha Fiscal** (*boat leaves Thu–Sun at 1pm, 2:30pm, and 4pm; ☞R$10, R$5 children*).

Museu Naval e Oceanográfico

Rua Dom Manoel 15. ◷Open Tue–Sun noon–4:45pm. ☞R$4. ✆21 2533 7626 /2233 9165.

This building in Eclectic style was inaugurated in 1900 as the headquarters of the Naval Club and opened to the public as the Naval and Oceanographic Museum in 1972.

Inside is a variety of objects related to the history of the Brazilian Navy, distributed over two floors. The museum boasts interesting relics and belongings of important historical personalities of the navy, as well as reproductions of ancient maps, and oil paintings. There are arms and items such as personal letters, photographs, and medals relating to wars in different periods, as well as naval uniforms. Also on display are tools for naval carpentry and navigation instruments.

ing an outstanding dragon on the prow. Also on show are numerous small-scale models of famous vessels, and an exhibition of sub-sea archeology, with relics of vessels wrecked off the Brazilian coast between 1648 and 1916.

CASTELO AND CINELÂNDIA★

Although geographically situated close to one another, "colonial" Castelo and "Belle Epoque" Cinelândia are two very distinct neighborhoods with their own history, architecture, and cultural identity. The Castelo area was originally a make-shift village that developed around Morro do Castelo (Castle Hill)—since leveled during one of Rio's urban reforms—it boasts one of the oldest churches in the city. Dating back to the opening of four movie theaters in the 1920s, neighboring Cinelândia ("Cinemaland") is a somewhat offbeat part of the city.

▶ **Orient Yourself:** Of the areas in the Historic Center, Castelo is the closest to Santos Dumont Airport. Right beside it, at the end of Avenida Rio Branco, near the Parque do Flamengo, lies Cinelândia. Both areas are easily accessed by the Cinelândia Metrô station

☺ **Don't Miss:** A performance from world-class artists at the Theatro Municipal.

◷ **Organizing Your Time:** Punctuate your visits through history with visits to some of the picturesque bars, cafes, and restaurants in this part of town (☞*see Your Stay in the City*).

Kids **Especially for Kids:** Don't forget that Cinelândia is right beside Parque do Flamengo (☞*see p 146*), a lovely area of wide-open green space, particularly on weekends when the roads through it are closed to traffic.

A Bit of History

About Castelo...

At the beginning of the 20C, Rio's mayors were keen to "modernize" the city. This often meant knocking down entire hills, creating landfills in the sea, widening existing streets, and creating new grand avenues. The Morro do Castelo was scratched from the cityscape for just such a scheme.

The historical importance of the hill was huge: it was here that the city of São Sebastião do Rio de Janeiro began life on March 1, 1567. It was a defensive settlement: its height afforded a good view of the entrance to the bay, the slopes were steep, and it was surrounded by swamps, lagoons, and beaches. As military concerns abated in the 17C, these attributes became less important, and the heart of the city was moved to the lowland area.

In 1922, Rio de Janeiro was to celebrate a century of independence from Portugal. In Castelo, the high concentration of poor housing on the slopes, around the hill and near some important historical buildings, was a source of concern for the authorities. The Morro do Castelo was leveled, and its rubble used for landfill in the coastal area of Glória (*see p 125*). The tangle of densely-populated steep alleyways was to be replaced with grand avenues (Churchill, Franklin Roosevelt, Marechal Câmara, Antonio Carlos) concentrating a large number of government buildings by architects with different ideologies. Among these were the huge, Neo-classical Ministry of Treasure, the Ministry of Labor, and a true masterpiece of Brazilian architecture: the modernist Ministry of Education, Culture and Health, currently known as the Capanema Palace (*see p 73*).

... and about Cinelândia

The emergence of "Cinemaland" is deeply connected to the construction of **Avenida Central** (now Avenida Rio Branco) and the demolition of the Convento da Ajuda (1750), which was opposite the National Library. Along with the convent went thousands of other colonial buildings in order to create Rio de Janeiro's first grand boulevard. With its central promenade, it quickly became the heart of the city's nightlife. In the area once occupied by the convent, four buildings went up—the Odeon, Glória, Capitólio, and Império—each of which contained a cinema. Of these, only the restored 600-seat **Odeon Petrobras** (*see Entertainment p 259*) is still a fully functioning movie theater.

Thus was born Cinelândia, the popular name for the **Praça Floriano** area.

In this square stands a monument (1910) dedicated to **Marshal Floriano Peixoto** (1842–1895), president of Brazil between 1891 and 1894. In 1906, beautiful Pálacio Monroe (former house of the Brazilian Senate) was built at the southern end of the square, toward the sea. But with the construction of the Metrô at the end of the 1970s, the square's original design was radically altered. The Monroe Palace was demolished and replaced with a large cast-iron fountain.

On weekdays, during the lunch break or after work, office workers like to congregate around the area, filling its cafes and bars. A platform for political and social debate, Praça Floriano is sometimes compared to London's Hyde Park: traditionally, political rallies and marches begin or end here, outside the City Counsel of Rio de Janeiro (Câmara dos Vereadores). During Carnival, the square really comes to life, with huge outdoor parties and events taking place there. One of Rio's most popular street Carnival bands, the **Cordão da Bola Preta,** heads downtown starting from Praça Floriano, attracting a large crowd of revelers.

Castelo

Igreja de Nossa Senhora de Bonsucesso★

Largo da Misericórdia. ⏰*Open Mon–Fri 7am–3:30pm (ring bell for entry).* ✉*Free Admission.* ✆*21 2220 3001.*

José de Anchieta (1534–1597) was a Canarian Jesuit priest who played a major role in the establishment of the new colonial settlements in Brazil and the evangelization of the Indians.

Museu Histórico Nacional

Museu Histórico Nacional

In 1582, he had a simple shack built by Morro do Castelo to treat the crew of Diogo Flores de Valdez affected by fever. Quite a modest start for what was to become **Santa Casa da Misericórdia de Rio de Janeiro,** a hospital complex that still plays a major role in the city's life.

Soon after, in 1584, Anchieta added a chapel built of wattle and daub.

The chapel underwent several renovations before becoming, in the 18C, a church dedicated to Our Lady of Bonsucesso. The elegant, rather sober façade of Nossa Senhora de Bonsucesso is typical of the overriding architectural style of Jesuit Baroque. Tones of gold and white traditionally dominated the interior of churches dedicated to the cult of the Virgin Mary, and this one is no exception. Its most precious relics are three **altars** and a **pulpit** that once graced the Jesuit church on Morro do Castelo, and were transferred here when the hill was demolished. These items are unique in exemplifying the early Mannerist style of the Jesuits. At the top of the main altar is the image of Christ crucified and below, Our Lady of Bonsucesso. The pulpit and the side altars are possibly among the oldest religious artefacts in Rio.

The pulpit would have witnessed the preachings of José de Anchieta *(see above)* and Manoel da Nóbrega (1517–1570), two instrumental figures in the early history of the colonial nation.

Museu Histórico Nacional★

Praça Marechal Âncora. ○*Open Tue–Fri 10am–5:30pm; Sat, Sun, major holidays 2pm–6pm.* ○*Some exhibits currently closed for restoration work.* ☞*R$6.* ✕ ✆*21 2550 9224. www.museuhistorico nacional.com.br.*

This is one of the largest and most important museums in the city, but also one that is not easily navigated. The museum was created in 1922, by decree of the then president Epitácio Pessoa. Set in an area of nearly 5 acres/2ha, it is made up of various interconnecting buildings of different architectural styles dating back to the original fortress that was built here in 1603.

The **collections**★★ at the National History Museum number nearly 300,000 pieces across fields as diverse as the decorative arts, arms and munitions, interior design, and transport. There is also a section about native Indians, with jewelry, ceramics, headdresses, and masks on display, along with explanations of the rituals of different tribes.

The Hall dos Arcazes showcases important pieces of religious art, including a number of ivory sculptures, and two major works of **Mestre Valentim** carved in wood: Saint John and Saint Matthew.

The **Pátio dos Canhões**, a beautiful internal courtyard with a fountain, displays an eclectic collection of cannons, statues, shields, and coats of arms.

Finally, an exhibition reveals the history of Brazil's Empire through a variety of documents, artefacts and paintings, including an impressive *Arrival of the Frigate Constitution in Rio de Janeiro* (1872) by **Edoardo de Martino** (1838–1912), and *Riachuelo Naval Combat* by **Victor Meireles** (1832–1903), showing a battle between Brazilian and Paraguayan naval forces in June 1865.

Cinelândia

Theatro Municipal★★★
Praça Floriano. ⏰*Open various times for performances.* 🚌*Tours available Mon–Fri 1pm–4pm.* ☎*21 2332 9191.* *www.theatromunicipal.rj.gov.br. The theater is currently undergoing extensive renovation and should reopen for its centennial, by the end of 2009; call the box office for information about tours and concerts (👜 see Entertainment p 257).*

Perhaps one of the most beautiful buildings in downtown Rio, and a rare surviving example of its period, the Theatro Municipal is also Brazil's premier artistic venue, with its own choir, symphonic orchestra and ballet ensemble. It has the capability of seating up to approximately 2,300 people over its main floor, lower and upper balconies and gallery. Modeled after the French Opéra Garnier, and built with the finest materials imported from Europe, the theater splendidly illustrates the Eclectic style favored by the Brazilian upperclasses at the beginning of the 20C. This ambitious project, designed by **Francisco de Oliveira Passos** with the collaboration of French architects Albert Guilbert and René Barba, was carried out between 1905 and 1909, at the same time as the city's central thoroughfare, Avenida Rio Branco, was being created. The involvement of major Brazilian artists such as Rodolfo Amoedo, Eliseu Visconti or Henrique Bernadelli, in decorating the façade as well as the interior, contributed to making this a monument of great historical, architectonic and artistic relevance for the city.

A subtle blend of clean, classical lines and typically Baroque forms give the **facade** a dynamic vigour. Theatrical symbology is abundant, with decorative elements such as sculptures by Bernardelli, or the names of great music and drama figures inscribed inside and out, among these Verdi, Carlos Gomes, Molière, and Martins Pena.

Lavishly decorated in the Louis XVI style with carrara marbles, onyx, bronze, crystals and gilded mirrors, the grand **foyer** boasts precious German stained-glass windows made in Stuttgart bearing allegories in honor of dance, theater, and music, and a glittering central chandelier on the vaulted ceiling; regarded as one of the theater's major pieces, it is surrounded by Visconti's *A Dança das Oréadas* (1899). Dance scenes from around the world (1916) by Amoedo are also noteworthy.

Opulent interior of Theatro Municipal

©Alexander Burzik/iStockphoto.com

New Wave

Casa Villarino *(Av. Calógeras 6; 21 2240 1627; www.villarino.com.br)* can lay a fair claim to being the birthplace of Bossa Nova. It was in this bar in the summer of 1956 that legendary musicians, Tom Jobim and Vinicius de Moraes, composers of the *Girl from Ipanema* *(see p 79)*, first heard the term "Bossa Nova" (New Wave). Together, they wrote music for the play *Orfeu da Conceição*, which had its first public performance just a few months later at the Theatro Municipal *(see p 109)*, complete with a black cast and Bossa Nova score. The music electrified not just the Brazilian, but also the world music scene, and continues to do so; performances still take place here.

Between performances, spectators should take a look at the Assyrio, a restaurant entirely covered with enamelled pottery inspired from ancient Babylon, or go to the upper level to enjoy a view of Sugar Loaf Mountain the windows overlooking Praça Floriano.

Museu Nacional de Belas Artes★

Av. Rio Branco, 199. Open Tue–Fri 10am–6pm; Sat, Sun and minor holidays noon–5pm. Some exhibits currently closed for restoration work. R$6, free Sun. 21 2240 0068. www.mnba.gov.br.

The imposing National Museum of Fine Arts contains around 20,000 works of art—mostly 18C and 19C European and Brazilian art paintings, but also sculptures and engravings. Furniture, medals, as well as examples of folk and African art, are also on display. The core works of the collection were brought over by the Portuguese royal family in 1808, and subsequently formed the collection of the School of Fine Arts, established by the French Mission. Inspired from the Louvre in Paris, the collection's current home (1908) was designed by Spanish architect Adolfo Morales de los Ríos. Visitors will appreciate works by landscape painters Frans Post (1612–1680) and Nicolas-Antoine Taunay (1755–1830), portraits by the official painter of the imperial court, **Jean Baptiste Debret** (1768–1848), and art works by one of Brazil's leading artists, **Victor Meirelles** (1832–1903). A real stand-out is *Navio Negreiro* (1961), a cubist tryptic by **Emiliano Augusto Di Cavalcanti** (1897–1976), Brazilian master of modernism who dared to break away from the traditionalism of European academic art.

Academia Brasileira de Letras

Av. Presidente Wilson 203. Open Mon–Fri 9am–6pm. Free Admission. 21 3974 2500. www.academia.org.br.

Built for the French Pavilion at Brazil's centennial celebration (1922), a copy of the Neo-classical Petit Trianon at Versailles houses the Brazilian Academy of Letters. Modeled after the French Academy, this great institution is charged with safeguarding the country's language and promoting its correct usage.

The prestigious group of 40 "immortals" (the leading lights of the academy) gather here to rule on the usage of new words and idioms and to hand out literary prizes. On the upper floor are personal effects that once belonged to great writers, such as the writing desk of **Joaquim Maria Machado de Assis** (1839–1908) *(see Art and Culture p 81)*. Considered perhaps the country's most important author, he was a founding member of the academy and its president until his death. The building is also

Sculpture gallery, Museu Nacional de Belas Artes

Y. Kanazawa/Michelin

Art-Nouveau staircase, Centro Cultural Justiça Federal

Centro Cultural Justiça Federal

home to two libraries, which concentrate on academic study of the written and spoken language.

Centro Cultural Justiça Federal

Av. Rio Branco 241. ◷*Open Tue–Sun noon–7pm.* ⊷*Free Admission.* ✕ ✆*21 3261 2550. www.ccjf.trf2.gov.br.*
In 2001, the former headquarters of the Federal Supreme Court were transformed into a lively cultural center. Designed by Spanish architect, Adolpho Morales de los Ríos, the building is one of the most impressive examples of the Eclectic style that was so in fashion here at the beginning of the 20C. Borrowing from different styles and epochs, the exterior with its massive doors exhibits influences from French Classicism, while

the marble and iron staircase provides a good example of Art Nouveau.
The **Hall of Sessions** is an imposing room, with enormous stained-glass windows, portraits of famous men of law, and two panels representing court scenes, painted by **Rodolfo Amoedo** (⟲*see Art and Culture p 76)*, who was one of the most highly regarded artists of his generation. In creating the cultural center, due respect was given to the sumptuousness and originality of the building, whilst modernizing and creating appropriate spaces, including 14 exhibition rooms, a theater, library, cafe, store, and even a cinema. The cultural center boasts a full program of events such as photography exhibitions.

Biblioteca Nacional

The nucleus of the National Library's collection was Dom João's royal library, which came with him from Lisbon in 1808. The collection became public in 1814, and has since grown from 60,000 to 13 million volumes, making it one of the largest libraries in the world. The depository of the bibliographic and documentary heritage of Brazil includes two complete Gutenberg Bibles dating back to 1462, 122 engravings by Albert Dürer (1471–1528), and a first edition of Handel's *Messiah*. The rare books are often put on display during small, changing exhibitions, but it is the building that houses them (built 1905–1910), and the history behind it, that is the main draw here. The library's facade shows obvious Neo-classical influences, particularly the Corinthian columns and triangular pediment.
Art Nouveau features can be seen in the interior decorative works such as statues, staircase handrails, and the impressive stained glass skylight (1910) made in France. The *ex-libris* of the National Library was designed by Eliseu Visconti who is considered a forerunner in Art Nouveau graphic design in Brazil. *(Av. Rio Branco 219; Open Mon–Fri 9am–8pm, Sat 9am–3pm; Free Admission, tours available Mon–Fri 1pm, must be booked in advance on* ✆*21 2220 9484 (R$2); 21 3095 3879; www.bn.br).*

LARGO DA CARIOCA

A happy collision of contemporary and colonial architecture awaits you at Largo da Carioca. Partly hidden by tall office buildings, the city's starkly modernist cathedral, an enchanting Art Nouveau cafe, and a jewel of a Baroque church are reasons enough to discover this bustling part of town.

▶ **Orient Yourself:** Carioca Metrô station is conveniently located right on the square. Confeitaria Colombo on Rua Gonçalves Dias, and the cathedral on Avenida República do Chile, are located along with the headquarters of various institutions and companies.

Don't Miss: The Catedral Metropolitana's outstanding interior, with its towering, vibrant stained glass windows.

Organizing Your Time: Spend a few hours soaking up old and new with a visit to the modern cathedral and the ancient church of San Antonio.

Especially for Kids: Delicious cakes and pastries at the Confeitaria Colombo.

A Bit of History

Humble beginnings

In the 16C two Franciscan friars erected a small chapel by a lagoon where Largo da Carioca square now stands. In the early 17C, the Franciscan Order went on to build a convent on top of Morro de Santo

Antônio (the very same convent which dominates the area to this day), and to drain the lagoon, by digging a trench that corresponds roughly to today's Rua Uruguaiana. Around the same period, a chapel of the Third Order of Saint Francis of Penance was built in the vicinity of the convent.

Confeitaria Colombo
Y. Kanazawa/Michelin

Confeitaria Colombo

Portuguese immigrants founded this lovely old *confeitaria* (sweet shop) in 1894. It expanded into a tea house and soon became a local institution. Today it is an evocative reminder of the days when it was fashionable to go shopping and take tea in the historic center. Its current appearance dates from 1913 and gives the place an irresistible Art Nouveau atmosphere that continues to delight locals and visitors alike. The exquisite, galleried interior features a high, decorated **stained-glass ceiling**, with delicate cornices and fleurons and window frames made from Brazilian jacaranda in the style of Louis XV.

Monumental Belgian mirrors each weigh as much as a car, the Portuguese tiled floor is covered with delicate drawings, and the tables have cast-iron feet with Italian marble tops. Well-known Brazilian writers and artists used to hold court here, and it has attracted some global names. Former U.S. President Teddy Roosevelt, Queen Elizabeth II of England, and every Brazilian president from the last hundred years have all taken tea here. There is now a sister cafe in the Copacabana Fort (*see p 161*), a very different and altogether breezier experience. *Rua Gonçalves Dias 32; Open Mon–Fri 9am–8pm, Sat and holidays 9:30–5pm; 21 2505 1500; www.confeitariacolombo.com.br; see also Where to Eat p 234.*

Inside Catedral Metropolitana

Y. Kanazawa/Michelin

At the Heart of it

In the 18C, the square was named Largo do Carioca, from the Carioca River, whose waters were carried from Santa Teresa *(see p 128)*, via the Arcos da Lapa aqueduct *(see p 122)* to a fountain here. Locals are still called "Cariocas" today after the river which sustained the colonial city centuries ago. The fountain, with its 16 waterspouts, put this square at the heart of city life. Slaves and children of the poor would queue here for hours in order to fill up jugs and barrels of water, for drinking and household use.

Moving on

In 1896, a tram line was established between Largo da Carioca and Santa Teresa, with the aqueduct adapted to allow the tram, instead of water, to run over it. Incredibly, it still runs today, but both the fountain and the original tram

station are long gone. These and other old buildings have made space for the ever-expanding square. During construction of the Metrô, boats and other relics of Rio's sea-faring past were excavated in this area—an indication of how different the area is now from what it once was. Today, Largo da Caricoa is a bustling part of the city center, sometimes invaded by hawkers and street vendors.

Sights

Catedral Metropolitana★★

Av. República do Chile 245. Open daily 7am–6pm. Mass Mon–Fri 11am, Sat, Sun 10am. Free Admission. 21 2240 2669. www.catedral.com.br. Locals, not always fondly, refer to the strikingly modern Catedral Metropolitana de São Sebastião as an upside-

Igreja e Convento de Santo Antônio

Y. Kanazawa/Michelin

down coffee cup, and indeed the ridged truncated cone can look like a plastic cup tossed away by a giant hand. However, hiding unexpectedly within is a striking and beautiful space where soft music plays, and tourists and locals mingle, bathed by the light filtering through the stained glass windows.

Seat of the Archbishop of Rio de Janeiro, the cathedral is dedicated to Saint Sebastian, the city's patron saint. Many churches have served as Rio de Janeiro's cathedral, beginning with the simple adobe chapel that once stood atop Morro do Castelo, flattened in the 1920s. The partial destruction of Morro de Santo Antônio in 1964, made space for this cathedral, which was consecrated in 1976.

Designed by Brazilian architect **Edgar de Oliveira da Fonseca**, the building soars to 328ft/100m, with a base diameter of similar dimensions. It has wonderful acoustics and can hold a staggering 20,000 people. The 598ft/18m-high congregational entrance features 48 figures on the theme of faith, in bronze relief.

Towering **stained glass windows** are each characterized by a dominant vivid color symbolizing the One (green), Holy (red), Catholic (blue) and Apostolic (yellow) Church. At the apex is a giant translucent cross made of Greek glass. In the basement of the cathedral, the **Museu de Arte Sacra** (*Open Wed 9am–noon,*

1pm–4pm, Sat and Sun 9am–noon; Free Admission) holds a collection of religious items.

The fonts used to baptize princes of the royal family, a statue of Our Lady of Rosário, and Dom Pedro II's throne are particularly noteworthy. The basement also houses a collection of archival documents (*Open Tue–Thu 2pm–6pm; Free Admission)* and a crypt.

Igreja da Ordem Terceira de São Francisco da Penitência★★

Largo da Carioca 5. Open Mon–Fri 9am–5pm, Sat and holidays 9:30–5pm. Free Admission. 21 2262 0197.

The stunning Baroque details, the glittering gold interior, and the painting on the nave's ceiling make this church, completed in 1736, a real architectural jewel. The church has no towers or bells, due to its proximity to the Igreja e Convento de Santo Antônio (*see below*). The simple Chapel of the Third Order, visible from the convent's church, to the right of the main alter, remains closed by curtains and grilles, due to continued friction between the Third Order and the Franciscan Order. Restoration of the church has been ongoing since 1988 as the church is one of Brazil's best examples of religious adornment, and certainly the most important in Rio de Janeiro.

The wood decoration—carried out between 1726 and 1743 by masters

Manuel and **Francisco Xavier de Brito**—is amongst the most impressive in the country.

Igreja e Convento de Santo Antônio★

Largo da Carioca (no number). ⏰*Open Mon–Fri 8am–6pm, Sat 8am–3pm.* 🎟*Free Admission.* ☎*21 2262 0129. At time of publication the church is open to visitors but the monastery is closed for restoration.*

Major restoration of the church and the monastery of Saint Anthony was begun in 2008, the date of its 400-year anniversary.

Sitting on what remains of Morro de Santo Antônio, the sprawling complex appears as if suspended above the Carioca Square, standing resolute amid the modern urban landscape. The structure has been modified several times during its history, yet it remains consistent with Franciscan architectural tradition, retaining its simple, brick construction with no towers or side chapels. In the porch leading to the entrance hall, a granite niche guards the famous statue of Saint Anthony, said to have protected Rio de Janeiro from French invasion, and to continue to protect the city.

The most celebrated feature of the monastery is the Baroque decoration of the three **altars** in the main chapel dating from the beginning of the 18C, and beautifully adorned with acanthus leaves and grapevines. Paintings relating the life of Saint Anthony, and two angels near the main altar, are highlights of the interior decoration.

The **sacristy**, to the right of the courtyard behind the monastery, is considered one of the most beautiful in Rio. Its floor and washbasin are made from marble, the furniture crafted from jacaranda, and there is a magnificent chest from the 18C. Delicate, traditional Portuguese tile panels and oil paintings illustrate passages from the life of Saint Anthony. To the right of the sacristy, through a garden courtyard, lies the **mausoleum** containing the remains of members of the royal family who died during childhood.

> ### 😊 A Bit of Advice 😊
>
> Take care walking around this area, as it can be unsafe, particularly after dark. The entrance to Igreja e Convento de Santo Antônio and São Francisco da Penitência can be hard to find. From Carioca Metrô station, follow the railings to the main gate and then find the entrance to the tunnel, at the end of which is an elevator.

PRAÇA TIRADENTES

By day, this square is at the heart of the city's commerce, but at sunset, the workers board buses headed to the suburbs. Praça Tiradentes then morphs into a bohemian enclave which, over the past few years has been given a new lease of life.

▶ **Orient Yourself:** Praça Tiradentes is located at one end of Rua do Lavradio, a lively, revitalized street that leads to Lapa and is dotted with upscale antique dealerships, restaurants, and bars. The three Metrô stations closest to the square are Carioca, Uruguaiana, and Presidente Vargas.

😊 **Don't Miss:** Brazilian music and dance at the Centro Cultural Carioca.

🕐 **Organizing Your Time:** A tour of the Itamaraty Palace is a leisurely affair that takes about an hour. Also consider coming to the area for an evening visit, taking in a show at a theater, or dancing in one of the local cabarets or *gafieiras* (😊don't wander around deserted streets at night).

🧒 **Especially for Kids:** Just for the experience, take a stroll along picturesque Rua da Alfândega, bargain hunter's paradise full of low-end stuff for sale spreading out from the stores onto the side walks.

Palácio Itamaraty

Y. Kanazawa/Michelin

A Bit of History

Toothpuller's Square

Praça Tiradentes is named in honor of **Joaquim José da Silva Xavier** (1746–1792). Nicknamed "Toothpuller," or Tiradentes, as dentistry was one of his many trades, he actively participated in the Independence movement at the end of the 18C. When the conspiracy was uncovered, Tiradentes was arrested and executed in 1792. It would be another 30 years before Brazil gained its independence, and almost a century before it became a republic, but Tiradentes was acknowledged as a national hero and the anniversary of his death declared a public holiday.

Legend states that Tiradentes was hanged nearby in what is known today as Toothpuller's Square. Many people wrongly assume that the statue in the center of the square is that of the Independence martyr. It is actually a statue of Dom Pedro, showing Brazil's first emperor on horseback, brandishing the declaration of Brazil's independence from Portugal. Dating from 1862, and created by French sculptor Luiz Rochet, it is one of the most beautiful and oldest statues in the city. A statue of the independence fighter can be found outside Palácio Tiradentes (*see p 99*), where he was imprisoned before being hanged.

Proclaiming the Republic

A short walk from Praça Tiradentes leads to **Praça da República**, where the end of the monarchy was announced to the people in 1889. There are several public buildings in the vicinity, mainly dating from the 19C. A modern one, on Avenida Presidente Vargas, houses the public library of the state of Rio de Janeiro. At the corner of Rua da Alfândega, the Igreja de São Gonçalo Garcia e de São Jorge, stands as a symbol of religious syncretism: the deity called Ogun in the Umbanda African-Brazilian religion is identified with the Catholic martyr Saint George whose feast is celebrated on April 23, a local holiday in Rio de Janeiro. The Museum of the Ministry of the Justice, on the corner of Constituição occupies the former headquarters of the National Archives. Behind Praça da República is the Quartel Central do Corpo de Bombeiros, a red- and silver-plated fire station. Inaugurated in 1902, it shows how deeply the architectural Eclecticism of the early century penetrated into daily life. Don't miss the former Mint, a monumental building which now houses the National Archives, and almost at the corner of Avenida Presidente Vargas, the home of **Marshal Deodoro da Fonseca** (1827–1892) who proclaimed the Republic on November 15, 1889.

Palácio Itamaraty★★

Av. Marechal Floriano 196. Free Admission. Admission only by pre-arranged guided tour (in Portuguese), with passport, Mon, Wed, Fri 2pm, 3pm, 4pm. 21 2253 2828.

The Itamaraty Palace is one of the most stunning examples of Neo-classical architecture in Rio de Janeiro. Only a few steps away from the hustle and bustle of city life, the pretty pink palace set around a pond with resident swans makes for a peaceful oasis, surrounded by elegant, imperial palms. Built by the son of the first Baron of Itamaraty, a wealthy coffee baron, between 1851 and 1855, the small palace served as the residence of his family in the city. **José Maria Jacinto Rebelo** (1821–1871), an architect of the French Artistic Mission, was personally in charge of the final phase of the construction. The building went on to serve as the headquarters of the Republican government from 1889, and was occupied by the presidency until 1898. The old palace then housed the Ministry of Foreign Affairs (until 1970 when it moved to Brasília).

The interior features the common characteristics of the great mansions of the 19C, including an imposing central staircase and entrance hall, fine furniture and precious art pieces. The star attraction is the **ballroom**, decorated in Napoleon III style. This hall is almost completely original, with the exception of the Republican coat of arms, in stucco, which decorate the four corners of the ceiling. Also take note of the dining

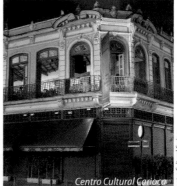

Centro Cultural Carioca

Centro Cultural Carioca

room with a huge jacaranda table and very striking **wallpaper** representing Amazonian scenes, painted in France in the 19C.

In the historical archives are a staggering six million documents relating to Brazilian diplomatic history, dating back to 1808. One real treasure-trove is the map library—an illustrated journey through Brazil's history.

Additional Sights

Centro Cultural Carioca★

Rua do Teatro 37. Open most days, times vary. Prices vary.
21 2252 6468.
www.centroculturalcarioca.com.br.

This is a picturesque two-story townhouse from the beginning of the 20C featuring Eclectic architecture, with a lovely upper balcony overlooking the Royal Portuguese Reading Room (*see p 118*). From the 1930s to the 1960s—a golden age of music and dance in Rio— the building functioned as the famous *Dancing Eldorado,* attracting legendary artists of the day. Today, the cultural center organizes various photographic and art shows and offers a full program of dance classes (*Mon–Fri 11am–8pm; 21 2252 5751*) deeply rooted in the history and culture of the city. The friendly dancehall atmosphere makes for great evening events, attracting beginners as well as devoted amateurs and semi-professionals. Enjoy some of the best of Carioca music and dance here *(for a program of events, check the website).*

Ball room, Palácio Itamaraty

Y. Kanazawa/Michelin

Central Station

Estação Dom Pedro II *(Praça Cristiano Ottoni, Av. Presidente Vargas; ℘21 2588 9494)* was put on the world map when it featured in the Oscar-nominated movie *Central Station* (1998).

Though a station has stood here since 1858, the present Art Déco building and splendid clock tower date from 1946. Trains continue to roar in and out, and a Metrô station of the same name stands right outside. The famous movie depicted hoards of people using the station; a scene repeated every weekday rush hour.

Real Gabinete Português de Leitura★

Rua Luís de Camões 30.
🕐*Open Mon–Fri 9am–6pm.*
🎫*Free Admission. ℘21 2221 3138.*
www.realgabinete.com.br.

This exquisite Portuguese library is remarkable for its collections, but also for the building itself, with its highly ornamental, late Portuguese Gothic style, known as Manueline. Statues of Luís de Camões, Vasco da Gama, Pedro Álvares Cabral and Infante Dom Henrique decorate its facade, inspired by the Jerônimos Monastery in Lisbon.

The interior decoration is even more impressive: the great **reading room**★★ covers 478sq yds/400sq m and soars to over 66ft/20m high, stacked with ancient books for much of its height. An exquisite **skylight** in red, white,

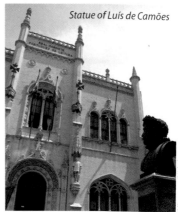

Statue of Luís de Camões

and blue allows the entire space to be bathed in natural light. Sixteen feet from the floor, a grand cast-iron **balcony** is ornately decorated in gold and bronze. Academics and researchers can be seen studying at delicate tables fashioned from jacaranda.

The library was founded in 1837 and currently houses more than 350,000 volumes, a number that increases every year. Some of these are extremely rare, including copies of the first edition of *The Lusiads* (1572), a Portuguese classic, and the "Bibliographical Dictionary" of Inocêncio Francisco da Silva that belonged to Camilo Castelo Branco, with notes in his own hand, as well as manuscripts of Gonçalves Dias and Machado de Assis. This library is one of the five largest libraries in the country and the second-largest in Rio de Janeiro, after the National Library (see p 111).

Real Gabinete Português de Leitura

Address Book

TAKING A BREAK

Within the Square of the Republic, a short walk from Praça Tiradentes, is **Campo de Santana** park, forming a little, if rather unkempt, oasis. Dotted with lakes, caves, fountains, and statues, it is surrounded by immense iron gates dating from 1873. With extensive greenery, a number of benches, and plenty of wildlife, it's a pleasant spot to take a break from Rio's often unrelenting urban landscape. The gardens were the project of French landscape painter and botanist **Auguste François Marie Glaziou**, who came to Brazil in 1858 at the invitation of Dom Peter II and who was also responsible for the gardens of Quinta da Boa Vista (*see p 123*). He introduced Brazilian plants into this garden, including thousands of deciduous trees, such as fig, casuarina, alamanda, baobab, and palm, which shade the paths and form leafy corners. Agoutis (a kind of rodent that looks a bit like a tail-less squirrel), peacocks, wild ducks, herons, and geese all run free around the park, creating a rather surprising pastoral scene. An artificial brook crosses the park, forming lakes and a simple waterfall. In the center of the park is a monument in honor of Republican leader, Benjamin Constant, (1836–1891) created by Décio Villares, with bas-relief by Eduardo de Sá.

ART GALLERIES

Durex Arte Contemporânea
Praça Tiradentes 85 Sobrado. Open Mon–Fri noon–6pm, Sat by appointment. Free Admission. ☎21 2508 6098. www.durexart.com.
This bright white art gallery in a historic, 19C building is just one of a new breed of modern galleries opening in the area. Its gleaming, pristine interior stands in sharp contrast to the rather faded square—which is however, under constant redevelopment. This gallery hosts work by local artists working in a range of media, from photography and painting to video and installation.

A Gentil Carioca
Rua Gonçalves Ledo 17. Open Tue–Fri noon–7pm, Sat noon–5pm. Free Admis-

Campo de Santana

Y. Kanazawa/Michelin

sion. ☎21 2222 1651. www.agentilcarioca.com.br.
The "Gentle People of Rio" art gallery is an ultra-modern space, incongruously on the edge of the sprawling SAARA open-air market (*see p 263*). Artist-run and determinedly eclectic, the gallery's changing exhibitions of installation and video, as well as more traditional art, are usually experimental and even off-the-wall. For every exhibition, a huge, corresponding wall-work decorates the building's facade.

SHOPPING

Something of a local shopping mecca, Rua da Alfândega is perhaps the most picturesque street in the center. This narrow, colorful artery is alive with traders during the week. Stroll down this pedestrianized street, part of SAARA (*see p 263*), absorbing its atmosphere and perhaps making some purchases.

LOCAL FESTIVAL

Dia de São Jorge (St Georges Day) is a popular saints day which is celebrated at the **Igreja de São Jorge** (*Rua da Alfândega 382*) on April 23 each year. A life-sized image of the Patron Saint of Portugal, an alter-ego of the Macumba warrior god Ogum, is carried through the streets accompanied by Catholics and followers of Afro-Brazilian religions, usually dressed in red.

Zona Norte

The North Zone of Rio de Janeiro is often only seen by tourists on the way to, or from, the international airport or inter-state bus station. The North Zone is a densely populated residential area, with the more affluent neighborhoods lying not far from the historic center. The districts here boast some major tourist and historical attractions and these unique sights are well worth making a little extra effort to visit, particularly if you have a longer stay in the city. The Maracanã Stadium, Quinta da Boa Vista (and the National Museum it houses), Solar de Marquesa de Santos, and the city zoo are all easily reached using the Metrô.

Museu Nacional, Quinta da Boa Vista

©Celso Pupo rodrigues/Dreamstime.com

Quinta da Boa Vista

One of Rio's major parks, the estate of **Quinta da Boa Vista** is located in the São Cristóvão neighborhood. It is made up of huge gardens designed in the French Romantic style, and a stately palace which was the official residence of Dom João VI, Dom Pedro I and Dom Pedro II and their families. The São Cristóvão Palace now houses the **Museu Nacional** *(Quinta da Boa Vista;* ◷*open Tue–Sun 10am–4pm;* ∞*R$3; ongoing restoration;* ✆*21 2562 6055; www.museunacional.ufrj. br)* which moved there in 1892. This natural history museum is one of the most impressive of its kind in South America, with particularly extensive collections of palaeontology and ethnology, and well organized exhibits. An exhibition on Brazil's indigenous population presents a large number of everyday and sacred objects relating to these cultures.

Solar da Marquesa de Santos

Conveniently located close to the imperial palace, the **Solar da Marquesa de Santos** *(Av. Pedro II 293, São Cristóvão;* ◷*open Tue–Fri 11am–5pm;* ∞*free admission;* ✆*21 2299 2148/4950)* was briefly home to Domitilia de Castro Canto e Melo, Dom Pedro I's mistress. A long-standing affair, their relationship caused much scandal and opposition at the time. The luxurious two-story house (1826) was built by French architect Pierre-Joseph Pézerat in the Neo-classical style, with touches of colonial Baroque. The exquisite interior decoration is attributed to some renowned artists of the time such as Francisco Pedro do Amaral *(Alegorias dos Quatro Continentes)* and to members of the French artistic mission. Today, the mansion houses the **Museu do Primeiro Reinado**, predictably dedicated to the reign of Dom Pedro I. Its decorative arts collection recreates the elegant lifestyle of the Brazilian aristocracy at the beginning of the 19C.

Museum, Maracanã Stadium
©Peter Treanor/Alamy

Maracanã★

The temple of football, the **Estádio do Maracanã**★ *(Rua Professor Eurico Rabello; ⏰open daily 9am–5pm (6pm summer); match days closed 5hrs before game; ⏰closed 2010–2013 for renovation; ☎21 2568 9962)* is one of the most popular sights in the city. Go for a game *(👣see p 274)* to experience the real thrill of the venue, but also try to take a tour *(booked in advance)* which includes a visit to the **museum** at Gate 18. Visitors experience the fascinating history of the stadium—the biggest in the world when it was finished in 1950. The sidewalk of fame features all the big names in football. An elevator to the sixth floor reveals a **panoramic view** of the whole ground, and all the seats from the bleachers to those used by Queen Elizabeth and Pope John Paul II. On the ground floor, visitors are taken through the tunnel, where the deafening roar of the crowd is recreated, through to the locker rooms and an indoor playing field with artificial turf. The Maracanã is also a world-class **music venue**; international stars such as Frank Sinatra, Madonna, and Paul McCartney have all played here.

Jardim Zoológico

The 🧒**Jardim Zoológico** *(Quinta da Boa Vista; ⏰open Tue–Sun 9am–4:30pm; 💰R$6, children under 1 meter tall free; ☎21 3878 4200)* is a small zoo home to around 2,500 reptiles, mammals, and birds from around the world, but many native to Brazil and particularly the Amazon. The entrance gate to the zoo is of particular note—a copy of the gate at Syon House in London, UK, and a gift from the Duke of Northumberland.

Jaguar in Jardim Zoológico
©Achilles Moreaux/Dreamstime.com

LAPA★

Lapa is among the most bohemian areas of the city, and a wonderful spot to enjoy a night out listening to the sounds of live Brazilian music. Time has taken its toll on this dilapidated neighborhood, but recent years have brought something of a renaissance to the area. A number of lively bars, restaurants, and clubs have opened up in old mansions, while a lively open-air party brings the streets to life at weekends.

▸ **Orient Yourself:** Lapa is an extension of Rio's historic center. In terms of atmosphere, it is similar to the Santa Teresa neighborhood (*see p 128*).

Don't Miss: The fair, Feira Rio Antigo, on the first Saturday of each month.

Organizing Your Time: After 10pm on weekends, the streets come alive. If you do happen to visit by day, make sure to come back after dark to get a better feel for the area.

Kids Especially for Kids: The green space of Passeio Público, and particularly for younger children, the unusual crocodile-shaped fountain found here.

A Bit of History

Level Playing Field
Before the middle of the 18C, Lapa was an unpopulated swamp land that spread out from the Boqueirão lagoon, around present-day Passeio Público. Rubble from one of the first hills in Rio de Janeiro to be leveled was used to fill the lagoon, and the destruction of Morro do Senado created the flat land on which most of Lapa was built. Where the lagoon once was, the famous aqueduct now stands – over which the *bondinho* (*see p 129*) still crosses.

A Roaring Success
The 1920s were positively roaring for Lapa. Barons and bohemians, poets, prostitutes, dancers and artists moved into grand old houses, living the high life and enjoying the *gafieiras* (dance halls). A slow deterioration began when Getulio Vargas closed down the brothels and casinos.
This downward trend accelerated in the 1960s when the capital was moved to Brasília. The historic parts of the city suddenly seemed of lesser importance, and buildings slowly began to crumble. However, recent years have seen new investment here, driven by a combination of tax incentives and hard work by committed locals. The old dance halls, re-invented, are thriving, and Lapa is, happily, roaring again.

Sights

Arcos da Lapa★★
With the resurgence of Lapa, the monumental aqueduct has crossed the barrier from local to city-wide icon. The striking construction of 42 arches made from stone and cement is impressive for its strength, but also for its beauty. Although the arched structure dates from the middle of the 18C, and was finished with slave-labor, the aqueduct project as a whole was started in the late 1600s, using natives. The aqueduct's purpose was to carry fresh water from the source of the Carioca river (Fonte das Caboclas), in the Tijuca Forest area above Santa Teresa, all the way down to Largo da Carioca (*see p 122*) at the base of Morro de Santo Antônio. In 1896 with the city now watered by pipelines, the aqueduct was adapted to carry Rio de Janeiro's **tram** (*see p 113*) from the city's historic center over Lapa and up to Santa Teresa, a role it continues to fill.

Igreja de Nossa Senhora do Carmo da Lapa★
Rua da Lapa 111. ⏰*Open Mon–Fri 6:30am–11am, 5pm–7:40pm.* ✎*Free Admission.* ☎*21 2221 3887.*
The construction of this church, designed by Portuguese military engineer José Fernandes Pinto Alpoim (architect of the Paço Imperial) began in 1751. It opened in 1775 as Igreja de Nossa Senhora do

Address Book

A BIT OF ADVICE

Lapa's raw nightlife is a world away (but only a 20-minute cab ride) from the slick and sometimes soulless clubs of the southern beaches. Arrive late (nothing gets going until 11pm or so), book a table at one of the live music venues (⌂ see Entertainment p 254), before joining the street party underneath the arches. Don't walk down any deserted streets and be prepared for some grime—it's all part of the charm.

NIGHTLIFE

Underneath the Arches

Every Friday and Saturday evening from around 10pm, mobile street vendors set up their carts for the night's festivities and don't pack up until the early hours, when the last revelers go home. At mobile cocktail stands, caipirinhas can be had for as little as R$3. Delicious Brazilian fast food comes in the form of home-made burgers served with crisps and a fried egg, or tender meat skewers—all cooked to order and therefore pretty safe on the stomach. Ice-cold beer is the most popular drink choice, and as there is always someone looking for cans and plastic to recycle, the party doesn't leave much mess behind.

Circo Voador

Rua dos Arcos (no number). Open weekends from 10pm. Admission price varies. ℘21 2533 0354. www.circovoador.com.br. Flying Circus is the name of this modern, tentlike construction right underneath the Arcos. This venue, complete with stage and large outdoor patio, holds as many as 3,000 people, and tends to attract a youthful crowd. A full program of events is listed on the website *(in Portuguese only)*, but also look out in the local press to see if something takes your fancy. Big name bands and international DJs like Franz Ferdinand attract their fair share of *gringos* (tourists), but the events here are truly eclectic and are just as likely to host a longstanding Brazilian crooner, such as Caetano Veloso. During the day, month-long circus courses in everything from acrobatics to trapeze acts take place.

CLASSICAL MUSIC

Lapa is home to the much-loved musical venues of Escola Nacional de Música and Sala Cecília Meireles (⌂ see *Entertainment p 257*). Both sights not only host orchestral concerts of a consistently high standard, but are also wonderful old historic buildings to visit.

Desterro and received its present name at the beginning of the 19C, after the Portuguese royal family took up residence in the Convento do Carmo at Praça XV (⌂ see p 98), causing the resident Carmelite friars to be moved.

A unique feature of this church is its elegant baroque façade flanked by two bell towers (one of them left unfinished) entirely covered with *azulejos*. Decorated in the rococo style, the interior presents some interesting peculiarities, among these the images of the church's two successive patron saints, Nossa Senhora da Lapa and Nossa Senhora do Carmo, one atop the other. Transferred from the Convento do Carmo at Praça XV, two curiously out-of-scale images of the prophets Elias and Eliseu, as well as the main altar attributed to Mestre Valentim himself highlight the interior.

Escadaria Selarón★   Kids

Rua Joaquim Silva, Lapa, to Rua Pinto Martins, Santa Teresa. ⏲Open 24hrs daily. ⊷Free Admission. www.selaron.net.

This brightly-colored mosaic staircase winding steeply up to Santa Teresa (⌂ see p 126) is the work of eccentric Chilean artist, Jorge Selarón, for whom it is named. The 215 steps are covered in recycled green, yellow, and blue tiles—the colors of the Brazilian flag—and represent Selarón's fond tribute to the people of his adopted country. When he began in 1990, Selarón would scavenge tiles from construction sites, but now they come from all over the world, sent or brought to him from admirers.

You might come across the artist. He lives next to the stairs, where visitors can buy his paintings and postcards and

Fundição Progresso

Y. Kanazawa/Michelin

Progressive Foundry

Fundição Progresso *(Rua dos Arcos 24; ℘21 2220 5070; www.fundicaoprogresso.com.br)* is an old foundry that was once condemned, but brought back to life as a vibrant cultural center.

Saved from demolition by public protest, the lovely old historic building and what goes on inside it stand as a symbol of the regeneration of Lapa.

A lively program of courses, from music and theater to circus and dance, take place throughout the year. One month may see an upbeat Cuban and Latin American rhythm workshop; the next, challenging acrobatic lessons.

A multitude of spaces here all take on their own role, with some of the larger areas hosting huge parties or acting as film sets. Big-name Latin American performers such as Manu Chau have put on shows here (&see Entertainment p 257), but it is the educational facilities that make Fundição Progresso one of the most important art institutions in the city.

Escadaria Selarón

Y. Kanazawa/Michelin

give donations so that he can continue with his work. Many of the tiles feature a pregnant African woman, whose image he claims to have painted more than 25,000 times. The artist says he will continue his work until his death, constantly replacing existing tiles with newer, prettier and more sophisticated pieces, so that this work of art is in constant flux.

Passeio Público

Between Ruas do Passeio, Teixeira de Freitas, Mestre Valentim and Luiz de Vasconcelos. ⊙*Open daily 9am–5pm.* ⊷*Free Admission. www.passeiopublico. com.*

This public park, inspired by the gardens of the royal palace in Lisbon, was built at the end of the 18C when the seat of government of colonial Brazil was transferred from Salvador to Rio de Janeiro. The project was commissioned by the Viceroyalty in 1779 as part of an effort to make Rio more attractive and modern through a series of sanitation and beautification works.

The location that was chosen for the park was very prestigious at the time, with a panorama of Guanabara Bay as a focal point. **Mestre Valentim** added his magic touch by creating various decorative elements such as the gateway and two granite pyramids. Exclusively frequented by the social elite, the Passeio did not open to the general public until 1793. Its French formal gardens, dotted with fountains, trees, and statues, were later remodeled along the lines of an English garden, with more natural forms.

GLÓRIA

This extension of Rio's historic center claims two landmark city sights—the charming 1930s Glória Hotel, which is currently undergoing restoration, and perched on a jutting hilltop, a picture-perfect 18C Colonial church which gave its name to the surrounding neighborhood. Behind Rua da Glória, the area's business main corridor, are some old-fashioned houses among newer apartment buildings on tree-lined streets.

- 🕐 **Orient Yourself:** Glória is nestled between Flamengo, Catete, Santa Teresa and the waterfront. It is served by the Glória Mêtro station.
- 👁 **Don't Miss:** The view over Parque do Flamengo, the Marina da Glória and the bay from the cobblestone Ladeira da Glória leading to the church.

Sight

Igreja de Nossa Senhora da Glória do Outeiro★★

Praça Nossa Senhora da Glória 135. 🕐*Mon–Fri 9am–5pm, Sat and Sun 9am–noon. Mass: Sun 9am–11am.* ✒*Free Admission.* 🖉*21 2225 2869. www.outeirodagloria.org.br. Consider going by taxi to visit the church, as it is at the top of a hill in a fairly deserted part of town.*

In the 1560's, Estácio da Sá took the strategic point on which the church now stands from Invading French forces (👁*see p 46*), paving the way for the Portuguese settlement. In 1671, Portuguese hermit Antonio de Caminha built a small chapel on the hill, replaced in 1739 with this attractive Baroque church. Its body is formed by two interlaced **octagonal prisms**, an important innovation in Brazilian Baroque architecture. The triple-arched entranceway supports a single **bell tower**. The **white facade** stands in stark contrast to the stone pillars at the vertices, each of which is crowned by a decorative spire. The "ox-eye" (eliptical) windows above the main windows were designed to bathe the altar in pools of light on certain days of the year.

Inside, despite its simplicity, the church is striking. Past the entrance are two 18C fonts, sculpted from Portuguese marble in the shape of seashells. Decorating the lower walls of the church are beautiful panels of **azulejos**—Portuguese tiles, with typical blue monochrome designs on white backgrounds. The finely carved 18C **high altar** is classic Rococo.

MARINA DA GLÓRIA

Open to visitors, the publicly owned compact circular inlet with two floating piers (*Av. Infante Dom Henrique, no number, Glória;* 🖉*21 2555 2200; www.marinadagloria.com.br*) is where sailing competitions often begin and end, and pleasure boat trips depart. There are two snack bars, a seafood restaurant, nautical store outlets, and a sailing school.

The Imperial Brotherhood of Nossa Senhora da Glória do Outeiro manages a small museum located across the church, **Museu Mauro Ribeiro Viegas** (🕐*Tue–Fri 9am–5pm, Sat 9am–noon, Sun 9am–1pm;* ✒*R$2*), with displays of liturgical items and 18C paintings that nicely illustrate the urban evolution of Rio de Janeiro.

Interior of Igreja de Nossa Senhora da Glória do Outeiro

Y. Kanazawa/Michelin

THE HILLS

Rio de Janeiro's striking hills, stretching across the city, are just one feature of its extraordinary geography. These morros (hills) afford some of Rio's most scenic views and beckon visitors from all over the world. Visitors can look out over Rio from the charming neighborhood of Santa Teresa, with its enticing craft shops and atmospheric restaurants, from stunning viewpoints in the beautiful, sprawling Tijuca Forest and of course savor the unforgettable panorama from the statue of Christ the Redeemer which crowns the Corcovado (Hunchback) Mountain—now one of the new seven wonders of the world.

Highlights

1 Strolling in Bohemian, laidback **Santa Teresa** (see p 128).

2 Admiring popular Brazilian art at **Pé de Boi** (see p 265).

3 Taking the Trenzinho do Corcovado to **Cristo Redentor** (see p 134).

4 Joining Terra Brasil on an eco tour in **Floresta da Tijuca** (see p 140).

5 Views from Mirante Dona Marta in **Parque Nacional da Tijuca** (see p 139)

Thrilling Rides

The journey up (or down) the city's steep hills can be as enjoyable as the sights themselves.

The ascent to see Christ the Redeemer (see p 135) is one of the most memorable in Rio de Janeiro, particularly if you ride the little cog railway up the densely forested Corcovado Mountain, but also if you take a taxi, admiring viewpoints along the way. Santa Teresa's little yellow bonde (tram) is a lovely way to reach the unique bohemian enclave.

🙂 A Bit of Advice 🙂

Pick a clear day, preferably in the fall, before taking to the hills in Rio. You might be surprised by how often—including in summer—the city can be engulfed by rain and even fog. In such weather, up on these high points, you might quite literally not to be able to see a thing—not even the Christ Statue while you are standing at its feet.

While the spectacular Tijuca National Park is best explored by car and on foot, the adventurous may choose to launch themselves from picturesque Pedra Bonita hang gliding ramp and fly like a bird all the way down to the beach of São Conrado (see p 179).

Hills with a View

These vantage points offer breathtaking, birds-eye views of the rest of the city. Mirantes (viewpoints) dot Tijuca National Park and the vista from Christ the Redeemer allows you to see the city of Rio de Janeiro stretched out at your feet—all the way from the historic center to the sands of the southern beaches. Plenty of spots, including the Centro Cultural Parque das Ruínas in Santa Teresa, offer a 360-degree panorama of the "Marvelous City", as its residents appreciatively call it.

History in the Making

From the 16C, people settled in the desirable neighborhoods of Santa Teresa and Tijuca because these high green enclaves provided cool retreats away from the heat below.

Some of the residences that once belonged to merchants and royal princes, today serve as fascinating reminders of Rio's history. Santa Teresa overlooks the city's historic center and is inextricably linked to it—both historically and physically—by Arcos da Lapa. These iconic arches support an aqueduct over which the hundred-year-old tram still rattles.

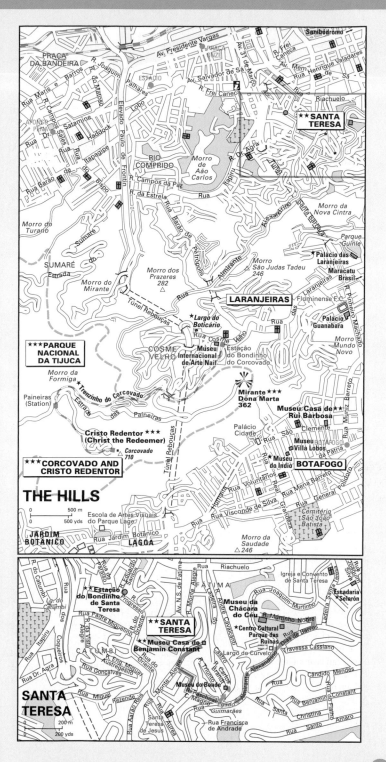

SANTA TERESA★★

Santa Teresa is one of the city's most delightful districts, home to writers, artists, lovely historic houses, and quirky museums. Day-trippers flock here to languish over lunch in friendly little restaurants, while boutique hotels, breathing new life into beautiful old buildings, invite visitors to relax in a picturesque setting. The tram follows the wriggling streets of this small but perfectly-formed neighborhood, stopping first at the lively little square of Largo do Curvelo and on to Largo do Guimarães and Largo das Neves, where the track ends.

▶ **Orient Yourself:** Not far from the historic center, Santa Teresa is a short (but steep) walk up from Lapa. With the exception of Rua Almirante Alexandrino, Santa Teresa's main thoroughfare, the other streets in this compact district wind back on themselves many times, making it easy to get lost.

😊 **Don't Miss:** A ride on the rattling, open-air tram and a meal in one of the quaint neighborhood restaurants. And another must-see: Largo das Neves, a picture-perfect square complete with a cute whitewashed church and vintage homes from the mid 19C, not to mention cozy little bars.

🕐 **Organizing Your Time:** It is safer to walk around Santa Teresa on weekends, although it may get a bit crowded. Take the tram up the hill mid-morning. Enjoy a leisurely lunch (😊 *see p 236*), take a look at the handful of arts and crafts shops, visit the magical Museu da Chácara do Céu *(closed Tuesday)*, and avoid walking around the backstreets on your own, especially after dark.

Kids Especially for Kids: Children will love to ride aboard the little yellow tram! You may then want to take them to the Museu do Bonde to learn about its history.

A Bit of History

The Hills are Alive...

An address in Santa Teresa was very much sought-after up until the early 19C. As infrastructure options evolved, richer residents drifted to the low coastal districts as it became clear these could be more easily connected to city utilities such as water, sewage, and (later) electricity. Today, Santa Teresa and other nearby areas have become desirable again, although they tend to suffer from the proximity of various *favelas*.

From a social and cultural standpoint, these impoverished hilltop communities may be quite interesting to study, but they should not be visited alone. Their makeshift homes were built along mountainsides to allow for the population to be closer to employment opportunities.

Getting on and off the bondinho in Santa Teresa

Y. Kanazawa/Michelin

Restored house in Centro Cultural Parque das Ruínas

Y. Kanazawa/Michelin

Walking Tour

▶ *2hrs/3km round trip. This tour begins with a ride on the tram from Carioca Metrô station.*

Bondinho★★   Kids
Carioca Metrô Station. ⏲*Open daily 6am–8pm.* ✆*R$0.60.* ☎*21 2240 5709.*
Santa Teresa's *bondinho* (little tram) is the last remnant of the historic transport system that once zig-zagged all over the city. Now electric, at one time the cars were pulled by donkeys. Today, the image of the yellow tram making its way over the aged white Carioca Aqueduct (Arcos da Lapa) appears on postcards all over the city. The *bondinho* is not only a popular tourist attraction. It is also an important transport link for locals and costs a fraction of bus and Metrô travel. You may see many of them make the bumpy journey standing on running boards and hanging onto the sides, thanks to a long-standing tradition that lets those who ride outside the cars travel for free.

☺ A Bit of Advice ☺

To guarantee a seat, join the tram at its starting point, next to the Carioca Metrô station. Trains run every 20min, with a one-hour guided tour on Saturdays at 10am. Keep an eye on your belongings and don't display flashy jewelry or expensive cameras.

▶ *Get off the Bondinho at Largo do Curvelo and walk along Rua Dias de Barros. After around 218yds/200m, turn left on Rua Murtinho Nobre.*

Centro Cultural Parque das Ruínas★
Rua Murtinho Nobre 169. ⏲*Open Tue–Sun 8am–8pm.* ✆*Free Admission.* ✕ ☎*21 2242 9741.*
The "Park of the Ruins" is all that is left of what was once the magnificent residence of the great patron of Rio's Belle Époque, **Laurinda Santos Lobo** (1878–1946). The "lady of a thousand dresses", as she was referred to by journalist, writer, and playwright João do Rio, was famed for bringing together intellectuals, artists, and politicians at legendary soirees held at the grand house.
The building fell into ruins before being adapted by architect Ernani Freire, who created a stunning contemporary structure of glass, brick and iron, with a 360-degree sensational **view**★★ taking in Guanabara Bay to Niterói and the Santa Cruz fortress; the Metropolitan Cathedral, Lapa arches, Santa Teresa Convent and churches, Santos Dumont Airport, and of course, the Sugar Loaf.
Today, the house hosts a charming cafe *(open weekends)*, exhibitions, and various cultural events, including musical and theatrical performances, which fittingly recall its function of nearly a hundred years ago.

Museu da Chácara do Céu

Y. Kanazawa/Michelin

▷ *Walk next door to the Museu da Chácara do Céu.*

Museu da Chácara do Céu★★

Rua Murtinho Nobre 93. ⏱*Open Wed–Mon noon–5pm.* ⏱*Closed all major holidays.* ✍*R$2. Free Wed.* ✆*21 2224 8981. www.museuscastromaya. com.br.*

The lovely little "Country house of the Sky" was once the home of industrialist, patron and benefactor **Raymundo Ottoni de Castro Maya** (1894–1968) and still contains his impressive art collection. Designed in 1954 by architect Wladimir Alves de Souza, its simple straight lines and windows beautifully integrate the interior with its surround-

ings. Visitors can enjoy spectacular views of the city from several angles, including the Guanabara Bay (⏱*see p 195)* and Sugar Loaf Mountain (⏱*see p 152)*. Works of European artists such as Matisse, Degas, Seurat, and **Jean-Baptiste Debret** sit alongside modern Brazilian art by Guignard, Di Cavalcanti, and Portinari and an exquisite collection of antique furniture and objects.

Up the first set of stairs, in the dining room are a large, sober dining table and English chairs in mahogany with bronze details from the 18C. A church chandelier made from Brazilian silver adds a touch of elegance and austerity to the decor. The library contains works of art, richly bound volumes and a large table made of jacaranda. The top floor showcases more Brazilian art and extensive archives of drawings and watercolors by Debret and Portinari. From the windows up here, take time to admire a lovely view of Santa Teresa and the city of Rio. In the peaceful, sheltered garden designed by **Burle Marx** (1909–1994), a stone patio gives way to a neat lawn and fish-filled pond. Partly shadowed by large deciduous trees, it is a good spot to relax for a while.

▷ *Return to the Bonde stop at Largo do Curvelo and follow the twisting tramline along Rua Almirante Alexandrino to Largo do Guimarães, a small triangular "square" that is the heart of Santa Teresa. Continue over Rua Carlos Magno, and follow*

LOCAL ENTERTAINMENT

Cine Santa Teresa

Rua Paschoal Carlos Magno, 136 , Largo do Guimarães. Open most days (irregular hours). R$8. ✆*21 2507 6841. www.cinesanta.com.br.*

This miniature cinema (there are only 46 seats) is the antithesis of the multiplex concept. Locals and Portuguese-speaking visitors enjoy Brazilian and art-house movies here, put on by an organization that works with social and cultural projects. Tourist information is on offer at the entrance, although publications available are limited and for sale only. The lobby hosts changing exhibitions with works by local artists.

What's in a Name?

1629, a small church dedicated to the Holy Child of God was built on Rua do Riachuelo where it still stands today. In the 18C, Jacinta and Francisca Rodrigues Ayres, two pious sisters who attended this church much frequented by pilgrims and devotees, bought a small piece of property on Morro do Desterro, where they had a chapel built. In 1750, answering the religious call, the women got permission from the colonial government to build a somewhat austere stone convent: **Convento e Igreja de Santa Teresa** *(Ladeira de Santa Teresa and Rua Joaquim Murtinho)*, from which the Santa Teresa neighborhood draws its name. Insulated from the outside world by its white walls and barred windows, the Santa Teresa Convent houses the contemplative, cloistered **Order of the Barefoot Carmelite Nuns**. You cannot visit the convent itself, but you may take a peak at the church . The entrance hall is decorated with traditional blue and white Portuguese ceramic tiles showing scenes from the *Book of Genesis*, while the rest of the interior is fittingly austere, complete with a locutory, where the nuns can talk to visitors through a grille.

the turns of the road downhill. Turn right into Rua Monte Alegre, where you'll see a gate at number 255.

Museu Casa de Benjamin Constant★★

Rua Monte Alegre 255. ⏰Open Wed–Sun 1pm–5pm. Gardens open daily 8am–6pm. ⮞⮞Free Admission. ⮞⮞Half-hour guided tours available by appointment Wed–Sun 1pm–5pm (⮞⮞free). ☎21 2509 1248.

Built around 1860, this wonderfully preserved house-museum was home to **Benjamin Constant Botelho de Magalhães** (1836–1891), the "Founder of the Republic" and one of the largest figures in Brazilian history. The building, typical of those in the district of Santa Teresa at the end of the 19C, was part of a small country estate which included exuberant gardens with fine views *(nowadays a little blocked out by trees)* over the city. Inside, paintings, photographs, sculptures, furnishings, medals, books, documents and personal effects provide insight into the daily life of the Constant family.

Various cultural activities and events take place on the premises: courses, temporary exhibitions, and open-air concerts. An annex of the museum also houses the Centro de Conservação e Preservação Fotográfica da Funarte (CCPF), specialized in the conservation and preservation of public and private photographic archives.

▶ *Retrace your steps following the tram tracks back uphill along Rua Almirante Alexandrino and take the second left into Rua Carlos Brant.*

Museu do Bonde   Kids

Rua Carlos Brant 14. ⏰Open daily 10am–4pm. ⏰Closed all major holidays. ⮞⮞Free Admission. ☎21 2242 2354.

This tiny Tram Museum, located next to Largo do Guimarães, displays many historic photographs, miniature *bonde*, and one of the original conductors' uniforms. Next door, a workshop still in use is home to various disused vehicles, including a hundred-year-old tram.

Museu do Bonde

Y. Kanazawa/Michelin

LARANJEIRAS

This primarily residential, low-key, upper middle-class neighborhood unexpectedly hides two well-known political landmarks in Rio: the Palácio das Laranjeiras, official residence of the Governor of the State of Rio de Janeiro, and the Palácio Guanabara, seat of the State government. Laranjeiras also offers picturesque musical corners such as Maracatu Brasil and Casa Rosa.

▶ **Orient Yourself:** This small enclave is located on the tourist trail to Corcovado. The Rebouças Tunnel gives access to the Zona Sul (South Zone).

🕓 **Don't Miss:** Architecture buffs will appreciate a curious juxtaposition of styles, with the refined eclecticism of Guanabara Palace coexisting with the bold modernism of nearby apartment buildings which served as a pattern for the residential "super-blocks" in Brasília.

🕓 **Organizing Your Time:** To visit either Pé de Boi (🛍 *see Shopping p 265*) or Maracatu Brasil, avoid Sundays when they are both closed. The cultural center of Casa Rosa, on the other hand, is only open on weekend evenings.

Kids **Especially for Kids:** Maracatu Brasil offers fun music classes for children.

A Bit of History

A River Runs Through It

Laranjeiras is one of Rio de Janeiro's oldest neighborhoods, having been inhabited since the 17C. At one time, it was covered with swathes of *laranjeiras* (orange trees), which gave the area its name. The clear waters of the pristine Carioca River ran all the way down from the Paineiras region at the foot of the Corcovado Mountain, and irrigated the flattest part near to the Flamengo beach, watering smallholdings that supplied the whole city—at that time sparsely populated—with fresh produce. Along with the Flamengo, Catete, Glória, and Cosme Velho districts, Laranjeiras formed part of the Rio Carioca basin.

From idyll to urban center

In the late 19C, when the city was dramatically modernized, Laranjeiras was one of the first neighborhoods to be transformed.

Large estates were broken up, the river was channeled, and new several-story homes were constructed. The Laranjeiras Palace is one of the main examples of the pioneering architecture of this period, while the Guanabara Palace is another important reminder of the district's glory days, currently serving as the seat of the state government.

Address Book

MUSIC

Maracatu Brasil

Rua Ipiranga 49. Open Mon–Sat 10am–6pm (studio and course times vary). ☎21 2557 4754. www.maracatubrasil.com.br. This treasure-trove of a music shop sells new and secondhand artisan instruments and celebrates the country's rich percussive traditions, which draw from Africa. Skilled teachers—many of them well known in the world of music—provide instruction for both aspiring and accomplished musicians, whether guitar, reggae, or samba.

Casa Rosa

Rua Alice 550. Open Fri–Sat 10:30pm–2am Sun 5pm–2am. R$5–12. ☎21 8877 8804. www.casarosa.com.br. The brightly painted "Pink House" is a popular music venue with a colorful history. The hundred-year-old building has a lively weekend program of music from samba and carnival music to funk and rock, as well as daytime arts and dance workshops. On Sundays, arrive early for *feijoda* (the traditional Carioca dish) which is served from 5pm—accompanied of course by music and dance.

Parque Guinle

Rua Gago Coutinho. 🕐*Open daily.*
This pleasant public park, with its lawns, its small pond and its paths, was built between 1909 and 1914. At the park entrance, note a fine iron gate flanked by sphinxes carrying bronze angels. This was actually the entrance gate to the former Guinle estate (🕐*see Palácio das Laranjeiras below*).
Perfectly integrated with the surrounding vegetation, the **residential complex** (1948–1954) at Parque Guinle should be noted. Conceived by **Lucio Costa** (1902–1998), known all over the world for having designed Brazil's new capital, the complex is regarded as a masterpiece of modernist architecture.

Palácio das Laranjeiras★

Rua Paulo César de Andrade 407.
🕐*Open Sat 9am–noon.* ✏*Free Admission. Guided tours only (Portuguese and English) must be reserved in advance on* ✆*21 2334 3229.*
This resplendent palace where **Eduardo Guinle** (1878–1941), a wealthy industrialist and engineer, once lived, overlooks Parque Guinle which at one time formed the gardens of the grand residence. Designed by **Armando Carlos da Silva Telles** and **Joseph Gire**, the mansion was built in the Eclectic style between 1909 and 1914, its main facade inspired from the Monte-Carlo Casino. Inside the imposing palace are columns of onyx, marble, and granite, enormous stained glass windows, Italian mosaic floors and European works of art (including paintings by Frans Post) and furniture. In 1947, the palace became the property of the Federal Government, before being passed to the government of the State of Rio de Janeiro in 1974.

Palácio Guanabara

Rua Pinheiro Machado. 🕐*Closed to the public for refurbishment until end 2010.*
Built in the eclectic style by Portuguese merchant José Machado Coelho, the Guanabara Palace (1853) was acquired in 1865 by the Imperial Government as residence to the Count of Eu and his

Parque Guinle and Palácio das Laranjeiras in the background

Y. Kanazawa/Michelin

wife, Princess Isabel, daughter of Dom Pedro II. Royal palms were planted on both sides of Rua Paissandu, which leads to the palace, making it one of the most picturesque streets in Rio.
With the advent of the Republic, in 1889, the palace fell into the hands of the federal, then state government. It became the official residence of the presidents from 1926 to 1947, and now serves as the seat of the State government.
Occupied by offices and formal halls, the white building boasts a grand staircase in marble and stucco decoration. Its beautiful French Renaissance style **gardens**, complete with a huge fountain of Neptune, were designed in 1908 by French landscape architect Paul Villon.

Playing Ball

The **Estádio das Laranjeiras** (Laranjeiras Stadium)—rarely referred to by its official title of Manoel Schwartz—was constructed in 1905 and today is one of Brazil's oldest stadiums. It is the home turf of local football team, **Fluminense**. One of the four most popular clubs in the city (along with Flamengo, Vasco, and Botafogo), Fluminense were winners of the Brazil Cup in 2007. Today the club uses the local stadium mostly for training as the large and modern **Maracanã**★ (🕐*see p 274*) hosts most games.

ORCOVADO AND
ISTO REDENTOR★★★

...ns of the statue of Christ the Redeemer atop Corcovado welcome thousands of visitors to Rio each day, and few will want to miss a visit to the city's most iconic sight. On the edge of Tijuca National Park, Corcovado ("Hunchback") is an immense block of vertical rock that rises 2,329ft/710m out of the dense forest and dominates its surroundings. You can go by taxi, or you can board the "trenzinho", a cog wheel train departing regularly for the almost vertical ride to the top.

- **Information:** www.corcovado.com.br.
- ▶ **Orient Yourself:** Built at the base of morro do Corcovado, the train station is located in the neighborhood of Cosme Velho, an extension of Laranjeiras.
- **Don't Miss:** Getting off the train at Paineiras station to take a walk through the lush Tijuca Park.
- **Organizing Your Time:** Allow an hour or two to visit Cristo Redentor, but plan three at weekends or on holidays. Consider combining it with a visit to the surrounding Tijuca National Park, and always try to visit on a clear day.
- **Especially for Kids:** The memorable train ride up to the top of Corcovado, which chugs slowly up the mountain through dense tropical forest.

A Bit of History

Through the Centuries

As far back as the 16C, the Portuguese attributed religious significance to this peak, which they dubbed **Pináculo da Tentação** (The Pinnacle of Temptation), in an allusion to the biblical passage where Satan, testing Jesus, took him to the top of a mountain where he could see all the great cities of the world.

In the early 19C, the dense undergrowth surrounding Corcovado, as it had by then become known, was a popular hide-out for runaway slaves from nearby plantations and farms. Nobles too, made their home in the pleasantly cool forest. **Emperor Dom Pedro II** himself frequently made the slow and laborious journey by donkey to the scenic summit. In 1882, to encourage more visitors to come and enjoy the beautiful scenery, the emperor authorized the construction of the Corcovado train line, which was completed two years later. The 4,156yd/3,800m long railroad was

Address Book

SHOPPING

Vitacura

At the Trenzinho Corcovado station. Open daily 8:30am–7pm.

The obviously touristy shop at the Corcovado train station is not necessarily the cheapest spot to get your Brazilian football t-shirt, Christ the Redeemer fridge magnet, or Corcovado keyring, but the quality of the goods on sale here is pretty good, and if you are short on time, it is a good place to stock up on souvenirs and gifts to take back home.

TRAIN CAFE

Café do Trem

In the Espaço Cultural. Open daily 9am–5pm.

This little stand at the train station, within the "cultural space" (&see p 135) sells good coffee, a variety of sandwiches, Brazilian snacks, and even beer. Although there is a terrace cafe at the top near the statue that offers fresh juices and hot pies, this cafe is a great place to kill some time if you have to wait for the next train.

Cristo Redentor

Y. Kanazawa/Michelin

then—and still is—considered a miracle of engineering, because it negotiates such a long, steep incline. The idea of erecting the Christ statue was originally suggested in 1921, to commemorate the centenary of Brazilian independence the following year. However, it wasn't until 1926 that construction began on the Christ the Redeemer statue, which was finally inaugurated in 1931.

A Work of Art

The finely sculpted Art Deco monument features delicately flowing robes and a face that is the picture of both serenity and strength. Frenchman **Paul Landowski** (1875–1961) actually had to create the statue in several parts. Until those pieces had been shipped from France to Brazil, and then carried up the mountain by train, the statue had never been assembled. Soapstone was used for the outer layer due to its resistance

to extreme weather. The giant figure is subjected to both scorching sunshine and heavy rain and storms, but has remained unscathed through the years, even surviving several dramatic lightning strikes.

An Illuminating Experience

Things didn't go so well at the inauguration ceremony of the monument, back in 1931. The new floodlights were supposed to be turned on by radio signal from a yacht off the coast of Naples, some 5,700mi/9,200km away. This ambitious plan had been hatched by **Guglielmo Marconi** (1874–1937) to promote his pioneering radio transmitter. Unfortunately, bad weather spoiled the grand plan, and in the end local workers in Rio had to turn on the lights manually. Today, powerful spotlights illuminate the Cristo Redentor statue so that it can be seen all over the city.

A Walk in the Park

One way to really enjoy Corcovado and to escape the well-trodden tourist trail that leads straight to the Christ statue, is to alight from the train halfway up at **Paineiras** station. This acts as unofficial gateway to the **Tijuca National Park** (☾ *see p 139*), since almost immediately from you find yourself in the depths of the thick, lush tropical vegetation. From the station it is just a half-hour walk through impressive scenery to a trio of pretty waterfalls. Alternatively, if you are feeling energetic, you could walk the remaining 1.9mi/3km to the summit and the Christ statue. The mountain of Corcovado is also a magnet for **rock-climbers**; the south face alone features more than 50 routes. Note that these are not walking trails, and should only be attempted by those with the proper equipment and training or supervision.

Visit

🕐 *Open daily 8:30am–6pm.* ☞*R$30.* ✗ 𝒫*21 2558 2359. www.corcovado.com.br.*
From the *favelas* to the rich suburbs of Rio, **Christ the Redeemer**'s open arms embrace the whole city, seemingly blessing the skyline of Rio de Janeiro, and protecting inhabitants and visitors alike. The iconic statue can be seen from just about anywhere in the city, and regardless of faith or convictions, the comforting, spiritual presence which emanates from it cannot be denied.

In 2007, this outstanding piece of art was deservedly named as one of the "New Seven Wonders of the World." The monumental 98ft/30m-high stone figure sits on a 26ft/8m-tall pedestal, its head alone weighing 30 tons and the arms 88 tons. From the station or the van drop-off near the top, a lift and then an escalator (or stairs) take you past cafes and souvenir shops to the viewing platform where tourists jostle for pictures, most of them with outstretched arms in imitation of the great figure.

From this vantage point, a breathtaking **view**★★★ of mountains, ocean, and city unfolds beneath you. If you turn your back on the statue of Christ and look out over the city as the statue does, to the right you will see Lagoa Rodrigo de Freitas, the Botanical Gardens, Gávea horse racing track, the sands of Ipanema Beach, Copacabana's high-rises, and far away, the islands in the Atlantic Ocean, appearing as specks. Straight ahead, the view encompasses the bulbous mound of Sugar Loaf and nearby Botafogo Bay dotted with tiny boats. More to your left, you will catch a glimpse of downtown skyscrapers, and just above, clearly vis-

The Only Way is Up

Locals love to jog or walk up Corcovado—especially at weekends. If you don't feel energetic enough to join them, you can make the ascent up Corcovado by the cog-driven train (☾ *see Trenzinho do Corcovado, right*), taking a taxi to the station. Tickets for the train are relatively steep *(although these do include the entrance fee to the statue)*, and a taxi for two can be had for a similar price, though it can be tough to negotiate a fair price with the taxi cartel at the base. It is now no longer possible for **private cars** or **taxis** to go right to the top of the Corcovado. All vehicles must stop at Paineiras station and from there passengers take one of the vans licensed by IBAMA *(a fixed fee)*. Smart visitors try to avoid the over-priced taxis that prey on tourists at the station down below. As an alternative, consider taking a taxi from your hotel or starting point to Corcovado, negotiating a price that includes taking you up to Paineiras and waiting for you while you visit the statue. Apart from cost, taking a taxi means you don't have to queue for train tickets, or wait for the train, which only runs every 30 minutes. If you do take the train, you can now purchase tickets in advance online *(www. ticketronics.net)*. Otherwise, on busy days at the booth, you can sometimes wait an hour or more for a ticket.

ble, the huge Maracanã stadium. If you walk around the statue, you will find, nestled at its base, the tiny **Capela de Nossa Senhora da Aparecida**. Named after the patron saint of Brazil, this unique place of worship hosts mass, baptisms, and weddings.

Night Vision

Just before sunset is a great time to visit Corcovado, when the city *(good weather permitting)* is bathed in a warm orange glow. Stay for a while, and just before nightfall, the floodlights switch on. Christ the Redeemer is beautifully lit, appearing as if it were suspended in mid-air like a vision. Gradually, Rio turns into a sea of twinkling lights, and a new enchanting cityscape appears. On some misty nights, the enormous figure of Christ appears to wear a golden halo, as if bathed in light from an other-worldly source.

Trenzinho do Corcovado★   Kids

Rua Cosme Velho 513, Cosme Velho. ⏰*Open daily 8:30am–6pm.* ✎*R$30.* ✕ ☎*21 2558 2359. www.corcovado.com.br.* The Corcovado train station is the start-ing point for the picturesque ascent to Christ the Redeemer (⟲*see p 132).*

The first train was steam-driven, but in 1910 it became the first electric train in the whole country. Trains run every 30 minutes and take 17 minutes, the car-riages slowly rising up the steep 30 per-cent incline through beautiful dense for-est, over a metal viaduct, and making a stop at Paineiras station.

You may see passengers getting off here and at other little stations along the way as, incredibly, people live up on this steep, jungle-covered mountain. At Paineiras, it waits for the descend-ing train to pass before climbing the remaining distance. The forest opens up on the left, offering a view of the whole of the south of the city, the beaches of Ipanema and Leblon, Niterói Bridge, and the whole of Guanabara Bay; just a taste of what awaits the visitor at the top. For the best view, sit at the back of the train on the way up—or on the right hand side. Samba buskers in a group often join the train, creating a carnival atmosphere.

Espaço Cultural

Rua Cosme Velho 513, Cosme Velho. ⏰*Open daily 8:30am–6pm.* ⛔*Closed all major holidays.* ✎*Free Admission.* ✕ This informal cultural space in Corco-vado train station is a good place to learn about the history of both the railway and the statue. Huge murals, blown-up historic photographs, and interactive displays tell the fascinating story of how such a tiny train and such an enormous statue came to be built on a steep, jungle-covered mountain. Copies of newspaper reports dating from the inauguration of the railroad on October 9, 1884 give a sense of the momentous occasion, attended by poli-ticians and celebrities of the day, with much fanfare and great solemnity, as this was also a religious affair. Emperor Dom Pedro II presided over the occa-sion and rode up in the train. Since then, famous names from around the world, such as Albert Einstein, Pope John Paul II and Princess Diana, and have made the ascent on the little cog railway.

Also on show here is an antique carriage manufactured in Switzerland in 1883. Visitors can also see the original electric engine that replaced the steam engine when the system was overhauled in 1910. Perhaps the most unusual exhibit is a model of the head of the Christ the Redeemer statue. Made of terracotta, 31.5in/80cm wide and on a concrete base, it was used as a basis for the real thing by Paul Landowski, the French sculptor who created the statue.

Trenzinho do Corcovado

R. Mills/Michelin

Largo do Boticário

Y. Kanazawa/Michelin

Additional Sights

Largo do Boticário★

*Rua Cosme Velho. ⏰Open daily 24hrs.
⊚Free Admission.*
The "Square of the Pharmacist" is a charming enclave that lies all the way down the tiny alley at the end of Rua Cosme Velho. This small bucolic plaza was named in honor of Joaquim José da Silva Souto, who leased the land here in 1831, and carried the title of Apothecary to the Royal Family. With its prettily painted neo-Colonial houses *(ongoing restoration work)* built beneath a backdrop of Atlantic rainforest, its

Museu Internacional de Arte Naïf

Y. Kanazawa/Michelin

fountain and old-style cobble pavement, this architectural composition is like a parenthesis in time. Looking at picturesque, colorful pink house *(⏷see picture above)*, you may be surprised to learn it is not as old as it appears. The mansion was actually built in 1937, and renovated nine years later by Lucio Costa, partially using materials saved from the demolition of old buildings undertaken for the opening of Avenida Presidente Vargas.

Museu Internacional de Arte Naïf

Rua Cosme Velho 562. ☎21 2205 8612. www.museunaif.com.br. A discount is given on presentation of your Corcovado ticket. ☹Sadly, the museum has suffered from financial troubles in recent years, so do check at your time of visit to verify that it is still receiving visitors.
Housed in a beautiful 19C mansion, next to the Corcovado train station, this museum has one of the largest collections of naïve art in the world. Characterized by vibrant colors and simple perspectives, many of these works of art are enchanting, particularly those depicting scenes from Rio. On display are more than 6,000 works created by artists in all the states in Brazil and from more than 130 countries.

PARQUE NACIONAL DA TIJUCA★★★

The exuberant vegetation of Tijuca National Park lies within the densely populated city of Rio de Janeiro, forming the largest urban forest in the world (8,154acres/3,300ha). The altitude of the park ranges from 262ft/80m at the bottom of the Jardim Botânico, to 3,349ft/1,021m at Pico da Tijuca, its highest point. Tijuca National Park is a natural playground which gives visitors a chance to enjoy walking, hiking, rock climbing or even hang gliding in a beautiful setting, just a stone's throw from the great metropolis.

▶ **Orient Yourself:** The huge swathes of forest stretch from Barra da Tijuca (see p 178), west of Rio, all the way to the coastal mountains overlooking Guanabara Bay, such as Morro do Corcovado (see p 134). The best way to make the most of a visit is to combine traveling by car with exploring on foot.

Don't Miss: The breathtaking view of Rio's most iconic sights from Vista Chinesa. The amazing collection of *azulejos* at Museu do Açude. A picnic at the beauty-spot of Bom Retiro.

Organizing Your Time: Avoid visiting on a rainy day, because foggy weather conditions and soggy paths could ruin the fun.

Especially for Kids: Spot cheeky monkeys, lazy sloths, agile squirrels, gentle butterflies and all the gorgeous birds that live in the forest.

A Bit of History

Tijuca National Park—*tijuca* means "swamp" in the native Tupi-Guaranian language, refering to the swamp-like lake located at the foot of the Tijuca hills, where the Tijuca Forest lays— includes the slopes of the nearby mountains, an area once entirely covered by a dense forest.

In the 16C, this vegetation was almost completely destroyed when large numbers of trees were cut down for firewood and coal. From the 17C until the end of the 19C, coffee plantations caused further destruction of the landscape. This resulted in a mass exodus of the farmers to more fertile lands.

Slave Labor

Meanwhile, the city was growing at a dramatic rate, causing the authorities to adopt urgent measures to guarantee the crucial water supply. At that time, Parque Nacional da Tijuca had as many as 150 freshwater springs, so the government decided to restore the vegetation to protect its precious water. **Major Manuel Gomes Archer**, with his team of six slaves, began the mammoth task

of **reforestation**—a job that lasted 13 years. This small group of individuals planted more than 60,000 trees in an area of 3,954 acres/1,600ha, adding to the native varieties exotic species which can still be seen today.

Success Story

In 1874, under the orders of **Dom Pedro II**, the area was placed under the care of the **Baron d'Escragnolle** (see p 142), who, with the help of French landscape architect **Auguste**

Parque Nacional da Tijuca

www.terrabrasil.org.br

François Marie Glaziou (1828–1906), embellished the forest with bridges, lookouts, and lakes. By 1887, the region boasted more than 100,000 trees. This large-scale intensive program of regeneration and reforestation ultimately lead to the creation of one of the world's largest urban parks.

A Bit of Geography

Wild at Heart
The Tijuca National Park was created in 1961, and just 30 years later, its status was raised to **Biosphere Reserve**. It is home to hundreds of species of plants, animals, and birds—many threatened by extinction as they thrive only in the rare, ancient *Mata Atlântica* (Atlantic Rainforest).

Many of the creatures are naturally shy, but visitors may be lucky enough to spot armadillos, anteaters, and monkeys. Multi-colored birds and butterflies are easy to see, while spiders and snakes are some of the less welcome inhabitants. Tijuca contains more bromelias (most likely to be seen on humid, rainy days) than the Amazon jungle, as well as a spectacular variety of orchids that grow amongst the rich vegetation which includes walnut, eucalyptus, and Jacaranda trees.

😊 A Bit of Advice 😊

If you want to do any extensive walking, hire a guide or join a tour. Although there is a comprehensive network of paths, it is easy to get lost and you should never visit the park alone. Try to visit the viewpoints on weekends during the day as there are plenty of other people around as well as police. Bring insect repellent, sunscreen, and something warm to wear in case the temperature drops (it is always considerably cooler than the beach areas). Floresta da Tijuca is a special place and deserves to be protected. Hunting, feeding wild animals, straying from the paths, picking flowers or any plants, leaving garbage, and lighting fires are all strictly prohibited.

Viewpoints

Mirante Dona Marta★★★
Estrada do Mirante Dona Marta.
Reached by car from the district of Cosme Velho, this low viewpoint, at just 1,194ft/364m, provides a relatively close panorama of Rio de Janeiro. On the left, in the north of the city, is the Maracanã stadium (*see p 274*), and the waters of the Bay of Guanabara cut through by the Rio–Niterói bridge. Ahead, the city of Niterói stands out against the horizon and the ocean; in the foreground is the historic center and Santa Teresa and to the right, Sugar Loaf and Copacabana.

Vista Chinesa★★
Estrada Dona Castorina, Serra Carioca.
The "Chinese View" gets its unusual name from the pagoda, topped by a dragon's head, built to honor the thousands of Chinese who worked tirelessly on the roads through the forest. It stands at 1,355ft/413m, along the access road to the park coming from the Botanical Gardens area. The viewpoint reveals Cristo Redentor, parts of Botafogo, Sugar Loaf Mountain, and the Bay of Guanabara, right down to the southern beaches.

Mesa do Imperador
Estrada Dona Castorina, Serra Carioca.
At 1,585ft/483m, the "Emperor's Table" is just a short distance up from the Vista Chinesa on the same road. It is formed by a natural stone recess which features two observation levels. On the lower level is a large square, with a stone table, from where a staircase leads to the upper level. A magnificent view, through the dense forest, reveals Rodrigo de Freitas lake, the beaches of Ipanema and Leblon, and the ocean.

Floresta da Tijuca 🚸

Estrada da Cascatinha 850, Alto da Boa Vista. ⏰*Open daily 8am–6pm.* 📞*21 2492 2252.*
The entrance to Tijuca Forest, which is just a part of the much larger National Park, is marked by a gate at Plaza de Alfonso Vizeu (called Praça do Alto), in the Alto da Boa Vista neighborhood.

Many of its sights can be seen from the main roads that lead through it. There is also a large number of trails—ranging from gentle walks to more strenuous hikes that require guides.

Cascatinha do Taunay

Just off the main Estrada da Cascatinha road is this 98ft/30m-high waterfall formed by the Tijuca, Caveira, and Cascatinha rivers. It is named after **Nicolas Antoine Taunay**, a French painter and member of the French Artistic Mission of 1816 which settled in the area. When the Taunay family first visited this peaceful spot, they were instantly enchanted by its beauty and tranquility.

Capela Mayrink

The tiny pink Mayrink Chapel, sitting in a coppice by the side of the road which goes through the forest, has a fairytale appearance. It was once part of the Boa Vista farm estate, in which coffee, sugar, and fruits flourished, and was often visited by the **Empress Leopoldina**, wife of Dom Pedro I. Built in 1863, the chapel was sold in 1888 to Counselor Mayrink, hence its name.

Centro de Visitantes

Praça Afonso Viseu. ○*Open daily 8am–7pm.* ℘*21 2492 2253.*
Drop into the Visitor Center, close to the chapel, for detailed information about the park and its trails, including maps, as well as up-to-date safety advice.

Bom Retiro

At 2,158ft/658m, on Estrada dos Picos, this is the highest point of the asphalted roads in Tijuca Forest, as well as an attractive **picnic spot**. From here a well-marked trail that takes about an hour leads to the **Pico da Tijuca**★.

Pico da Tijuca★

This moderately easy trek follows a clearly marked trail through scenic forest, past small streams to the highest point in the park, at 3,349ft/1,021 meters. The very last section features over 100 steps with a metal handrail looking over a dizzying drop. From the top a dazzling view of the whole of the city more than rewards hikers for their

Cascatinha do Taunay

Y. Kanazawa/Michelin

ECOTOURISM

Terra Brasil
Rua da Passagem 83, Room 314, Botafogo. ℘*21 2543 3185. www. terra-brazil.com.*
Many Brazilian adventure and outdoor tour companies misleadingly say they offer "ecotourism". Created in 1990, Terra Brasil is a highly recommended nonprofit institution whose activities center around conservation, environmental education, and eco-tourism. They offer genuine eco-tours in Floresta da Tijuca, as well as the rest of Rio.

efforts. Set off early to avoid the scorching midday sun on this south-facing slope. Although it is possible to walk it without a guide, it is recommended that walkers travel in groups.

Ruínas do Archer

The ruins of the house of **Major Archer** (see p 139)—the man who oversaw the reforestation of Tijuca—does not have any significant features, as only the walls still stand. However, it is an important landmark next to the Estrada dos Picos road. The slave quarters once attached to the house have been transformed into a restaurant.

Os Esquilos

Estrada Barão d'Escragnolle. ○*Open Tue–Sun 10am–6pm.* ✕ ℘*21 2492 2197. www.osesquilos.com.br.*

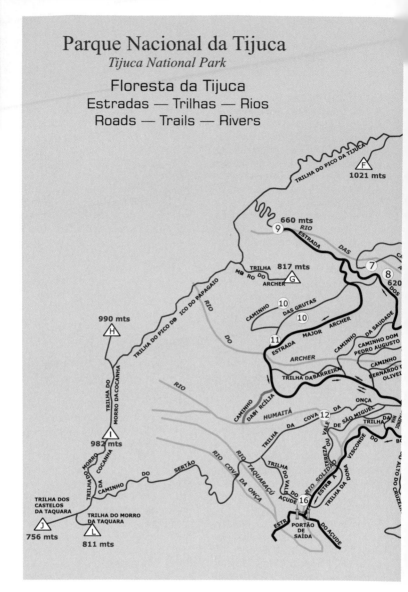

Parque Nacional da Tijuca
Tijuca National Park

Floresta da Tijuca
Estradas — Trilhas — Rios
Roads — Trails — Rivers

This is the place where **Baron d'Escragnolle**'s residence once stood. The French aristocrat, who went into exile during the French Revolution, came to Rio in 1808. From 1874 on, he assumed responsibility for the reforestation of the area. As a nature-lover eager to share the beauty of Tijuca with others, he made its natural beauty spots accessible, and gave them names that visitors would remember (mostly names of family members or favorite literary works).

By 1945, his former home was practically in ruins and had lost all its original characteristics. A new house— built using materials from demolition works in old Rio—was built, and now houses a restaurant (🕯 *see p 237*).

Museu do Açude★
Estrada do Açude 764, Alto da Boa Vista. 🕐*Open Wed–Mon 11am–5pm.* 🎟*R$6. Free Thu.* 📞*21 2492 5443. www. museuscastromaya.com.br.*

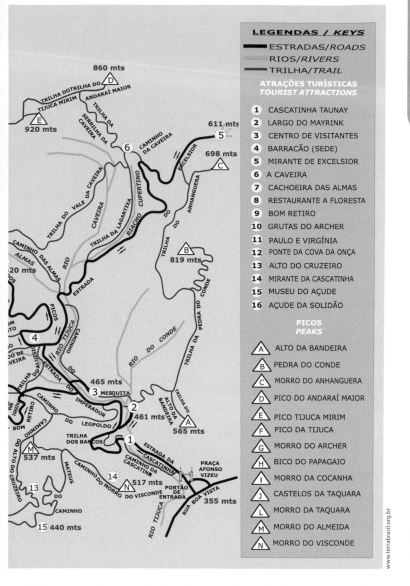

LEGENDAS / KEYS

ESTRADAS/ROADS
RIOS/RIVERS
TRILHA/TRAIL

ATRAÇÕES TURÍSTICAS
TOURIST ATTRACTIONS

1. CASCATINHA TAUNAY
2. LARGO DO MAYRINK
3. CENTRO DE VISITANTES
4. BARRACÃO (SEDE)
5. MIRANTE DE EXCELSIOR
6. A CAVEIRA
7. CACHOEIRA DAS ALMAS
8. RESTAURANTE A FLORESTA
9. BOM RETIRO
10. GRUTAS DO ARCHER
11. PAULO E VIRGÍNIA
12. PONTE DA COVA DA ONÇA
13. ALTO DO CRUZEIRO
14. MIRANTE DA CASCATINHA
15. MUSEU DO AÇUDE
16. AÇUDE DA SOLIDÃO

PICOS
PEAKS

A. ALTO DA BANDEIRA
B. PEDRA DO CONDE
C. MORRO DO ANHANGUERA
D. PICO DO ANDARAÍ MAIOR
E. PICO TIJUCA MIRIM
F. PICO DA TIJUCA
G. MORRO DO ARCHER
H. BICO DO PAPAGAIO
I. MORRO DA COCANHA
J. CASTELOS DA TAQUARA
L. MORRO DA TAQUARA
M. MORRO DO ALMEIDA
N. MORRO DO VISCONDE

www.terrabrasil.org.br

Set in an enchanting neo-Colonial-style house nestled deep in the forest, this museum was the summer residence of **Raymundo Ottoni de Castro Maya** (1894–1968), entrepreneur, patron, and art collector—who also lived in today's Museu da Chácara do Céu (see p 130), in Santa Teresa.

Inside, an extensive collection of 17C–19C **azulejos** (tiles from Portugal, but also from France, Spain, and Holland), precious Portuguese and Brazilian works in silver and crystal, and oriental art (mainly porcelain from the West Indies Company) decorate the rooms.

Outside, the house is enclosed by a beautiful **garden** and exuberant tropical vegetation. The external walls and the garden benches and fountains display more tile work. The garden also has installations of contemporary Brazilian artists such as Iole de Freitas, Anna Maria Maiolino, Hélio Oiticica, Lygia Pape, Nuno Ramos, and José Rezende.

143

SOUTH ZONE BESIDE THE BAY

A few neighborhoods have spread along the curve of Guanabara Bay, covered for much of its length by Flamengo Park's huge sweep of coastal greenery. These neighborhoods do not only present significant historical interest. They also claim some of Rio's most impressive natural features. The bay itself, a beautifully formed natural haven, today busy with commercial shipping lanes as well as pleasure boats, provides the foreground for the bay's main marker and Brazilian icon: Sugar Loaf Mountain, located on a narrow strip of land between peaceful Botafogo Bay and the ocean.

Highlights

1 The dazzling interior of the **Museu da República** (☙see p 149).

2 World-class exhibitions at the **Museu de Arte Moderna** (☙see p 146).

3 Panoramic sunset views from **Pão de Açúcar** (☙see p 152).

4 Sitting on the ocean wall outside **Bar Urca** (☙see p 250).

5 Strolling along the **Cláudio Coutinho** nature trail which hugs the coastline around Morro da Urca (☙see p 153).

A Place to Discover

Until the end of the 18C, the area was little more than a passageway to the forts on the southern coast and to what is now known as Lagoa Rodrigo de Freitas (☙see p 170). The bay area's subsequent occupation came about thanks to its privileged location and its rare beauty: the Guanabara Bay (☙see p 195) on one side, Rodrigo de Freitas Lake on the other, as well as lush green mountains such as Corcovado Mountain (☙see p 134). Sandwiched between the historic center (☙see p 94) and the south zone beaches (☙see p 154), this part of Rio should definitely be visited for the unique insights it brings to understanding the city's history, and for its beauty, with the unforgettable spectacle of world-famous Sugar Loaf Mountain (☙see p 152).

Origins of a Name

Sugar Loaf Mountain, or *Pão de Açúcar* in Portuguese, is assumed to have derived from its resemblance to a sugar loaf, or "bread of sugar". In the 16C and 17C refined sugar was molded into a conical shape (like a loaf) in order for it to be transported. Another theory relates to the indigenous Tamois name for the granite monolith, *Pau-nh-açuquã*, meaning high, isolated hill; to the Portuguese settlers this must have sounded remarkably similar to *Pão de Açúcar*.

Walking on the Beach

There are several beaches in this part of town. Their sands and views out to the bay make for peaceful, pleasant strolls. On a fine day, you may see plenty of racing dinghies, sail boats, and motor yachts, all making use of the bay. Few sunbathers are found on the beaches though, and swimming is not recommended, as the waters of Guanabara Bay are polluted. Attempts are being made to restore the area to its former glory.

Birthplace of the City

This area of Rio de Janeiro was the first to be populated by Europeans. When the Portuguese arrived here on January 1, 1502, they thought Guanabara Bay was the estuary of a great river, and named the place "January River" (or Rio de Janeiro in Portuguese). For hundreds of years, the area had been inhabited by native Indians from the Tupi culture.

😊 A Bit of Advice 😊

This area is punctuated by a row of five Metrô stations, closely packed together, from Catete at the northern end down to Botafogo in the south. The Metrô is regarded as clean, efficient, and safe (☙see p 21).

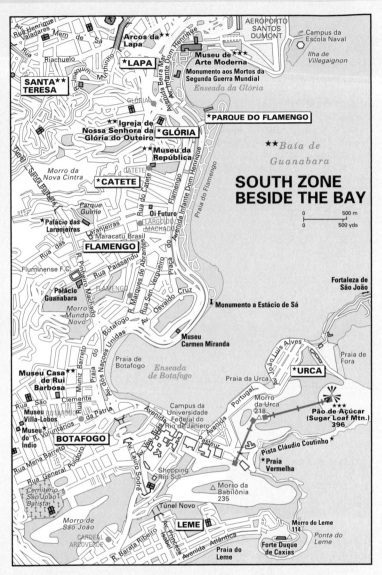

South Zone Beside the Bay

Map labels:

Av. Henrique Valadares · Rua · Mem · de · Sá · Riachuelo · **Arcos da Lapa** · AEROPORTO SANTOS DUMONT · Campus da Escola Naval · Ilha de Villegaignon · **★LAPA** · **Museu de ★★★ Arte Moderna** · **Monumento aos Mortos da Segunda Guerra Mundial** · **SANTA★★ TERESA** · Avenida Beira Mar · Avenida Infante Dom Henrique · *Enseada da Glória* · GLÓRIA · **★PARQUE DO FLAMENGO** · **★★Igreja de Nossa Senhora da Glória do Outeiro** · **★GLÓRIA** · **★★Museu da República** · **★★***Baía de Guanabara* · CATETE · Morro da Nova Cintra · **★CATETE** · Flamengo · Praia do Flamengo · **SOUTH ZONE BESIDE THE BAY** · 0 500 m / 0 500 yds · Parque Guinle · **★Palácio das Laranjeiras** · **Oi Futuro** · LARGO DO MACHADO · Maracatu Brasil · Rua das · Laranjeiras · **FLAMENGO** · Fluminense F.C. · R. Pinheiro Machado · Rua Paissandu · Rua Marquês de Abrantes · Rua São Vaqueiro · Praça Cruz · **Fortaleza de São João** · **Palácio Guanabara** · FLAMENGO · Av. Osvaldo · **Monumento a Estácio de Sá** · Morro Mundo Novo · Botafogo · Av. das Nações Unidas · **Museu Carmen Miranda** · Praia de Botafogo · *Enseada de Botafogo* · João Luís Alves · Praia de Fora · **Museu Casa de Rui Barbosa** · Rua Muniz Barreto · Praia de Botafogo · Praia da Urca · Portugal · **★URCA** · Rua São Clemente · **Museu Villa-Lobos** · Rua da Pátria · Campus da Universidade Federal do Rio de Janeiro · Avenida · Pasteur · Avenida · Morro da Urca 218 · **★★★Pão de Açúcar (Sugar Loaf Mtn.) 396** · **Museu do Índio** · Rua Voluntários · **BOTAFOGO** · Av. Lauro Sodré · Av. Venceslau Brás · **Pista Cláudio Coutinho★** · Rua Mena Barreto · Rua General Polidoro · Shopping Rio Sul · **★Praia Vermelha** · *Cemitério São João Batista* · △ Morro da Babilônia 235 · Túnel Novo · Morro do Leme 114 · CARDEAL ARCOVERDE · Morro de São João · R. Barata Ribeiro · R. Princesa Isabel · Avenida Atlântica · **LEME** · *Ponta do Leme* · Praia do Leme · **Forte Duque de Caxias**

Converted by Jesuit missionaries, and depending on the priests' countries of origin, either French or Portuguese, the Indians showed allegiance to that country. Over time, Tupi Indians disappeared from the region.

European Influence

The European influence first manifested itself in the historic center, with the emergence of a localized Portuguese style of architecture.

Rio's historic core then saw, in the 19C, the arrival of the French-inspired Neoclassical Style (Casa França-Brasil), a trend which soon spread to São Cristovão (Solar da Marquesa de Santos) and Botafogo (Casa de Rui Barbosa).

Toward the end of the 19C and in the early 20C came a strong wave of Eclectic style which literally swept the entire city, along with Art Nouveau and Art Deco styles still visible in some of Flamengo and Urca's architectural landscape today.

PARQUE DO FLAMENGO★

Opened to the public in October 1965, this landscaped park offers spectacular views of Sugar Loaf Mountain and Christ the Redeemer. The monumental public space stretches the waterfront from the historic center, past Glória, Catete, and Flamengo, before eventually being halted by the sands of Botafogo Beach.

▸ **Orient Yourself:** The main road through the park, Avenida Infante Dom Henrique, runs parallel to the bay. The Modern Art Museum is in the far north, on the fringes of the historic center.

🕒 **Don't Miss:** The strikingly contemporary Modern Art Museum (MAM) and its gardens, landscaped by Burle Marx.

🕐 **Organizing Your Time:** A visit to the park can be combined with the surrounding districts of Flamengo and Catete (see p 148), Botafogo (see p 150), or the historic center (see p 94). On Sundays and holidays, between 7am and 6pm, the main roads through the park are closed to traffic. Avoid visiting on Mondays when the Modern Art Museum is closed.

Kids **Especially for Kids:** The playgrounds and wide-open spaces.

Visit   Kids

Flamengo Park, also known as **Aterro** (landfill) **do Flamengo**, was created from the decimation of the huge hill of Saint Antonio, which was poured into the ocean to make the park.

Completed under the governorship of **Carlos Lacerda** (1961–1965), the working group included architects, engineers, an urban planner, a botanist, and a graphic designer.

Eduardo Reidy was responsible for the civil and building works, while **Burle Marx** designed the immense gardens that stretch the length of the park, replete with hundreds of species of birds, plants, and trees.

This beautiful park provides a pleasant place for a stroll (🕒during daytime only). Sports facilities include cycle and roller-blading tracks, football pitches, and volleyball courts.

Sights

Museu de Arte Moderna★★★

Av. Infante Dom Henrique 85, Parque do Flamengo. 🕐*Open Tue–Fri noon–6pm; Sat, Sun, and holidays noon–7pm. Last entry half an hour before closing time.* *R$8.* ✕ 🖉*21 2240 4944/21 2240 4899. www.mamrio.com.br.*

The Museum of Modern Art was founded in 1948 on the initiative of a group of

Museu de Arte Moderna

Y. Kanazawa/Michelin

art enthusiasts at the Capanema Palace (*see p 73*), which today houses the Ministry of Education, Culture and Health. In 1952, the museum began the move to Aterro do Flamengo, where it was inaugurated in 1958. The building was designed by urban architect **Affonso Eduardo Reidy** (1909–1964).

The museum is notable for its large glazed facade, with robust modernist pillars propping up a concrete shelf that provides external shade and forms a continuous line down to the ocean. Its striking, contemporary design allows for fluid interior spaces infused with light. In the gardens, designed by Burle Marx (*see p 74*), vegetation bursts from the ground in regimented rectangles, with pools, flowerbeds, and pebbles to soften the overall effect.

In 1978, fire destroyed almost all of MAM's exhibits, including masterpieces by Picasso, Miró, Dalí, and Magritte. In dire straits, the museum received a huge boost 11 years later, when **Gilberto Chateaubriand** donated his entire 4,000-piece collection. Today the museum is once again at the forefront of the art scene, displaying works by the greatest Brazilian artists. Look for gems from **Candido Portinari** (1903–1962) and **Emiliano Di Cavalcanti** (1897–1967). **Anita Malfatti's** (1889–1964) iconic *Lighthouse* and **Tarsila do Amaral's** (1886–1973) dramatic *Urutu* also must not be missed.

There are over 11,000 pieces here, including masterful sculptures by the likes of **Henry Moore** and **Alberto Giacometti**. Mesmerizing images by **Pierre Verger** and more than 1,000 other photographs make up the contemporary Joaquim Paiva Collection. MAM is also home to an important archive of Brazilian and world cinema, and hosts regular screenings and short film courses.

Monumento aos Mortos da Segunda Guerra Mundial

Av. Infante Dom Henrique 85, Parque do Flamengo. Open Tue–Sun, 9am–5pm.

This monument to the World War II dead was built between 1957 and 1960, the second project of architects Hélio Ribas Marinho and Marcos Konder Netto. An

Parque do Flamengo
Y. Kanazawa/Michelin

underground mausoleum contains graves of Brazilians transferred from the cemetery at Pistóia, near the Italian city of Florence. The men of the Brazilian Expeditionary Force (FEB) fought alongside the Allies and were the only South American troops to fight in Europe during World War II.

In the mausoleum are 468 graves with marble tombstones. Two graves are empty, and 13 unidentified, with the following inscription: "Here lies a hero of the F.E.B., God knows his name." Outside, on each side of the mausoleum's entrance, are two panels by the painter **Anísio Araújo de Medeiros**, made of enameled and glazed ceramics, in tribute to the navy (which took part in allied U-boat patrols in the Atlantic). Little is remembered of such contributions beyond the borders of Brazil—a country known as "The Forgotten Ally" among war historians.

Museu Carmen Miranda

Av. Rui Barbosa, Parque do Flamengo. Open Tue–Fri 10am–5pm, Sat and Sun 1pm–5pm. Free Admission. 21 2299 5586.

Born in Portugal, but raised in Brazil, the name Carmen Miranda (1909–1955) is synonymous with Brazilian exuberance and style. This small museum in the south of the park is set in a modernist circular building designed by architect Affonso Eduardo Reidy. Dedicated to the famous Hollywood star and with over 3,000 items of memorabilia *(only some of them on display at one time)*, the collection includes her famous platform shoes, turbans, costumes, and jewelry.

FLAMENGO AND CATETE★

These districts are home to a scattering of historic remnants, including palaces and museums—the highlight of which is undoubtedly the Museum of the Republic housed in the dazzling Catete Palace. The area also boasts interesting 19C and 20C homes and apartment buildings, which lend a faded grandeur to the pleasant tree-lined streets, as well as some down-at-heel office buildings.

▸ **Orient Yourself:** The districts of Catete and Flamengo lie between Glória (◉see p 125) and Botafogo (◉see p 150) and each has a namesake Metrô station.

⊚ **Don't Miss:** Enjoy the lavish interior decoration of Catete Palace, former residence of Brazilian presidents. And make sure you stop by the wonderful shop of the National Center of Folklore and Popular Culture, located on the grounds of the Museum of the Republic.

◔ **Organizing Your Time:** Note that the Museum of the Republic is closed on Monday. And remember to avoid wandering around the neighborhood at night, when the streets become empty and potentially unsafe.

Kids **Especially for Kids:** The Museum of the Republic's gardens have plenty of space to run around and a small playground for children under 10. If you have teenagers, take them to Oi Futuro for the gallery's innovative exhibits of digital art or art with interactive media.

A Bit of History

A Natural Link
The districts of Catete and Flamengo expanded in the 16C as a link between the historic center (◉see p 94) and the

---

CULTURAL CENTER

Casa de Arte e Cultura Julieta de Serpa
Praia do Flamengo. ✕ ℰ*21 2551 1278. www.casajulietadeserpa.com.br.*
Billed as a "House of Art and Culture," this beautifully restored home is more about having fun and socializing in an exquisite 20C Eclectic building. The **Salão D'Or** (Salon of Gold) **tea room** provides delicate sandwiches, pretty little cakes, and pastries all presented on fine china *(Open Tue–Sat 4pm–7pm).* At the **J. Club piano bar**, enjoy cocktails and live music from MPB (Brazilian popular music) to Jazz *(Open Fri and Sat from 9pm).* There is also a **French restaurant** (Restaurante Blason) and **bistro** (Bistro BS) *(both open Mon–Fri noon–4pm, Tue–Sat 7pm–11pm).* Call ahead to find out about changing exhibitions and look out for regular cultural events.

---

south zone beaches (◉see p 154). At that time Rua do Catete was known as Caminho do Boqueirão da Glória. It bordered a marsh fed by a branch of the Carioca River that flowed down from Corcovado through the Laranjeiras Valley, draining into the ocean at Flamengo Beach. According to some, the name Flamengo comes from the flocks of beautiful red flamingos that once frequented this beach, others insist it originates from Flemish prisoners of war who lived here in the 17C.

Rich Residents
In the 18C, Catete and Flamengo began to be populated by smallholders and potters, taking advantage of the abundant water supply in the area. The character of the districts changed as the 19C progressed, when wealthy residents attracted by the close proximity to the city center, moved here from the hills. Flamengo and Catete became aristocratic neighborhoods, as evidenced by the Catete Palace (◉see Museu da República, opposite), built by a well-to-do Rio coffee planter. The Rua do Catete retains traces of its grandiose past, with facades and some complete houses—mainly between numbers 126 and 196—dating from the late 19C.

Commercial Success

In the 20C, because of its proximity to Rio's historic core and also because of the increasing value of **Zona Sul** (South Zone) districts, Catete was transformed into a commercial area. Dramatic urban growth ensued, and the neighborhood charm was difficult to preserve.

Sights

Museu da República★★

✕*Rua do Catete 153.* 🕐 *Tue–Fri, 10am–6pm; Sat, Sun, and holidays 1pm–6pm.* ✆*R$6. Free Wed and Sun.* ✆*21 3235 2650. www.museudarepublica.org.br.*

In 1897, shortly after the creation of the Republic, the **Catete Palace** officially became the presidential residence—a role it filled until April 1960, when the new capital of Brasília was inaugurated.

The Catete Palace then became home to the Museum of the Republic. The building is a beautiful example of mid-19C urban architecture and a visit is an education in Brazilian history from Empire (1840–1889) to Republic (1899–1930). As one of the country's most luxurious palaces, the interior is suitably dazzling, with lavish decoration, furniture, and works of art. Later additions included electric lights—one of the first such installations in Brazil—and bronze eagles, created by sculptor **Rodolfo Bernadelli**, which gave the building the nickname "Palace of the Eagles."

A series of opulent halls were used for entertaining. Official guests would

Lavishly decorated hall of Palácio do Catete

Y. Kanazawa/Michelin

gather in the fine **Venetian Salon**, where an enormous crystal chandelier drips from the ceiling, while the **Moorish Hall**, exquisitely decorated with Islamic art, was reserved as a smoking and games room for men only. Presidential meals took place in the grand **Banqueting Hall**, beneath a copy of Domenichino's celebrated *Diana* which adorns the ceiling.

On the top floor were the private rooms of the President of the Republic where, in 1954, **Getúlio Vargas** committed suicide by shooting himself though the heart. The austere **bedroom** is preserved with the suicide note, the 32-caliber Colt revolver that Vargas used to shoot himself, and his pyjamas—complete with bullet hole.

Oi Futuro

Rua Dois de Dezembro 63. 🕐*Open Tue–Sun 11am–8pm.* ✆*Free Admission.* ✕✆*21 3131 3060. www.oifuturo.org.br.* Owned by the Oi telecommunications company, this cultural center occupies eight levels.

Apart from a small permanent display on the history of the telephone, this is an achingly high-tech space. Changing exhibitions of contemporary and emerging art, performances, and cultural events are broad-ranging and of varying quality, but tend to focus on the avant-garde. On the top floor, a **cyber-café** serves lunch and snacks.

FOLK ART

The **National Center of Folklore and Popular Culture** or **CNFCP** *(181 Rua do Catete; Open Tue–Fri 11am–6pm; Sat, Sun and holidays 3pm–6pm; ✆21 2285 0441; www.cnfcp.gov. br)* has a little shop in the grounds of the Museu da República selling Brazilian art and handicrafts from communities who have participated in the exhibits of its **Popular Artists' Room**. It also offers a selection of books, CDs, and postcards relating to Brazilian folk art and culture.

BOTAFOGO

During the colonial period, Portuguese landowner José Pereira de Souza Botafogo settled here, giving his name to the neighborhood and its small beach, Praia de Botafogo. Part residential, part commercial, housing headquarters for many major corporations, Botafogo is undeniably quieter than its nearby beachfront neighbors. The area has recently become more upbeat with a number of cozy bars and restaurants, two great shopping centers and a few interesting museums to discover.

▶ **Orient Yourself:** Botafogo is due north of Copacabana, with the Bay of Guanabara and Urca to the east, and Flamengo to the north. The three main streets running through the neighborhood are Rua São Clemente (going towards Lagoa and Jardim Botânico), Rua Voluntários de Pátria (leading to Laranjeiras and Catete), and Avenida Praia de Botafogo (running parallel to waterfront Avenida Infante Dom Henrique).

☺ **Don't Miss:** For the studious, the splendid house-museum of legendary Brazilian political figure, Rui Barbosa. And for shopaholics, the gigantic Rio Sul shopping mall (☝ *see Shopping, p 261*), is very close to the tunnel connecting Botafogo to Copacabana, and its smaller counterpart, Botafogo Praia Shopping.

🕐 **Organizing Your Time:** Do not plan on spending any time at Botafogo's beach, as its waters are not be suitable for swimming. And if you are visiting the neighborhood on a Monday, note that only Villa-Lobos Museum will be open.

Kids **Especially for Kids:** Museu Casa de Rui Barbosa has a children's library, information about the museum in game form for little ones, and a spacious garden. Museu do Índio is another great spot for children, complete with child-friendly activities.

Sights

Museu Casa de Rui Barbosa★★   Kids
Rua São Clemente 134. 🕐*Open Tue–Fri 9am–5:30pm; Sat, Sun, and holidays 2pm–6pm.* ✆*R$2.* ✆*21 3289 4600. www.casaruibarbosa.gov.br.*

Rui Barbosa de Oliveira (1849–1923) was a liberal statesman, journalist, and later a judge at the International Court of Justice in the Hague. He played a key role in the Brazilian abolitionist movement.

In 1895, Rui Barbosa purchased this Neoclassical home which had been built in

Museu Casa de Rui Barbosa

Y. Kanazawa/Michelin

1859 for Bernardo Casimiro de Freitas, baron of Lagoa. When Rui Barbosa died, the Federal Government bought the house, opening it as a museum in 1930. Today, the museum, along with a center for research and documentation, is part of the Rui Barbosa House Foundation.

The house and gardens offer an interesting window into the domestic world of the Brazilian middle classes in the late 19C. Stucco detailing decorates the windows and doors, while rooftop statues represent the continents. Inside, the main rooms at the front look out onto a porch with a wrought-iron balustrade (typical of the period), but this entrance was used only for receptions and social events. The entrance to the museum, the same used by its first inhabitants on a daily basis, is actually off to the right side of the house.

Nearly 1,500 of Barbosa's belongings can be seen within the beautifully preserved interior—from Japanese porcelain to fine European furniture, not to mention Rui Barbosa's 1913 Benz automobile, parked in the garage. The statesman's personal, 37,000-volume **library**, along with the dining, music, and visiting rooms, represent an important page in Rio's social history. This lively museum also houses concerts, courses, and theatrical performances. Its lovely gardens offer a real respite for families with young children.

Museu do Índio★ `Kids`

Rua das Palmeiras 55. ○*Open Tue–Fri 9am–5:30pm; Sat, Sun, and holidays 1pm–5pm.* ◌ *R$3. Free Sun.* ♪*21 3214 8702. www.museudoindio.org.br.*

Inaugurated in 1953 with the objective of preserving and displaying the cultural heritage of the indigenous population of Brazil, the Museum of the Indian has operated from Botafogo since 1979.

It is managed by the National Foundation of the Indian (FUNAI), the only government body representing the more than 220 Indian ethnic groups in the country.

The main building dates from 1880, and within and around it lies a circuit of informative exhibitions divided into various aspects of indigenous life.

Museu do Índio

Y. Kanazawa/Michelin

An exhibition displays adornments, weapons for hunting and warfare, pieces made of pottery and straw, and a canoe made from a tree trunk. Photographs and videos allow visitors to observe some of the traditional rituals of indigenous groups, such as the exhausting races of the Timbira Indians, where logs serve as relay batons. Another exhibit explains the intricate Kwarup funerary rites of the Alto Xingu tribes, alongside a display of ritual masks belonging to different ethnic groups. A small reproduction of the interior of a Xingu home is also noteworthy. Visitors will also be able to buy various artefacts made by Brazilian Indians at the museum's shop.

Museu Villa-Lobos

Rua Sorocaba, 200. ○*Open Mon–Fri 10am–5pm.* ◌*R$2.* ⟋*Tours available by appointment.* ♪*21 2266 1024/2266 3894. www.museuvillalobos.org.br.*

Heitor Villa-Lobos (1887–1959), the famous Brazilian composer, was a master of integrating the most diverse musical genres. Many consider his greatest work to be *Bachianas Brasileiras*, which mixed the modulations and countermelodies of Brazilian folk songs with the music of Bach. Housed in a charming 19C mansion is this small collection relating to the rich life of Villa-Lobos, including an extensive library and sound archive. Visitors can peruse his personal letters, photographs, and sheet music and watch a short film about his life and works. In the pleasant garden is an acoustic "shell" where concerts are sometimes held.

URCA ★

...uiet haven in the middle of Rio's urban hustle and bustle stands out from ...e other neighborhoods for its natural beauty, its history, and its rich architec-...ural heritage. Stroll along Urca's streets, past its small beach and ocean wall, and toward Bar Urca, nearby São João Fortress, just to sit and enjoy an ice-cold beer while watching the boats in Guanabara Bay. Urca also boasts one of the city's major landmarks: world-famous Sugar Loaf Mountain, the top attraction of the area, and a must-see for any visitor to Rio.

▶ **Orient Yourself:** Urca is a compact neighborhood of less than one square mile, occupying a mountainous peninsula on the southern edge of Guanabara Bay.

☺ **Don't Miss:** Swaying up Sugar Loaf in a cablecar to enjoy breathtaking views. Walking between tropical forest and the ocean on Pista Cláudio Coutinho.

🕐 **Organizing Your Time:** To beat the crowds, visit Sugar Loaf early, or at sun-set when the scenery gets particularly beautiful.

Kids **Especially for Kids:** Colorful birds and butterflies, and even little monkeys, can be seen on the flat, easy walk along Pista Cláudio Coutinho.

A Bit of History

Of the many stories behind the origin of Urca's name, the most colorful describes the resemblance of the neighborhood's hill to the shape of the Flemish ships, called *urcas*, which often moored close by in the bay. The Urca neighborhood developed in the 1920s, which accounts for its amazing variety of unblemished architectural styles (*see sidebar*), mostly Art Deco and Eclectic with a South American and Neo-colonial touch.

Pão de Açúcar★★★ Kids

Av Pasteur 520. ⏰*Open daily 8am– 7:50pm.* ☞*R$44.* ✕ ♿ ☎*21 2461 2700. www.bondinho.com.br. Choose a clear day to visit.*

Rising up between the two smaller hills of **Morro da Urca** and **Cara de Cão**, the iconic sight of **Sugar Loaf Mountain** (👣*see also p 144*) is at the heart of Rio de Janeiro's history. It was here that Estácio de Sá disembarked on March 1, 1565, to build the original nucleus of the city. Standing at the entrance of Guanabara Bay (👣*see p 195*), this massive block of solid rock is 1,296ft/395m high.

Brazilian engineer Augusto Ferreira Ramos had the visionary idea of an aerial route up Sugar Loaf mountain in 1908. The daring design, using German equip-

ment and Brazilian and Portuguese labor was, when it was inaugurated in 1912, the first cablecar in Brazil, and only the third in the world. Passengers traveled up in wooden trams with curtained windows, as a small exhibition at the entrance to the cablecar station shows. Renovated in 1972, the *bondinho* was featured in the movie *Moonraker* (1979), which sees James Bond in a death-defy-ing fight atop one of the cablecars.

The two-leg ride up to the top of Sugar Loaf is beautiful but short, with each ride taking just three minutes. From the cablecar, on the right, you will see **Praça General Tibúrcio**, and beyond, Praia Vermelha, where a bust of Chopin contemplates the ocean.

The first leg carries passengers 1,886.5ft/ 575m, to **Morro da Urca** (735ft/224m high), which boasts a restaurant and a beautiful panoramic **view** of the sur-roundings, although this is just a taste of what visitors will get to see from the top of Sugar Loaf Mountain.

The ride's second leg leads to the much-awaited viewing platforms of **Morro do Pão de Açúcar**. This outstand-ing vantage point affords a sweeping **view**★★★ of Corcovado, with the Christ the Redeemer statue (👣*see p 134*), the tangle of buildings of Botafogo and Fla-mengo, and the outline of their beaches, dotted with small boats. To the east, you can see the beaches of Copacabana and

Cablecar up to Pão de Açúcar

Y. Kanazawa/Michelin

Ipanema and the open ocean; and on the other side, Rio's center, the Rio–Niterói bridge crossing Guanabara Bay, and the city of Niterói with its ocean beaches.

Additional Sights

Pista Cláudio Coutinho★ [Kids]

Praia Vermelha. ⊘*Open daily 6am–6pm. The trail's location in a military zone makes it a very safe place to walk.*
One of the most enjoyable walks in the area, this nature trail starts at a corner of Praia Vermelha. It was named after a former coach of the Brazilian soccer team, but is also known as the Estrada do Costão or the "Caminho do Bem-Te-Vi." It is a 8,200ft/2,500m round-trip walk, with distance markers every 164ft/50m. Strolling the trail which hugs the coastline around Morro da Urca and Morro do Pão de Açúcar, amidst lush vegetation inhabited by cheeky capuchin monkeys, is a truly special experience.

Monumento aos Heróis de Laguna e Dourados

Praça General Tibúrcio, ♿.
This granite and bronze monument pays tribute to the soldiers and all those who died as a result of Paraguay's invasion of Brazil in 1864.
In Dourados, a Brazilian garrison of just 15 soldiers, led by Antonio João Ribeiro fought to the death against a vastly superior invasion force.

Praia Vermelha

The small, sheltered "Red Beach" sitting at the foot of Morro da Urca gets its name from the minerals that color its sands. Swimming is not recommended here because of high pollution levels, but the beach does boast lovely views of the waves crashing against the rocky coastline. You may even see kayakers making their way out to Cotunduba, an island fairly close to the coast, at the entrance of Guanabara Bay.

Architectural Showcase

Urca boasts a wonderful medley of architectural styles. A private residence located at 26 Rua Urbano Santo, and the Praia da Urca's former casino are fine Art Deco examples. Chalet-style homes can be found at 75 and 85 Rua Otávio Correia, and at 17 Rua Urbano Santos. The area also features modernist houses, low-rise buildings typical of the 1960s–1970s, and more recent, higher condominiums. The much-favored 20C Eclectic style is also present, with the Insituto Benjamin Constant and the Companhia de Recursos Minerais, respectively at 350 and 404 Avenida Pasteur. Located on the same avenue at number 250, the former **Hospício D. Pedro II** (1852) is perhaps Urca's most remarkable architecture. Today, this grand Neo-classical building houses the rectorship of the Federal University of Rio de Janeiro (UFRJ).

SOUTH ZONE BEACHES

A spectacular sweep of scalloped coast runs all the way from Leme and Copacabana to Ipanema and Leblon. Each of these coastal neighborhoods has its own character, but together they contribute to the undeniable allure of Rio de Janeiro. From morning until night , the sidewalks and sands are filled with tourists and locals alike, all enjoying one of the most beautiful stretches of beach in the world. Vendors selling everything from suntan lotion to fresh fruit caipirinhas add the finishing touches to this lively scene.

Highlights

1   When the ocean is calm, following the delightful **Caminho dos Pescadores** around Morro do Leme (*see p 158*).

2   Having morning coffee or brunch at the legendary **Copacabana Palace Hotel** (*see p 160*).

3   Enjoying the view from the charming outside terrace of the **Café do Forte** (*see p 240*).

4   Strolling through the streets and browsing the chic boutiques of **Ipanema** (*see p 163*).

5   Heading for **Arpoador** (*see p 164*) to get one of the best sunset views in Rio.

History in the Sand

The Leme, Copacabana, Ipanema, Leblon, and Lagoa neighborhoods were once part of the same isolated area, known by the Tupi Indians as "Sacopenapã", referring to the Sacopenapã lake (now called Lagoa Rodrigo de Freitas). Right up until the middle of the 18C, the southern beaches formed a remote area of coast and marshland, cut off from the rest of the city, covered with *pitanga* (Surinam cherry trees) and cashew trees, and frequented only by humble fishermen and the occasional birds and whales.

Marking the Way

The endless sweep of sun-drenched sand is punctuated by Morro do Leme, the jutting rock of Arpoador, and Morro

Sunset at Praia de Ipanema, Morro Dois Irmãos in the background

Y. Kanazawa/Michelin

COPACABANA

0 ————— 400 m
0 ————— 400 yds

Dois Irmãos. Today, the beaches are subdivided into sectors demarcated by lifeguard stations called *postos*, acting as directional as well as social-markers,

some *postos* having a culture all of their own. Buildings which sprung up along the coastal areas, block the view of the hills, which once came right up to the

Playing football on *Praia do Leblon*

I. MacIntyre/Michelin

water's edge, but are now blocked from view, and can only be glimpsed through sidestreets or from the Forte de Copacabana (see p 161)

Safety First

Currents, undertows, and riptides can be dangerous at all the beaches here. Even experienced swimmers aware of the risks have been known to get into trouble, and even drown. Take care and look for flags and warnings. Lifeguards, stationed at the tall *postos* that rise from the sands, are generally on duty from 8am to 8pm throughout the summer, with winter seeing shorter hours. Waves in winter reaching more than 10ft/3m high may bring joy to the heart of surfers, but can spell disaster for careless swimmers. Water quality off these beaches can be poor, depending on the current and the weather. A light blue color is usually a good sign. Even though the sands are floodlit at night, do not walk by the water after dark.

Taking a break

Quiosques (kiosks) can be found at regular intervals along the beaches here. Those at Copacabana have enjoyed a facelift and now boast clean underground toilets, showers, and even

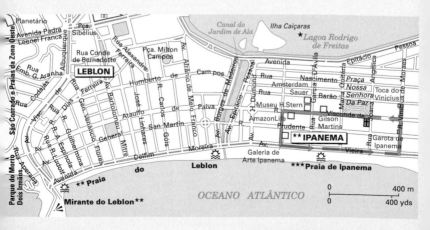

baby changing facilities. In Ipanema and Leme, the lifeguard stations have indoor showers and toilets that can be used for a small fee. On the sand itself, are *barracas* (beach stands) that will supply deck chairs and parasols for a charge. The attendants will bring you drinks at a reasonable price. Most Cariocas have their favorite kiosk, and you may find your own. Service is invariably friendly and trustworthy and owners will often look out for you. At the kiosks along the sidewalk, enjoy *caipirinhas* in the cooler late afternoon, but stick to hydrating *água de coco* (coconut water) during the hot midday sun. Once you've finished sipping it through a straw, hand the shell back to be cut in half and then scoop out the tender, nutritious flesh.

When in Rome...

It goes without saying that Brazilian beaches are relaxed. But appearance is all and it is a good idea to try and fit in a little with the locals. Women can wear tiny bikinis, but should never go topless. Only *gringos* (tourists) wear socks and sandals; instead get yourself a pair of stylish yet practical *havaianas* (flip-flops). These international exports are practically compulsory beachwear in Rio—for both men and women.

Beach towels (bring a sarong and rent a deck chair instead) and non-"Brazilian" bathing suits are other give-aways that you are a tourist. If you dare, buy a bikini at an Ipanema boutique (see p 260)

A Sporting Chance

Rio de Janeiro's beaches are not just about sunbathing. They double as bar, restaurant, meeting place, and gym—in particular the latter. At all times of day, you can see power-walkers, volleyball players, surfers, joggers, and impromptu aerobics sessions on the sidewalk or on the sand. **Beach soccer** is popular—as evidenced by all the goal nets, with Copacabana regularly hosting the world beach soccer championships. A distinctly Brazilian variation of volleyball is **futevolei**, played across a net like the normal game but with ball contact only allowed with the head, shoulders, and feet; it is an acrobatic, absorbing spectacle that is exhausting just to watch. On Sundays and holidays, the beachside part of Avenida Atlântica is closed to traffic along its length. Cyclists, roller-bladers, and joggers all come out in force, joined by *capoeira* performers and musicians.

where you can purchase a top and bottom in different sizes. Local men wear *sungas* (pronounced soon-gas), the Carioca version of Speedos, and these are no less revealing. For those finishing touches, pedicures in Rio de Janeiro are some of the best in the world, and a real bargain.

😊 A Bit of Advice 😊

At the Copacabana **kiosks**, try to sit at a table away from the vendors that stream along both the beach and the sidewalk. When going to any beaches in Rio, dress casually and take the minimum of cash. If you want to take photos, bring your camera out for a limited time and then return it to your hotel. Avoid getting a taxi outside any luxury hotel—instead, walk a short distance first and then hail one in the street, to avoid being overcharged.

Morro do Cantagalo

Morro do Pavão

R. Saint Roman
R. Sá Ferreira
R. Sousa Lima
R. Francisco Sá
Raul Pompéia
Copacabana
R. Bulhões Carvalho
R. Rainha Elizabeth

Silva
Rua Farme de Amoedo
da
Torre
Praça General Osório
Pirajá
R. Gomes Carneiro
de
Morais
Souto
Casa de Cultura
Laura Alvim

Rua Francisco Otaviano

ARPOADOR

IPANEMA AND LEBLON

LEME

Graced with coconut palms along its sidewalk, this small beach stretches for little over half a mile at the northern end of Copacabana. With its smattering of restaurants and hotels, it offers an altogether quieter experience than its more touristy neighbor. A stone's throw from densely populated areas and on land belonging to the Brazilian Army, the slopes of beautiful Morro do Leme hide an unexpected nook of the original Atlantic forest and native vegetation.

▶ **Orient Yourself:** Leme's layout consists of a main thoroughfare crossed by smaller streets. Avenida Princesa Isabel is the bordering line between Leme and Copacabana. From Leme, a street leads to Morro Chapéu Mangueira, on which stands one of Rio's oldest *favelas*. If you intend on using the subway to go to Leme, the closest Metrô station available is Cardeal Arcoverde.

◉ **Don't Miss:** The enchanting Fishermen's Walk around Morro do Leme (in calm water conditions only) and a visit to the fort to enjoy spectacular views of Copacabana, Morro da Urca, Sugar Loaf, and the Atlantic Ocean.

◷ **Organizing Your Time:** Sunset and sunrise are lovely times to visit, when there is less heat, fewer people, and wonderful photo opportunities.

▦ **Especially for Kids:** Families will appreciate this beach with calm waters.

Sights

Forte Duque de Caxias

Praça Almirante Júlio de Noronha (no number). ◷*Open Sat, Sun, and holidays 9am–5pm.* ⊚*R$3.* ☏*21 2275 7696.*
Although this is part of a military compound, it is possible to make the 689ft/210m walk up to this fort at weekends and holidays. **Views** of Copacabana's long stretch of sand and the beaches of Nitéroi, on the opposite side of the bay, can be seen from this vantage point. A Brazilian flag marks the original Forte do Vigia (Lookout Fort) built in 1779. Visitors to the Caxias Fort

(built in 1913) can stroll along the battlements and see the 280mm *obuseiros* that are mounted in sunken gun emplacements. The curved-trajectory canons, made by the German armaments firm Krupp, were installed in 1919 to be used against ships that tried to hide behind small islands in the bay.

Morro do Leme

⊚*Rough sea conditions can make the trail unsafe to walk.*
Around the base of this large hill lies a charming trail known as **Caminho dos Pescadores** (Fishermen's Walk), marked out in 1985. Shaded by trees and hugging the water's edge, you are likely to see birds, butterflies, and perhaps even monkeys, as well as the amateur anglers who gave the place its name.

Praia do Leme

This compact beach—little more than half a mile long—is popular with families, who appreciate the calm waters and low-key ambiance here. Surfers can often be seen attempting to catch a wave near Morro do Leme, and volleyball players congregate on the free, sandy court. Toward its northern end is the lifeguard post Posto 1, the first of 12 along the beaches of Copacabana, Ipanema, and Leblon.

Praia do Leme and Morro do Leme

Y. Kanazawa/Michelin

COPACABANA★

Squeezed in between the hills and the ocean, the vast expanse of Copacabana Beach has long enjoyed a world-wide reputation. These days, the former neighborhood glamor has somewhat faded and Copacabana has been sharing the spotlight with its younger, hipper sister, Ipanema. However, the beach area still manages to maintain some of the myths that made it famous in decades past as a lively and cosmopolitan Rio playground.

▶ **Orient Yourself:** Avenue Nossa Senhora de Copacabana, a block back from the beach, is lined with shops. The beach stretches south from Leme to the headland of Arpoador, which separates Copacabana from the sands of Ipanema. Cardeal Arcoverde, Siqueira Campos and Cantagalo are nearby Metrô stations.

🐵 **Don't Miss:** Treat yourself to a morning coffee or brunch by the pool of beautiful Copacabana Palace Hotel. Then take a stroll along Copacabana's black-and-white wave sidewalk designed by Burle Marx, relax and just enjoy the beach scene.

🕐 **Organizing Your Time:** After 7pm, the night market Feira Avenida Atlântica comes alive (*see Shopping p 263*).

Especially for Kids: On Sundays, rent bikes and take to the beach road.

A Bit of History

What's in a Name?

The world-famous **Copacabana Beach**★★★ takes its name from the church of Our Lady of Copacabana, which was located in the southern end of the area, where today stands Forte de Copacabana (*see p 161*). Most likely built in the 17C, the church was destroyed to make way for the fort. Legend has it that traders and smugglers who had visited the Spanish colonies came here with images of the miraculous virgin of Copacabana, a settlement on the shores of Lake Titicaca in Bolivia.

An Isolated Beach

For much of the 19C, Copacabana was little more than a church, some summer cottages, a few cashew trees, and battered fishing boats. Land access was extremely difficult due to the impenetrable hills that surrounded the pristine beach. In 1892, a tunnel (called Túnel Velho, "the old tunnel") was opened, linking Copacabana to Botafogo. Mayor Pereira Passos then had a second tunnel built, known as Túnel Novo ("the new tunnel"). This short, two-way tunnel was completed in 1906, and is the main access to Copacabana. At the start of the 20C, with the arrival of the electric tram

Praia de Copacabana

©Celso Pupo Rodrigues/iStockphoto.com

Forte de Copacabana

Y. Kanazawa/Michelin

and construction of Avenida Atlântica, the district had a bright new future.

Elegance and Style

Some old pictures from the early 1920s show the Copacabana Palace Hotel standing all alone on the beachfront. When this innovative hotel opened in 1923, it broke the mold, and literally started a new trend: living a healthy life by the ocean was suddenly fashionable. The small fishermen's houses in the neighborhood were gradually replaced with large, almost palatial summer residences, often built in the much-favored Eclectic style. Later, multi-leveled Art Deco buildings began to flourish, and still grace some of Copacabana's cross streets today.

Urban Growth

Copacabana has been growing skyward ever since, but unfortunately architectural merit has given way to ease of construction and sheer size. The large condominiums and the cramped shacks

☺ A Bit of Advice ☺

Many first-time visitors are surprised that Copacabana is noticeably cheaper than Ipanema. This holds true for the hotels, restaurants, supermarkets, and stores, which tend to be oriented to locals, rather than tourists.

on the nearby hills, together constitute one of the highest urban densities in the world. The beachfront road Avenida Atlântica is crowded with an eclectic mix of shabby versus gleaming high-rise hotels, with restaurants spilling out onto the sidewalk. Avenida Nossa Senhora de Copacabana is crammed with shops along its length. The one quiet spot in the area is the tiny Bairro Peixoto, nearby Túnel Velho. With its small buildings, this quiet, residential enclave provides a glimpse of how Copacabana might have looked decades ago.

Sights

Praia de Copacabana★★★

The busy six-lane **Avenida Atlântica**, lined by coconut palms and almond trees, runs for the beach's 2.5mi/4km length. So does the wide black-and-white **wave sidewalk** made up of mosaic basalt and limestone designed by the great **Burle Marx** as a highly modern, abstract interpretation of a traditional Portuguese pattern.

The beach is punctuated by lifeguard posts from number 2 at the Leme end to 6, near the Forte de Copacabana (©see p 161). All human life is here, from bronzed pensioners and young lovers to newly-arrived visitors, teenagers and children. Posto 3, in front of the Copacabana Palace, tends to attract tourists who can be targets for thieves—so it is wise to be vigilant. Posto 4 has a soccer school for local children and teenagers. The scene around Posto 5 remains generally quiet, and at Posto 6 the distinctive bronze statue of poet Carlos Drummond de Andrade, can be found sitting on a bench on the sidewalk. Nearby, at the western end of the beach, are nets and boats belonging to the fishermen who sell fish here early most mornings.

Copacabana Palace★★

Ave. Atlântica 1702. ◷*Open 24hrs (poolside bar open daily until midnight).* ✕ ℘*21 2545 8790. www.copacabana palace.com.br.*
Designed for Octavio Guinle by French architect **Joseph Gire** (1872–1933) and inspired by two French Riviera hotels (the Negresco in Nice and the Carlton in Cannes), the Copacabana Palace has long been renowned as the hotel of choice for politicians, artists, and celebrities. Constructed in 1923, this dazzling landmark Eclectic-style building is an imposing sight for the visitor, its white-washed facade exuding elegance and style.

Inside, the glamor of the roaring 1920s comes alive, with marble, chandeliers, and a grand ballroom. Famously, Fred Astaire and Ginger Rogers first danced together in the Copacabana Palace in a movie classic, *Flying Down to Rio* (1933). In reality, the actors were just hot-footing it in a Hollywood studio replica of the hotel... When the picture premiered, though, it sealed Rio de Janeiro's reputation as a glamorous destination, with the Copacabana Palace at the heart of it.

A SPECIAL TREAT

Marriott
Avenida Atlântica 2600, Copacabana. Open daily 9am–9pm (fitness center 11pm). R$60. ℘*21 2545 6500. www. marriott.com.* If you want to enjoy the facilities of this hotel without the price tag, the **day use option** here is a good one. For a set fee, non-guests can make use of the rooftop pool, showers, sauna, and fitness center with gym and spa.

Over the years, an impressive line-up of famous guests stayed at the "Copa" and continue to do so, as illustrated by the photos covering the walls of the first-floor corridors.

Forte de Copacabana★

Ave. Atlântica, Posto 6. ◷*Open Tue–Sun and holidays 10am–5pm (exhibition), 10am–8pm (external area).* ⌔*R$4.* ✕ ℘*21 2521 1032. www. fortedecopacabana.com.*
The fort lies at the southern end of Copacabana Beach. Built between 1908 and 1914, it is now the headquarters of an army history museum called **Museu Historicio do Exército**.

Visitors enter through the main gate *(beachwear not permitted)*, and past the wonderful **Café de Forte** (◷*see p 240*) and small souvenir shop. Impressive cannons line the battlements. The main attraction of the fort are the spectacular **views** of Copacabana and Sugar Loaf Mountain from the terrace and fortifications. Temporary art exhibitions and shows are also held at the fort.

Goddess of the Sea

Second only to Carnival in popularity, New Year's Eve festivities in Rio are concentrated in Copacabana (◷*see p 37*). Alongside the flashy hedonism of **Reveillon** on Copacabana Beach, **Yemanjá**, the Goddess of the Sea, is honored in a touching, spiritual ritual. Celebrants launch their offerings of flowers (white roses in particular), candles, silver jewelry, sweets, and champagne in little boats onto the ocean. Regal and protective, Yemanjá is an Afro–Brazilian mermaid-like religious figure who is commonly associated with the Virgin Mary. Cariocas, all dressed in white as is customary, gather in large numbers on the beach to greet the New Year. The religious spectacle adds a unique element to traditional champagne-popping celebrations.

IPANEMA★★

Cariocas and visitors alike love to congregate in this laid-back, relaxed and fashionable beachfront area. But there is a lot more to this trend-setting neighborhood than the legendary beach. With its leafy streets and squares, attractive boutiques, art galleries and an assortment of cozy cafes and bars, all within walking distance, beautiful Ipanema provides an atmosphere equal to none.

▶ **Orient Yourself:** Ipanema is a narrow strip of land which separates the Rodrigo de Freitas lake from the ocean. Ipanema's beach road is called Avenida Vieira Souto. The main commercial street, Rua Visconde de Pirajá, is just two blocks away. As yet there is no Metrô station closer than Copacabana.

☺ **Don't Miss:** Ipanema beach scene offers a picturesque glimpse into Cariocas' lifestyle. Stroll along the beachfront sidewalk, soak up the sun, watch the crowds go by, and enjoy the spectacular setting.

🕐 **Organizing Your Time:** Weekends and holidays can get particularly crowded here. Sunday is a good day to come though, because the beach road is partly closed to cars, but all of the shops may not be open.

Kids **Especially for Kids:** Give your kids a slice of Brazilian style. Buy them a pair of funky flip-flops known as Havaianas—they'll love the colors and designs!

A Bit of History

The native Indians gave Ipanema its name, which means "bad water" in Tupi-Guarani. This is most likely to be a reference to the dangerous undertow here, which can be a threat even to the strongest and most experienced of swimmers.

For a number of years, Ipanema lived in the shadow of its more famous "Copa" neighbor, but during the 1960s, bohemian artists and intellectuals started to hang out in the area's restaurants and bars, or at the beach.

Ipanema's profile has been on the rise ever since, as have the buildings that occupy the area. One of Ipanema's distinctive features is its Burle Marx mosaic sidewalk pavement, more geometric than the one in Copacabana.

Ipanema's son, poet **Vinicius de Moraes** (1913–1980), who composed world-famous Bossa Nova classic, *The Girl from Ipanema*, has one of the neighborhood streets named after him.

Families gather around Posto 7 at weekends

Y. Kanazawa/Michelin

Walking Tour

Ipanema is loved for its boutiques and bars, and a walking tour of the area would not be complete without stopping for a caipirinha or to browse CDs or beachwear. The commercial addresses included below are just a select few highlights (☉ see Your Stay in the City).

▶ *Begin at Posto 9 on the beach.*

Praia de Ipanema★★★

Ipanema Beach has almost mythical status around the world, and rightly so. On a sunny day, with the soaring twin peaks of the "Two Brothers" at its western end, the jutting rock of Arpoador to the east, and its three islands in the ocean, it is one of the most beautiful places on earth. As in Copacabana, the beach is divided by numbered lifeguard posts. The beach close to Arpoador tends to attract families and children; gays and lesbians congregate around Posto 8, marked with a giant rainbow flag in front of Rua Farme de Amoedo. Legendary Posto 9 (gone down in legend with *The Girl from Ipanema* song) and Posto 10 are particularly crowded meeting points.

▶ *Walk up Rua Vinicius de Moraes, to the corner of the junction with Rua Prudentes de Moraes.*

Garota de Ipanema

Rua Vinicius de Moraes 49 A.
☉*Open daily noon until last customer.*
✖ ☏*21 2523 3787.*
www.garotaipanema.com.br.
This corner bar, open to the street, was where de Moraes and Tom Jobim composed the famous Bossa Nova song, after watching the eponymous girl go by—"tall and tanned and long and lovely", as she walked toward the beach. Note the posters on the wall with reproductions of the song which was supposedly written on a napkin. The service is good here, and so is the food. But don't expect to see many locals in this highly touristic spot which changed its former name, Veloso, to honor the famous song. Have a drink and a snack rather than dinner: try *picanha* (strips of sizzling steak) and *caipirinhas*.

Promenade along Praia de Ipanema

R. Mills/Michelin

▶ *Continue along Rua Vinicius de Moraes to number 129, on the left.*

Toca do Vinicius

Rua Vinicius de Moraes 129. ☉*Open April–Nov daily 10am–8pm, 10am–5pm Sun, Dec–Mar 9am–10pm.* ☏*21 2247 5227. www.tocadovinicius.com.br.* This CD, book, and souvenir store was named after Vinicius de Moraes (☉see p 162). Expect friendly, helpful service from aficionados who genuinely love music. Free sidewalk concerts take place on occasional Sundays (☉*7:30pm summer, 8pm winter*).

▶ *Retrace your steps to Rua Visconde de Pirajá, turn right, and continue to the square on the right.*

Praça Nossa Senhora da Paz

The square of "Our Lady of Peace" takes its name from the nearby **church**, which is decorated with German stained-glass windows and an Italian marble altar *(Rua Visconde de Pirajá 339;* ☉*open Mon–Sat 6am–8pm, Sun 6am–10pm;* ☏*21 2241 0003).* Every year for Christmas, the nativity scene exhibited outside the church is a very popular attraction.
The square itself is a lovely, leafy spot, where nannies bring their charges to the **Kids playground** and locals relax while sitting on shady benches.
Every Friday morning (☉*6am–1pm*), a **farmers market** sells fresh, local produce, including fish, flowers, fruit and vegetables.

> *Continue along the residential street of Rua Visconde de Piraja to number 462B.*

Gilson Martins

Rua Visconde de Pirajá 462. 🕐*Open Mon–Sat 10am–8pm.* 📞*21 2227 6178. www.gilsonmartins.com.br.*
The much-loved Brazilian designer takes simple silhouettes of Rio icons, such as Corcovado, the Lapa arches, and Sugar Loaf, and emblazons them onto suitcases, holdalls, makeup bags, and pencil cases; anything he can get his hands on really—all using his unique color palette. Note that none of the products are leather, but all vinyl. There is another store in Copacabana.

> *Continue along Rua Visconde de Pirajá, to the corner of the junction with Rua Garcia D'Ávila.*

Museu H. Stern

Rua Garcia D'Ávila 113. 🕐*Open Mon–Fri 9am–6pm, Sat 9am–noon.* 🎫*Free Admission and free transportation provided to and from any hotel in the South zone.* 📞*21 2106 0000. www.hstern. net/hsterninrio.*
Brazil's mineral rich valleys and mountains account for an estimated 65 percent of the world's gem production. With this figure in mind, visitors may be interested in seeing the beautiful collections of this museum, housed in the famous jeweler's headquarters.

Rock of Arpoador

Y. Kanazawa/Michelin

The museum includes a permanent exhibition of uncut precious stones such as topaz, aquamarines and citrines, and the largest collection of cut **tourmalines** in the world, in shades of pink, red, fuschia, green and a rare blue. The insightful **workshop tour** *(12min; available in 18 languages)* shows the different steps involved in the process of jewelry making, from mining to finished product. The store also offers great souvenirs, with absolutely no pressure to buy.

> *Cross over Rua Visconde de Pirajá to number 449.*

AmazonLife

Rua Visconde de Pirajá 449, 2nd floor. 🕐*Open Mon–Fri 10am–8pm, Sat 10am–6pm.* 📞*21 2511 7686. www.amazonlife.com.br.*
Make a purchase here and save your conscience. A wide range of products includes bags and clothing made from latex extracted from the Amazon rain forest. The company operates on social and ecological fair trade principles, aiming at helping local producers and promoting sustainability.

> *Continue along Rua Visconde de Pirajá to number 27.*

Galeria de Arte Ipanema

Rua Aníbal de Mendonça 27. 🕐*Open Mon–Fri 10am–7pm, Sat 10am–2pm.* 📞*21 2512 8832. www.galeria-ipanema.com.*
Created in 1965, this art gallery showcases the works of important Brazilian artists, such as Hélio Oiticica and Candido Portinari.

> *Make the short walk to the beach and treat yourself to a refreshing coconut water at one of the kiosks around Posto 10.*

Additional Sights

Arpoador

The small headland that separates Ipanema from Copacabana is a lovely, scenic spot. Every early evening, people gather on the *pedra* (rock) to watch the

Bohemian Banda de Ipanema

Particularly famous for its raucous spirit of celebration, this informal Carnival street band began back in the 1960s, and played a significant role in the politics of the city. In 1965, Brazil went under military dictatorship, almost all forms of expression—other than football and carnival—being then controlled or censored. Many artists and intellectuals were imprisoned or left the country. The Banda taunted the dictatorship by adopting a totally meaningless slogan, "Yolhesman Crisbeles!"—that the power in place believed to be a rallying call for its overthrow. The Banda's irreverent humor is even said to have brought Rio's Street Carnival spirit back to life. Today, this truly democratic troupe attracts all ages, sexes, and colors, but remains a particular favorite of drag queens.

sunset, with the distinctive shape of Morro Dois Irmãos in the distance. In the 19C, whales would gather just off the rock, and it is thought that the name Arpoador ("harpoon thrower") comes from the hunters who used to gather here. On the eastern side of the small headland, **Praia do Diablo** (Devil's Beach) attracts surfers who appreciate its big swells. Behind is the small **Kids** **Parque Garota de Ipanema**, with a playground and skating rink, and near the beach, a fitness area. On the western side of the rock is the 550yd/500m-long **Arpoador Beach**. Its calm waters are very popular with surfers practicing their skills.

Praça General Osório

In the center of this square, you will notice a fountain called **Chafariz das Saracuras** (1795). This work by Mestre Valentim used to stand in a courtyard of the Ajuda convent in Cinelândia, and was moved here in 1911 when the convent was demolished.

Every Sunday sees the spectacle of Ipanema's Handicrafts Fair: **Feira de Artezanato de Ipanema** (◎ *see p 262*). Commonly known as the "Feira Hippie", it has taken place here since the 1960s. All manner of souvenirs are on sale, from clothes to leather products, musical instruments and paintings. Admittedly touristy, it is a fun place to visit. Be sure to try the hot, spicy food from the Bahian stalls.

COOLING REFRESHMENT

Sorvete italia
Ave. Visconde de Pirajá 187 (also at 395 and at Ave. Henrique Dumont 71). Open daily 9am–10pm. ☏*21 2247 2842. www.sorveteitalia.com.*
This ice-cream parlor serves up cooling, fruit flavored sorbets, including Amazonian Açai and passionfruit, as well as chocolate ice-cream in a range of permutations. Diet versions and yoghurt cups are also on offer.

Banda de Ipanema

©WPN/Photoshot

LEBLON

Mile-long Leblon Beach lies at the western end of Ipanema Beach, separated from it by the Jardim de Alah channel between Postos 10 and 11. Discretely elegant, and quieter than its hip eastern neighbor, charming Leblon has fine restaurants and sophisticated cafes around Rua Dias Ferreira, upscale boutiques and a fantastic beach for children.

▶ **Orient Yourself:** Most of the district's commerce is situated on Avenida Ataulfo de Paiva, which runs parallel to the beach.

☺ **Don't Miss:** The spectacular beach and mountain vista of the "Two Brothers," viewed at sunset while sipping a *caipirinha*.

🕐 **Organizing Your Time:** Spend the afternoon at the beach and the evening in one of Leblon's fine restaurants, theaters, or nightclubs.

🄺🄸🄳🅂 **Especially for Kids:** Leblon has one of the best beaches in Rio for children. Its Baixo Baby beach playground, complete with toys and plenty of sand to build sandcastles is a sure hit with little ones!

A Bit of History

Slave Sanctuary

Leblon owes its fairly recent name to Frenchman Charles Leblon who sold much of his property here to a notary in 1857. The man resold it in 1878 to Portuguese businessman **José de Seixas Magalhãe**. Sympathetic to the abolitionist cause, Magalhãe allowed runaway slaves to retreat to his Leblon's farms, transitioning them into *quilombos* (communities of escaped slaves). Although the African slave trade was abolished in 1830, slavery continued to be legal in Brazil until 1888.

By the beginning of the 20C, Leblon was essentially made up of smallholdings. Because it was located at the end of the tram line that connected it with its nearest neighbor, development in Leblon was much slower than in Ipanema, and the area was able to preserve some of its cozy, small town atmosphere. These days, Leblon stands as one of the most desirable residential areas anywhere in Rio, with a sophisticated mix of individual homes, small apartment buildings and highrise blocks.

A Road with a View

One of Rio's most scenic drives, **Avenida Niemeyer** begins where Leblon Beach ends. Originally designed as a railroad, it connects Leblon to São Conrado (◉ *see p 181*).

It took some 30 years to carry out such a monumental project and meet the major challenge of cutting through the sheer cliff, but the work was finally completed in 1916.

From 1933 until 1954, the avenue hosted a 6.8mi/11km-long car racing event. Today, Avenida Niemeyer is an important link between the south and west zones. It offers spectacular views of the ocean, but don't attempt to pull over to take photos, as this is a very busy two-way road.

Sights

Praia do Leblon★★

Always make sure that you check sea conditions and the pollution level before heading out into the water.

Leblon Beach is much more low-key than the achingly cool Ipanema Beach, partly because of its lower population density. Early mornings see nannies staking out their piece of sand at 🄺🄸🄳🅂 **Baixo Bebê**,

☺ A Bit of Advice ☺

It is advisable to go up the Leblon **lookout** early in the morning or just before sunset to avoid the heat of the day, and also to get the best views. Although it is a popular spot with romantic couples in the evening and is usually policed, avoid going up here after dark.

Vidigal

View from Mirante do Leblon —Vidigal on the hill

Y. Kanazawa/Michelin

The name of a *favela* perched on the slopes of Morro Dois Irmãos, near Leblon, Vidigal, in the last few years, has benefited from the **Favela Bairro program,** an initiative launched in the 1990s which seeks to turn shantytowns into safe and stable neighborhoods through their urban, social and economic restructuring.

Infrastructure may remain poor in Vidigal today, but the community has been improving its living standards, with child day care, health services, a sports complex and even an actors' studio, **Nós do Morro** ("Us from the hill"), which has participated in projects with the Royal Shakespeare Company.

---

an area specifically set up for little ones. Located between Posto 11 and 12 in front of Rua General Venâncio Flores *(closer to the Posto 11 end)*, this place offers clean sands throughout the day and baby care services. You will also find a diaper changing station, jungle gym and slides, and inflatable castles. If you are traveling with youngsters, this is a good place to spend a few hours under a parasol, which can be rented for a fee. As at all the beach areas, cold drinks and snacks are readily available.

Morro Dois Irmãos

The towering "Two Brothers" hill owes its name to its distinctive double peak. One of Rio de Janeiro's many iconic picture postcards shows the sun setting behind this popular local landmark, with Leblon and Ipanema in the foreground.

Up on Avenida Niemeyer, **Mirante do Leblon** offers a wonderful **view**★★ of the rock formations near the lookout, as well as of Leblon and Ipanema beaches, with the rock of Arpoador at the opposite end. The view from the lookout is all the more spectacular when the water is rough. Take some time to enjoy the scene, with a coconut water from one of the nearby kiosks.

Part of the Two Brothers hill, **Parque do Penhasco Dois Irmãos** *(steep, paved access road)* is a good place to relax. This large area is made up of parkland, playground, soccer fields, and four other lookout points revealing spectacular views of Leblon, Ipanema and Rodrigo de Freitas lake standing out on the mountainous background.

JUICE BARS

In Rio de Janeiro, you are never too far from a fresh *suco* (juice) bar... Rio's most famous one is **Bibi Sucos** *(Avenida Ataulfo de Palva 591; ℘21 2259 4298)*, which also has branches in Copacabana, Barra, and Jardim Botânico.

You may also want to try **Hortifruti** *(Rua Dias Ferreira 57; ℘21 2586 7000; www.hortifruti.com.br)*, with branches across the city.

They both have salads and sandwiches on the menu, but don't leave without sampling a refreshing *água de coco* or a perhaps you might prefer a delicious juice; mango, melon, cashew, or pineapple with mint.

LAKE AND SURROUNDS

Rio de Janeiro's magnificent coastline and mountain backdrop is further enhanced by the large, still, mirror of its lake, Lagoa Rodrigo de Freitas, right in the middle of what is so justly called the "Marvelous City." The lake and its surrounds offer a large sample of sights to discover, from the Lagoa neighborhood, with its desirable condominiums along the lake shore, to Gávea's mix of exclusive mansions and lower income houses, and Jardim Botânico standing like a green oasis in the center of urban activity.

Highlights

1   Strolling through the lush gardens of **Jardîm Botânico** (&see p 175).

2   Admiring the art and atmosphere at **Instituto Moreira Salles** (&see p 172).

3   An evening of culture at the **Eva Klabin Foundation** (&see p 171).

4   Getting star struck at the planetarium, **Planetário da Gávea** (&see p 171).

5   Relaxing with a drink at one of the waterside kiosks at **Lagoa Rodrigo de Freitas** (&see p 177).

Location, location, location...

A trio of neighborhoods: **Lagoa**, **Gávea**, and **Jardim Botânico** occupy the heart of this area, which is bordered by Morro do Corcovado (&see p 134) to the north and the slopes of the Serra da Carioca to the northwest. The Botanical Gardens neighborhood stands on the western edge of the Rodrigo de Freitas lake. Ipanema and Leblon (&see p 166) occupy the strip of land between the lake and the ocean, while two impenetrable hills separate it from Copacabana (&see p 159) to the east.

The Beginnings

Development of the area by the Europeans began in the 16C with a sugar cane plantation which passed hands until 1660 when the land was acquired by **Rodrigo de Freitas Mello e Castro**. In 1808, the whole area was expropriated by order of Dom João VI, who wanted the land in order to build the Botanical Gardens and a gunpowder factory (Fábrica de Pólvora).

After 1831, when the factory was transferred close to Petrópolis (&see p 208), the royal estate was gradually broken up and sold as smallholdings.

Lagoa Rodrigo de Freitas viewed from Corcovado

©Ricardo De Mattos/iStockphoto.com

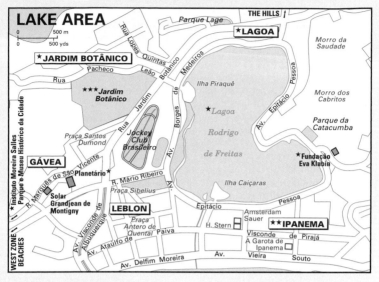

LAKE AREA

0   500 m
0   500 yds

★ **JARDIM BOTÂNICO**

THE HILLS

★ **LAGOA**

Parque Lage

Morro da Saudade

Rua Lopes Quintas

Pacheco

Leão

Rua

★★★ *Jardim Botânico*

Ilha Piraquê

Morro dos Cabritos

Parque da Catacumba

Jardim

Rua

de Borges

Botânico

Medeiros

Av. Epitácio

Pessoa

★ *Lagoa Rodrigo de Freitas*

Praça Santos Dumond

Jockey Club Brasileiro

GÁVEA

R. Marques de São Vicente

Planetário

R. Mário Ribeiro

★ **Fundação Eva Klabin**

Praça Sibelius

Ilha Caiçaras

Solar Grandjean de Montigny

Av. Visconde de Albuquerque

LEBLON

Praça Antero de Quental

Paiva

Epitácio

Pessoa

Amsterdam Sauer

H. Stern

★★ **IPANEMA**

Instituto Moreira Salles
Parque e Museu Histórico da Cidade

WEST ZONE BEACHES

Av. Ataúlfo de

Av. Delfim Moreira

Visconde de Pirajá

A Garota de Ipanema

Av. Vieira

Souto

A Wealth of History

Besides King Dom João VI, to whom Rio owes its outstanding Botanical Gardens, which helped preserve rare plant species from around the world, two illustrious area residents have left a wonderful legacy behind. One was a private collector; the other a banker. Their former homes, filled with priceless works of art, have been turned into modern cultural centers—the Eva Klabin foundation and Instituto Moreira Salles— for all to enjoy. Another wonderful historic sight in this area is the Eclectic style 1920s mansion in the Parque Lage (see p 177).

Oh Christmas Tree...

Every year since 1996, an enormous floating Christmas tree has been installed in the middle of the lake. As high as a 27-story building, it takes more than 1,000 workers and costs over a million dollars, to set up and light. The tree is illuminated every night from the end of November until the beginning of January. Thousands come to see the decorations, which vary from year to year, along with the three million lights and the fireworks displays.

😊 A Bit of Advice 😊

There are many different ways to access this part of town, but assuming you come from the North Zone or from the Laranjeiras or Cosme Velho neighborhoods, one of the best is through the **Túnel André Rebouças**. Slicing through the enormous Corcovado mountain, the tunnel connects Rio's South and North Zones. At 3,062yd/2,800m long, it is one of the biggest urban tunnels of the world. As you emerge from its darkness, the magnificent image of the enormous lake comes into view.

Café du Lage at Parque Lage

©Matthew Levine/CC-by-2.0

LAGOA★

The 4.8mi/7.8km pleasant path along Lagoa Rodrigo de Freitas shores lends itself to jogging, walking, biking and all sorts of other relaxing activities. Quite understandably, locals just love their lake, and apartments along its edges are much sought after. The road around Lagoa Rodrigo de Freitas connects the neighborhoods of Lagoa, Ipanema, Leblon, Jardim Botânico, and Gávea. The lake is the uncontested star attraction in this area, although some other interesting sights nearby merit a visit as well.

▶ **Orient Yourself:** "Lagoa Rodrigo de Freitas" refers to the lake itself, while "Lagoa" describes the neighborhood around it. The closest Metrô station, on the lake's east side, is Cantagalo (in Copacabana).

⊜ **Don't Miss:** Relive art collector Eva Klabin's refined soirees by attending one of the Quintas com Musica events offered at Fundação Eva Klabin.

🕓 **Organizing Your Time:** Visit in late afternoon to stroll around the lake's edges, then enjoy a *suco* (juice) or a delicious *água de coco* (coconut water often served in the coconut itself) at an outdoor kiosk. This is a busy, lively spot at weekends, and you may have to stand in line at the kiosks...

Kids Especially for Kids: Take them on the water in a fun, swan-shaped paddle boat *(boat rentals available at Parque do Cantagalo; ⚓see below).*

Sights

Lagoa Rodrigo de Freitas★ Kids

This lake plunges to 1,410ft/430m deep and is 1.9mi/3km across at its widest point, with a perimeter of 4.8mi/7.8km. Though always referred to as "the lake," Lagoa Rodrigo de Freitas is really a salt-water lagoon. Close to the coast, it is separated from the ocean by a strip of land and linked to it by the Jardim de Alah canal. Over time, many thousands of square yards, equivalent to a third of its area, have been absorbed by successive landfills.

The lake is surrounded by parkland. On the Botanical Gardens' side, **Parque dos Patins** *(Avenida Borges de Medeiros)* boasts a skating rink, soccer field, children's playground, and an amphitheater. On the other side of the lake, close to Copacabana, paddle boats can be rented from the little pier at **Parque do Cantagalo** *(Avenue Epitácio Pessoa).* Both parks have recreation areas and bike rental as well as casual waterside **kiosks**. Particularly popular at weekends, these places sometimes have live music. Two small islands near the shore are home to various clubs. A heliport

Riding four-wheel bikes around the lake

Y. Kanazawa/Michelin

at Parque dos Patins is used for scenic panoramic flights (see p 29) over the city and beaches.

Fundação Eva Klabin★

Av. Epitácio Pessoa 2480. Open Tue–Sun 2pm–6pm. R$10. Tours available on request. 21 3202 8554. www.evaklabin.org.br.

In 1952, art collector **Eva Klabin** (1903–1991) bought one of the very first residential homes built on Rodrigo de Freitas lake. Located within walking distance of Parque do Cantagalo, the mansion (1931) was dramatically modernized in the 1960s. The ten rooms contain one of Brazil's most important art collections, with over 1,000 pieces, including paintings, sculptures, furniture and silverware, from all over the world and stretching back to antiquity.

Eva Klabin counted David Rockefeller and Henry Kissinger among her friends, along with legendary landscape designer, Burle Marx. The **Quintas com Musica**, held at the house-museum on Thursdays from March to December, recreate her magical soirees *(check the website for further details)*. Guests are taken on a guided tour, and can enjoy a concert of Brazilian music in the auditorium, followed by cocktails in the garden.

Parque da Catacumba

Ave. Epitácio Pessoa 3000. Open Tue–Sun 8am–5pm. 21 2521 5540.

This park owes its name to a former hillside slum called Favela da Catacumba which used to stand here until it was removed by order of Governor Carlos Lacerda in the 1960s. To preserve the area, the upper part of the hill was reforested, while the bottom section opened as a sculpture park in 1979.

People relaxing at a kiosk by the lake

Rio Convention and Visitors Bureau

WATERSIDE ALFRESCO
Arab Quiosque
Parque dos Patins, Quiosques 7 and 9. Open daily 9am–last customer. 21 2540 0747.

Many peoples' favorite kiosk on the lake offers Syrian and Lebanese cuisine as well as live music. It's a lovely spot to relax, eat and drink under the stars, and soak up the atmosphere. If this kiosk is too crowded, there are plenty of others nearby, from which you can still enjoy the music.

Here in the open air, among the fruit trees, is a nice collection of 32 sculptures by internationally known artists, such as Norberto Moriconi, Franz Weissmann, Antonio Manuel, Caribé, Bruno Giorgio, Mário Cravo, and Sérgio Camargo. A pleasant trail leads to the top of the green hill of Morro dos Cabritos. The short but steep walk is rewarded with stunning **views**★★ of the city.

A Living Lake

Shrimp and crabs, along with more than 30 species of fishes, live in the waters of the Rodrigo de Freitas lake. Fishing is controlled, although some small-scale activity does take place, with special licences. The connection to the ocean by **Jardim de Alá**, a 913yd/835m-long man-made canal, is controlled by floodgates. This is essential to preserve the fragile balance of the ecosystem; although algae provides food for the fish, its growth must be kept in constant check in order to prevent the destruction of plant and animal life.

GÁVEA

Tucked between the Tijuca Forest and Leblon, this mostly residential area was named after Pedra de Gávea, a local rock in the shape of a topsail (*gávea*). As with Leblon, there is an upper Gávea, largely filled with beautiful mansions. Higher is the green space of Parque de Cidade, and the Instituto Moreira Salles. And still higher, sprawling up the mountain side, stands Favela da Rocinha, an area which should not be visited without proper guidance. Lower Gávea has a high concentration of bars and restaurants. Marques de São Vicente is the main artery, where the Shopping da Gávea mall is located.

▶ **Orient Yourself:** Out on the western wing of the Rodrigo de Freitas lake, this neighborhood is dominated in its lower part by the huge Jockey Club.

Don't Miss: Contemporary Brazilian art exhibits at the Instituto Moreira Salles, and perhaps a quick refresher on Rio's history at the Museu Histórico da Cidade.

Organizing Your Time: Consider visiting on weekends when the area gets more lively and there are races at the Jockey Club.

Especially for Kids: Stargazing at the state-of-the-art Planetário da Gávea.

Sights

Instituto Moreira Salles★

Rua Marquês de São Vicente, 476.
Open Tue–Sun 1pm–8pm. Free Admission. Tours available Tue–Sat 5pm. 21 3284 7400. http://ims.uol.com.br/ims.

Designed by Olavo Redig de Campos, the former residence of the Moreira Salles family (who owned one of Brazil's biggest banking concerns) is an elegant, modern building (1951) surrounded by beautiful **Burle Marx gardens**.

The Moreira Salles Institute is opposed to the traditional ideas of passive patronage. Here the individual is empowered to engage with the art—and it shows. The institute's superb exhibitions mainly focus on contemporary Brazilian art. In addition to sculptures, paintings and drawings, the Moreira Salles Institute also holds a sizable **photography archive** which includes historic records of Rio's transformations, and an extensive collection of Brazilian **music recordings** (visiting both archives may be arranged upon request).

Planetário da Gávea★

Rua Vice-Governador Rubens Berardo 100. 21 2274 0046. www.rio.rj.gov.br/planetario.

Rio de Janeiro's Planetarium includes two state-of-the art domes as well as the **Museu do Universo** (Tue–Fri 9am–6pm; Sat, Sun, holidays 3pm–7pm; R$6) which boasts interactive displays, including moon phases and tides and photos of the cosmos from NASA. At the **Praça dos Telescópios** (Square of Telescopes), four modern telescopes allow you to observe the sky under the guidance of a team of astronomers from the foundation (closed during cloudy and rainy weather; open Tue–Thu 6:30pm–7:30pm, summer 7:30pm–8:30pm; Free Admission).

Educational material with cartoon characters is available, with events and programs for children (in Portuguese).

A Bit of Advice

Be sure to pick up a free copy of a plan of the Moreira Salles Institute at the entrance; all the text is in Portuguese but it is useful to find your way around. Take time to have tea or a light lunch in the outdoor cafe, relaxing at one of the tables next to the fish-filled pond. Walk past the swimming pool here, to take a look at the little creek that runs through the backyard behind it. Don't miss the wonderful store, selling art and photography books and postcards, including those of old Rio.

An interactive map of the Milky Way and a device to find out what you would weigh on another planet are fun displays. Consider returning for the slick 00 (Zero Zero) nightclub (🎧 *see p 253*) in the same building.

Jockey Club Brasileiro

Praça Santos Dumont 31. ⊗Free Admission. ✕ ✆*21 3534 9000. www.jcb.com.br.*
The city's Jockey Club occupies a huge site between the lake and the Jardim Botânico, overlooked by the green slopes of Tijuca's National Park. Also known as the **Hipódromo da Gávea**, it was designed in Louis XV style by architect Francisco Couchet and inaugurated in 1926. Some areas are reserved for club members and their guests, but the general public is allowed entry for horse races (🕐*Fri 5pm, Sat and Sun 2:45pm, Mon 6:15pm; subject to change*).
The first Grand Prix horse race took place here in 1933 and is still an August institution. Other events, concerts, and receptions are sprinkled over the social calendar, among these the monthly **Babilônia Feira Hype** *(www.babilonia hype.com.br)* selling clothes, food, and local crafts.

Parque e Museu Histórico da Cidade

Estrada Santa Marinha (no number).
🕐*Open Tue–Fri 10am–4pm; Sun, holidays 10am–3pm.* ⊗*R$2.* ✆*21 2512 2353/2294 5990. www.rio.rj.gov. br/culturas.*
Dominating the Parque da Cidade (City Park), this 19C mansion is home to a museum that chronicles Rio de Janeiro's history. Art, furniture, coins, and armor are on permanent display, but the museum also organizes temporary exhibits. Built in 1920, the **Capela de São João** contains a painting by Bahian artist Carlos Bastos.
Outside in the pleasant park, marmosets, sloths and other animals from the Atlantic rain forest roam about.

Solar Grandjean de Montigny

Rua Marquês de São Vicente 225.
🕐*Open Mon–Fri 8:30am–5pm.* ⊗*Free Admission.* ✆*21 3527 1435. www. puc-rio.br/sobrepuc/depto/solar.*

Garden in Instituto Moreira Salles

Y. Kanazawa/Michelin

Auguste Henri Victor Grandjean de Montigny (1776–1850) arrived in Rio in 1816, as part of the French Artistic Mission. He was responsible for the design of Casa França Brasil (🎧 *see p 103)* and played a significant role in the development of architecture in Brazil.
Located at the entrance of PUC campus (Pontifícia Universidade Católica), his former home has been turned into a cultural center. It forms a social and cultural link between the public and the academic institution, hosting temporary art exhibitions as well as an extensive art and architecture library.
Montigny's mansion *(solar)* is a perfect example of how Neo-classical standards in architecture can be adapted to life in the tropics.

Local Square

At the heart of the Gávea district, **Praça Santos Dumont**, also called Praça do Joquei (Jockey Square), is a small urban park with trees, playground, and a fountain. It is surrounded by restaurants and bars where people like to congregate until the late hours. The area gets particularly busy towards the end of the week. Sundays see a traditional **antique and flea market** *(9am–5pm)* around Rua Marques de São Vicente.

JARDIM BOTÂNICO ★

This predominantly residential neighborhood, dotted with shops and restaurants, enjoys a privileged location. It was named after the landmark attraction around which it grew: Rio's splendid Botanical Gardens, created in 1808 for Dom João VI. Under the watchful gaze of Christ the Redeemer, these gardens form one of the most impressive botanic collections in the world, a treasure of such ecological importance as to be granted the Biosphere Reserve distinction by the UNESCO in 1992.

▶ **Orient Yourself:** The neighborhood's main street, Rua Jardim Botânico, runs parallel to the shores of Rodrigo de Freitas lake. Further in, a compact network of little streets extend across the area.

◉ **Don't Miss:** Take a rare glance at the Gardens' *Pau-brasil* (Brazilwood), the national tree of Brazil which gave its name to the country. Due to the shrinking of the Atlantic rain forest and extensive export of its dyewood, this extremely dense hardwood has now been classified as an endangered species.

◷ **Organizing Your Time:** The Botanical Gardens are always a good option, even on a cloudy day and whatever the season! Just make sure to allow a couple of hours for a guided tour, or to complete the walk suggested below.

▦ **Especially for Kids:** Watch out for the scampering squirrels, monkeys, brightly colored parakeets in the trees, and fascinating insect-eating plants.

A Bit of History

A Growing Concern

When Prince Dom João arrived in 1808, he initially set up the gardens to grow the spices that otherwise would have to be transported from the East Indies. Nutmeg and avocado plants, brought over from Mauritius, were among the first to be introduced here. In 1810 came exotic species from French Guiana, and tea seeds. The prince was enthralled by the exuberance of the vegetation and the gardens quickly grew. When his son, Dom Pedro I, became Regent in 1821, the Royal Garden, then private, was opened to the public. Lakes and waterfalls were built, the botanic collection significantly expanded, and an extensive library was created.

Visitors today can follow in the footsteps of the men in top hats and the ladies in long dresses, shaded by parasols, who once walked these paths.

The Birds and The Trees

At the Botanical Gardens, stretches of wild rain forest alternate with carefully manicured green expanses, creating a wonderfully subtle balance. The air is filled with the sweet smells of exotic fruit trees and flowers and the sound of tropical bird song. Marmosets, squirrels and other little animals can be seen jumping between the treetops. Multicolored parakeets and toucans show off their stunning plumage, while owls and swallows build their nests, and vultures observe it all from high up in the trees. Magical, tiny hummingbirds and brightly colored butterflies punctuate the landscape with their beautiful colors.

Lago Frei Leandro with Victoria Regia

Y. Kanazawa/Michelin

Jardim Botânico★★★

Rio de Janeiro's Botanical Gardens are an amazing tropical, plant-filled oasis. Follow this walking tour to ensure you visit the highlights. Then take time to make discoveries on your own. *Rua Jardim Botânico 1008.* ○*Open daily 8am–5pm.* ○*Closed Dec 25, Jan 1.* ○*R$5.* ○*Tours available (ideally arranged in advance) in Portuguese, Spanish, and English 9am–3:30pm. 90min.* ✕ ℘*21 3874 1808/3874 1214. www.jbrj.gov.br.*

Aleia Barbosa Rodrigues, avenue lined with royal palms

Y. Kanazawa/Michelin

Walking Tour

▷ *Begin at the entrance at 920 Rua Jardim Botânico. Turn right along Aleia Karl Glasl.*

Looking to your right, note the **Japanese Corner**. Successfully designed as a restful space, it features a carp-filled lake surrounded by striking bamboo, bonsai and cherry trees.

▷ *Continue along Aleia Karl Glasl, past the Rose Garden on the left, until you reach Região Amazônica.*

A typical Amazonian thatched hut and the statue of a "Caboclo" fisherman (meaning of mixed European and American Indian descent) recreate the **Amazon Region**, draped by dense vegetation, nutmeg and banana trees. Admire the magnificent *bombax Munguba* planted in 1899 and whose trunk is nearly 22yd/20m in diameter!

▷ *Turn left along Aleia Frei Leandro.*

On your right, housed in a former violet greenhouse (1942), the **Memorial Mestre Valentim** contains two of the artist's pewter and lead sculptures of the nymph, *Echo* and the hero, *Narcissus*.

▷ *Continue to the Fountain of the Muses with the monument to composer Antonio Carlos Jobim on your right, and turn right up Aleia Barbosa Rodrigues.*

You are now looking at one of the Gardens' most famous symbols, which was created in 1842: majestic 809yd/740m-long **Palms Alley**. This beautiful aisle starts at the Gardens' entrance gate, and is lined with 142 imperial palms with an average height of 82ft/25m and 1.1yd/1m in diameter, descending from one single specimen known as *Palma Mater* (○*see p 177*).

▷ *For a little detour, go all the way down Palms Alley to take a quick look at the Portal da Real Academia de Belas Artes (1821).*

Designed by French architect Grandjean de Montigny, the **Royal Academy of Fine Arts** was formerly located near Praça Tiradentes. Demolished in 1908,

---

😊 A Bit of Advice 😊

Pick up a leaflet with a map at one of the two entrances of the Botanical Gardens: at 920 Rua Jardim Botânico or at 1008, where there is a visitor center. **Electric car tours** are available for seniors (over 60), pregnant women, and visitors with special needs *(Mon–Sun 9am, 10am, & 11am, 1pm, 2pm, 3pm, & 4pm; 40min; free; advanced reservations only; ℘21 3874 1808; canceled in bad weather).*

GARDEN REFRESHMENT

Café Botânica

Rua Jardim Botânico 1008. Open daily 8:30am–5pm. ✆21 2512 1848
This is a lovely outdoor cafe. Sit underneath the trees of the Botanical Gardens and enjoy a light lunch of quiche and salad, or perhaps coffee with a slice of cake.

BEAUTIFUL CAFE

Café du Lage

Rua Jardim Botânico. Open Mon–Thu 9am–10:30pm, Fri–Sun 9–5:30pm (subject to change according to events taking place). ✆21 9639 9650.
Come here for brunch, a light lunch, or just morning coffee, served in the inner patio. Bread and cakes, as well as sandwiches and homemade soups are on the menu.

its façade was dismantled and re-assembled on the Gardens' grounds.

▶ *Retrace your steps and turn left at Aleia Bento Pickel, following the Rio dos Macacos, a major source of irrigation for the Gardens, as it crosses much of its territory. Pass, on your right, the ruins of the old gunpowder factory (1808), and a cafe. Turn right onto Aleia John Wills.*

You are now coming across the **Medicinal Plants Collection,** made up of over 150 species that are part of the Brazilian healing tradition (some of them as common as mint, rosemary, and lavender).

▶ *Return to Aleia Bento Pickel, turn right, and follow it to the junction with Aléa Frei Velloso.*

The **Bromeliads Greenhouse** contains 1,700 species of these amazing ornamental plants. During periods of drought, they play a vital role for the ecological balance of the forests by storing water, which will be drunk by insects and animals.

▶ *Walk down Aleia Frei Velloso to the Orquidário.*

The magnificent, octagonal-shaped **Orchidarium**, made of iron and glass, was modeled on English hothouses. Inside, are more than 3,000 specimen belonging to 600 different species of orchids and exotic flowers, with their heady perfumes and delicate forms. Mostly Brazilian, there are some non-native species and hybrids too. Look out for the strong lilac shade of the *Laelia pumila*, native to Minas Gerais and Rio de Janeiro. You can't miss the *Oncidium papilio*, a native of Central and South America, with haughty, striped flowers of yellow and orange, reaching a height of 6in/15cm, and the *Colombian miltoniopsis*, with its blood-red blooms.

▶ *Walk down Aleia Guilherme Guinle for a short distance.*

On the right you will pass a statue of Xochipilli (prince of flowers), the Aztec god of love.

▶ *Turn right down Aleia John Wills to the Casa dos Pilões (Pesles House).*

As part of the Royal Gunpowder Factory, which was located by the Rodrigo de Freitas lake, the **Oficina do Moinho dos Piloes**—a little white building (1800)— is where the gunpowder was compacted. As a reminder of this dangerous activity, you can see a number of millstones used to grind the coal, one of the key ingredients necessary to the making of gunpowder.

▶ *Return up Aleia John Wills, and turn right almost immediately onto Aleia Alberto Löefgren, which snakes around a lake to the left, Lago Frei Leandro.*

Built in 1884, today the lake boasts floating 2.2yd/2m-wide waterlilies, **Victoria Regia**, from the Amazon.
While you are still in this area, look for a place known as **Cômoro Frei Leandro,** which offers a nice vantage point of the Gardens. On an artificial hillock stands a little square-shaped pavilion, Casa dos Cedros, in front of which a granite table provided a place for Emperors Dom Pedro I and II to have lunch while visiting

the Gardens. A little further down, note a sundial carved in stone and a beautiful 150 year-old jackfruit tree still bearing impressive fruit.

▷ *Turn left down Aleia J.J. Pizzaro for a short detour to the Estufa de Plantas Insetívoras.*

The first insectivorous plants, attracting their prey with a sweet-smelling scent before consuming, were installed in the **Insectivorous Greenhouse** in 1936. One of the most easily recognizable is the common flycatcher. Originally from Madagascar, India, Australia, and Southeast Asia, its tubelike leaves form a long, sinister neck that can reach up to 20in/50cm.

▷ *Return back down Aleia J.J. Pizzaro, turning right to follow the the path around the Frei Leandro Lake and down Aleia Pedro Gordilho, where soon you will see a small waterfall on your right. Just past this is a little square with a bust of Dom João VI, a rare Pau-brasil (👁 see p 174) and an imperial palm.*

In 1809, Dom João VI planted, with his own hands, the seed of a palm tree brought from Mauritius. As the origin of all palms found today in Brazil, it was known as the *Palma Mater*, or **Mother Palm**. Sadly, the tree was struck by lightning in 1972 on this spot, but was symbolically replaced by another plant grown from its seed.

▷ *Continue the short distance to the end of Aliea Peter Gordilho.*

Sponsored by the Michelin tire corporation, the **Jardim Sensorial** (Sensory Garden), to your right, was specifically designed for visually-impaired visitors. It contains medicinal, edible and aromatic plants, such as fragrant jasmine, ginger, and oregano, all labeled in braille.

▷ *Walk down Aleia João Gomes, left down Aleia Warming and right along Aliea Custódio Serrão. About halfway along, note one of the Gardens' many treasures: an abrico*

Jardim Sensorial

Michelin

de macao. This unusual tree from the Amazon bears flowers and large, round-shaped fruits, giving rise to its nickname "arvore canhão" (Cannonball tree).

▷ *At the very end of Aliea Custódio Serrão, you will find the entrance where you first arrived.*

Additional Sight

Parque Lage
Rua Jardim Botânico 414.
This lovely park, located at the base of Morro de Corcovado (👁 see p 134), owes its name to Commander Antonio Martins Lage who acquired the property in 1859. Its focal point is an Eclectic style mansion from the 1920s, which now houses the School of Visual Arts (🕐 Mon–Thu 9am–8pm, Fri 9am–5pm, Sat 10am–1pm; 📞 21 3257 1800; www.eavparquelage. org.br) and is where visitors can enjoy temporary exhibits.
The mansion was built for industrialist Henrique Lage whose wife, lyric singer Gabriela Bezanzoni Lage, founded the Lyrical Theater Society. Note the extraordinary theater to the left of the entrance hall, and the exquisite swimming pool, flanked by colonnades, which appeared in one of the masterpieces of the Brazilian cinema, Terra em Transe (1967) and was also featured in US rapper and actor Snoop Dogg's music video, appropriately named Beautiful (2003).
As for the gardens, they were originally designed in the Romantic style by English landscape painter **John Tyndale** back in 1840.

WEST ZONE BEACHES

Beyond São Conrado, the next stop along the coast is the urban district of Barra da Tijuca with its mega shopping malls and seemingly neverending stretch of sand. Those who venture farther will be rewarded with charming seafood lunches, peaceful beaches, and stunning cultural highlights. The beaches of the Zona Oeste (West Zone) are some of the most beautiful and rugged in the city, as this part of Rio de Janeiro forms the beginning of the Costa Verde (Green Coast)—a real taste of things to come if you are venturing on an excursion out of the metropolis.

Highlights

1 Flying like a bird in a hang glider over **São Conrado** (see p 181).
2 Cycling along the track at **Barra da Tijuca** Beach (see p 185).
3 Viewing Brazilian Folk Art at **Museu Casa do Pontal** (see p 186).
4 Marveling at the art and gardens of **Sítio Burle Marx** (see p 187).
5 Taking in the wild beauty of the beach at **Grumari** (see p 189).

A State of Preservation

Barra da Tijuca literally means "rotten water, swamp," which accurately described this area of ponds and wetlands in the plains between the mountain and sea. The neighborhood also featured a large expanse of shrub-covered sand dunes, which is now sliced through by the Avenida das Américas highway

GETTING THERE

City buses (see p 180) do serve this stretch of coast, although Barra enjoys greater frequency than the farther outlying beaches.

If you want to explore, and visit any of the sights away from the coast, or complete our **driving tour** of west zone beaches (see p 180), having your own vehicle is essential. Rather than renting a car, you may want to consider hiring a **taxi** for several hours or a full day. To avoid possible over-charging later, just make sure that you clearly agree on a total fixed price before setting off—as a guide, R$300 a day would not be a bad deal. Better still, get a Brazilian (perhaps your tour agent, or hotelier) to do the negotiating for you.

Praia de Guaratiba

Y. Kanazawa/Michelin

(part of the BR-101) and by highrise blocks and large commercial centers. Today, "Barra", as it is commonly known, is a mini modern city, with development encroaching ever-westward. Condominiums are quickly sprouting up at **Recreio**, Barra's nearest neighbor. Further away, the beaches of **Guaratiba** and **Grumari** have managed to preserve much of their wilderness. Backing much of this part of the coast is a wide belt of **Atlantic rain forest** that is now permanently preserved.

Surf City

Ipanema and Arpoador's crowded shorelines provide less than perfect surfing conditions. As a result, dedicated surfers tend to migrate to these west zone beaches to catch some of the best waves in Rio. **Barra**'s beach features fast, strong winds, which attract wind and kite surfers; it also has numerous surf schools, along with surf board and body board rentals. The further afield beaches of **Recreio**, Macumba and **Prainha** feature more consistently good breaks, even drawing a large number of professional surfers.

WEST ZONE BEACHES

Driving Tour
West Zone Beaches

74mi/120km—two hours driving round trip, but allow a full day for the tour, including lunch and visits to the significant sights of Sítio Burle Marx and Museu Casa do Pontal.

Begin at Avenida Prefeito Mendes de Morais in São Conrado, and watch—or even join in—the hang gliders landing on the beach of **Praia do Pepino** *(weather permitting).*

▶ *Make a short detour, turning up Estrada das Canoas to the house of the same name.*

Casa das Canoas (*see p 183*)
A rare treat to look around the former home of world-renowned architect Oscar Niemeyer.

▶ *Return to the coastal road and drive over the overpass of Elevado do Joá, with sweeping views out to sea, and through the Túnel do Joá, to get to Barra da Tijuca. Continue on the coastal road, Avenida Lúcio Costa (previously known as Sernambetiba, a name which is still often used).*

Praia da Barra da Tijuca★★
(*see p 185*)
Find a parking spot on the right-hand side of the road, and cross over to the beach, taking extra care. There are kiosks selling coconut water and refreshments all along Barra Beach: just take your pick. At the western end is the mile-long beach of **Recreio** (*see p 185*).

▶ *Continue past the small beaches of Praia do Pontal and Macumba, keeping to the coastal road which becomes Avenida do Estado da Guanabara.*

Prainha★★ and **Grumari★** (*see p 188*)
Stop at one of these lovely beaches, depending on availability of parking spaces. As a popular surfing spot, Prainha is often crowded with cars, whereas vehicular access is limited at Grumari beach, with even buses prohibited.

▶ *From Grumari, the road that begins at the end of the beach climbs upward, offering spectacular views over the Sepetiba plain and the Restinga da Marambaia.*

Point de Grumari (*see p 245*)
The terrace of this restaurant is a stunning spot for a leisurely seafood lunch.

▶ *Follow the Estrada de Guaratiba to the beach of the same name.*

Barra de Guaratiba★ (*see p 189*)
This beach marks the beginning of the wild and magnificent expanse of the Restinga da Marambaia. This is located on military property and access is strictly prohibited.

▶ *Take the Estrada Roberto Burle Marx de Guaratiba to number 2019.*

Sítio Roberto Burle Marx★★★
(*see p 187*)
Designed by a legendary landscape artist, the spectacular gardens and museum can only be visited as part of a guided tour arranged in advance. Parking spaces are readily available on site.

▶ *Return the way you came along Estrada Roberto Burle Marx de Guaratiba and follow the wriggling Estrada do Grumari. Turn right onto Estrado do Pontal and continue to number 3295.*

Museu Casa do Pontal★★
(*see p 186*)
The entrance to this wonderful Folk Art museum can be hard to find—numbering along this road is not sequential and the house is set back from the road.

▶ *Continue along Estrada do Pontal which leads into Avenida Lúcio Costa to return to the south zone beaches.*

SÃO CONRADO

Dominated by a massive, wind-etched granite formation, this neighborhood is technically part of Rio's South Zone, but serves as the first stop of the many beaches stretching West from the metropolis of Rio. It may not be the best place to quietly practice your backstroke because of strong, powerful breaking waves, but the area has a lot more to offer in terms of tourism. You can choose between the modernist architecture of Casa das Canoas and a guided tour of Rocinha favela, or a daring, adrenaline-pumping ride as a flighty hang glider. Or simply relax and soak up the sun on the long stretch of sand of São Conrado Beach, or maybe partake in some serious shopping in the enormous São Conrado Fashion Mall.

▶ **Orient Yourself:** To the east, Morro Dois Irmãos separates São Conrado from Leblon and Gávea. To the west, Pedra da Gávea stands as a boundary between São Conrado and the West Zone, mainly Barra da Tijuca.

🙈 **Don't Miss:** Taking to the skies from Tijuca Forest in a hang glider. Having Sunday lunch at Villa Riso. Visiting Oscar Niemeyer's former home at Casa | das Canoas.

🕐 **Organizing Your Time:** Hang gliders tend to take off in the morning, so arrive early *(on clear days only)* to see—or join them—landing on Praia do Pepino.

Kids **Especially for Kids:** A choice of more than 30 cakes and pies at Torta & Cia.

A Bit of History

Farming Country
Until the 19C, much of the land in this part of the city was taken up by huge, lucrative farm estates, known as *fazendas*. In these, coffee and sugar were grown. Even as recently as the beginning of the 20C, this area remained decidedly rural. The little church, **Igreja de São Conrado** (1903), from which the district gets its name, still stands here *(to the right of the main road toward Barra)*. It was built for **Conrado Jacob**

Niemeyer (no relation to the famous architect), after whom Avenida Niemeyer was named. Until this road was built in 1916, São Conrado was largely cut off from the rest of Rio.

Geography

The official name of the beach at São Conrado is **Gávea Beach** because it lies in the shadow of **Pedra de Gávea**. This huge mountain, which can be scaled with the help of a qualified guide, offers

Hang glider flying down to Praia do Pepino

©Ricardo De Mattos/iStockphoto.com

Address Book

A BIT OF ADVICE

Reputable hang-gliding companies are detailed in Planning Your Trip (ⓒ see p 31), all of whom provide free pick-ups from your hotel. It is strongly recommended that the company you choose is accredited by the **Associação de Voo Livre do Rio de Janeiro** (www.abvl.com.br). Many of the "instructors" that hang out on Pepino Beach looking for business are not reputable.

GETTING THERE

Bus Travel

Numerous buses ply the coastal road from São Conrado to Barra de Guaratiba. These buses don't run to a timetable, but services are frequent during daylight hours. A single journey to any of the west zone beaches should cost a very reasonable R$2.20.

SHOPPING WITH SOUL

Art and Society

Most guided tours of Rocinha take in a visit to one of the community's crafts stores, run and operated by women as cooperatives (for instance, Cooparoca—Rocinha Cooperative of Women's Artisans and Seamstresses —sells high design around the world). To show your support, you may want to buy an item of clothing, a bag, or piece of jewelry.

CAKE TIME

Torta & Cia   Kids

Estrada da Gávea 820 (Posto Shell). Open daily 9am–10pm. ☎21 3322 5933. www.tortaecia.com.br.

Call in at "Cake and Co" for more than 30 kinds of pies and cakes—the chocolate, coconut, and lemon are particularly recommended, as well as quiches, pies, and snacks. They have a full range of coffee too—whether you like it iced, mocha, or Viennese style. Either eat in at this pleasant, neighborhood-style cafe, or take away.

---

a spectacular panorama of Rio and the neighboring city of Niterói (ⓒsee p 192), on the other side of Guanabara Bay. The wooded hills of **Tijuca National Park** (ⓒsee p 139), in the background, nicely echo the green expanses of the **Gávea Golf and Country Club**, located beneath the massive Gávea rock, which stretches from the base of the mountain down to the beach.

Gávea Golf Club and Praia de São Conrado from above

F. Klingen/Michelin

Avenida Niemeyer, which links São Conrado to Leblon, is the most scenic route into the neighborhood.

To get to Barra da Tijuca from São Conrado, you may want to take the **Joá overpass and tunnel** (Elevado e Tunel do Joá) by the ocean, or drive along **Estrada do Joá,** an old, winding access road. Either way, you will enjoy beautiful views of the ocean, with the solitary island of **Redonda** standing alone far out in the ocean.

Sights

Villa Riso

Estrada da Gávea 728. Art gallery: ⓞOpen Mon–Fri 11am–7pm, Sat–Sun 1pm–5pm. ⬤Free admission. ✗ Sunday lunch served from 1pm onward. ☎21 3322 1444. www.villariso.com.br.

Built in 1770, this colonial-style mansion was once part of a huge farming estate, Fazenda São José da ALagoinha da Gávea, which stretched all the way from Gávea to Jacarepaguá and Tijuca. In the

Rocinha

The makeshift homes clinging to the slopes of Morro Dois Irmãos, in São Conrado, share the same view as the neighboring upmarket condominiums which were built in the flat part of the neighborhood. An estimated population of 250,000 live in the chaotic tangle of streets that make up the *favela* (slum) of Rocinha, with basic amenities and services such as sewerage, medical care and community policing. Upward of four million people—around a third of Rio de Janeiro's population—live in neighborhoods like this one. However, Rocinha is not only the largest of its kind in Rio, but in the whole of Latin America.

Most people living in Rocinha come from the northeastern part of Brazil, having brought their families here in search of work. Favelas are actually the powerhouse of the city: the housekeeper in your hotel, the waiter serving coffee, the cashier at the supermarket, and the Ipanema store assistant most likely live in such neighborhoods. Rio's state government is trying to free these communities from both the control of gang leaders involved in drug trafficking activities, and the increasing power of the militias, a parallel force imposing its clandestine scheme of security. The Dona Marta Favela, in Botafogo, has benefited from one such initiative and is now experiencing relative peace. However, none of the favelas should be visited unaccompanied—go either on the invitation of a resident you trust, or with an organized tour (*see p 29*).

19C the house was acquired by Ferreira Viana, advisor to Dom Pedro II.

In 1934 the house was sold to Italian banker Osvaldo Riso, patron of the arts and an instrumental figure in the creation of the Brazilian Symphonic Orchestra.

You may want to visit Villa Riso for the quality exhibits of its **art gallery**, presenting the works of local and foreign artists, or you may just want to treat yourself to a great **Sunday lunch**, complete with authentic Brazilian dishes served in a refined setting.

Casa das Canoas

Estrada das Canoas, 2310. ◷*Open Tue–Fri 1pm–5pm.* ⬯*R$10.* ✆*21 3322 3581. www.niemeyer.org.br.*
World-renowned architect **Oscar Niemeyer** built this "House of the Canoes" in 1951 as a home for himself and his family. He created the building with smooth, curved lines to integrate with its environment. Huge boulders and thick vegetation actually make their way into the beautiful interior space, made up of large, open rooms around a cool blue swimming pool.

Trees and shaded areas deliberately do away with the need for curtains, creating a transparent living space that blurs the lines between interior and exterior. Visitors can peruse some of the original furniture, as well as Niemeyer's models and designs, some of which are presented in an interactive, multimedia display.

Praia de São Conrado

(☹*Because of huge swells, this beach is not a safe place to swim.*)
At the end of Avenida Niemeyer, approaching from Leblon, the two-mile stretch of São Conrado Beach (officially called **Gávea Beach**) comes into view. The sands tend to be popular with kids from the nearby Rocinha favela (*see sidebar, above*), as well as surfers and residents of the large upscale condominiums nearby.

Behind the beach is the Gávea Golf and Country Club (*see p 32*) and the **São Conrado Fashion Mall** (*Estrada da Gávea 899;* ◷*Mon–Sat 10am–10pm, Sun 3pm–9pm;* ✆*21 2111 4444; www. scfashionmall.com.br.*), with more than 150 stores, an impressive food court, and several movie theaters.

The hang gliders that jump from the rock of Pedra Bonita, in Tijuca National Park, are a colorful, dramatic sight as they float down from the sky to the beach of **Praia do Pepino**, at the western end of São Conrado. The sands come to a halt just afterward at the **Túnel São Conrado**.

BARRA DA TIJUCA

Heading farther west, the city's newest neighborhood is an area of explosive growth and modernization. There is definitely an American feel to "Barra", with its sprawling shopping malls, soaring apartment buildings, and challenging traffic. Barra da Tijuca's beach is Rio's longest and one of the best around the city. It attracts a mixed crowd of casual swimmers, avid surfers, windsurfers and divers, making Barra a lively scene, particularly on weekends.

▶ **Orient Yourself:** The long, multi-lane Avenue das Américas is the district's main thoroughfare. Avenue Lúcio Costa runs parallel, along the beachfront.
🐾 **Don't Miss:** Catching a wave with the help of a local surf school (👓 see p 34).
🕐 **Organizing Your Time:** Avoid rush hour and weekends due to heavy traffic.
Kids Especially for Kids: Waves can be powerful here, but fortunately there is plenty to do on the sand! Also consider a stroll or bike ride in Bosque da Barra, a nature park at the intersection of Av. Ayrton Senna and Av. das Américas. If the weather is bad, check the malls for indoor activities specifically for children.

A Bit of History

American Model

Right up until the end of the 1960s, Barra was largely a wild coastal region of lakes, marshland, and sand dunes. In 1969, architect **Lúcio Costa**, the man responsible for creating Brasília, came up with a pilot plan which involved the urban occupation of the region of Barra, where the city of Rio de Janeiro could grow. The project followed the guiding principles of rationalist city planning. Doggedly road-oriented and modernist—just like the design of the new capital—it was a deliberate break from Rio's urban past and a conscious assertion of a new lifestyle. In the end, Costa's dream of creating a socially integrated urban landscape turned into a vision of freeways and isolated condominiums, with public greenspaces being walled up or consumed by shopping malls. What visitors see today in Barra is a modern neighborhood, part residential with rows of high rise condos, part commercial with large shopping centers, stretching out for miles and miles along the ocean.

Entertainment Central

To many, Barra da Tijuca represents a safe space in the chaotic city and is a nucleus for entertainment. Barra Shopping (👓 see p 262) is one of the largest malls in Latin America—it even has its own monorail; other "shoppings" (as

Long beach of Barra da Tijuca

Y. Kanazawa/Michelin

Praia do Pepê

Y. Kanazawa/Michelin

Brazilians like to call them) are sprouting up all the time. Some of Rio's best cinemas, theaters, restaurants and nightclubs (*See p 248*) are found here. **Cidade da Musica** (*see p 73*) is the latest addition, a hugely ambitious, multimillion dollar "City of Music" designed by world famous architect, Christian de Portzamparc. Dogged by delays, once completed it will include concert halls, rehearsal spaces, stores, and restaurants and serve as the headquarters of the Brazilian Symphonic Orchestra.

Sight

Praia da Barra da Tijuca★★   Kids

Rio's longest beach (14km/8.7mi) is dotted with kiosks for a quick bite and drink, and lifeguard stations with showers and bathrooms, although facilities tend to thin the closer you get to Recreio dos Bandeirantes (*see p 186*) . The first few miles has the biggest concentration of bars and restaurants, where fresh fish is the local specialty.

Praia do Pepê is a 275-meter/300-yard stretch of beach between Postos 1 and 2 that tends to attract a young crowd. Both beach and beach-stand were named after a popular hang glider and surfer known as Pepê, who was killed in a hang gliding competition in Japan in 1991.

Bikers and joggers enjoy the well-maintained **cycle track** which backs the whole beach. As everywhere in Rio, **beach volleyball** is popular and there are nets at regular intervals, but Posto 3 is considered as "the" place to play this sport. The beach also lends itself to the challenging sport of **foot volley**. Finally, **surfing** schools are found along the length of the beach, with the oldest one in Brazil still operating in front of the Sheraton Barra Hotel

Address Book

GETTING THERE
Taxi!
☎ *21 2209 9292. 24hrs. www.radio-taxi. com.br.* Getting a cab to Barra from Rio is easy enough; just hail one from the street. Be aware they do charge a higher meter rate (twice as much) for any destination west of São Conrado. Finding a cab for your return journey may not be straightforward depending on the time of day *(rush hour is difficult)*. If your Portuguese is good enough and you are prepared to pay a bit more, call a radio cab company. An air-conditioned omnibus and "surf buses" also go to Barra (*see p 186*).

BEACH EATS
Barraca do Pepê, quiosque 11
Av. do Pepê. Open daily 8am–8pm.
☎ *21 2433 1400. www.pepe.com.br.*
Delicious snacks, sandwiches, and shakes can be had at this well-known *barraca,* which is a magnet for surfers and health-conscious clients.

RECREIO DOS BANDEIRANTES

Often simply referred to as "Recreio", this neighborhood has long been enjoyed by families and locals who favor its more peaceful atmosphere over neighboring Barra da Tijuca. They particularly appreciate the calm waters of its 1mi/1.5km long beach, protected by a large outcrop at its western end. Recreio had escaped the urban sprawl that has swallowed up the coastal landscape around Rio, but today urbanization is fast encroaching, particularly at its beachfront.

▶ **Orient Yourself:** Tucked up into the western corner of Barra, the beach of Recreio is really an extension of Praia da Barra.

🐊 **Don't Miss:** The animated Carnival parade with samba school performers and audience at Museu Casa do Pontal. A walk through native forest at Parque Ecológico Chico Mendes.

🕐 **Organizing Your Time:** The Casa do Pontal museum is closed on Monday.

Kids **Especially for Kids:** The baby alligators at Parque Ecológico Chico Mendes.

Sights

Museu Casa do Pontal★★ Kids

Estrada do Pontal, 3295. 🕐*Open Tue–Sun 9:30am–5pm.* 🎫*R$10.* 📞*21 2490 3278. www.museucasadopontal.com.br.*

Located between the rock of Pedra Branca and the beach of Prainha, this wonderful museum houses an outstanding collection of rural and urban Brazilian folk art. This collection consists of more than 5,000 works (and a further 3,000 in reserve) created by over 200 artists from 1950 until the present day, with new acquisitions all the time.

Such a range and depth of information about Brazilian culture is on show that this little treasure has been deservedly described by UNESCO as a true anthropological museum. Delightful wood carvings, clay, cloth, straw, and even dough figures as well as moving mechanical forms are imaginatively displayed. Pieces are organized by theme; eroticism *(adults only permitted to this room)*, festivities, and religion are explored and get to the very heart of daily Brazilian life.

This extensive collection is the work of Frenchman **Jacques Van de Beuque**, who lived in Brazil from 1944; since his death in 2000, the museum has been run by his widow and son. Explanatory texts accompany the exhibits in English.

Parque Ecológico Chico Mendes Kids

Jarbas Avenida de Carvalho, 679. 🕐*Open 8am–5pm.* 🎫*Free Admission.* 📞*21 2437 6400*

This ecological park was named after Chico Mendes, the Brazilian environmentalist who campaigned to save the Amazon and set up a union of rubber tappers before he was murdered in 1988. The park was created to preserve the endangered fauna and flora of Lagoinha das Tachas: bromeliads, ingas, three-fingered sloths and yellowthroat alligators. It is the only area in Rio where native **restinga** (unique marshy sandbanks) can still be seen. Visitors to the park can follow trails through native forest, enjoy picnics in designated areas, and visit an alligator nursery.

Museu da Casa do Pontal

Museu Casa do Pontal

GUARATIBA AND SURROUNDS

Beyond Barra da Tijuca, further along the coastline past Recreio dos Bandeirantes, the population becomes less dense. Fishing communities, nature reserves and uncrowded, unspoilt beaches transition to stretches of virtually deserted sands as you travel even farther west. No less impressive, the Inland showcases one of Brazil's most beautiful tropical gardens, designed by the father of modern landscape architecture.

▸ **Orient Yourself:** The road at the end of Grumari Beach climbs through thick forest to hilltop views of Guaratiba and Sepetiba Bay, closed by Restinga da Marambaia.

Don't Miss: Treat yourself to a delicious *alfresco* seafood lunch with a view of the ocean at a local restaurant (*see p 244*). Then enjoy one of the most important collections of tropical plants in the world at Sítio Burle Marx.

🕐 **Organizing Your Time:** A highly recommended visit to Sítio Burle Marx is only possible on a guided tour booked in advance. Make sure to call ahead and plan to spend a couple of hours at this outstanding sight.

Geography

In the language of the Native Indians, Guaratiba means "gathering place of herons"—birds who continue to frequent this peaceful spot. The beaches here are special for having managed to preserve some **restingas**. Home to native crabs and birds, these shrubby or herbaceous coastal sand-dune habitats used to cover most of Rio de Janeiro's verdant coastline, but they have now largely disappeared due to human activity. As an environmental conservation area, Grumari has taken up the challenge of preserving this unique ancient habitat from the fate of other urbanized beaches.

Sítio Burle Marx★★★

Estrada Roberto Burle Marx 2019.
🕐*Open open by guided tours arranged in advance Tue–Sat 9:30am and 1:30pm. Bookings taken 8am–4pm.* ✍*R$5.* ✆*21 2410 1412.*

Brazilian landscape architect **Roberto Burle Marx** (*see p 73*) bought this huge estate—an old banana plantation—in 1949, and he lived here from 1973 until his death in 1994. He handed over the 100-acre/40-ha site to the government in 1985, and today it is owned by the National Institute for Historical and Artistic Heritage (IPHAN).

Sítio Burle Marx

F. Klingen/Michelin

Modern Man

When, in 1965, the American Institute of Architects proclaimed Burle Marx "the real creator of the modern garden" they credited him, even then, with being a man ahead of his time.

Burle Marx believed strongly that man must work in harmony with nature and warned of the destruction of the rain forest long before it became a popular cause. His creative impulses always defined his work, and his landscape design was never a mere backdrop to architectural forms. And most importantly, he almost single-handedly wrenched native Brazilian garden design from the grasp of the Europeans, freeing it from neat lines and constricting formality.

GETTING THERE

Surf Bus

Largo do Machado, Botafogo to Prainha. ☎21 8702 2837. www.surfbus.com.br.
For those without their own transport, the orange Surf Bus does the rounds of Rio de Janeiro's best surf beaches daily 7am–7pm with English speaking guides. Leaving Largo do Machado at 7am, 10am, 1pm, and 4pm, it stops at the southern beaches, São Conrado, Barra da Tijuca, Recreio, Macumba, and Prainha, with each circuit taking an hour and a half *(see website for full details)*.
You can embark and disembark at any point. There is room for boards or any other equipment, and non-surfers are welcome too, making it a good way of exploring some of the remote west zone beaches.

Nature as a Work of Art

Burle Marx was above all an artist who had studied in Europe, and had a highly developed sense of the esthetic.
For him, Brazil's natural vegetation was his canvas, and the plants the paint for the picture he was creating in his work. He not only introduced tropical landscaping to the Brazilians, but combined it with modern art to create a new, truly international, esthetic language. In this way, all his sensibilities came together in his gardens to form works of art.

A Gardener's World

The spectacular gardens here contain more than 3,500 plant species that were gathered from around the world by Burle Marx, beginning at the tender age of six. Together they comprise one of the most important collections of tropical plants anywhere on the planet. Plants are presented as works of art, often grouped together as single species or color, or against a body of water, for maximum effect. Delicate **orchids**, spiky **bromeliads** and stately **palms** abound. They include dozens of indigenous plants named for him, testament to his skill as a botanist, such as the *Heliconia burlemarxii*—which is used as the stylish logo for the site.

A Living Museum

Burle Marx lovingly restored both the country house and the **chapel** built here in the 17C. He built the studio himself—out of Victorian stones from buildings demolished in the city—and used this space as his office and workshop until he died. Burle Marx was often quoted as declaring: "One needs to surround oneself with objects of poetic emotion." It was a quote he had borrowed from the French architect Le Corbusier, but it was very much how he lived his life. The rooms of the house are filled with his beloved collections from around the world, from jugs and decorative pots to religious icons.

Burle Marx was typically Brazilian in that he loved to socialize, and a pavilion next to the house was designed for the sole purpose of entertaining. He regularly hosted large Sunday lunches and lively parties, and his birthday is

Surfing at Prainha

F. Klingen/Michelin

still celebrated with live music every August 4. Visitors pass agave cacti and royal palms on the way up to sweeping **views** of the valley from the hilltop chapel, where villagers still gather for mass every Sunday.

Additional Sights

Prainha★★

This "little" beach, as its name means, is nestled between the mountains and the ocean. Here, you will find clear waters and powerful waves, ideal for **surfing**. Needless to say the beach and its small cluster of kiosks are often full with professional and amateur surfers. Don't miss the round boulders on the shore which almost look as if they had just rolled down from the mountains.

Praia de Grumari★

Grumari is one of the few beaches in the area that maintains a truly wild aspect. Backed by low, rolling hills densely carpeted in Atlantic forest, it forms an environmental protection zone where buses are banned and car access limited. The only commercial activity is that of a handful of kiosks and a basic restaurant. Between Grumari and Prainha, hidden behind the rocks, is Rio's only nudist beach: **Praia do Abricó**.

Barra de Guaratiba★   Kids

Guaratiba has long been a fishermen's colony, and still retains its traditional atmosphere, with fishing boats, flocks of patrolling seagulls, and several rustic fish and seafood restaurants.

Popular with locals, its small family-friendly beach is the last on Rio's south coast. Backed by a number of trees, such as almond and apricot, as well as houses that climb up the slopes, the beach is protected by the peninsula of Restinga da Marambaia and by Picão point, and enjoys generally calm waters.

From the Restinga da Marambaia, trails lead to deserted, unspoiled beaches *(authorization from the Army required).*

Praia de Grumari

F. Klingen/Michelin

EXCURSIONS

Just a few hours away from Rio de Janeiro are several stunning destinations to explore. Start with the city of Niterói, a short ferry ride from Rio's downtown, with its impressive Museum of Contemporary Art overlooking beautiful Guanabara Bay. Driving eastward, you will come across the pristine beaches and splendid bays of Brazilian Costa do Sol, and the famous beachside resort of Búzios. Heading west from Rio you'll find the beauty of yet another coast, the lush corridor of Costa Verde, home to Ilha Grande and the colonial town of Paraty. For a total change of scenery, head inland to the Coffee Valley, or to Petrópolis, the old imperial city, nestling in the hills of Serra do Mar, and experience a pleasantly cooler climate and rich cultural history.

Stepping Back in Time

A ferry trip on the **Bay of Guanabara** reveals the Neo-gothic Ilha Fiscal and on the other side of the bay, **Niterói**, with its imposing fortresses, then farther still, the timeless island of Paquetá.

Inland, the "Valley of the Coffee Barons" (**Coffee Valley**) offers visitors a glimpse into a culture once so vital to Brazil's economy. **Petrópolis**, founded by Dom Pedro II as a summer retreat, retains an air of royalty with grand historical buildings and horse drawn buggies clip-clopping through its wide avenues.

Along the coast, **Paraty** boasts a colonial past beautifully preserved in the cobblestoned streets of its historic center.

The paradise of **Ilha Grande** retains its natural state of beauty protected by eco-tourism, and its status as a reserve.

Making Time

Explore the beauty outside the city. Take the slower ferry to Niterói; pull over to

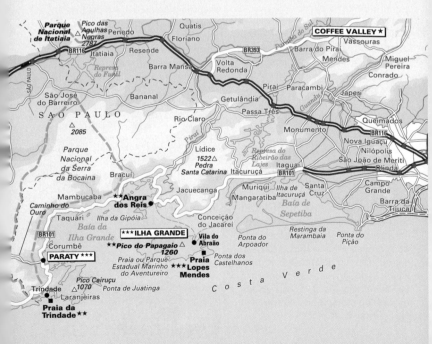

Highlights

1 Admiring the bay from the gallery of the contemporary art museum in **Niterói** (👁 *see p 192*).

2 Relaxing on the beautiful beaches of charming **Búzios** (👁 *see p 196*).

3 Hiking through pristine rainforest on **Ilha Grande** (👁 *see p 200*).

4 Taking a boat trip on the turquoise waters around **Paraty Bay** (👁 *see p 204*).

5 Marveling at the rich history and architecture of Imperial **Petrópolis** (👁 *see p 208*).

covered mountains tumbling down to a stunning coastline fringed with palm trees and white sand beaches.

The **Costa do Sol** (Sun Coast), true to its name, attracts sun worshipers all along the 60mi/100km stretch from Niterói to fashionable, laidback Búzios. Pristine beaches and beautiful lagoons dot the coast. Take the scenic route and stay overnight in one of the many fishing villages or upmarket resorts along the way.

😊 A Bit of Advice 😊

Other than Guanabara Bay and Niterói, the places described in this section are popular **weekend getaways** *(and holiday destinations, mainly Dec–Feb)* for Brazilians. Avoid traveling at these times, when their tranquil appeal diminishes, prices increase and accommodation is hard to come by.

take pictures on the winding road to Petrópolis; stay overnight in a magnificent fazenda in the Coffee Valley.

The journey to Paraty, Ilha Grande or Búzios is part of the adventure. Between the emerald of the Atlantic forest and the aquamarine ocean of the **Costa Verde** (Green Coast), highway BR-101 snakes its way west revealing jungle-

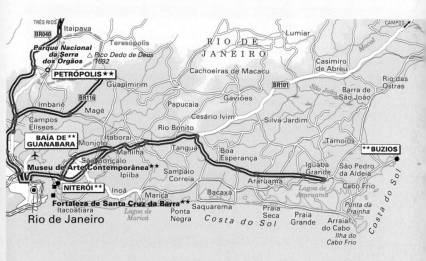

EXCURSIONS FROM RIO

BAÍA DE GUANABARA AND NITERÓI★★

Located on the other side of Guanabara Bay, Niterói is just a short ferry ride from Rio's downtown, or an 8ml/13km-long drive across the Rio–Niterói Bridge. Home to an estimated half a million residents, this city has venerable fortresses guarding the once much-coveted bay, and its landmark giant white flower (or is it a flying saucer?) Museum of Contemporary Art brings a modern architectural touch to the landscape. Niterói also has pleasant beaches, some by the bay, others by the ocean, breathtaking viewpoints from where you can capture stunning images, and striking Niemeyer architecture.

▶ **Orient Yourself:** Niterói's major sights tend to be concentrated along Guanabara Bay, while beautiful, open sea beaches line its more remote Atlantic shore.

Don't Miss: Oscar Niemeyer's Museum of Contemporary Art, for its incredibly bold architecture and the gorgeous view of Rio and the Guanabara Bay it offers from its circular gallery.

Organizing Your Time: Try to plan a morning or late afternoon visit to the Santa Cruz da Barra Fortress, as this beautiful place does not offer any protection from the scorching sun.

Especially for Kids: Hire an old-fashioned horse-drawn carriage and explore the picturesque Ilha de Paquetá. Straight out of a fairy tale book, the colorful castle on Ilha Fiscal should also be a sure hit!

Niterói

Museu de Arte Contemporânea (MAC)★★

Mirante da Boa Viagem. ⏰*Open Tue–Sun 10am–6pm (7pm summer weekends), box office closes 15min before exhibition space. External courtyard 9am–7pm, Sat and Sun 9am–8pm.* ⮑*R$4.* ☎*21 2620 2400. www.mac-niteroi.com.br. To reach MAC, turn right from the ferry terminal and take bus number 47B up to the museum.*

On a high promontory that juts out into Guanabara Bay, this landmark building appears to hover above the water, like a giant white flower on a huge stalk, as architect **Oscar Niemeyer** (b. 1907) likes to describe it. The Museum of Contemporary Art is an extraordinary spectacle and justifiably one of the most visited sights in Niterói. The reflecting pool lying beneath the impressive **cupola** (53ft/16m-high with a diameter of 55yd/50m) creates a mirror effect. The MAC was originally built to house João Leão Sattamini Neto's extensive

Museu de Arte Contemporânea

Y. Kanazawa/Michelin

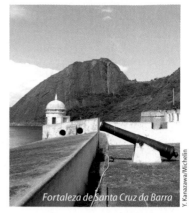

Fortaleza de Santa Cruz da Barra

Y. Kanazawa/Michelin

😊 A Bit of Advice 😊

The fort of Fortaleza de Santa Cruz da Barra is about a 15-min drive from MAC and, as it still has an army division posted here, visitors must pass through checkpoints to enter. The whole area is open to the elements, and particularly to the beating sun, so wear a protective hat and sunscreen and bring water. To see the inside of the fort, you must take a guided tour *(in Portuguese only; however, a free leaflet with map and information in English is available).*

collection of contemporary Brazilian art, which had been spread across the city in various locations. Today, temporary exhibits highlight selections from the permanent collection which now totals more than 12,000 pieces of art from the second half of the 20C. The Niemeyer building is reached by a wide spiral ramp which leads visitors to a splendid **viewing gallery** through which they can admire Guanabara Bay, Rio de Janeiro and the Sugar Loaf mountain.

Fortaleza de Santa Cruz da Barra★★

Rua General Eurico Gaspar Dutra, Jurujuba. ◷*Open Tue–Sun 10am–5pm.* ✆*R$4. Entry with guided tour only.* ☎*21 2710 2354.*
An improvised fortification was built on this site in 1555 by Frenchman **Nicolau Durand de Villegaignon**, to defend the colony of "French Antartica" he had founded in Rio. The French forces

having been expelled from Brazil in 1567, the fortress was expanded by the Portuguese as the key point of defence for Guanabara Bay.
The drive from Niterói takes you up a hill past a few other coastal fortifications *(see sidebar)* and small coves filled with fishing boats. You then arrive at Santa Cruz da Barra, a beautiful setting, with the white walls of the fortress extending along the lines of the steep cliff on which it stands.
The Santa Cruz fortress is a huge compound, complete with prison cells, 20 casemates on the first floor and 21 on the second floor, and impressive rows of high-caliber cannons. Some parts of the walls date back to the mid-16C. Note the lovely colonial-style **Santa Bárbara Chapel**★, built in 1612, and the lighthouse, turned into a small cultural space with temporary exhibitions. Don't miss the spectacular **view** across Guanabara Bay, Niterói, and Rio de Janeiro, with

Niterói Forts and Fortresses

Some claim that the city of Niterói concentrates one of the highest number of forts and fortresses in Latin America. The listing is indeed quite impressive. Beside Fortaleza de Santa Cruz da Barra, which played a key role in the defense of Guanabara Bay, there is, among others, a particularly interesting trio: **Forte do Imbuí**, **Forte Barão do Rio Branco** and the ruins of **Forte de São Luiz**. Located on top of Morro do Pico (755ft/230m), the highest point in this area, the latter affords a breathtaking view of Fortaleza de Santa Cruz da Barra, Morro da Urca and Sugar Loaf Mountain on one side, and Forte do Imbuí and the ocean on the other. *Access to the three forts through Forte Barão do Rio Branco entrance gate at Alameda Marechal Pessoa Leal, 265, Jurujuba;* ◷ *Guided tour Sat–Sun and national holidays 9:30am–4pm;* ✆*R$10;* ☎ *21 2711 0566/2711 0462.*

GETTING THERE AND AROUND

Ferries for Niterói depart from behind Praça XV in Rio's historic center (📖 see p 98) every 15min, taking 20min. Hydrofoils and catamarans take between five and eight minutes and are a quicker and more pleasant way to travel.

Return at dusk to see the city of Rio de Janeiro bathed in a beautiful golden light. Outside the ferry terminal in Niterói is a tourist information office (open daily 9am–6pm), that provides up-to-date information about transport around the city, maps, and directions. Frequent buses leave for Niterói from Praça XV, crossing the 8mi/13km Rio–Niterói Bridge. Otherwise, drive or take a cab.

Sugar Loaf Mountain and the statue of Christ the Redeemer, particularly lovely at sunset.

Parque da Cidade

Estrada da Viração. 🕐 *Open Mon–Fri, 9am–6pm (7pm during daylight saving time). Cafe Mon–Fri 9am–5pm.*
✕ 🖉 21 2610 3157
Located at 886ft/270m above sea level on Morro da Viração, the city park is reached by taxi or on foot from São Francisco Beach *(you may need to ask for directions)*. The main reason to visit this place is the fantastic birds-eye **view**★★★ of Guanabara Bay from the bayside hang gliding ramp—particularly memorable at sunset. A second ramp offers views across the ocean. The park itself, full of wild plants and flowers, is a pleasant spot for strolling and relaxing. A small cafe sells snacks and cold drinks.

Niterói Beaches

To discover Niterói's **bayside beaches**, start with **Praia da Icaraí**, the main beach in town. At its end, the Leopoldo Fróes road hugs the rocky coast and leads to **Praia de São Francisco**, famous for its nightlife and its beautiful São Francisco Xavier Church, founded in the 16C by José de Anchieta.

Continuing along the coast, you will come across **Praia de Charitas,** then **Praia de Jurujuba**, a short stretch of sand with fishing boats—both really extensions of São Francisco Beach. Next come **Praia de Adão** and **Praia de Eva**, separated from one another by a large rock formation.

To discover Niterói's **ocean-side beaches**, from downtown Niterói, the way to go is to follow the Leopoldo Fróes coastal road. Then, instead of turning right towards São Francisco Beach, keep going straight and take Avenida Presidente Roosevelt. The first ocean side beach you reach is **Praia de Piratininga**. You can swim off this 1.5mi/2.5km-long beach, with a great view of Rio, although the water can sometimes get rough.

A short trail leads to the small **Praia do Sossego** with relatively calm, clear waters. The next beach, **Praia de Camboinhas**, specializes in watersports. Popular **Praia de Itaipu** is a pretty beach with sand dunes and a fishing community. Finally, surfers like to hang out at **Praia de Itacoatiara**, with its beach bars and trails leading into the hills behind.

Caminho Niemeyer

The Niemeyer Corridor or "Way" is a bayside architectural trail of cultural and religious buildings designed by the renowned architect, **Oscar Niemeyer**. Among them are the MAC and the Juscelino Kubitschek Square. The latest addition is the Teatro Popular (People's Theater) to the left as you exit the ferry terminal, opened in 2007 on Niemeyer's 100th birthday. A new ferry terminal, a museum of Brazilian cinema, a Roberto Silveira memorial, both a Catholic and a Baptist cathedral, and a building for the Oscar Niemeyer Foundation are also due to be completed soon, and together will represent the largest collection of Niemeyer-designed projects outside the capital city, Brasília.

Baía de Guanabara

Ilha Fiscal★   Kids

Av. Alfredo Agache. ○*Boat tours Thu–Sun, 1pm, 2:30pm and 4pm. Tickets are available from Espaço Cultural da Marinha (○ see p 105) from 11am on visit days.* ○*Ilha Fiscal closed Jan 1, Carnival, Good Friday, All Soul's Day, Dec 24, 25, and 31.* *21 2104 6721.*

Like a floating fairy tale castle in Guanabara Bay, this extraordinary green neo-Gothic building may seem rather whimsical for a customs house. Designed by architect **Adolpho Del Vecchio** in 1881, the project was personally approved by Emperor Dom Pedro II, and eventually garnered a gold medal at the Imperial Academy of Fine Arts.

In April 1889, the castle was inaugurated in the presence of the emperor. Less than seven months later, it hosted a celebration in honor of the Chilean Navy. A painting by Aurélio de Figueiredo, entitled *O último baile da Ilha Fiscal*, portrays what would be known as the "Last Ball of the Monarchy," Brazil having been proclaimed a republic very shortly afterward.

In 1913, the building was taken over by the Navy and, since 1998, houses exhibitions depicting both the history of the building and of the Navy. Needless to say, part of the building's main appeal—a building that Dom Pedro II is said to have referred to as "a delicate jewel box, worthy of a dazzling jewel"—is its refined decorative interior.

Ilha de Paquetá   Kids

This is Guanabara Bay's second-largest island, the largest one being Ilha do Governador where Rio's main airport is located. An isthmus in the middle of Paquetá gives the island its distinctive, hourglass shape. Its landscape is characterized by a combination of low hills toward the interior, and along the coast, a large numbers of boulders sculpted by the wind and sun.

Shells can still be found in various parts of Paquetá, hence its Tupi name meaning "many shells."

The island makes for a pleasant change from the bustle of Rio, with a few colonial houses and a slower pace of life. Hydro-

Ilha Fiscal

Y. Kanazawa/Michelin

foils and catamarans *(taking 20mins)* and ferries *(taking 1hr)* leave from behind Praça XV in the historic center around every two hours throughout the day. The website *(www.ilhadepaqueta.com. br)* has information about transport links and tours. A small tourist office (○*open daily 11am–5pm*) also operates from the boat terminal.

On the island, motorized vehicles are prohibited, so visitors get around on foot or on rental bikes. Horse-drawn carriages are also available, and a tourist train (pulled by a tractor) tours the island *(R$4, 50min)*. Because of water pollution, the beaches on Paquetá are not crowded. Located at the end of Praia José Bonifácio, **Parque Darke de Mattos** is an attractive wooded area with flowers. **Solar d'El Rey**, the island's main historic building, is a manor house which belonged to slave trader Francisco Gonçalves da Fonseca and where Dom João VI liked to spend his summers. Today, the mansion houses a small local library *(Rua Príncipe Regente 55;* ○*open Tue–Sat 8:30am–4:30pm).*

BAY BOATS

Saveiros Tour
Av. Infante Dom Henrique (no number), Shop 13/14, Marina da Glória. *21 2225 6064. www.saveiros.com.br*
Cultural tours on schooners around the bay visit Niterói, Santa Cruz da Barra Fortress, and Ilha Fiscal. They leave morning and afternoon, daily.

BÚZIOS★★

"Brazil's Saint-Tropez" has somehow managed to stay both endearingly rustic and highly sophisticated. Fringed with attractive small beaches, clear blue ocean, secluded coves, and picturesque islands off its coastline, this wonderfully scalloped peninsula hasn't lost a bit of its charm. Visitors from all over the world love the exuberant nature around Búzios, but they also come here to enjoy its narrow cobblestone streets lined with boutiques and quaint restaurants, its lovely inns and the overall friendly, relaxed atmosphere which have contributed to making it one of Brazil's favorite seaside resorts.

▶ **Orient Yourself:** 105mi/169km east of Rio de Janeiro, on the Brazilian Costa do Sol, Búzios peninsula is about 5mi/8km long. The eastward extension of Rua das Pedras, Búzios' main entertainment venue, is a promenade called Orla Bardot which overlooks Búzios' central beach: Praia da Armação.

⊘ **Don't Miss:** Enjoy two spectacular viewpoints on Búzios' peninsula: one from Mirante do Forno, the other from Mirante de João Fernandes. Discover the picturesque islands around the peninsula by boat: Ilha Feia, Ilha dos Gravatás, Ilha do Caboclo, Ilha Da Âncor and Ilha Branca. Find your way to Ponta da Lagoinha, a limpid water lagoon nearby Ferradura Beach, created by an impressive rocky formation referred to as the "Brazilian Himalayas".

🕐 **Organizing Your Time:** If you happen to be in Búzios on June 29, you will see local fishermen celebrate their patron saint with decorated boats and a procession starting at charming Sant'ana Church (1740), located between Armação and Ossos beaches.

🧒 **Especially for Kids:** Snorkeling in the clear, shallow waters is good fun and a great way to learn about the local underwater life.

A Bit of History

A thousand years before the Portuguese arrived in Brazil, the region around Búzios was already inhabited by Indians from the Tamoio and Goitacás tribes. In the 16C, the European colonization process and the ensuing over-logging forced the local people to turn to **whaling** to survive. Both Armação ("carcass") and Ossos ("bones") beaches still bear the long-faded memory of a time when the sands were scattered with the bones from whales who had been processed for their oil. The area's full name of Armação dos Búzios is now seldom used.

Praia da Ferradurinha

©iStockBrazil/Alamy

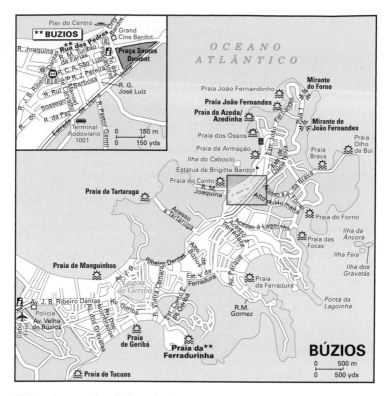

Today, when people talk about the history of Búzios, they usually cite **Brigitte Bardot** strolling on the sand streets with her Brazilian boyfriend in 1964 as its most defining moment. Until then, Búzios had been an unassuming fishing community, but when photos of the starlet on holiday here appeared in the international press, it shot to fame as one of the most desirable destinations in the world.

Downtown

Rua das Pedras★★

Lined with art galleries, bars, eateries, and boutiques selling everything from designer clothes and sunglasses to souvenirs, Búzios' most famous street, the Rua das Pedras, little more than 550yds/500m long, lies at the heart of the historic center.

People love to stroll along the pedestrianized cobblestoned street at any time of day, but it really comes alive from sunset until the small hours of the morning. A popular spot for celebrities, the area overflows with tanned, beautiful people from around the world, creating a lively atmosphere, and offering great people-watching too.

Many of the boutiques along Rua das Pedras do not open until 5pm and do not begin closing until 11pm onward. The restaurants (♻ *see p 245*) here are truly international, and cuisine includes French, Italian, Argentinian, Thai, Moroccan, or delicious Brazilian seafood.

At the eastern end of Rua das Pedras is **Orla Bardot**, a lovely waterfront promenade graced with a bronze statue of the famous French actress by local artist Cristina Motta. A little farther on, boat excursions to the nearby islands leave from Armação Beach's remodelled **Pier do Centro** where water taxis, dive boats and *escunas* (schooners) wait for passengers to board.

The Beaches

With over twenty five beaches to choose from, Búzios offers great opportunities

Nature Hiking

There is more to Búzios than crystal-clear waters and an old fishermen's village charm. Beautiful, exuberant natural sights are here to explore and enjoy.

Take a guided walk through the **Emerências Reserve** to get a feel for the Atlantic Forest's unique ecosystem, complete with Golden Tamarin monkeys and bromeliads. *Call the Instituto Ecológico Búzios Mata Atlântica (IEBMA) at ✆22 2623 2200 or 22 2623 2446 for more details.*

Visit the **Tauá Reserve** where remarkable private efforts are leading to the gradual restoration of the Cabo Frio *restinga* environment. ⏰*Open 8am–6:30pm.* *Free entrance. Check www.reservataua.com for more details.*

Also note that Búzios is home to the state's largest reserve of **Pau-Brasil** (or Brasilwood), a most endangered species of tree. This protected area extends from Tucuns Beach all the way to Cabo Frio.

to surf, kite surf, dive, snorkel, swim or just relax by the water. The northern beaches, closer to town, tend to have calmer, warmer waters, while the southern ones, less easily accessible, are a bit colder, but with better surf. The beaches listed below offer a good sample of what the area has to offer.

Praia da Ferradurinha★★

"Little Horseshoe" is a lovely deep cove with turquoise waters, and one of the prettiest (and safest) beaches on Búzios. Families flock to this natural swimming pool, formed by long, low rocks flanking shallow, warm waters. On a warm day, the rock formations that slide into the ocean are dotted with sunbathers, while kayakers serenely paddle in the cove.

There is a small kiosk peddling drinks and snacks, as well as large parasols for rent—which are very welcome on this treeless beach. In the area surrounding the rocks, underwater visibility is ideal for going snorkeling. The beach is a pleasant, 10-minute walk from Geribá, which can be reached by car.

Praia de Geribá

Búzios' most popular beach is located on the narrowest part of the peninsula. Dotted with kiosks all along its length, the beach has more than its fair share of restaurants, *pousadas* (inns) and summerhouses.

Here, the wide expanse of sand makes the perfect playground for sports such as volleyball and beach soccer. As one of the longest beaches around, with consistent waves and winds, Geribá

also boasts some of the best surfing in Búzios. Its most remote and less urbanized part can be dangerous because of strong waves and currents, but the sea is much calmer and the waves much smaller on its opposite end, known as **Canto de Geribá**.

Praia de Tucuns

A little way past Geriba, this beach is a 15-minute drive from downtown Búzios. Backed by large sand dunes, the wild beauty here is a continuation of a series of coastal beaches that begins at Cabo Frio. Surfers and kite boarders can be observed, along with a sprinkling of *pousadas* nearby.

Praia de Manguinhos

This huge, 2mi/3.2km-long scoop of sand sits on the other side of the peninsula's neck from Geribá. Windsurfers and kite surfers like to congregate on this beach which serves as Búzios' windsurfing club (Búzios Vela Clube) headquarters. The area offers good fishing, and an impromptu fish market often takes place in the early morning. In the 19C, after the abolition of slavery, the secluded coves and bays around Búzios were perfect hideouts for slave traders who continued to trade illegally, using the site as a clandestine landing point for many slaves.

Praia da Tartaruga

Actually comprising two beaches, the smaller one is frequented by fishermen, while the larger stretch is a hang-out for swimmers. Snorkelers also love Tartaruga's nearby reefs. Beach huts sell grilled fish, fresh oysters and drinks.

Praia Azeda/Azedinha

Particularly popular with families because of the shallow water, these twin beaches are two of the most delightful on the peninsula and only a 15-minute walk from Praia dos Ossos. Descend the path off the cobblestoned road, down the granite steps, then along the rocky path, in order to get to Azeda, a compact crescent of sand with good snorkeling. Just past Azeda, along the rocky trail, lies Azedinha ("little Azeda"), an even smaller beach. Morning visits offer shade, and do be aware that there are no facilities, but there are vendors selling drinks and snacks.

Praia de João Fernandes

Of all the beaches on the Peninsula, this one has the greatest concentration of accommodation and restaurants, and some of the best transport connections.

Orla Bardot

©snaptitude/Fotolia.com

However, it does get very crowded, especially at weekends or holidays, so arrive early to enjoy it at its best. Calm, pool-like waters make this beach one of the best for snorkeling *(equipment rental available)*. Beyond a low cliff lies the next beach, **João Fernandinho** (little Fernandes).

Address Book

GETTING THERE AND AROUND

Búzios is approximately three and a half hours from Rio de Janeiro—travelling by car, bus or taxi. Auto Viação 1001 *(www.autoviacao1001.com.br; ℘21 4004 5001)* operates buses every two hours during daylight hours. Consult the website, which has an English option, for full details, including an up-to-date timetable. Most of the *pousadas* in town can arrange transport from Rio, with the advantage that your driver will know where he is going. There are plenty of options for getting around the peninsula; all of the beaches can be reached by taxi, car, bike (not easy though, because some streets are unpaved), even beach buggy. If you prefer to travel by water, choose from fishing boat, glass-bottomed catamaran, schooner *(day passes)*, or water taxi.

DIVING DEEP

Búzios has been described as a living aquarium, thanks to its clear, warm waters—filled with creatures from tiny anchovies and eels to big-game fish like barracuda, giant manta rays,

and sea turtles. Divers can visit key dive spots near the beaches or head to the island of Ancora 6mi/10km and a 30min boat ride from the coast that enjoys average visibility of 39ft/12m. "Baptisms" for novices offer basic theory and an accompanying instructor, and non-divers can normally join trips and just snorkel. Choose from morning or afternoon sessions, or even a night dive. Búzios generally enjoys good year-round diving conditions. *(Casamar Dive Resort, Rua das Pedras 242; ℘22 2623 2441; www.casamar.com.br.)*

COCKTAILS ON THE BEACH

Deck

Alto do Humaitá 10, Pousada Casas Brancas. Open 6pm–1am daily. ℘22 2623 1458. www.casasbrancas.com.br.

If you take a short stroll out of town along Orla Bardot, you will reach this sophisticated joint with a panoramic bar overlooking Búzios' central beach: Praia da Armação. Savor a batida with fresh fruit of the season and contemplate the magical view of the sea in the tropical breeze.

ILHA GRANDE ★★★

Swaths of rare Atlantic forest, crisscrossed by scenic hiking trails cover more than half the surface of the spectacular Costa Verde "Big Island". Transparent green water ebbs and flows on a hundred white sand beaches, while its interior jealously hides crystal clear rivers, waterfalls, and bright blue and green lagoons. Vila do Abraão, the island's "capital", is a tiny village with sand and cobblestoned streets, where fishing boats bob in the bay. No roads anywhere... No cars in sight... Ilha Grande is a true island getaway.

▶ **Orient Yourself:** Ilha Grande is 100mi/161km south of Rio, about 1hr 30min from Paraty (*see p 204*) by powerboat or from Angra dos Reis by ferry. Vila do Abraão is 11 nautical mi/20km from the mainland.

☺ **Don't Miss:** Praia Lopes Mendes, consistently voted as one of the world's nicest beaches. The outstanding views from the top of Pico do Papagalo, which can reach as far as Pedra da Gávea, some 100mi/161km away from the island.

🕐 **Organizing Your Time:** To appreciate the tranquility of the island, spend at least three nights here. Ferries to the island usually leave once a day (*see Address Book*) and the island is quieter during the week.

🧒 **Especially for Kids:** Tales of pirates on a boat trip around the island.

A Bit of History

Checkered Past

Around 100 Indians skilled at hunting and fishing lived peacefully here until the Portuguese arrived in the 16C. French, Dutch, and English pirates followed, hiding in the many coves and ambushing Spanish ships laden with gold from the Spanish colonies. In the 19C, and even after slavery was abolished in Brazil in 1888, traders continued to hide in the area and sell slave labor to the coffee and sugar plantations. Because of its isolation, the island became home to a leper colony before being turned into a prison. Criminals and dissident intellectuals were held here during the military regime in the 1960s. The prison was demolished by order of the state government in 1994, when the island was opened to the public for the first time.

Geography

Island Idyll

There are no large hotels on this beautiful, unspoiled island where building restrictions are stringent. All of the

Angra dos Reis ★★

Portuguese explorers "discovered" Angra in 1502 and today it is an important tourist destination. The stunning natural setting is the major draw; the village sits surrounded by greenery on the magnificent *costa verde* shoreline. Offshore lies 365 secluded islands waiting to be explored, and Angra is not only a popular jumping off point for Ilha Grande, but also for other islands, including Ilha da Gipóia.

Angra's interesting historic sights include the Igreja e Convento de Nossa Senhora do Carmo and the ruins of the 18C Convento de São Bernardino de Sena. The small historic center with its cute *sombrados* is also well worth a visit.

Resorts and hotels in the region organize boat trips to offshore islands. *EcoResort Angra dos Reis: Estrada do Contorno 8413, Praia de Tanguá; ☎0800 703 7272; www. ecoresortangra.com.br. Novo Frade & Golf Resort: Rodovia Rio Santos, BR 101, km 508, Praia do Frade; ☎0800 881 9500; www.hoteldofrade.com.br. Melia Angra: Access by Rodovia Rio Santos, BR 101, km 488; ☎0800 703 3399; www.solmelia.com.br.*

Praia Lopes Mendes

©Ricardo De Mattos/Michelin

island's fragile ecosystem, along with the water that surrounds it, is protected by law. Different kinds of monkeys and tropical birds, including colorful parrots, live in the dense forest, with its banana, almond, and coconut trees. Pico da Pedra D´Água (3,383ft/1031m) and Pico do Papagaio (3,146ft/959m) are the island's main visual landmarks.

Sights

Praia Lopes Mendes★★★

Lopes Mendes is one of the most beautiful beaches in the world—and is regularly voted as such. One of the reasons for this is that no human intervention has occurred here allowing for preservation of its natural state.

Framed by low, rolling hills, a thick carpet of deep green Atlantic forest reaches right to the edge of the 2 mi/3.2km-long crescent of blinding white sand facing the clear waters of the Atlantic Ocean. Consistent surf—the best on the island—attracts boarders (Santo Antônio and Aventureiro are other good surfing beaches). There are no beach bars or even vendors so bring water, although shade is provided by the many leafy almond trees.

Half a mile out to sea is the little island of Jorge Greco, complete with beach and great diving and snorkeling.

According to legend, the tiny island is named after a Greek pirate who once made his home here.

Pico do Papagaio★★

A steep, three-hour slog leads you to the top of "Parrot Peak," which gets its name from its beaklike formation. Those who manage the ascent are rewarded by panoramic **views**★★★ across the island and on clear days even to Pedra da Gávea, 100mi/161km away in Rio. Guides are a must as getting lost is easy to do, and they enhance the visit by pointing out plants and wildlife such as monkeys, squirrels, and even iguanas.

Vila do Abraão

The "capital" of the island is little more than a few streets of simple, prettily painted buildings. This is where the

😊 A Bit of Advice 😊

When exploring the island, take special care not to interfere with your surroundings, paying particular attention to the following rules:

- No fishing within .62mi/1km of the shore.
- No feeding the animals.
- No picking or damaging plants or flowers.
- Do not destroy the vegetation.
- Do not bathe in drinking water reservoirs.
- Do not use soap or shampoo when bathing in the rivers, lakes, and waterfalls.
- Do not light fires.
- Do not camp on the beaches.

Island Life

Of course, if all you want to do is relax, there is nothing to stop you just swinging in a hammock or lying on the beach for your entire stay, but if you really want to enjoy the island, the best thing to do is get active. Snorkeling the clear waters around the reefs and diving the numerous shipwrecks on the ocean floor are unforgettable experiences. Hiking the numerous short, clearly marked trails as well as mountainous treks is particularly pleasant between May and July when the temperature drops and rainfall is minimal. The ambitious (and fit) could even consider trekking around the entire island—the circuit trail takes about a week to complete. Ocean kayaking, in the usually calm waters of the inlets, is a wonderful way to enjoy the scenery, as well as a rewarding way to reach a few deserted beaches. Surf lessons can be booked and boards hired on Lopes Mendes beach, by prior arrangement in Vila do Abraão.

vast majority of visitors arrive and where most of the local population of 3,000 or so have made their home.

The one-time fishing community caters almost exclusively to tourists, although pockets of this industry still remain. Most tourists base themselves here, as Vila do Abraão contains the only real infrastructure on the island.

The main street is called **Rua da Praia** (Beach Street). Around the pier is the one place on Ilha Grande not suitable for swimming due to pollution from the ferries that dock here.

Lazareto

It is a pleasant 20-minute walk from the village of Abraão along a dirt path to the haunting ruins of this old building. Built between 1884 and 1886, the structure originally functioned as a hospital for infectious diseases such as cholera and leprosy brought in by the large numbers of immigrants. The hospital was closed in 1913, and in 1940, it became the Cândido Mendes prison. Behind the ruins lies the well-preserved old aqueduct, built in 1893 to supply water to the island.

Freguesia de Santana

Once the focus for all economic activity on the island, this beach now serves as a popular stop-off with boats as it is the midway point between Vila do Abraão and the Blue Lagoon. Tourists are invited to take a dip in the clear waters and make the short walk to visit Santana's solitary, simple church, built in 1796.

Dois Rios

A river runs to both ends of the stretch of sand here, giving the place its name, "Two Rivers." The beach comes a close

Vila do Abraão

©Photononstop/Tips Images

Address Book

A BIT OF ADVICE

Accommodation (☞ see p 228) is generally simple on the island; don't expect luxury and air-con or even uninterrupted electricity. A big part of the charm of Ilha Grande is living the simple life. Rustic *pousadas* (little inns) are found in the Vila do Abraão, the tiny "capital." Slightly more swish "resort hotels" are situated on outlying beaches but you will be at their mercy for transport as access is only by hotel boat, with prices for drinks and food often unreasonably high. The island also has a number of campsites—although camping is not permitted on the beaches. There are no banks, ATMs, or foreign exchange offices and few establishments take credit cards, so bring enough funds in *reais* (not foreign currency) for the duration of your stay.

GETTING THERE AND AROUND

Boat Trips and Rides

The island is a 1hr 30min ferry ride from Angra dos Reis (Bay of the Kings) or 1hr and 45 minutes from Mangaratiba.

Barcas S/A—Ferry from Angra dos Reis and Mangaratiba to Ilha Grande *(R$6.50 from Angra, R$6.35 from Mangaratiba, R$14 Sat, Sun, and holidays; ✆0800 70 44 113; www.barcas-sa.com.br)*. **Angra dos Reis:** Mon–Fri 3:30pm, return 10am. Sat, Sun, and holidays 1:30pm, return 5:30pm. **Mangaratiba:** daily 8am (also Fri 10pm), return 5:30pm.

You can also hire a private powerboat from **Paraty** to Ilha Grande—the price depends on how many people on the boat, the time of year, the day of the week... (☞*contact the tour operators below for more information)*.

Once here, take your pick from the boat trips on offer, or arrange your own, tailor-made. A variety of boats from fishing tugs to elegant schooners *(buy tickets from agencies or authorized selling points, not from individuals)* leave from Vila do Abraão pier *(ask in the village for full information)*. One highly recommended trip is a return boat ride *(50min each way)* to the stunning **Lopes Mendes beach**. The Vessel drops passengers at Pouso pier, from where it is an hour-long scenic hike to the beach. Otherwise, it is a beautiful three-hour walk from Vila do Abraão. There are also bikes for hire in the village.

Phoenix Turismo – *Rua da Praia 703, Vila da Abrãao. ✆24 3361 5822. www. phoenixturismo.com.br.*
Paraty Tours – *Av. Roberto Silveira 11. ✆24 3371 1327. www.paratytours. com.br.*

These well-established operators run boat trips around the island and to islands in the bay, by schooner and speed boat. They also offers diving for the experienced as well as novices, and night dives. Guided walks to nearby tourist sights or longer trails to beaches and up the main peaks, as well as kayaking, cycling, and mountaineering trips are also on offer. Make sure lifejackets are provided on boats, no matter which company you choose.

CAKE O'CLOCK

Cake Cart

When the boats unload hungry daytrippers at Vila do Abraão every day at about 4pm, a local with a cart of homemade cakes for sale is there to welcome them. Tuck into slices of delicious chocolate, caramel, and apple cake—or whatever the flavor of the day happens to be. The seller normally hangs around for about an hour.

second to Lopes Mendes, but staying on it after 5pm without special permission is forbidden. A little store sells supplies to visitors.

Aventureiro

Because this remote beach is only accessible by motor boat, it is nearly always deserted, apart from the presence of a few local fishermen. The charming half-mile-long expanse has a scattering of large boulders, and although the water is shallow, the waves can get rough. A little wharf allows small boats to dock, and inland lies a church and school for the local fishing community, who sometimes serve meals to visitors in their houses.

PARATY★★★

Framed by the emerald green Serra da Bocaina in the background, pretty little Paraty is a wonderfully preserved colonial town, its cobbled streets lined with 19C houses that are now family-run boutiques, pousadas (little inns), and restaurants. Just a few miles from its historic center, the town gives way to the exuberant vegetation of the Costa Verde, where the mountainous Gold Trail snakes past clear waterfalls. As if that were not enough, the clear turquoise waters of Paraty's huge bay are dotted with spectacular beaches and sprinkled with dozens of desert islands, creating a tropical paradise.

▶ **Orient Yourself:** Paraty is the southern and westernmost city in Rio de Janeiro state. It is located 150mi/241km south of Rio, on the lush corridor called Costa Verde which runs along the state coastline. Its pedestrianized historic center is bordered by the Perequê Açu River and the ocean.

⊛ **Don't Miss:** Take a leisurely walk through Paraty's exceptional historic center, which is listed as a national heritage site. The city is also a gateway to beautiful islands and quiet sand beaches that can be discovered by boat. If you have time, walk part of the legendary Gold Trail or enjoy the unspoiled charm of Trindade, an old fishing village south of Paraty.

🕐 **Organizing Your Time:** Paraty becomes unpleasantly crowded during any holiday, or during major events such as the Carnival or the Paraty International Literary Festival (FLIP).

🄺🄸🄳🅂 **Especially for Kids:** The beaches here are a natural playground for children. Walking the Caminho do Ouro trail, children can learn about the history of Paraty and its use as a port for the Portuguese to send precious gold to Lisbon.

A Bit of History

Mixed Fortunes

Indians were the original inhabitants of this area, naming it "Parati" (as it is still sometimes spelled), which means "white fish." The natives endured the back-breaking work of cutting trails through the thickly forested mountains, and from the 17C, the Portuguese went on to make full use of them. Gold, diamonds, and emeralds from landlocked Minas Gerais were carried on the backs of slaves and mules to Paraty from where they were shipped to Rio de Janeiro. Paraty quickly became one of the wealthiest towns in Brazil until in the 18C an alternative trail to Rio bypassed

Paraty—no cars are allowed in the center of the town

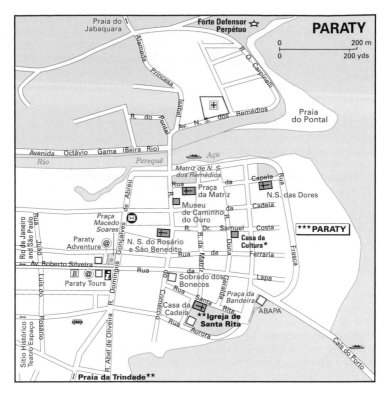

the port. Fortunes did rise again in the mid-19C, when coffee from the nearby plantations was exported to Europe, and luxury goods such as pianos and porcelain were shipped in for the wealthy coffee barons.

But the population shrank from 16,000 in 1851 to just 600 women, children, and the elderly by the end of the 19C—an indication of how much the town had relied on slave labor (outlawed in 1888). In 1966 the town was declared part of the Brazilian Historical Heritage but until the Rio–Santos road was built in the 1970s, the town was largely forgotten—one of the reasons, of course, it remains so beautifully preserved.

Discovering the Islands by Boat

Every day from around noon until the early afternoon, boats leave on half-day trips from Paraty's little pier, near the Santa Rita church (see p 206), on the edge of the historic center. You may choose from sailboats, ramshackle fishing boats, well-equipped purpose-built schooners, or slick speedboats.

Most visitors will want to buy their tickets *(from agencies and pousadas)* in advance. The normal rate per person for a boat trip is R$40 per hour and up to R$50 or even R$80 in high season.

Larger group tours that include lunch can be more like booze cruises, with cocktails and loud music, and little serious attention to the beautiful surroundings. Smaller tailor-made tours are generally much more enjoyable—although much more expensive too.

It is worth paying more to take a trip on a faster boat because this is the only means to get out to the outlying islands and back in a day. Check to see if guides speak English and pay attention to onboard safety in all cases.

Islands in the Bay

Your captain, or tour guide, will usually make suggestions for stops depending on his local knowledge, the weather, and even the time of day. Unfortunately for

Spirit of Paraty

By the end of the 18C sugar and cachaça production had become an important part of Paraty's economy. At one time, there were several hundred sugar plantations and distilleries and the town was producing such a high quality brew that the name Paraty became synonymous with cachaça. The town still exports bottles of its famous firewater to the rest of the country.

tourists, many of the islands are private so it is illegal to land on them.

Most operators stop at **Ilha Comprida** for snorkeling, while **Ilha dos Meros** is a hotspot for diving. Farther outlying beaches require a speedboat to be reached. **Praia Grande de Cajaíba** is a beautiful, pristine beach with nearby waterfalls to visit.

Mamanguá *(50min by boat from Paraty)* is the only fiord in Brazil, with a spectacular 5mi/8km-long entrance, bordered by mangroves and Atlantic rain forest, forming the Mamanguá Ecological Reserve.

Praia de Paraty-Mirim, which is 11mi/18km east of Paraty by dirt road, is a tranquil beach with a few *barracas* (foodstalls), the ruins of a few houses, and the delightfully simple Nossa Senhora da Conceição Chapel, built in 1720 and partially restored.

Schedule time for a seafood lunch at one of the island restaurants. Located on **Ilha do Algodão**, Restaurante do

Pier and Igreja de Santa Rita
Y. Kanazawa/Michelin

Hiltinho (◷ *open Fri–Sun and holidays 11am–5pm;* ✆*24 3371 1488*) is an upmarket seafood restaurant. Equally enchanting and specializing in grilled seafood is Eh Lahô (◷ *open noon–6pm;* ✆*24 3371 2253*) on the tiny island of **Catimbau**—little more than a bundle of rocks in the ocean.

Sights

Igreja de Santa Rita★★

Largo Rosário, corner of Rua Samual Costa and Rua do Comércio. ◷*Open Wed–Sun 10am–noon, 2pm–5pm.*
The church's tower rising above the town, with the blue waters of the bay in the foreground, is the perennial picture-postcard image of Paraty. Built in 1722, Santa Rita was one of Paraty's churches used by freed slaves. Despite its elegant simplicity, this is a Baroque church, with fine wood carvings on the doors and side altars. At the back of the church, the small **Museu de Arte Sacra** presents a collection of religious artefacts.

Casa da Cultura★

Rua Dona Geralda 177. ◷*Open Wed–Mon 10am–6:30pm.* ◈*R$5.* ✆*24 3371 2325. www.casadaculturaparaty. org.br.*
Located in Paraty's historic center, the "House of Culture" sits within a well-preserved house built in 1754. A room dedicated to indigenous peoples showcases various artefacts and works of art. Made of colored sawdust and flowers, a striking ceremonial floor covering has been protected by glass to accommodate foot traffic

Upstairs, an interactive permanent exhibition, with computer terminals offers programs on Paraty's history. As a touching tribute to the city's cultural heritage, an entire wall has been covered with video monitors showing interviews with locals of all backgrounds and ages *(English and Portuguese versions available)*. Everyday objects, rescued from houses and workplaces, illustrate their stories. The Casa da Cultura also presents temporary exhibitions, and has a pleasant cafe as well as a small shop selling local souvenirs and crafts.

Forte Defensor Perpétuo

The only remaining fort in Paraty today is reached by a 15-minute walk from the town center. Built in 1703, the fort was renovated and extended in 1793. In 1822, the site was renamed Fort of the Perpetual Defender in honor of Dom Pedro who became emperor in that year. Featuring eight guns and sweeping views of Paraty Bay, it boasts a small but interesting **Museu de Artes e Tradições Populares** (*open Wed–Sun 9am–noon and 2pm–5pm*) that showcases local arts and crafts.

Excursions

Caminho do Ouro★★

The departure point is the Centro de Informações Turísticas Caminho do Ouro on the Paraty–Cunha road (9km from the center of Paraty). ⊷R$20. Tour agencies in town can arrange English language tours, including lunch and transport to and from the departure point.

Roughly paved in the 18C, the **Gold Trail** was part of the gold and diamond export route from Minas Gerais to Paraty. Almost 2km of the 746mi/1,200km-long cobbled pathway has been cleared and opened to visitors, so that they may follow it on foot *(approx 1hr)*. Set within the scenic **Parque Nacional da Serra da Bocaina**, the trail is a wonderful opportunity to discover the fauna and flora of the Mata Atlântica. You will pass waterfalls and ponds to cool off in along the way. Self-guided maps lead for a mile to the nearest farm, where there is a restaurant and wonderful views of Paraty and the surrounding countryside.

Trindade★★

Make the effort to venture to this former hippy enclave *(16mi/26km south of Paraty)*. Due to its growing popularity, local fishermen have turned their simple houses into stores, bars, and restaurants. The dirt road has now been paved, but Trindade continues to exude its unspoiled charm.

PETRÓPOLIS★★

tic setting of the hills of Serra dos Órgãos, "Pedro's City"
home for the imperial family in their quest to escape the
Janeiro. An air of aristocratic elegance permeates the old
...y. The former summer palace, now an outstanding museum, and the
charming historic houses and mansions which grace some of Petrópolis' lovely
tree-lined streets attract many visitors who also enjoy the European flavor of
the city's restaurants, and its surprisingly cool climate.

- ▌ **Information:** www.petropolis.rj.gov.br.
- ▶ **Orient Yourself:** Petrópolis is 44mi/71km north of Rio, and 2,625ft/800m above. It is located in the Serra dos Órgãos (inland part of the larger Serra do Mar coastal mountain range), part of the Mata Atlântica Biosphere Reserve.
- ☺ **Don't Miss:** The impressive Crown Jewels at the Imperial Palace, or the tomb of Dom Pedro II at the San Pedro de Alcantara Cathedral.
- ⏲ **Organizing Your Time:** A day-trip is feasible, but may feel rushed. Consider a relaxing overnight stay in one of the city's charming *pousadas* (☙*see p 230*).
- **Kids** **Especially for Kids:** Donning comical felt slippers to explore the Imperial Palace. (Although it may be tempting, remind the kids they must not slide with them on the beautiful Brazilian hardwood flooring!)

A Bit of History

Hillside Honeypot

On his way to to inspect the mines of Minas Gerais in 1830, Dom Pedro I purchased land here after becoming enchanted by its undeveloped beauty. His son went on to found Petrópolis in 1843, along with Teresópolis 30mi/48km away, named in honor of Empress Teresa Cristina. As an alternative to slave labor, Dom Pedro II encouraged immigration and the population quickly swelled with Germans, Swiss, and Austrians, attracted by the cool climate. As the summer residence of the Imperial family, the city did not only attract nobles, but also the wealthy and the intellectual elite. Even after the Republic was declared and the royal family exiled in 1889, Petrópolis

was not forgotten. It served as state capital from 1894 to 1903. Around 300,000 people live in Petrópolis today.

Historic Houses

Grand summer residences that once accommodated the barons, dukes, industrialists, and politicians that made up Dom Pedro II's court are scattered around the city. Adopting European architectural traditions—first the Neo-classical style of the Empire, followed by Eclecticism from the end of the 19C—most of these houses are still privately-owned and can only be seen from the outside.

Avenida Koeller, the lovely tree-lined avenue named after the architect who designed Petrópolis' city plan and the Imperial Palace, boasts the greatest

---

Palácio Quitandinha

Located on the outskirts of Petrópolis, this former "palace" was built in 1944 as the largest casino-hotel in South America, with enough space for a staggering 10,000 guests. While its exterior is Norman in style, the interior is pure Hollywood, with hundreds of marble bathrooms, monumental chandeliers, an indoor pool as well as indoor tennis and soccer courts, and even a theater with three revolving stages. The dome of the hotel's great hall is said to be one of the largest in the world, its diameter being comparable with St Peter's basilica in Rome. Gambling was banned in 1946, the casino was closed and part of it was sold as apartments.

GETTING THERE AND AROUND

Petropólis is a couple of hours from Rio by either bus, car or taxi *(sit on the left for the best views on your way there)*. Even though the historic district features tree-lined avenues, canals crossed by pretty bridges, and leafy squares, it can be congested and not too pleasant for extensive walking. Instead consider a horse-drawn carriage ride starting in front of the palace *(choose from one of three circuits 20min–1hr; R$20–R$50; daily 8am–5pm; see Petrópolis website for more detail)*.

concentration of historic stately mansions. The most impressive, at number 255, is **Palácio Rio Negro**. Bought from a coffee baron, the "palace" became the official summer residence of Brazilian presidents, including Getúlio Vargas. Koeller Avenue's other highlights include number 42 *(opposite the cathedral)*, the **Casa da Princesa Isabel**, former home of Dom Pedro II's daughter and her husband, Count d'Eu; number 260, **Palácio Sérgio Fadel**, current city hall; number 376, **Solar Dom Afonso**, which houses the Solar Empire Hotel; and across the river, enchanting Vila Itararé.

Other buildings of note can be found in Petrópolis. **Casa de Stefan Zweig** *(Rua Gonçalves Dias 34)* is the house where the celebrated Austrian writer committed suicide in 1942. Surrounded by lovely gardens, **Casa do Barão de Mauá** *(Praça da Confluência 3)* belonged to Irineu Evangelista de Sousa, Baron of Mauá, the man responsible for Brazil's first railroad, which was built between Petrópolis and Rio de Janeiro in 1854.

Museu Imperial★★★

Rua da Imperatriz 220. ⏱*Open Tue–Sun 11am–6pm.* ⌷*R$8.* ✕ ✆*24 2237 8000. www.museuimperial.gov.br.*
The pink, Neo-classical **Palácio Imperial de Petrópolis** houses the most visited museum in Brazil. This museum was inaugurated in 1943, the first centennial of the founding of the city of Petrópolis. Elegant yet simple, it appears to be designed more in the style of a grand country house than a palace and it leaves the visitor with a strong impression of a warm family life.

🧒 On passing through the entrance decorated with Ionian and Corinthian columns, visitors are asked to put felt slippers on over their shoes to pro-

tect the highly polished floors. Brazilian hardwood flooring and furniture crafted from mahogany, rosewood, and jacaranda is found throughout, although bear in mind that not all the furniture and works of art are original to the palace.

Sala de Música

Recitals were regularly held in the Music Room, which contains a noteworthy **gilded harp** by Pleyel Wolff, a fine **piano**, crafted in England by Broadwood, and a **spinet** made by a master craftsman in Lisbon. The ceiling is fittingly decorated with musical instruments as well as heraldic dragons.

Sala de Visitas da Imperatriz

In her Visiting Room, Empress Teresa Christina would sit embroidering, as she entertained guests. Diminutive sofas and chairs, reflecting the short stature of the empress, are made of fine rosewood and upholstered with a crown and "T" for Teresa.

Gabinete de Dom Pedro II

Dom Pedro II spent much of his time in this study, considered his favorite place.

Museu Imperial

Y. Kanazawa/Michelin

Imperial crown of Dom Pedro II

Museu Imperial

Crown Jewels

Dom Pedro II's beautifully crafted gold crown is encrusted with 639 diamonds and 77 pearls. The emperor wore it for his coronation in 1841, when he was just 15 years old.

One of the world's first telephones still sits on his desk, brought back from a meeting in 1876 with its inventor Alexander Graham Bell in Philadelphia.

Sala Dourada

In addition to the fine gilt furniture in the "Gold Room," two oil paintings depict important political moments in the life of Dom Pedro II. One, by painter **René François Moreaux**, shows the coronation in 1841; the other, by **Pedro Américo** in 1872, illustrates the opening of the General Assembly, with Dom Pedro II sporting the royal costume, crown, and scepter. The actual coronation clothes are on display opposite the painting of Dom Pedro II, who is depicted wearing them.

Sala de Estado

The once state room is now a reconstruction of the throne room in the São Cristóvão Palace (see p 120). Note the sévres porcelain urns on either side of the majestic throne, which were gifts from the French president to the Brazilian emperor.

Palace Grounds

There was no kitchen in the palace proper—food was cooked in one of the out buildings and brought into the stucco-decorated dining room in metal-lined boxes heated with charcoal. Don't miss the carriage collection housed in the former slave and servant quarters (which doubled as a storeroom) behind the palace. Here, a gold carriage built in London in 1837 and used by Dom Pedro II on special occasions, is extravagantly decorated with the imperial coat of arms, gold-embroidered upholstery, and finely painted panels. The palace gardens, designed by famous botanist Jean Baptiste Binot under the supervision of the emperor, feature imperial palms, tropical plants and trees, fountains, and Greek statues.

Additional Sights

Catedral de São Pedro de Alcântara★★

Rua São Pedro de Alcântara 60.
⊙*Open Mon–Sat 8am–noon; Tue–Sat 2pm–6pm; Sun 8am–1pm, 3pm–6pm.* ✆ *24 2242 4300.*
The 230ft/70m-high tower of the Neo-gothic cathedral, dedicated to San Pedro de Alcantara, is one of Petrópolis visual landmarks. The construction of the cathedral, inspired by the cathedrals of northern France, began in 1884, but the tower, with its huge bronze bells from Germany, is a more recent addition. Made of stone and granite, the building is divided into three naves with two side chapels. Much of the interior is Carrara marble. Note the impressive organ, designed and built in Rio de Janeiro in 1937 by **Guilherme Berner**, pioneer of Brazil's organ industry. To the right of the entrance, light floods in through the stained-glass windows of a peaceful **chapel** which houses the tombs of Dom Pedro II, Dona Teresa Cristiana, Princesa Isabel, and the Count d'Eu.

Casa de Santos Dumont★

Rua do Encanto 22. ⊙*Open Tue–Sun 9:30am–5pm.* ☞*R$5 with guided tour only.* ✆ *24 2247 5222.*
The Brazilian inventor **Santos Dumont** (1873–1932) fondly called his tiny summer house "A Encantada"—the Enchanted One. Built in the style of an alpine chalet, it is imbued with the quirky personality of its creator.

A life-long bachelor, Dumont created a compact home with no kitchen, an alcohol-powered hot shower, and a desk that was transformed into a bed at night. The observatory, positioned on the roof of the house, is another highlight, not to mention the quirky stairs leading to the house. Rumor has it that these stairs were designed so that visitors would always climb them using their right foot first for good luck.

Known as the father of aviation, Dumont created the first plane to fly without assistance (the Wright brothers made use of a catapult) as well as the first wristwatch (Cartier still produces a timeless Santos-Dumont model in his honor). Depressed by the increasing use of his "babies" in aerial warfare, Dumont took his own life in 1932.

Catedral de São Pedro de Alcântara

Y. Kanazawa/Michelin

Palácio de Cristal★

Rua Alfredo Pachá (no number).
◷Open Wed–Sun 9am–6:30pm.
⊷Free Admission. ℘24 2247 3721.
Inspired by London's Crystal Palace, this splendid steel and glass construction was built in France and inaugurated in 1884 to be used for special events. During Easter 1888, Princesa Isabela, accompanied by her children, presided over a manumission ceremony. The elegant building now stands empty, except for occasional cultural events. A small gift store and tourist office sit near the entrance to the gardens.

Casa da Avenida Ipiranga

Rua Ipiranga 716. ◷Open Thu–Tue noon–6pm. ⊷R$6, includes guided tour. ✕℘24 2231 5711.
This Victorian-style house (1884) now serves as a cultural center. Its original interior with French chandeliers, Carrara marble fireplaces, Belgian crystal mirrors, and 300 paintings has been beautifully preserved.

A lively program of events takes place here, with classical music concerts, plays, and exhibitions.

Auguste Glaziou, the botanist and landscaper responsible for among other things, Quinta da Boa Vista (*&see p 121*), designed the gardens. The adjoining barn is home to the Bordeaux Restaurant (*&see p 247*).

Centro de Cultura Raul de Leoni

Praça Visconde de Mauá 305. ◷Open Mon–Sat 1pm–7pm. ℘24 2247 3747.
This other cultural center is named in honor of Raul de Leoni, poet and former president of the Petrópolis Academy of Letters. It hosts temporary art and sculpture exhibitions, painting and music courses, and cultural activities relating to theater and arts, and also contains the Petrópolis City Library (*◷open Mon–Fri 8am–6:30pm, Sat 8am–noon*).

ENTERTAINMENT
Armazém 646

Rua Visconde de Itaboraí 646. Open daily 8am–2am. ℘24 2243 1001.
www.armazem646.com.br.
This traditional bar, located in one of the oldest parts of town, is a friendly place which serves snacks and meals. Live music take place on Friday and Saturday evenings from 9pm.

OUTLET SHOPPING
Rua Teresa

Rua Teresa. Open Mon 2pm–6pm, Tue–Sat 9am–6pm, Sun 10am–5pm.
Some Brazilians travel to Petrópolis just to visit this shopping street, which is lined with stores selling clothes and fashion accessories. These locally produced goods are great value for money.

COFFEE VALLEY★

Brazil's coffee boom of the 19C made this fertile valley of paramount economic importance to the state of Rio de Janeiro. Today, many of the magnificent *fazendas* (coffee farms) of the golden era have been restored to their former glory; some are still working farms, some offer leisure activities such as horseback riding or hiking, and some are hotel retreats set deep in the lush green countryside.

▷ **Orient Yourself:** The Rio Paraíba Valley (otherwise known as "Coffee Valley") is a few hours drive inland on the Via Dutra, the main Rio–São Paulo road.

🕒 **Organizing Your Time:** An overnight stay in a *fazenda* is recommended.

A Bit of History

Coffee served as the basis of the economy both for the Empire and the Old Republic (1889–1930). The number of coffee plantations and of slaves to cultivate them indicated a person's wealth—powerful families owned countless farms. Farms were usually located close to a stream and were organized around a main square used for coffee drying. There was a main house (where business was conducted), silos (for storage), the mill (where sugar and corn were processed), and the slave quarters. Dams, chapels and imperial palm trees were also indications of the owner's prestige.

Life on a coffee farm

Work on the coffee farm was on an annual cycle basis. Manual labor included clearing the natural habitat, and harvesting, drying, stocking and processing the grain. A slaves' day began with prayers in the square, then they worked from before dawn until nightfall, after which they bagged coffee grains for shipment. Slaves were only allowed limited leisure hours, particularly Sundays and holidays. The plantation owner's family remained in the main house where the women supervised the domestic chores and the men managed the farm activities or received the merchants. Parties and social gatherings (weddings, christenings and evenings of music) seldom interrupted the farm's routine.

Sights

Barra do Piraí, Valença, Rio das Flores and Vassouras are good areas to use a base to visit the fazendas. Some fazendas offer meals and accommodation and others can be visited with the owner's permission.

Barra do Piraí

The city of Barra do Piraí used to be a railroad junction to Minas Gerais, São Paulo, and Rio de Janeiro, and an important coffee shipping center. After the decline of coffee production the city became a commercial and industrial center.

Fazenda Ponte Alta

Av. Silas Pereira da Mota, 880, Parque Santana. 🚌*Guided tour R$59 (one day incl. lunch). Accommodation R$297.* 📞*24 2443 5159/2443 5005. www.pontealta.com.br* Much of the original 19C architecture and furnishing of this picturesque fazenda is intact. A small museum on slavery is also on site.

Valença

In the 19C this city had the largest number of slaves in the state. Valença was prosperous and had a theater, a school, and a hospital. The Igreja Matriz de Nossa Senhora da Glória, and some houses on Praça XV and Visconde do Rio Preto squares survive from the golden era.

Fazenda Veneza

Estrada Veneza, Valença. 📞*24 2452 2235. Grounds only.* The main house has Neo-classical decorative characteristics on its facade. The coffee square and the mill, with its water wheel, are preserved.

Fazenda Florença★

Estrada da Cachoeira 1560. ⌂Accommodation R$870 (weekend); R$1,600 (five nights Mon–Fri). ℘24 2438 01 24.
In spite of its simple architectural style, the main house shows Neo-classical detail in the original porch with carved wood columns and a pediment at each end. Restored some years ago, the house contains antique furnishings and a quaint chapel. Accommodation is in a colonial-style building, and the main house can be visited by appointment.

Fazenda Santa Rosa

Rod. Valença, Rio das Flores (RJ-145), km 82. ℘24 2453 0144. Grounds only.
The small main house is simple in its architecture style. The old coffee square and the processing facilities are well preserved. At present, the sugar mill, water wheel and a *still* are in operation and open to visitors. The farm produces the famous Santa Rosa spirits.

Fazenda Paraíso★

Estrada Rio das Flores, Tres Ilhas, Km 9, Paraibuna. ⌂R$30 (snack incl.). ℘24 2458 0093. Visits must be arranged in advance.
This two-story Neo-classic mansion was one of the most sophisticated of the 19C and the first place in Brazil to use gas lighting. In the lounge a 10m-long panel painted by José Maria Villaronga shows Rio de Janeiro in 1860. Nearby, the silos, the mill and the old coffee square are well preserved.

Fazenda Santa Mônica

Embrapa-Rua Barão de Santa Mônica. Barão de Juparanã. ℘24 2453 1888. Visits must be arranged in advance.
Easily recognized by its imperial palm trees and located close to the Paraíba do Sul riverbanks, this early-19C house is a wide and impressive two-story building with 1m-thick walls. The farm received the Emperor Dom Pedro II as a guest on several occasions.

Vassouras

The city of Vassouras originated as a overnight stop between Minas Gerais and Rio de Janeiro. Despite the decline of its coffee output, Vassouras maintains

GETTING THERE

For information about visiting the Coffee Valley and its fazendas contact **Preservale**, an organization created in 1994 to promote and preserve the cultural heritage of this area (℘24 2453 5116/21 8118 0007; www.preservale.com.br; soniamlucas@preservale.com.br).

some interesting architectural and historical monuments. The houses and street layout, church, fountain, cemetery and train station all merit a look.

Museu da Hera★

Rua Dr. Fernandes Júnior 160, Vassouras (300m from Praça Barão de Campo Belo, downtown). ◷Open Wed–Mon, 11am–5pm. ℘02 4471 2144/4471 2342.
This ivy-covered museum surrounded by imperial palm trees sports an unpretentious facade. A peek inside reveals Neo-classic architecture in the living room, salons, and hallway. Note the imported original wallpaper, gold framed mirrors, crystal chandeliers, candlesticks and grand piano.

Fazenda Santa Eufrásia

Estrada BR-393 km 42, Vassouras. ℘24 2471 1065/24 9994 9494. fazstaeufrasia@hotmail.com. Visits must be arranged in advance.
Surrounded by trees, the main house is one of the oldest in the region. This simple farm has conserved some of its 19C furniture and old farm vehicles.

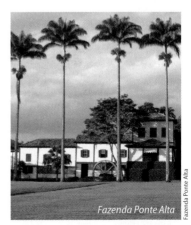

Fazenda Ponte Alta

Fazenda Ponte Alta

Maracanã Stadium
TurisRio

WHERE TO STAY

Roughly 1.56 million foreign visitors arrive every year in Rio for pleasure, business or both—and that doesn't count domestic visitors. Though there are 20,000 hotel rooms available in the city, you'll need to book well ahead to find the best room in your chosen neighborhood if you're visiting for Carnival, New Year's Eve, or during a large business convention.

The properties described in this section have been chosen for their ambience, comfort, location and general high standard relative to the respective budget. They are organized according to geographical areas in the guide and each of these is broken down into neighborhoods. Where areas are not included, it's because there are either no hotels or there are better ones in adjacent communities. Prices reflect the cost of a double room in the high season, outside of Carnival or New Year.

$	Under R$100		$$$$	R$300–R$400
$$	R$100–R$200		$$$$$	Above R$400
$$$	R$200–R$300			

Choosing a District

The cost of staying in Rio de Janeiro reflects its status as an international city and a coveted tourist destination. Considered by Brazilians as the country's playground, it's popular for conventions so participants can relax after work. Consequently, hotels fill quickly and room prices inflate. However there are deals to be had, and if like Brazilians, you can use the *jeito* (a knack for unconventional solutions) and negotiate with charm, you are sure to find something you can afford. As with any big city one needs to pick a safe neighborhood and one that suits your chosen itinerary. The **south zone beaches** (*see p 220*) are considered a safe part of town, and are the most popular with tourists. Busy **Copacabana** has the largest number of hotels, where all price ranges and standards of accommodation are available. It is well-placed for the beach, within walking distance to pricier Ipanema, and served by the Metrô for downtown historical sights. Claiming fewer hotels but a great selection of bars and restaurants, **Ipanema** and **Leblon** are sophisticated and lively neighborhoods—and of course, their prices reflect this. The **historic center** (*see p 218*) is handy for visiting both the historic

sights and Lapa's samba clubs, but it is farther from the beaches and one is not as safe walking around alone at night. The center is deserted on weekends and very busy during the week. **Flamengo** (*see p 219*) is a good compromise, the Metrô runs from here to Copacabana, and the central historic sights are nearby. Reasonably priced hotels are here for those with a lower budget.

In the hills above Rio, bohemian **Santa Teresa** (*see p 218*) offers bars, restaurants, shops, and galleries. Popular with tourists, although nighttime wandering is not recommended. **Gávea** and **Jardim Botânico** in the Lake Area (*see p 225*) are largely residential areas, but don't be put off—the pousadas in Gávea are surrounded by greenery, offer great views, and are only a short bus or cab ride to the beach.

Outside of the city (*see Excursions p 227*), some wonderful mountain and beachside inns wait to be discovered.

Seasonal Rates

Rio's busiest season begins roughly a week before Christmas and goes until the end of March, after Carnival. The period around New Year's Eve and the week of Carnival see prices elevated,

Swimming pool at night, Copacabana Palace

©Alessandro Batistessa/Orient-Express Hotels (UK)

and hotels demand a minimum stay for premium rates during these times. The rest of the year is low season, but be aware of the Brazilian holidays at Easter, in July, and the bank holiday weekends (🕮 *see p 40*), when it can be harder to find a room. In May, June, and August to November, prices drop and bargains are easy to find. Winter can be a great time to visit as temperatures rarely drop below 18ºC.

Discounts

Room rates are subject to a minefield of variables in Rio. Higher-end, larger establishments with more rooms tend to offer cheaper deals according to occupancy, so if they're only half-full you might be able to negotiate a cheaper price on their website or by phoning in advance. Some offer 10 percent if you book by email; others offer discounts for rooms with no view. Neighborhoods affording an ocean view, or anywhere with a view of Sugar Loaf or Christ the Redeemer spell higher prices. The lower end of the market is more likely to offer a discount (around 10 percent or more) if you pay in cash. They will also often charge a sliding scale that works out cheaper per person the more people that stay in a room. However, these establishments might also charge more for rooms with air-conditioning—this should be made clear when you check in.

Hotels that cater to the business market, especially in Flamengo, Centro and Botafogo, frequently offer cheap weekend rates and are less likely to raise their prices during Carnival and New Year. Almost all hotels will offer lower rates for longer stays.

Apartments

Although serviced apartments exist the world over, they are especially plentiful in Rio de Janeiro thanks to the domestic business market, which requires longer stays and self-catering facilities. Apartments are also ideal for those on holiday who want to experience the Carioca lifestyle. Many *apart-hotéls* require a minimum stay of three months, but **Mercure** (www.mercure.com) and **Promenade** (www.promenade.com.br) also offer short stays. **Rio Bay Housing** (www.riobay housing.com) comes highly recommended and has a selection of tastefully decorated options located on or a few minutes' walk from the south zone beaches. Apartment rates generally hover at the level of a 3- to 4-star hotel, but for this you get a suite that includes a living room, a kitchenette, and one or two bedrooms.

217

Address Book

HISTORIC CENTER AND SURROUNDS

CENTRO

$$$

Windsor Guanabara Palace Hotel – Av. Presidente Vargas 392, Centro. 📞21 2195 6000. www.windsorhoteis. com. 531 rooms. The biggest hotel in downtown Rio, situated along one of the busiest avenues of the city, Guanabara Palace caters toward the high-end business market with 36 meeting rooms. Of the four room categories, the most exclusive are the 47sq-meter suites: mini-apartments complete with private saunas. The rooftop pool overlooks the spires of Candelaria church's and Guanabara Bay at one end, and Corcovado and Christ the Redeemer at the other.

$$

Windsor Asturias Hotel – Rua Senador Dantas 14, Centro. 📞21 2195 1500. www.windsorhoteis.com. 166 rooms. Considered to be the "economical" option of the Windsor Hotels brand, this is still a well-located and very pleasant option for a city-center stay. All rooms feature broadband access, central air-con, cable TV, safe and radio, and 24 hour room service. You can take in the magnificent vista of the city, Guanabara Bay and Lapa's arches from the pool, fitness room and bar on the 22nd-floor rooftop terrace .

$$

Hotel OK – Rua Senador Dantas 24, Centro. 📞21 3479 4500. www.hotelok. com.br. 156 rooms. Built in 1949 to impress visitors to the 1950 World Cup in Brazil, the hotel lobby resembles a 1940s movie set. The 18 floors surround an open gallery of stucco balconies, which are guaranteed to challenge those with vertigo. The rooms were renovated recently.

LAPA

$$

Arcos Rio Palace Hotel – Av. Mem de Sá, Lapa. 📞21 2242 8116. www. arcosriopalacehotel.com.br. 130 rooms. Perfectly located for Samba-bar crawls in Lapa, the Arcos Rio Palace claims clean, modern rooms including air-conditioning, cable TV and a safe. A tiny pool offers an oasis, which makes it easy to escape the city's heat.

THE HILLS

SANTA TERESA

$$$$$

Hotel Santa Teresa – Rua Almirante Alexandrino 66, Santa Teresa. 📞21 2222 2755. www.santateresahotel.com. 44 rooms. Built in 1855, the Santa Teresa Hotel recently reopened following a three-year renovation. The rooms and common areas are decorated with a number of contemporary Brazilian artworks. The effect is a simple elegance, with an ethnic touch. The hotel has treatment rooms, **Le Spa**, a bar called **Bar dos Descasados** (a reference to the nickname given to the hotel that once stood here) and one of the best French cuisine restaurants in the city, **Térèze**.

Mama Ruisa – Rua Santa Cristina 132, Santa Teresa. 📞21 2242 1281. www. mamaruisa.com. 7 rooms. Step back in time to 1871 in this unique house where the Brazilian wooden floors are polished to perfection, reflecting an elegant and eclectic mix of carefully chosen furniture and art. Just minutes away from the center of Santa Teresa, the hotel boasts a pleasant garden and a refreshing pool. Breakfast is served on a terrace facing out toward Guanabara Bay.

Casa Amarelo – Rua Joaquim Murtinho 569, Santa Teresa. 📞21 2242 9840. www. casa-amarelo.com. 5 rooms. A taxi to

Swimming pool, Windsor Asturias

Windsor Hoteis

and from the hotel is recommended. The Yellow House is discreetly hidden on a quiet hillside. Enter the lovingly restored 1904 home using the original tunnel and lift, where *Azulejos* (blue and white tiles) and a stained-glass Maltese Cross attest that the first owners were Portuguese. Rates include complimentary non-alcoholic drinks should you choose to lounge by the pool. Let go with a Samba dance class.

Rio 180 – *Rua Dr.Júlio Otoni 254, Santa Teresa. ℰ21 2205 1247. www. rio180hotel.com. 8 suites.* A little off the beaten track from the center of Santa Teresa, Rio 180 is worth the trip just for the view. There is no name on the huge white wall in front, but once you find this new hotel, you can choose between eight suites among three confidently named categories; "Cosy," "Very Chic" and "Oh La La!." As you dig into the tropical breakfast or sip an evening caipirinha, you can soak up the staggering panorama that stretches 180 degrees from hills and forests, across downtown's skyscrapers to Sugar Loaf and Guanabara Bay, then to Niterói and the mountains beyond.

$$$$

Solar de Santa – *Ladeira do Meireles 32, Santa Teresa. ℰ21 2221 2117. www. solardesanta.com. 5 rooms.* Surrounded by tropical gardens, this boutique property is a tranquil TV-free oasis just minutes from the heart of Santa Teresa. Sit on the spacious veranda and gaze out at the gardens against a background of chirping birds and crickets. Or laze by the pool with its spectacular Sugar Loaf backdrop. The house is also available to rent as a villa with optional butler service and yoga classes.

$$

Villa Laurinda – *Rua Laurinda Santos Lobo 98, Santa Teresa. ℰ21 2507 2216. www.villalaurinda.com. 6 rooms.* Set on a quiet side street, this 1888 house is named after one of Rio's best-known early 20C art patron and collector. Rooms are on the small side, but the high ceilings and garden and pool views compensate for the size. The basement is a workshop for the artist-owners.

Pousada or Hotel?

Brazil offers accommodation in both pousadas and hotels. The difference between the two can be defined by the style of the accommodation and the service. Usually pousadas have fewer rooms that might be individually decorated. Generally located outside of major cities, pousadas are sometimes family-owned and run, and they always offer a warm welcome, less standardization, and a high level of service. Some offer a similar décor and "feel" to a boutique hotel.

Pousada Pitanga – *Rua Laurinda Santos Lobo 136, Santa Teresa. ℰ21 2224 0044. www.pousadapitanga. com.br. 5 rooms.* This stylish, intimate B&B claims a peaceful setting, yet is situated close to the boho neighbor-hood's bars and restaurants. The guest-room decor is inspired by Brazilian fruit; in one room the accessories and colors are purple for açaí. The lodging takes its name from the pitanga fruit trees that grow in its garden, where there is also a small pool.

SOUTH ZONE BESIDE THE BAY

FLAMENGO

$$$

Hotel Novo Mundo – *Praia do Flamengo 20, Flamengo. ℰ21 2105 7000. www.hotelnovomundo-rio. com.br. 231 rooms.* Situated on Praia do Flamengo, this grand hotel was originally constructed for Brazil's 1950 World Cup. The hotel faces Flamengo

Villa Laurinda

Hotel Paysandú

Hotel Paysandú

Park and Sugar Loaf Mountain; to one side, it peers out on the former Catete Palace, now the Museum of the Republic. The complicated structure of room rates depends on which floor of the twelve you choose, and whether you're willing to pay for a Sugar Loaf view. Both non-smoking and non-allergic rooms are available.

$$$

Hotel Florida – *Rua Ferreira Viana 69, Flamengo. ☎21 2195 6800. www. windsorhoteis.com.br. 312 rooms.* A stone's throw from Sugar Loaf, walking distance to Flamengo park and beach, and five minutes from the downtown sights, Hotel Florida makes a good base for exploring the city. Enjoy a drink in the evening at

Cama e Café

Experience the real deal by staying with a local using this B&B network. **Cama e Café** will find you a room in the house of a local resident who lives, for example, in the charming historic neighborhood of Santa Teresa. (*We recommend that you check with TURISRIO that the residence is registered and recognized by the authorities.*) You can discover romance in the neighborhood's landmark fairytale gothic castle, where the owner, an IT consulatant, rents out the top tower. (*Cama e Café, Rua Laurinda Santos Lobo 124, Santa Teresa. ☎21 2225 4366. www. camaecafe.com.br.*)

the rooftop pool bar, then drift off to sleep in your sound-proof quarters. Weekend rates are less expensive, because it is popular with business travelers during the week.

Hotel Paysandú – *Rua Paissandú 23, Flamengo. ☎21 2558 7270. www. paysanduhotel.com.br. 75 rooms.* From the elegant Imperial palm-lined side street to the Hollywood-style 1940s decor, this hotel is a gem. Another 1950s World Cup structure, this one actually housed the Uruguay team during the games, and later the Brazilian team for their 1958 Champions city parade. Breakfast in the delightful restaurant is like stepping out with Fred and Ginger in the 1933 film Flying Down to Rio.

BOTAFOGO

$$$$

Caesar Business Botafogo – *Rua da Passagem 39, Botafogo. ☎21 2131 1212. www.caesarbusiness.com.br. 110 rooms.* Close to Botafogo Praia Shopping, where there are cinemas, shops and restaurants, this place boasts large, clean and bright rooms, each with its own balcony. The hotel appeals to business travelers for its location, also room rates don't skyrocket during Carnival.

$$$

Mercure Apartments Rio de Janeiro Botafogo – *Rua Sorocaba 305, Botafogo. ☎21 2266 9200. www. mercure.com. 64 apartments. Breakfast not included.* Tucked away in the heart of Botafogo, this apartment hotel doesn't charge for parking or Wi-Fi access. There is a large, well-stocked supermarket across the road. Each apartment has a balcony; the best views take in Christ the Redeemer. The hotel also offers a fitness room, a pool, and a sauna.

SOUTH ZONE BEACHES

COPACABANA

$$$$$

Copacabana Palace – *Av. Atlântica 1702, Copacabana. ☎21 2548 7070. www.copacabanapalace.com.br. 242 rooms.* A Rio icon (*see p 161*), this grand hotel was constructed in 1923.

Designed to recall the grand hotels in the South of France, the Copa Palace is a favorite of artists, statesmen, and famous personalities, including in the past, Princess Diana, Ava Gardener and Ginger Rogers. With a staff of 500 in the high season, the service is impeccable. The **Cipriani**, considered to be one of the best restaurants in town, overlooks the swimming pool. The **Pérgula** restaurant at the other end of the pool serves a great breakfast, Saturday *feijoada*, or Sunday brunch.

Sofitel – *Av. Atlântica 4240, Copacabana.* ✆*21 2525 1232. www.sofitel. com.br. 388 rooms. Breakfast not included.* Sofitel brings well-located luxury at the Ipanema end of Copacabana Beach. All rooms have balconies, but some overlook the street rather than the beach and are therefore cheaper. There are two pool's, one at the front of the hotel and one at the back. The hotel's main restaurant enjoys a sweeping view of Copacabana Beach and Sugar Loaf. Windows in the rooms are double-glazed to cut the Avenida Atlântica traffic noise. Sample the exceptional-menu in the **Le Pré Catelan** restaurant, which combines to perfection French cuisine with regional Brazilian touches.

JW Marriott Hotel – *Av. Atlântica 2600, Copacabana.* ✆*21 2545 6500. www. marriott.com.br. 245 rooms. Breakfast not included for some price categories.* This hotel, midway along the ocean-front road, has small rooms. Some of them face the ocean, but the windows are not large. The best view is from the swimming pool area at the top of the hill, where there is also a fitness room.

$$$$

Pestana Rio Atlantica – *Av. Atlântica 2964, Copacabana.* ✆*21 3816 8530. www.pestana.com. 216 rooms.* In the heart of Copacabana's oceanfront Avenida Atlântica, the best rooms at this hotel have balconies and birds'-eye views of Copacabana Beach. During Rio's New Years Eve celebrations, these front rooms are sought-after perches from which to watch fireworks displays that are second to none. Book a room on the 8th floor or above for peace and quiet plus sensational sunrise views.

Now 10 years old, Pestana's rooms are gradually being refurbished. There are two suites for the disabled. The rooftop pool, which doesn't close until 10pm, is particularly pleasant.

Windsor Excelsior – *Av. Atlântica 1800, Copacabana.* ✆*2195 5800. www. windsorhoteis.com.br. 233 rooms.* This member of the Windsor chain boasts an enviable location on the oceanfront and has recently been renovated. Staff are helpful; and the spotless rooms bear the standard Windsor décor... Small windows are the rule, and some rooms have no view at all—but these are rented for a lower rate.

$$$

Rio Othon Palace – *Av. Atlântica 3264, Copacabana.* ✆*21 2525 1500. www. othon.com.br. 572 rooms.* This 30-floor landmark hotel in the heart of the Copacabana Beach area is the second-largest in the city—meaning the views from the rooftop pool area are spectacular. Some of the rooms have been recently refurbished.

Ouro Verde – *Av. Atlântica 1456, Copacabana.* ✆*21 2543 4123. www.dayrell. com.br. 64 rooms.* One of the few moderately priced hotels on Av. Atlântica, this hotel seems frozen in time. Ouro Verde opened in 1950 for the World Cup, and the room decor appears to be untouched since then—check out the original '50s cupboards and bubble-gum-pink bathroom tiles. They are well-kept, however, and the lack of renovation means that the original large size and high ceilings are intact.

Mar Palace Copacabana Hotel – *Av. Nossa Senhora de Copacabana 552.* ✆*21 2132 1500. www.hotelmarpalace. com.br. 103 rooms.* A pleasant hotel,

Swimming pool, Sofitel

©Fabrice Rambert/Accor

set on Copacabana's main shopping street two blocks back from the beach. Renovated five years ago, rooms are pleasant and extremely large at 30sq meters. The rooftop terrace houses a small pool and steam room with a view of Christ the Redeemer.

$$

Premier Copacabana – *Rua Tonelero 205, Copacabana. ℘21 3816 9090. www.premier.com.br. 110 rooms.* Situated three blocks back from the beach, this hotel is perfectly situated for city travel since it sits right next to Siqueira Campos Metro station. Recently renovated rooms are smart and spotless. There is a rooftop pool with bar, fitness and steam rooms, in addition to a 360-degree panorama of mountains, city, Christ the Redeemer, and the ocean in the distance.

Residencial Apart – *Rua Francisco Otaviano 42, Copacabana. ℘21 2522 1722. www.apartt.com.br. 24 rooms.* This small hotel is conveniently placed just one block from Posto 6 and near to Arpoador. Wi-Fi is available for a minimal cost per day, and breakfast—included in the rate—is served in your room. There is a kitchen for cooking up a storm, or you can step out of the front door to sample the food from a host of local eateries.

Hotel Santa Clara – *Rua Décio Vilares, 316, Copacabana. ℘21 2256 2650. www.hotelsantaclara.com.br. 25 rooms.* Small and attractive with a friendly staff, the Santa Clara is buffered from Copacabana's clamor seven blocks from the beach in a little residential quarter known as Bairro Peixoto. Four rooms on the front have balconies. There's no breakfast room, but there is room-service in the morning.

Stone of a Beach Backpackers – *Rua Barata Ribeiro 111, Copacabana. ℘21 3209 0348. www.stoneofabeach.com.br. 10 dorms, 6 rooms.* No frills come with this hostel on Copacabana's busy thoroughfare near Leme, three blocks from the beach. Yet the staff is obliging, and the rooftop terrace boasts a bar and Jacuzzi. Wi-Fi is free, as are the three computer terminals in the lobby.

LEME

$$$

Golden Tulip Continental – *Rua Gustavo Sampaio 320, Leme. ℘21 3545 5300. www.goldentulipcontinental.com. 280 rooms.* Tucked away in Leme at the end of Copacabana beach, the Golden Tulip inhabits a quieter neighborhood. The nearby beach is tranquil beneath the huge rock after which this residential community takes its name. Rooms are comfortable and well-decorated, with those on the back looking out on the Morro Chapéu Mangueira favela. Views from the rooftop pool are of Pedra do Leme, Sugar Loaf and the vast beach of Copacabana.

ARPOADOR

$$$

Hotel Arpoador Inn – *Rua Francisco Otaviano 177, Arpoador. ℘21 2523 0060. 50 rooms. www.arpoadorinn. com.br.* Right on the ocean, this hotel has an excellent location next to Ipanema. Guest rooms on the front not only have a sea view, but as there is no road between the hotel and the beach, they are blissfully quiet. All accommodations and shared areas have been recently refurbished. Take an early-morning dip in the city's calmest waters before savoring breakfast on the beachside terrace. At day's end, stroll two minutes to see the best sunset in town from Arpoador rock before popping into the **Azul Marinho** (on the hotel's ground floor) to experience one of Rio's best-loved seafood restaurants.

$$

Hotel Cristal Palace – *Rua Francisco Otaviano 56, Arpoador. ℘21 2548 7070. www.hotelcristalpalace.com.br. 24 rooms.* Located between Ipanema and Copacabana, this glass-front hotel is classically decorated and comfortable. Rates are reasonable, and rooms without a balcony are cheaper.

IPANEMA

$$$$$

Fasano – *Av. Vieira Souto 80, Ipanema. ℘21 3202 4000. www.fasano.com.br. 91 rooms. Breakfast not included.*

Step into Philippe Starck's fantasy world, where luxury, taste and contemporary style blend together. Celebrities such as Madonna, Naomi Campbell, Lenny Kravitz and Diana Krall have all visited this exclusive and newly opened hotel. Starck's furniture punctuates the almost triangular corridors, while perspective and lighting play sensory illusional tricks—à la Alice in Wonderland. It's quite an art finding your room door as it's hidden in a wall of dark wood. Once inside, the luxurious chambers have king-size beds with Egyptian cotton sheets, a 32-inch LCD TV screen with 59 channels, and an iPod dock. The fantastic view from the pool is of Ipanema and Leblon beaches, with Morro Dois Irmãos in the background. For a taste of Rio's best nightlife, head to the ground floor and hip **Londra** bar. Also on-site is the exclusive **Al Mare** restaurant.

Caesar Park – *Av. Vieira Souto 460, Ipanema.* ✆ *21 2525 2525. www. caesarpark-rio.com. 222 rooms.* This hotel has comfortable and traditional spacious rooms with those at the front overlooking Ipanema Beach. The restaurant and pool on top of the hotel offer a spectacular view of the surroundings.

Ipanema Plaza – *Rua Farme de Amoedo 34, Ipanema.* ✆ *21 3687 2000. www. goldentulipipanemaplaza.com. 140 rooms.* This hotel is located on a street with a great choice of restaurants and is close to Posto 8 of Ipanema Beach (designated by the giant rainbow flag as the gay area). Some rooms are small and offer a side view of the beach, whereas the swimming pool overlooks the lagoon.

$$$$

Best Western Sol Ipanema – *Av. Vieira Souto 320, Ipanema.* ✆ *21 2525 2020. www.solipanema.com.br. 90 rooms.* A tall building close to Ipanema Beach, this hotel is pure understated chic. With only six rooms per floor, it's also very quiet. The rooms are sleekly decorated with white floors contrasting with the dark wood furniture. Room safes are big enough to hold a laptop. Although there are two room catego-

ries, the only difference is the view; you'll pay more for an ocean vista.

Promenade Visconti – *Rua Prudente de Morais 1050.* ✆ *21 2111 8600. www. promenade.com.br/visconti. 48 apartments/rooms.* Conveniently located in the heart of Ipanema, this apart-hotel has both rooms and apartments to rent. Most rooms have a decent street or garden view. Although there's no pool, there is a Jacuzzi, and the beach is only one block away.

$$$

Hotel Ipanema Inn – *Rua Maria Quitéria 27, Ipanema.* ✆ *21 2523 6092. www. ipanemainn.com.br. 56 rooms.* A lovely hotel, the Ipanema occupies a fantastic spot just one block from Rio's hippest part of the beach, Posto 9. The rooms have been recently redecorated, but the less expensive rooms are darker and have no view. If you stay more than one week, you can get a discount.

Hotel Vermont – *Rua Visconde de Pirajá 254, Ipanema.* ✆ *21 3202 5500. www.hotelvermont.com.br. 86 rooms.* This clean, basic hotel is located two blocks from the beach, on Ipanema's busiest street—perfectly placed for Ipanema's bars, restaurants and shops. All rooms have tile floors, and those on the 9th and 10th floors at the back of the small property have great views of the Christ the Redeemer statue. Two computers and Wi-Fi are available for guest use for a fee.

$$

Hotel San Marco – *Rua Visconde de Pirajá 524, Ipanema.* ✆ *21 2540 5032. www.sanmarcohotel.net. 56 rooms.* An unassuming hotel in a buzzing site close to hip shops, bars and restaurants, the San Marco is just two blocks from Ipanema Beach. Rooms are slightly worn, but are well-kept and are great value for this prime location in Rio's sought-after Zona Sul.

Ipanema Beach House – *Rua Barão da Torre 485, Ipanema.* ✆ *21 3202 2693. www.ipanemahouse.com. 7 dorms, 4 rooms.* This popular hostel is set on a quiet street just off Ipanema's ritzy Rua Garcia D'Ávila. There's a small pool with a bar and pool tables. All rooms have a street or pool view, and Wi-Fi is free.

Pool Bar, Marina Palace

Epoque Hotels

LEBLON

$$$$$

Mercure Apartments Leblon – *Rua Joao Lira 95, Leblon. 21 2113 2400. www.mercure.com. 38 apartments. Breakfast not included.* You'll feel right at home in your mini apartment in the center of chic Leblon. Each apartment has a living room with a kitchenette, bedroom and bathroom. There are supermarkets nearby that will deliver if you don't want to do the shopping. There's also a pool, but you're only one block from the fantastic beach. Parking and Wi-Fi are free.

Marina All Suites – *Av. Delfim Moreira 696, Leblon. 21 2172 1100. www.marinaallsuites.com.br. 39 rooms. Breakfast not included.* A boutique hotel in the sky, this all-suite property has a tiny reception area that belies the exclusive luxury spread behind it over 18 floors. With only three suites per floor, the whole concept of this elite establishment is to make guests "feel at home." In the nine design suites, you'll stay in style. Each have a different theme and are titled after Brazilian gems. Gisele Bündchen has sampled the "Diamond" suite, and actor Gael García and musician Lenny Kravitz have also checked in. There's a tiny but glamorous rooftop pool, a cinema room with eight comfy chairs to kick back in, and a cozy lounge on the 16th floor where you can watch TV or play cards. The hotel's **Bar d'Hotel** is famous for its sophisticated menu and contemporary setting overlooking the sea.

Sheraton – *Av. Niemeyer 121, Leblon. 21 2274 1122. www.sheraton-rio.com. 559 rooms. Breakfast not included.* Slightly off the beaten path on the beautiful coast road that runs from Leblon to São Conrado. Right on the ocean, the hotel has its own little beach with stunning views of Leblon, Ipanema, and Arpoador. All the rooms have views, some taking in Vidigal favela. Excellent leisure facilities include a large outdoor pool and a children's pool, tennis courts, plus tons of space under the trees to enjoy the lounge chairs and the ocean horizon in peace. In the health center you'll find a spa, a gym with dance studio, and a steam room and sauna. Guests have 30 minutes free Internet time per day, and there is also a free shuttle service that skirts the beaches all the way to Botafogo.

Marina Palace – *Av. Delfim Moreira 630, Leblon. 21 2172 1000. www.marinapalacehotel.com. 150 rooms. Breakfast not included.* This four star hotel is right on Leblon's oceanfront. The highest building on the Leblon oceanfront strip, Marina Palace also affords some of the best views. Rooms are a decent size with large windows. There is a rooftop pool and bar.

$$$$

Leblon Flat – *Rua Antônio Maria Teixeira 33. 21 2125 4000/3722 5054. Central Reservations. www.redeprotel.com.br. 16 apartments.* Right next to Shopping Leblon and only three blocks from Leblon beach, this apart-hotel personifies convenience. All the suites have balconies and living rooms with a kitchenette. One- and two-bedroom apartments are available for long stays or short rentals of a few days. By calling the reservation number in advance, you can negotiate a better deal.

Ritz Plaza Hotel – *Rua Ataulfo de Paiva 1280, Leblon. 21 2540 4940. www.ritzhotel.com.br. 56 rooms.* A few paces from Leblon's Dias Ferreira Street where trendy bars and restaurants stand shoulder to shoulder, this hotel is one of Rio's best-kept secrets. You can top up your tan and enjoy the hotel's cozy deck and pool, with its huge, colorful mosaic. One block from the beach, this constantly renovated hotel is always in tip-top condition.

Gávea Tropical

Gávea Tropical

$$

Lemon Spirit Hostel – *Rua Cupertino Durão 56, Leblon.* ✆*21 2294 1853. www.lemonspirit.com. 4 rooms, 5 dorms.* Friendly staff greet guests at this laid-back hostel, one block from Leblon beach and close to cafés, bars, shops and cinemas. Rooms all have air-con and all, except one, have a street view. Most of the dorms have triple-bunk beds, but the hostel also offers private rooms. A TV lounge and a kitchen with good facilities is also on-site.

LAKE AND SURROUNDS

GÁVEA

$$$$$

La Maison – *Rua Sérgio Porto 58, Gávea.* ✆*21 3205 3585. www. lamaisonario.com. 5 rooms. Close to the favela of Rocinha; a taxi to and from the hotel is recommended.* A fusion of boutique hotel and guesthouse, each of the rooms is an eye-catching, eclectic mix of modern and Victorian design. Four rooms claim breath-taking panoramas of the lake, with tropical forest in the background. One room compensates for its lack of view with a private terrace.

$$$$

Gávea Tropical – *Rua Sérgio Porto, Gávea.* ✆*21 2274 6015. www. gaveatropical.com. 6 rooms. Close to the favela of Rocinha; a taxi to and from the hotel is recommended.* At the very end of a jungle-lined residential street behind a high wall, this charming guesthouse is a well-hidden gem on the border of South America's biggest favela, Rocinha. The manager insists his guests are safer here than in Copaca-bana. Arranged across terraces spilling down the hillside (which means lots of stairs), all of the rooms have balconies peering out on the jungle-strewn mountains with Christ the Redeemer as a backdrop. The spacious rooms have bohemian French/Asian decor, but be warned the bathrooms in the rooms do not have doors.

WEST ZONE BEACHES

SÃO CONRADO

$$$$$

Intercontinental – *Av. Prefeito Mendes de Moraes 222, São Conrado.* ✆*21 3323 2236. www.intercontinental.com. 418 rooms.* In situ since 1974, this is one of Rio's oldest large-scale luxury resort hotels. The pool has just been reno-vated and is now raised to overlook the ocean. All rooms come with a balcony, and the rooms are all the same size, unless they are in the superior category. Some rooms overlook Gávea Golf Club. Since there's a twenty-room convention center here, be forewarned that rates rise when major meetings hit town. Rio's chic fashion mall, housing a good selection of eateries and upmar-ket shops, is just a stone's-throw away from the hotel.

$$$$

La Suite – *Rua Jackson de Figuereido 501, Joatinga.* ✆*21 2484 1962. 7 rooms. Access is only possible by car or taxi.* A 5-minute drive from São Conrado, and 20 minutes to Leblon, this boutique hotel offers fantastic views; from the large open-sided sitting room you can look back at a part of Rio's coastline most never get to see. And the view from the infinity pool is sensational. Rooms

Green Room, La Suite

La Suite

use vibrant colors to a striking effect, and all seven rooms take advantage of the panoramas with either full-length windows or private balconies. Often booked for fashion shoots, this hotel makes the perfect lair for a honeymoon or a romantic weekend.

BARRA DA TIJUCA

$$$$$

Sheraton Barra – *Av. Lúcio Costa 3150, Barra da Tijuca.* ☎ *21 3139 8000. www. sheraton.com/barra. 292 rooms.* The vast white beach outside the front door, coupled with a luxurious pool area, and a six-room business center spell broad appeal here. With two restaurants, a bar in the lobby and by the pool, a hairdresser, convenience store, children's play area, and two squash courts, Sheraton Barra is part condominium, part hotel. Rounding out the amenities, the gym claims the best hotel fitness facility in town, and **Vila Spa L'Occitane** operates five massage bungalows in a serene palm-lined courtyard. Wi-Fi is available in all the shared areas.

Windsor Barra – *Av. Sernambetiba 2630, Barra da Tijuca.* ☎ *21 2195 5000. www.windsorhoteis.com.br. 340 rooms.* Right on Barra's beach, this Windsor has views over either the sweeping beach in front or mountains in back—the higher the room the better the view. Decent-size rooms each have a sumptuous marble bathroom. Modern amenities include cable TV with 48 channels, while the rooftop pool has phenomenal views of both the ocean and mountains. The hotel has the largest convention center in Rio de Janeiro,

which does mean booking rooms in advance is essential.

$$$

Royalty Barra – *Av. Do Pepê 690, Barra da Tijuca.* ☎ *21 2483 5373. www. royaltyhotel.com.br. 249 rooms.* At the end of Praia da Barra, the views from this hotel take in the entire length of the beach. Rooms at the back look over mountains, side rooms face the beach and mountains, and front rooms have magnificent beach views. Spacious accommodation are done in neutral schemes, with tile floors and fresh white bathrooms.

RECREIO

$$$

Atlântico Sul Hotel – *Av. Professor Armando Ribeiro 25, Recreio.* ☎ *21 3418 9100. www.atlanticosulhotel.com.br. 100 rooms.* Lap up some serenity at the end of Recreio dos Bandeirantes, by a beach with clean, clear water—quiet in the week, but busy at weekends. Great views abound: Barra and Recreio beaches from the front rooms, and the mountains from those at the back. Far from the city bustle and major attractions (1hr 30mins from Copacabana) this hotel has a holiday vibe.

BARRA DE GUARATIBA

$$$

Le Relais de Marambaia – *Estrada Roberto Burle Marx 9346, Barra de Guaratiba.* ☎ *21 2394 2544. www. lerelaisdemarambaia.com. 5 rooms.* Located just on the edge of the village, this chic pousada is a new kid on the Guaratiba block, offering beach-house style and comfort. Each of the rooms has its own contemporary decor, with an ocean-view balcony and a Jakusi ou Ofuro bath. Perched right on the edge of the ocean, the pool deck is just a flight of steps away from a private beach that is perfect for snorkeling. Relax on the veranda and savor the sweeping view across the region.

$$

Pousada Refúgio das Bananeiras – *Estrada da Vendinha 81, Barra de Guaratiba.* ☎ *21 2410 8166. www. refugiodasbananeiras.com. 7 rooms.*

Royalty Barra

Hotel Royalty Barra

Step out of your chalet into the tropical gardens. The view of the river and surrounding *Restinga* (a specific type of indigenous tropical forest) stretches as far as the eye can see and nature's own soundtrack can be enjoyed 24/7. It's a 10min walk to the beach.

EXCURSIONS

BAÍA DE GUANABARA AND NITERÓI

NITERÓI

$$$

Mercure Apartments Niterói Orizzonte – *Rua Cel. Tamarindo 321, Gragoatá, Niterói.* 📞21 2707 5700. *www.mercure.com. 139 rooms.* All rooms in this modern building have balconies that overlook Guanabara Bay and offer spectacular views of Rio.

Tower Hotel – *Av. Alm. Ary Parreiras 12, Icaraí, Niterói.* 📞21 2612 2121. *www. towerhotel.com.br. 110 rooms.* It's a 10min drive from the Tower Hotel to the center of Niterói or a 20min walk to the Museu do Arte Contemporânea (MAC). It's close to Icaraí beach, where panoramic views of Rio rise across the bay. The rooms are well-kept; those on the front have views of the beach and those on the back overlook the mountains. Wi-Fi and parking are free.

$$

Icaraí Praia Hotel – *Rua Belizário Augusto 21, Icaraí, Niterói.* 📞21 2710 2323. *www.icaraipraiahotel.com.br. 63 rooms.* One block back from Icaraí beach, this simple hotel is perfect for a night or two. Laminate flooring and fresh, cream-colored walls décorate the rooms. Wi-Fi and parking are free. A 10min stroll will get you to the Museu do Arte Contemporânea; 10min by car lands you in Niterói.

PAQUETÁ

Hotel Farol de Paquetá – *Praia das Gaivotas 796/816, Paquetá Island.* 📞21 3397 0402. *www.hotelfaroldepaqueta. com.br. 23 rooms.* This modest little place is right by the beach, just a 10min walk from the ferry. Geared for leisure, the hotel has a football/volleyball pitch, a games room and two swimming pools. The restaurant borders the beach, and there's also a snack bar on-site. If you stay more than three nights in low season (mid-March to June), you can negotiate a good deal.

BÚZIOS

$$$$$

Casas Brancas Boutique Hotel & Spa – *Alto do Humaitá 10, Centro, Búzios.* 📞22 2623 1458. *www.casasbrancas. com.br. 32 rooms.* The wow factor here hits you as you climb the dark stone steps to the terrace. Overlooking Búzios' rambling center with its azure bay framed by Flamboyant trees, Casa Brancas' split-level patios and classy stone pool offer the ultimate in relaxation. The pousada is Búzios' most renowned luxury hideaway and spa. Inspired by Mediterranean architecture, the simplicity of the exterior and interior is what gives Casas Brancas its charm. At dusk, wander down the steps for a sundowner at the **Deck** bar, then climb back up for Brazilian-Mediterranean fusion cuisine at **Café Atlántico**—the restaurant with the best view in town.

Insólito Boutique Hotel – *Praia da Ferradura, Rua E1, Condomínio Atlântico, Búzios.* 📞22 2623 2172. *www.insolitos. com.br. 12 apartments.* Located on Ferradura Beach, this exclusive hotel is an oasis for the senses. Overlooking the blue ocean and integrated with lush greenery, this truly is a place to get away from it all. Each stylish apartment contains works of art and books about art and culture. Recycled wood furniture and crafts made by low income Brazilian communities share space with LCD TVs, DVD players, Wi-Fi, and iPod docking stations. Facilities for guests include the use of two boats, bicycles,

Insólito Boutique Hotel

Chez Pitu Praia Hotel

Chez Pitu Praia Hotel

fresh and salt water pools, sauna, jacuzzi, and spa.

$$$$

Chez Pitu Praia Hotel – *Av. Geribá 10, Aldeia de Geribá, Búzios.* ☎22 2623 6460. *www.chezpitu.com.br. 27 rooms.* Located by Geribá Beach, known for its surfing and busy on weekends, this lovely hotel has a terrace, bar, and pool. From the ground-floor rooms you step right out to the pool area. After watching the sun set over the ocean from your room, you'll fall asleep to the sound of the surf (there's no road between the guesthouse and the beach). Rooms are cozy and well-maintained. A light tea (included in the room rate) is served from 6–7pm.

$$$

Perola Búzios Design – *Av. José Bento Ribeiro Dantas 222, Centro, Búzios.* ☎22 2620 8507. *www.atlanticahotels. com.br. 49 rooms/11 suites.* In central Búzios, this hotel boasts a lovely swimming pool with a stunning deck area and hanging beds. The hotel also offers transfers to the beach. There is a fitness room (with instructor) and a massage room.

Pousada Corsário – *Rua Agripino de Souza 50, Praia dos Ossos, Búzios.* ☎22 2623 6403. *www.pousadacorsario. com.br. 32 rooms.* This stylish and comfortable inn has direct access to the Praia dos Ossos, and is also close to the beaches Azeda and Azedinha (10 min walk) and João Fernandes (20 minutes walk). The service is impeccable.

Pousada Vila do Mar – *Travessa dos Pescadores 88, Centro, Búzios.* ☎22 2623 1466. *www.viladomar.com. 18 rooms/*

7 suites. Located near Rua das Pedras and Orla Bardot, this pousada opened in 1981 and was one of the first in Búzios. Some rooms have an exceptional view of the Praia da Armação and all are decorated in a contemporary style. The swimming pool is sheltered by plants and trees.

$$

Alegravila – *Av Jose Bento Ribeiro Dantas 1475, Centro, Búzios.* ☎22 2623 2329. *www.alegravila.com.br. 12 rooms.* Located on the main road into Buzios, rooms at this simple, quiet pousada overlook the tropical gardens and small pool. The nightlife at the center of Buzios is just a 15min walk away. A 20min stroll will take you to tranquil Tartaruga beach, or to Ferradura for a more lively atmosphere.

ILHA GRANDE

$$$$

Pousada Sankay – *Praia Bananal, Ilha Grande.* ☎24 3365 1090. *www.pousa-dasankay.com.br. 11 rooms.* Situated off the beaten track (six hours by trail from Abraão, Ilha Grande's main village, or one-and-a-half hours by boat from Angra dos Reis), Pousada Sankay enjoys utter peace and quiet amid the virgin rain forest by the Bay of Angra dos Reis. All rooms have a balcony with an ocean view and a hammock to relax in. If you want to swim, both the pool and the sea are just steps away. You can take diving lessons at the on-site dive school, and the hotel will take you out diving if you're already certified... Breakfast, dinner and boat transfers to and from the mainland are included in the price.

Pousada Sítio do Lobo – *Enseada das Estrelas, Ilha Grande.* ☎24 3361 4438. *Reservations:* ☎21 2227 4138. *www.sitiodolobo.com.br. 6 suites.* This pousada is located at Enseada das Estrelas (cove of the stars) and offers spectacular ocean views. Nearby is the exclusive Feiticeira Beach. The comfortable suites are both rustic and sophisticated at the same time. Accessible only by boat (10 minutes from Praia do Abraão).

Sagu Mini Resort

Sagu Mini Resort

$$$

Sagu Mini Resort – *Praia Brava, Vila do Abraão, Ilha Grande.* ℰ24 3361 5660. *www.saguresort.com. 9 rooms.* A cozy guesthouse on the palm-lined fringes of Ilha Grande's main village, the resort lies between the ocean and the jungle in a pristine natural setting. All rooms have a sea view and a balcony or terrace. Although there's no pool, you can dive off the jetty into the turquoise ocean or relax in the hot tub on a deck surrounded by tropical forest. Try delicious nouvelle Brazilian food for your evening meal at the magical **Toscanelli** restaurant. Rates include boat transfers to and from Abraão.

$$

Pousada Casablanca – *Rua da praia 34, Jardim Buganville, Abraão.* ℰ24 3361 5040. *www.casablancapousada. com.br. 9 rooms.* This simple but attractive bed and breakfast is centrally located in a peaceful part of the village of Abraão, just a 3min walk from the main beach and a 5min stroll to the little port. All rooms have a minibar, air-con and TV. Six rooms have mountain and garden views, and the other three peer out on the ground-floor veranda.

PARATY

$$$$

Pousada Casa Turquesa – *Rua Doutor Pereira, 50 ,Centro Histórico.* ℰ24 3371 1037. *www.casaturquesa. com.br. 9 suites.* Located in front of the pier and near the Church of Santa Rita, Casa Turquesa opened in May 2008 and combines charm, warmth and modernity. The suites are comfortable. An inner courtyard with swimming

pool is the ideal place for rest after a day of sightseeing. The restoration project recreated the facade of the 18C building, destroyed by fire thirty years ago, but the interior has all the comforts associated with a modern hotel.

Pousada Porto Imperial – *Rua do Comércio (Centro Histórico).* ℰ24 3371 2323. *www.portotel.com.br. 50 rooms.* This charming 19C colonial house sits behind the town's main church, Igreja Matriz, in the heart of the historic center. Every room is named after a famous Brazilian woman such as Elis Regina, Tarsila do Amaral, Chiquinha Gonzaga, and Rachel de Queiroz, and each room has a little board telling their history.

Pousada do Ouro – *Rua Dr. Pereira 145 (Old Rua da Praia), Paraty.* ℰ24 3371 4300/3371 2033. *www.pousadaouro. com.br. 18 rooms/8 suites.* This traditional pousada near the pier has had singer Mick Jagger as a guest in the past. In the main building there are several types of rooms with two levels, which can house two adults and children. Over the road are smaller rooms and a passage leading to another area of the inn, where you have breakfast. One of the few hotels in Paraty with parking, the hotel also has a spa and a restaurant.

Pousada do Sandi – *Rua Largo do Rosario 1, Paraty.* ℰ24 3371 2100. *www. pousadadosandi.com.br. 26 rooms.* This elegant 18C building sits in the center of the historic quarter. Large, comfortable rooms have high ceilings, and are decorated in vibrant hues. Bright primary tones color the furnishings and paintings in the reception area, while

Pousada do Sandi

Pousada do Sandi

Pousada da Alcobaça

Miriam Cutz

wooden ceilings are painted yellow, and the door and window frames wear colonial Portuguese bright blue. Out in the cobbled courtyard there's a curving pool in which to unwind on hot tropical nights.

Santa Clara Hotel – *Rodovia Rio-Santos, Km 563, Paraty. ℘24 3371 8900. www.santaclarahotel.com.br. 34 rooms.* Located 10km from Paraty, this Mercure hotel is set in an area of 500,000sq meters of lush greenery—partly Atlantic rain forest. The swimming pool overlooks the ocean, as do some of the luxury rooms.

$$

Pousada Santa Rita – *Rua Santa Rita 335, Centro Histórico, Paraty. ℘24 3371 1206. www.paraty.com.br/santarita. 6 rooms.* A winsome old colonial house, Pousada Santa Rita shines as a little Paraty gem. All rooms are affordable, clean and comfortable; five of them boast ocean views. Right beside Santa Rita Church, you're a stone's throw from all the sights, cafés and restaurants lining Paraty's cobbled streets.

PETRÓPOLIS

$$$$$

Solar do Imperio – *Av. Koeller 376, Petrópolis. ℘24 2103 3000. www. solardoimperio.com.br. 24 rooms.* This superb hotel in a great location lies within walking distance of all the local sights. The majestic structure was built in 1875 by a coffee baron. The iron gates are studded with coffee beans and the beautiful gardens at the front have a pond with carp. Rooms are designed for comfort, and the cheerful

staff make every guest feel at home. The hotel has a small convention center, a spa and a heated swimming pool with sauna. Recently a new annex was opened with high ceilinged, large rooms. The hotel's restaurant is the elegant **Leopoldina**, under chef Claudia Mascarenhas.

$$$$

Pousada da Alcobaça – *Rua Agostinho Goulão 298, Correas. ℘24 2221 1240. www.pousadadaalcobaca.com.br. 11 rooms.* This traditional pousada is a 15 minute drive from Petrópolis. The building is a pretty 1914 mansion set in beautiful gardens. Antique furniture and attentive service contribute to the warm ambiance. The excellent restaurant is also open to the public.

$$$

Pousada Monte Imperial Koeller – *Av. Koeller 99, Petrópolis. ℘24 2237 1664. www.pousadamonteimperial.com.br.* Located in the beautiful Avenue Koeller, almost in front of the cathedral, this tall, quirky 1875 former home has been lovingly restored to retain its original features. There's a small, elegant swimming pool in the back where you can take a dip.

$$

Hotel York – *Rua do Imperador, Petrópolis. ℘24 2243 2662. www. hotelyork.com.br. 32 rooms.* Flowered bedspreads and wooden furniture fill the rooms in this clean, small hotel, which is well-located in the city center within walking of the Imperial Museum. Prices are reasonable, but rooms with air-con cost extra. Some rooms have no view at all.

NEARBY PETRÓPOLIS

VALE DO CUIABÁ

$$$$

Pousada Tankamana – *Estrada Júlio Cápua, Vale do Cuiabá, Petrópolis. ℘24 2222 9181. www.pousadatankamana. com.br. 15 chalets.* An hour's drive from Petrópolis, the accommodation here is a complex of comfortable chalets that blend in with the natural forest setting. As well as a swimming pool, jacuzzi and sauna, there is a natural pool with

Brazilian Motels

Motels are scattered around Rio, but be warned, these are not equivalent to our roadside motels. An everyday part of Brazilian culture, these are *"love motels"* used by couples and young people who have no privacy at home. The lower-end motels are basic and affordable, but Brazilians take pleasure seriously, so there are plenty of stylish, sophisticated establishments too. Jacuzzis, steam rooms and saunas are common, as are swimming pools—some of which even have waterfalls.

Many motels have music systems and dance floors, complete with disco lighting. Then there's the naughty element, including ceiling mirrors and revolving beds. Rooms can be rented by the hour instead of by the day. Some have a system that ensures total privacy, with private garages. Although there's no reception area per se, the rooms themselves resemble hotel rooms. The most famous *love motel* in Rio is the **Vips Motel** which has balconies overlooking stunning ocean views. Often, when the city hosts a big event, these motels are used as regular hotels. *(Vips, Av. Niemeyer 418, Leblon; 21 3322 1662; www.vipsmotel.com.br.)*

Pousada Tankamana

a waterfall. Tankamana also boasts a fantastic restaurant.

TERESÓPOLIS

$$$$

Pousada Urikana – *Estrada Ibiporanga 2151, Parque do Imbuí, Teresópolis.* 21 2641 8991. www.pousadaurikana. com.br. 20 chalets/3 suites. This charming pousada lies 50km from Petrópolis at the top of Serra dos Órgãos. The comfortable chalets and apartments are traditionally furnished. In summer the climate here is pleasantly cool. Mini-golf keeps kids entertained!

$$$

Pousada Toca-Terê – *Rua Reinaldo Viana 257, Ingá, Teresópolis.* 21 2642 1100. www.tocatere.com.br. 9 chalets. Not far from the city of Teresópolis, but surrounded by forest, this hotel is a mountain getaway. Chalets perch on the mountainside overlooking the lush gardens and river. Chalets have balconies, fireplaces and whirlpools baths.

ITATIAIA REGION

$$$

Pousada Serra da India – *Estrada Vale do Ermitão (no number), Penedo, Itatiaia.* 24 3351 1185. www.serradaindia.com.br. 14 chalets. On the hillside in a beautiful natural setting, this hotel is typical of the region with little chalets surrounded by gardens with brightly colored flowers. There is a jacuzzi, swimming pool and sauna, with the option of a shower under ice-cold mountain spring water.

Pousada Terraço – *Estrada do Ermitão, 520, Penedo, Itatiaia.* 24 3351 2525/3351 2500. www.terracopenedo. com.br. This boutique hotel set in the middle of the forest has a beautiful view of Serra da Índia. From the unheated pool and its stylish decking area you can breathe in the pure mountain air and listen to the sounds of the birds. The rooms on the second floor boast a fantastic view over the forest and all rooms have a balcony.

Pousada Urikana

WHERE TO EAT

The pleasant temperature and magical setting of Rio de Janeiro make outdoor dining a best bet—whether on wonderful terraces in the hills or overlooking the ocean. Lunch is an important meal of the day for Brazilians, particularly at weekends, and having your main meal at lunchtime can be an inexpensive option. In the evening you could go to one the many lovely bars for a drink and to graze on bar snacks. If you are self-catering, the city's "Zona Sul" chain of supermarkets are popular for fresh bread, salad, and imported cheeses.

The venues described in this section have been chosen for the standard of the food, ambience, setting and/or value for money.
Rates indicate the average cost of an appetizer, main course, and dessert for one person (not including tax, gratuity or beverages). They are organized according to seven geographical areas and each of those is broken down into neighborhoods.

$	Under R$50	**$$$**	R$100–R$200
$$	R$50–R$100	**$$$$**	Above R$200

Choosing a District

Lapa is the best place for bar snacks at nighttime. In **Santa Teresa**, *Rua Almirante Alexandrino* has a selection of eateries including Japanese, Italian, and Brazilian food. **Botafogo**'s restaurants are mostly on *Rua Visconde de Caravelas*. **Copacabana**'s seafront road *Avenida Atlântica* is teeming with international eateries, although you'll often find better value and service on the side streets leading away from the main tourist strip. **Ipanema** offers a wide choice of stylish restaurants, centered particularly around *Rua Barão da Torre, Rua Garcia D'Ávila,* and *Rua*

Anibal de Mendonça. **Leblon**, although pricier than other parts of town, has a good selection of award-winning restaurants—on *Rua Dias Ferreira* they can be found back to back.
Rio de Janeiro's tourist board, RioTur, publishes a free bi-monthly guide, *Guia do Rio*, that includes a comprehensive list of restaurants organized by type of cuisine. The magazine is distributed throughout Rio's hotels or can be found at the RioTur Office (see p 16). Alternatively, if you're a serious foodie, invest in a Rio de Janeiro restaurant guide, *Guia Danusia Barbara*, available in most Rio bookshops. The entries are also in English.

Y. Kanazawa/Michelin

Juice Bars

The colorful juice bars spread about the city are much-loved for their fresh and inexpensive tropical juices. Rio de Janeiro juice bars first opened in the 1980s when the health movement was in full swing. A famous local hang-glider, known simply as "Pepê," further encouraged the scene with healthy sandwiches and juices served at the beach in Barra da Tijuca. These days everyone has caught on and there are chains such as "Bibi" and "Beach Sucos" and "Hortifruti" which have juice bars all over the city selling blends including *açai* (an Amazonian berry), *manga* (mango), and maracujá (passionfruit).

Cafes and Bakeries

Traditionally Rio has always had *padarias* which have their origins in the Portuguese style of bakeries. Offering bread, buns, pastries and a selection of Portuguese sweets such as *brigadeiros*, made with condensed milk and sweet cocoa powder, bakeries can be found throughout the city. The European-style cafe scene is relatively recent (excepting the famous Confeiteria Colombo *see p 112*), but you will still encounter serious jostling for tables late on Sunday mornings, particularly in Ipanema.

Bar Urca

International Restaurants

Due to the waves of immigration in Brazil over the centuries, the cuisine is varied, with Portuguese food, with an African influence, part and parcel of Brazilian fare. German, Japanese, Italian, French, and Lebanese cuisine can all be enjoyed throughout the city, as well as regional Brazilian food. All along the beach front from Flamengo, Copacabana, Ipanema to Leblon are large hotels that have restaurants with an international menu.

Specialties
*See also Food and Drink p 51*

Churrasco

The *churrasco*, or barbeque, is not strictly Carioca, but from South Brazil. However, Rio has adopted this form of cuisine as its own and it was here that the much-loved nationwide chain Porcão (*see p 246*) began. You'll find churrasco restaurants in every neighborhood and they all focus on meat, offering a wide variety of pork, lamb, chicken and beef. They all run with the same concept of table service and an all-you-can-eat fixed price meal. On your signal, hovering waiters bring huge skewers and slice grilled-to-perfection meat on to your plate. Also included is a sumptuous buffet and numerous side-dishes.

Bar Snacks

Many of the best neighborhoods for bar snacks are in Lapa, close to the samba clubs. Busy neighborhoods, particularly Leblon and Ipanema, are littered with *botequim* (bars that serve snacks). They are the perfect antidote to all the healthy juice bars, offering an array of high-calorie nibbles.

Kilo Restaurants

Although found all over Brazil, Rio is particularly fond of the pay-per-weight-meal. The food is low priced, quick, nutritious—and can also be ordered as take-out. Kilo restaurants can be found throughout the city and many have also been adapted as high-end eateries with delicacies such as sushi, duck and frog added to the buffet.

Buffet at Porcão Rio

Porcão

Address Book

HISTORIC CENTER AND SURROUNDS

CENTRO

$$$

Cais do Oriente – *Rua Visconde de Itaboraí. ☎21 2203 0178. www. caisdooriente.com.br. Open daily.* **Contemporary Mediterranean.** Occupying a restored 1878 building, Cais do Oriente shows off its original brickwork, and high ceilings, which give it a grand feel and enough room for a mezzanine area. There's also a terrace decorated with tropical plants. The cuisine blends influences from Thailand, Malaysia and even Morocco, as in the grilled tuna with sesame seeds and grape.

Eça – *Av. Rio Branco 128 inside the H.Stern shop. ☎21 2524 2401. www. hstern.com.br/eca. Open Mon–Fri lunch only.* **French.** For a sophisticated break from jewelry shopping, stop by Eça. You'll feel like royalty as you indulge in warm foie gras, vegetarian risotto with crisp vegetables, and the delectable chocolate desserts (the chef is Belgian—say no more).

$$

Aspargus – *Rua Senador Dantas 74, 17th floor. ☎21 2533 1098. Open Mon–Fri lunch only.* **International.** Take a rest from the downtown racket 17 floors above it all, with a stupendous view of the Lapa Arches to boot. Such dishes as green salad with gorgonzola dressing, and medallions of beef tenderloin with brie and baked potatoes will vie with the view for your attention.

Brasserie Rosário – *Rua do Rosário 34. ☎21 2518 3033. www.brasserierosario.*

Confeitaria Colombo
Y. Kanazawa/Michelin

com.br. Open Mon–Sat. **Brazilian.** In the old part of the historic center, this brasserie resides in an Azulejo-fronted building that dates back to 1800, when it was the first gold depository in Brazil. **Rosário** is famous for its cakes and pastries, all freshly made on the premises. Chef Frédéric Monnier recommends the grilled cherne, a fish from northeastern Brazil that is similar to turbot and is considered the country's best fish. Typically served with couscous, this dish is a real crowd pleaser.

Confeitaria Colombo – *Rua Gonçalves Dias 32. ☎21 2232 2300. www. confeitariacolombo.com.br. Open Mon–Fri 9am–8pm; Sat and holidays 9.30–5pm.* **Brazilian.** *For information about the history of the building see p 112.* Rio's best selection of hand-made sweet biscuits, pastries and cakes all huddle invitingly behind quaint glass cabinets here. The petit-fours, lemon meringue pie, mini cheesecakes and brigadeiro sweets are sublime. Or, for the ideal snack, try the empadas (individual crumbly pies filled with hearts of palm, cheese or prawns etc), quiche, and pastel (fried dough with meat or prawns etc). Upstairs, the restaurant serves a sumptuous buffet lunch.

O Navegador – *Av. Rio Branco 180, Edifício Clube Naval, 6th Floor. ☎21 2262 6037. www.onavegador.com.br. Open Mon–Fri.* **Brazilian.** This restaurant in the city center features traditional dishes that run from grilled lamb chops with mint sauce and lime-parmesan risotto to grilled Amazon fish with a garlic-thyme crust atop a bed of ratatouille. Check out the tea bar at the back; it's the only one in Rio. The dessert trolley is laden with goodies such as walnut pie, and guava cream with fresh cheese.

Rio Minho – *Rua do Ouvidor 10. ☎21 2509 2338. Open Mon–Fri 11am–4pm.* **Seafood.** Ownership here has only changed four times since the original building was completed in 1884. Locals love the famous Leão Veloso soup, a consommé of seafood invented in the 19C at this location. The seafood mixed grill with fish, squid, shrimp, lobster and mussels is also a winner.

$

Brasserie Brasil – *Rua Primeiro de Março 66, Centro Cultural do Banco do Brasil. ☎21 2299 2874. Open Tue–Sun.* **International**. A small space on the first floor inside the Bank of Brasil's Cultural center, Brasserie Brasil is the perfect spot for a lunch or early dinner after seeing an exhibition. The simple menu offers salads, sandwiches, pastas, steak, soups and omelettes. Refresh yourself with a cold beer before hitting the historic center for more cultural sights.

LAPA

$$

Adega Flor de Coimbra – *Rua Teotônio Regadas 34, Shop A. ☎21 2224 4582. www.adegaflordecoimbra.com.br. Open daily.* **Portuguese.** Tuck into a fine, authentic Portuguese feijoada made with butter beans and prime-quality meats. The wine-marinated goat wins raves, and is served with broccoli, rice and roasted potatoes. Customers are fiercely loyal, including those who ate here as students and now bring their grandchildren on Sundays.

Cosmopolitan – *Rua da Assembléia 13. ☎21 2220 9008. www.cosmopolitanrio.com.br. Open Mon–Sat.* **International**. A global vibe pervades the Cosmopolitan, where the hip young crowd who comes for happy hour after work (Tue–Fri) favors the X14 cocktail, made with tequila, cointreau and blue curaçao. Filet mignon with Dijon mustard and gnocchi made from sweet potato, parsnips and Irish potato will give you a taste of the menu. .

Mangue Seco – *Rua do Lavradio 23. ☎21 3852 1947. www.mangueseco cachacaria.com.br. Open Mon–Sat.* **Brazilian**. Mangue Seco, in the state of Sergipe, is an environmentally protected area of rivers, dunes and beaches. Thus, the menu looks to the waters for crab and moqueca, and seafood stew features prominently. Dance the night away after your meal as the live music kicks in. The vast choice of cachaça is mind-boggling, especially after a glass or two.

Bobó de camarão, Mangue Seco

Mangue Seco

Santo Scenarium – *Rua do Lavradio 36. ☎21 3147 9007. www.rioscenarium.com.br. Open Mon–Tue 10am–5pm, Wed–Sat 10am–midnight.* **Brazilian**. This chic bi-level eatery, with its exposed stone walls and warehouse-height ceiling, is one of the highlights of Lapa nightlife. Patrons are greeted by a suspended angel, and more religious artifacts, including paintings and chapel cabinets upstairs, adorn the space. Menu options include grilled salmon with a mustard sauce, or tournados of filet mignon served with a Madeira sauce, potato puree with gorgonzola, and peanut rice. After dinner, head for the samba clubs to burn off all the calories.

Nova Capela – *Av. Mem de Sá. ☎21 2252 6228. Open daily 11am–5am.* **Portuguese.** Established in 1903 as a family business, this stalwart provides nourishing fare for clubbers and non-clubbers alike throughout the night. Proprietor Aires, who turns up daily to keep an eye on things, makes sure that entrées are big enough to share. Try the wild boar, the house specialty, washed down with a bottle from the voluminous list of Portuguese reds.

Pizzaria Carioca da Gema – *Av. Mem de Sá 77. ☎21 3970 1281. Open Tue–Sat 6pm. www.barcariocadagema.com.br/pizzaria.htm.* **Pizza.** Pizza stars here in almost every possible iteration, even a sweet version topped with bananas, sugar and cinnamon. A young crowd piles in for sustenance before or after hitting the Lapa samba circuit.

GLÓRIA

$$$

Casa da Suíça – *Rua Cândido Mendes 157. ☎21 2252 5182. www.casa-dasuica.com.br. Open Sat evening only.*

International. This charmer opened in 1956 and is now practically part of Rio's heritage. Chef and owner Volkmar Wendlinger works in the kitchen with his daughter, Claudia, and it's obvious they are both equally passionate about their food and making their customers comfortable. Resembling a cozy Alpine hunting lodge, the dining room is adorned with original artwork painted by the chef himself. Originally from Austria, Wendlinger can whip up a fondue, a flambé and a steak tartare that make Brazilians proud. The Menu Degustaçao offers an array of dishes at a good value. And don't pass up the Swiss chocolates to finish.

THE HILLS

SANTA TERESA

$$$

Térèze – *Rua Almirante Alexandrino 660, Hotel Santa Teresa.* ℘*21 2221 1406. www.santateresahotel.com.br. Open daily.* **International.** This trendy restaurant has a diverse menu that ranges from mozzarella ravioli to Magnifica tiger prawns risotto (grilled tiger prawns flamed with Magnifica brand cachaça, served with mango chutney), there's great choices for every palate.

$$

Aprazível – *Rua Aprazível 62.* ℘*21 2507 7334. www.aprazivel.com.br. Open Tue–Sun.* **Brazilian.** One of Rio's most well-known and established restaurants, Aprazivel draws crowds for its charming location and great Brazilian food. Sit under the trees at big wooden tables and sample the tropical fish from the Maranhão coast in the north, grilled in an orange sauce, with coconut and cashew nut rice and a roasted banana. Wash it all down with some Brazilian wine, or sip one of the artisan-made cachaças in the well stocked Cachaçaria bar.

Asia – *Rua Almirante Alexandrino 256.* ℘*21 2224 2014. www.asia-rio.com. Open daily.* **Asian.** The Brazilian version of Asian food here sweeps broadly across China, Singapore, Malaysia and Thailand. Nine types of tea are served throughout the meal, and the dim sum is superb. The owners are Gordon Lewis (he's from Ireland) and Malaysian native Yewweng Ho. The deck on the top floor has a stunning view of the neighborhood and you might even see a monkey or two stroll by.

Espírito Santa – *Rua Almirante Alexandrino 264.* ℘*21 2508 7095. www.espiritosanta.com.br. Open Wed–Mon.* **Brazilian.** This little culinary jewel up in the hills sports bohemian-boutique decor and brightly colored walls, the main dining room lies just past the bar, over which hangs a cozy mezzanine. Walk past the bar to the little terrace with its magical vista of the grand old houses of Santa Teresa. Chef Natasha Fink has won awards for a reason; try a refreshing fruit juice with the crabmeat-stuffed plantain medallions, then choose from the delectable dessert menu.

Sobrenatural – *Rua Almirante Alexandrino 432.* ℘*21 2224 1003. www.restaurantesobrenatural.com. Open daily.* **Brazilian Seafood.** On Santa Teresa's main stretch, this is a long-time favorite with Cariocas. The decor is homespun and the staff is friendly and attentive. As for the Amazonian fish from Pará, it's tender, full of flavor, and a great reason to make the trip to Santa Teresa.

Mike's Haus – *Rua Almirante Alexandrino 1458, Shop A.* ℘*21 2509 5248. www.mikeshaus.com.br. Open daily.* **German.** This union of German and Brazilian cuisine came about after Michael Wanke came from Bavaria 15 years ago to take a holiday here. He met his Brazilian wife in Paraty, and their marriage resulted in Mike's Haus. Now German food and wheat draft beer (Erdinger and Paulaner) are available in Santa Teresa in the restaurant's rustic

Espírito Santa

surroundings. Wannke commands the kitchen with his wife and family all chipping in. The menu also offers several different kinds of sausages as well as smoked pork.

Adega do Pimenta – *Rua Almirante Alexandrino 296.* 📞 *21 2224 7554. www.adegadopimenta.com.br. Open daily, closed Nov 2.* **German.** Spend the afternoon watching the trams rattle past as you dig into a hearty meal. Owner William Guedes offers a choice of 21 kinds of German sausage. The house specialty Eisbein (pork knee) takes 15 hours to cook, so you'll need to be organized enough to reserve a place 24 hours in advance. Take a crowd ready to feast as this dish serves eight.

$

Ora Pro Nobis – *Rua Almirante Alexandrino 1458, Shop D.* 📞 *21 2508 6188. Open Mon–Sat 8am–8pm. Closed bank holidays.* **Contemporary Brazilian.** Edson Meirelles multitasks as owner, manager, chef and sommelier in this bistro-style restaurant. Go for the original recipes he's been perfecting since opening in 2004, especially the vegetable bobó served with rice and dendê flour. Chicken fried in sugar-free granola, served with rice and salad is another of his winning dishes. Author of a book about Aphrodisiac cookery, Meirelles knows how to set up a romantic meal!

TIJUCA NATIONAL PARK

$$

Os Esquilos – *Estrada Barão D'Escragnolle (no number).* 📞 *21 2492 2197. www.osesquilos. com.br. Open Tue–Sun noon–6pm. Cash only.* **Brazilian.** This touristy restaurant in the Tijuca forest has two homey rooms with dark wood floors and ceilings, and old bentwood chairs. One room has a large fireplace. The kitchen cooks up a great *feijoada* on weekends, made with top-quality meat and sausage, and served with all the trimmings: rice, farofa, green cabbage, oranges and cracklings. Equally popular is the steak served with a madeira sauce and roasted potatoes.

LARANJEIRAS

$$

Sushimar – *Rua São Salvador 72.* 📞 *21 2285 7246. www.sushimar.com.br. Open daily.* **Japanese.** Sample Japanese fare here in a beautifully restored 1909 house boasting its original skylight and wooden staircase. The second floor has a balcony from which you can survey the streetscape. Japanese comic characters lend their names to menu items like "National Kid," "Speed Racer" and "Ultra Seven." Enjoy the 36-piece Akira combination with a friend, or choose the sushi with Philadelphia cream cheese.

Luigi's – *Rua Senador Correa 10.* 📞 *21 2205 7343. Open Tue–Sun.* **Italian.** Luigi's has carved out a niche with the locals, including Brazilian TV artists, who are often spotted here. There's a mouthwatering selection of homemade pasta such as beetroot fettuccine with rocket pesto. Risotto, fish and meat are featured, and pizza is served at night.

Churrascaria Gaúcha – *Rua das Laranjeiras 114.* 📞 *21 2558 2558. www. gauchachurrascaria.com.br. Open daily.* **Barbecue** One of the oldest and most traditional restaurants in Rio, this simple BBQ house was established 79 years ago. Their buffet displays more than 100 hot and cold dishes to accompany all that skewered meat. Live music entertains diners Tuesday to Sunday.

$

Severyna – *Rua Ipiranga 54.* 📞 *21 2556 9398. www.severyna.com.br. Open daily.* **Northeastern Brazilian.** Although Severyna serves northeastern food, the chef/owner is actually of Portuguese descent. One of his signatures is Fandango, sautéed sun-dried beef covered in pumpkin purée, and topped with grated mozzarella. At lunch, go for the Baião de Dois, a rice dish with black-eyed beans, chopped sun-dried beef, and curd cheese. There's also a bar where you can sample a the cachaça of the region and enjoy live music, including northeastern forró.

Espaço Rio Carioca – *Rua das Laranjeiras 307.* 📞 *21 2225 7332. www. espacoriocarioca.com.br. Open daily.*

Alcaparra

Alcaparra/Manuscodesign

Contemporary. In an annex of historic homes dating back to 1883, this space hosts shows, a CD shop, a bookstore and a cafe. The menu isn't extensive, but what's on offer is delicious, and the vibe is cool. Pumpkin soup with brie, and ratatouille with goat cheese mousse seasoned with herbs show off the kitchen's talent.

SOUTH ZONE BESIDE THE BAY

FLAMENGO

$$$

Blason – *Praia do Flamengo 340.* 📞*21 2551 1278. www.casajulietadeserpa. com.br. Open daily.* **French.** Blason makes an elegant setting for a special meal. This magnificent Eclectic-style mansion built as a home in 1918, is now a popular choice for wedding receptions. The property was purchased by its current owner in 2003 and was restored it to its former glory. It's now part of Rio State's heritage program. Walk past the pretty Salon D'Or (site of the superb high-tea buffet) and you'll reach the restaurant. Smartly dressed diners enjoy grilled lobster with rouille and artichoke hearts, and ostrich filet with tarragon sauce and potato ravioli.

Empório Santa Fé – *Praia do Flamengo 2.* 📞*21 2245 6274. www.emporiosantafe. com. Open daily.* **International.** Traditional style fills this upstairs restaurant, which has starched white tablecloths—not to mention exquisite food. The head waiter recommends the lamb cutlets, a favorite of the politicians who frequent Santa Fé. If you just fancy a drink, the cozy wine bar downstairs stocks some 500 types of wine, mostly South American.

Alcaparra – *Praia do Flamengo 150.* 📞*21 2558 3937. www.alcaparra. com.br. Open daily.* **International.** A classic, formal restaurant, Alcaparra sports a warm vibe to match its bright decor. At the entrance the bar is decked out like a gentleman's club with dark wood and forest-green leather chairs, perfect for the businessmen regulars. The extensive menu encompasses pastas, poultry, meat, fish and seafood. Highly recommended is the mignonnettes à Alcaparra, grilled filet mignon in a lemon sauce with parsley and the all-important capers, for which the restaurant is named.

CATETE

$

Rotisseria Sírio Libaneza – *Largo do Machado 29, Shop 19.* 📞*21 2557 2377 Open Mon–Sat.* **Lebanese.** Tucked away inside an eclectic shopping center, this simple cafe-style restaurant has been on the premises since the shopping center opened in 1967. Order any half-meal and you'll get two kafta's included in the price. The Arabian Savory snacks virtually melt in your mouth.

BOTAFOGO

$$

Yorubá – *Rua Arnaldo Quintela 94.* 📞*21 2541 9387. Open daily.* **Brazilian.** A little off the beaten track for tourists, Yorubá is worth the cab ride. Chef Neide Santos is a genuine Bahiana, and her cuisine reflects that with terrific versions of *moqueca* (fish stew), *vatapá* (bread, shrimp, coconut milk and palm oil mashed into a creamy paste) and *caruru* (okra, onion, shrimp, palm oil and toasted nuts) on the menu. Santos' Brazilian food is simple, but as she says, "very real." All dishes are made fresh on the premises and served on banana leaves.

Miam Miam – *Rua Gal Góes Monteiro 34.* 📞*21 2244 0125. www.miammiam. com.br. Open Tue–Sat from 7:30pm.* **Contemporary.** Chef-owner Roberta Ciasca bills her cuisine as "cozy comfort food" since it's prepared with love—just like your mum would make. In an old colonial building, the dark wood floors and stone walls contrast with 1950s, 60s and 70s retro furniture and lamps.

But it works. So does the food, like the popular fish-prawn moqueca in a mild curry sauce with coconut rice. Other favorites include the tenderloin served with potato gnocchi, rocket and crispy cheese farofa; and the wild-grain risotto with fresh mushrooms.

URCA

$$$

Zozô – *Av. Pasteur 520, Urca. ✆21 2542 9665. www.zozorio.com.br. Open Tue–Thu noon–midnight, Fri–Sat noon–1am, Sun noon–10pm.* **Barbeque.** This large restaurant is at the bottom of Sugar Loaf, and through its glass ceiling you can see the cablecar swinging up to the summit. The kitsch decoration includes pictures of saints and their related Brazilian entities, and a tree in the center of the restaurant. Fill up with all you can eat of Chorizo Argentino, Prime Rib Red Angus, T.Bone Steak Red Angus... there is also sushi, sandwiches, salads, and seafood included. Great selection of wines.

$$

Bar Urca – *Rua Cândido Gaffrée 205. ✆21 2295 8744. www.barurca. com.br. Open daily.* **Brazilian.** Right at the very end of Urca near the entrance to Fort São João, Bar Urca is a traditional restaurant, located on the upper floor of a bar. The best tables are at one end of the small room, where the building curves at the corner and a row of tables look out over the bay. The menu is extensive, the seafood especially good. Prawns in a pumpkin—prawns in a cream cheese sauce served in a whole pumpkin shell with white rice—makes a divine entrée.

Garota da Urca Restaurante e Bar – *Av. João Luiz Alves 56. ✆21 2541 5040. www.garotaipanema.com.br. Open daily.* **Brazilian.** Garota da Urca's location right by Urca's former Casino is the restaurant's big draw. Sit in the front veranda section and you'll have a view of Urca Beach and the bay, with Corcovado and Christ the Redeemer rising in the background. There are many choices on the a menu, but you can't go wrong with the picanha, rice and chips.

Praia Vermelha Restaurante e Bar – *Praça General Tibúrcio (no number), Praia Vermelha. ✆21 2543 7284. Open daily.* **Brazilian.** Enter the main Military Club building and march past the canteen to find one of Rio's best-kept secrets. The restaurant rests on quiet terraces overlooking Red Beach, and boasts an extraordinary view of Sugar Loaf. The menu is huge and the food can differ in standard. Locals typically go for pizza, served in the evenings only. Caipirinhas here pack a powerful punch.

SOUTH ZONE BEACHES

COPACABANA

$$$$

Cipriani – *Av. Atlântica 1702. ✆21 2545 8747. www.copacabanapalace.com.br. Open daily.* **Italian.** Next to the glamorous swimming pool at the Copacabana Palace, the restaurant reveals luxury in plush carpets and lounge chairs, large classical paintings of tropical Rio in days gone by, crystal chandeliers and waiters in starched white jackets. Take a taste of Italy in such dishes as partridge with dried figs, stuffed pear and Chianti wine sauce, and veal with foie gras and truffles, roesti potato and a glazed tomato tart.

$$$$

Le Pré Catelan – *Av. Atlântica 4240. ✆21 2525 1160. www.sofitel.com.br. Open daily.* **French-Brazilian Fusion.** A beautifully designed space divided into cozy sections by long white satin curtains that contrast with the dark wood floors, Le Pré Catelan is a truly elegant spot. The room curves along the front windows, offering a romantic and sweeping view of Copacabana Beach up to Sugar Loaf. The refined

Cozido, Bar Urca

Bar Urca

menu created by chef Roland Villard mixes exotic Brazilian accents with French cuisine. The fixed-price 10-course "Gastronomic Trip in Amazonia" is phenomenal; there's even a booklet that explains the exotic ingredients.

$$

Copa Café – *Av. Atlântica 3056. ✆21 2235 2947. Open Mon–Sat 7pm.* **International.** The smart doorman makes you feel like you're heading into somewhere special. The warm yet stylish dining room could be in New York or Munich, in contrast to many of Copacabana's steak, rice and salad restaurants. There's a wide range of international food including first-class house burgers, seafood, pasta and salads, all served up by the helpful and unobtrusive waitstaff. Take a seat at the big, shiny bar where you can sip a cocktail before dinner, or retire to the stylish mezzanine for privacy and a laid-back vibe.

Atlântico – *Av. Atlântica 3880. ✆21 2513 2485. Open Mon–Sat.* **International.** Funky chandeliers and flashes of red faux velvet surround the small group of white-clothed tables here. The focus of the relatively small menu is seafood. The VG in Shrimps VG must stand for Very Good; they're grilled with fresh tomatoes, truffle oil and parsley, and plated aside black rice. Later in the evening, the club crowd shows up at the long steel bar, the DJ steps in and pumps up the volume, and the cocktails flow freely. This restaurant hosts an exclusively gay evening on Mondays.

$

Café do Forte – *Praça Coronel Eugênio Franco 1, Forte de Copacabana. ✆21 3201 4049. www.confeitariacolombo. com.br. Open daily.* **International.** Within the Copacabana Fort and sibling

to the famous Confeitaria Colombo in Centro, this elegant cafe has a lovely view of Copacabana Beach, Leme and Sugar Loaf. The menu includes savory and sweet pastries and cakes, divine coffee and also light meals such as salads, quiches, omelets and crêpes. There's a queue for the best tables along the sea wall, so come early during peak times on weekends—breakfast is served from 10am. You have to pay a R$4 entrance fee to the fort area, but that's a small extra price to pay for a meal here.

IPANEMA

$$$

Gero – *Rua Aníbal de Mendonça 157. ✆21 2239 8158. www.fasano.com.br. Open daily.* **Italian.** One of the best Italian places in town, Gero attracts the chic Brazilian set, including Gisele Bundchen, Caetano Veloso, Gilberto Gil and Chico Buarque. Part of the Fasano emporium from São Paulo, it can't help but be stylish. The tuna medallion with lemon and golden potatoes seduces the celebs every time.

Esplanada Grill – *Rua Barão da Torre. ✆21 2239 6028. www.esplanadagrill. com.br. Open daily.* **Grill.** Meat and more meat stars at this traditional Ipanema grill, which has been going strong for some 20 years now. The room may be small, but the quality and portions of T-bone, sirloin strip, or Red Angus cap of rump steak are big. Non-meat-eaters appreciate menu items such as tuna with endive and shiitake mushrooms.

Satyricon – *Rua Barão da Torre, 192 ✆21 2521 0627. www.satyricon. com.br. Open daily.* **Mediterranean.** In Satyricon's case, the extensive menu of Mediterranean fare focuses on fresh seafood such as fish baked in rock salt with roast potatoes, and spaghetti with clam sauce. An equally generous wine list is available for pairing.

Ten Kai – *Rua Prudente de Moraes 1810. ✆21 2540 5100. www.tenkai.com.br. Open daily.* **Japanese.** Located on the corner of Rua Paul Redfern at the end of Ipanema, this elegant and intimate Japanese restaurant is one of the best in Rio. Delicious starters, sushi and hot dishes are served, along with less tra-

Copa Café

Y. Kanazawa/Michelin

ditional desserts such as brownies and cheesecake. On the second floor, two low tables give a more oriental touch to the environment.

$$

Forneria – *Rua Aníbal de Mendonça 112. ✆21 2540 8045. Open daily.* **Italian.** Here, the simple menu comes with understated but chic contemporary environs. Salads, pizzas, carpaccio and pastas fill the bill, along with more substantial fare—like steak alla milanese—for those who've worked up an appetite playing volleyball on the beach . Look for tiramisù in the puddings section of the dessert menu.

Gula Gula – *Rua Henrique Dumont 57. ✆21 2259 3084. www.gulagula. com.br. Open daily.* **Brazilian.** Opened in 1984 by Fernando de Lamare, Gula Gula now ranks as one of Rio's tried-and-true eateries, serving up delicious fare time after time. Today Fernando's granddaughter oversees the famously healthy menu of salads, quiches, and mains such as the potato salad with chicken, peas and rose sauce—one of Fernando's '84 originals. Spread over two floors, the restaurant provides a terrace area for smokers.

Bazzar – *Rua Barão da Torre 538. ✆21 3202 2884. www.bazzar.com.br. Open daily.* **Contemporary.** To start your meal at this hip restaurant, try cream of corn soup with goat cheese and mushrooms served with Italian bread and olive oil. Customers can't get enough of Bazzar's beef; the grilled filet mignon accompanied by rice flavored with brie cheese and apricot sauce is the most-ordered dish.

Da Silva – *Rua Barão da Torre 340, Shops A and B. ✆21 2521 1289. Open daily.* **Portuguese.** This restaurant has one of the best kilo buffets and a la carte menus, which accounts for the fact Da Silva has been going strong for 30 years. The "spiritual codfish" (a codfish soufflé with cheese and cream) is one of the classics here, (as is the Da Silva codfish, made with shredded dried cod, onion, sliced baked ham, chips, eggs and fresh parsley. End your meal in traditional Portuguese style with, siricais, a dessert marvel made with eggs, condensed milk and grated cinnamon.

Bazzar

$

Pizzaria Stravaganze – *Rua Maria Quitéria 132. ✆21 2523 2391. www. stravaganze.com.br. Open daily.* **Pizza.** Chef/owner Dudu Camargois is a cookbook author several times over. The Dudu Camargo pizza involves a long list of ingredients, including fresh grilled figs in Port, goat cheese, balsamic vinegar and honey, and sliced Parma ham.

Frontera – *Rua Visconde de Pirajá 128. ✆21 3289 2350. www.frontera.com.br. Open daily.* **Kilo.** Not a run-of-the-mill restaurant, Frontera is kilo gone posh. The pile-it-on-the-plate concept has been adapted by Dutch chef, Mark Kwaks, who stocks the buffet with such marvels as duck confit served with sugarcane and shoyu. The place is rustic in a hip sort of way and is always busy.

LEBLON

$$$

Antiquarius – *Rua Aristides Espínola 19. ✆21 2294 1049. www.antiquarius. com.br. Open daily.* **Portuguese.** Inside Antiquarius feels like a seaside shack, with touches of a British pub. Antiques and artwork tastefully decorate the place; these are available for purchase. A menu with more than a hundred options keeps the likes of Pelé, Diana Ross, Prince, Roger Moore and Mick Jagger happy. They escape the paparazzi to wolf down owner Carlos Perico's favorite dish, the duck rice, or to sample one of the countless ways in which the kitchen prepares *bacalhau* (dried codfish).

$$

Aquim – *Av. Ataulfo de Paiva 1240, Shop B, Leblon. ✆ 21 3235 9750. www.aquimgastronomia.com.br. Open Tue–Sun.* **Contemporary French.**

With a chic ambience and delicious food, Aquim provides a cafe and a fancy lunch/dinner space all in one. This business started in the family's home near Corcovado and then moved on to catering. A typical bistro, Aquim offers meals at any time of day. Purple seats and smoked mirrors give the place a sleek lounge feel, and the glass cabinet displaying the family's china is an elegant reference to the afternoon tea served here. Owner and chef Samantha Aquim recommends the black rice with lamb, as well as the grouper fillet baked in grape leaves served with yellow manioc (farofa) and Brazil nut pureé.

Carlota – *Rua Dias Ferreira 64, Shops B and C.* ☎ *21 2540 6821. www.carlota.com.br. Open daily.* **Contemporary.** Located on Leblon's restaurant row, Carla Pernambuco and her husband Fernando pride themselves on hosting some of Brazil's most talented chefs. Carla is a former actress who has also written five books about gastronomy. Her creativity extends to experimenting with Carlota's recipes, as can be seen in the grilled salmon with Peruvian orange sauce and Moroccan couscous, or the Parma ham risotto served with crispy prawns.

Nam Thai – *Rua Rainha Guilhermina 95.* ☎ *21 2259 2962. www.namthai.com.br. Open daily.* **Thai.** A cozy boho vibe and terrific freshly cooked Thai food make this a must-eat. The Gaen Kiew Wan Gai (sliced chicken breast with green thai curry, basil and sweet pepper) is mellow and flavour-packed. End with a White Orchid Coconut cocktail, made with gin, cointreau, coconut milk and pineapple, to complete this heavenly experience.

Zuka – *Rua Dias Ferreira 233B.* ☎ *21 3205 7154. www.zuka.com.br.*

Open daily. **Contemporary.** Zuka says cool by placing the glass-walled kitchen in the middle of the room. From the wood balcony, customers can watch the chef grill, steam, fry, bake and roast. The menu classifies its fare as being "from the sea," "from the air" or "from the earth." That translates to delicacies like prawns inside a garlic-bread crust with Sicilian lemon risotto.

LAKE AND SURROUNDS

GÁVEA

$$

Photochart – *Praça Santos Dumont 21, Jockey Club.* ☎ *21 2512 2247. www.photochart.com.br. Open daily.* **International.** For a novelty night out, Photochart has a very appropriate theme for its location next to the Gávea Jockey club (☉ *see p 173*. The decor is racing-themed, but be sure not to race through traditional grub that runs from snails to calamari kebabs. The chef is justifiably proud of his duck with gravy and banana pancakes.

Victoria – *Rua Mario Ribeiro 410.* ☎ *21 2540 9017. www.complexovictoria.com.br. Open daily.* **Contemporary.** Though it's hidden inside the Jockey Club, Victoria restaurant is open to the public. You can eat in the dining room, or out on the terraces with a spectacular view of the racecourse and Christ the Redeemer in the distance. The eclectic cuisine ranges from pasta and pizza cooked in a wood-burning oven to modern fare such as duck with jabuticaba (a tropical fruit) and parsnip puree. This is the perfect setting for a romantic meal, but come early to get one of the best tables with a Corcovado view.

Guimas – *Rua José Roberto Macedo Soares.* ☎ *21 2529 8300. Open daily.* **French.** This traditional restaurant is hidden behind the jockey plaza on a quiet street. With the tasty bar snacks, delectable Gallic classics, and the jazz piano playing softly in the background, you can easily imagine you're in Paris at this intimate bistro, where cut-outs along the wall allow you to see that the waiters are preparing your cocktails correctly. The Filé Boursin is a specialty.

Nam Thai

Bacalhau do Rei – *Rua Marquês de São Vicente 11.* ☎*21 2239 8945. Open daily.* **Portuguese.** No-frills characterize the bunker-like establishment, but this is the place to go if you're serious about cod. The classic Portuguese dish, *bacalhau* (dried cod), is available here in every possible version; the grilled cod is especially popular as a light dish. Bring some friends, since dishes are sized to share. Portuguese wine makes an ideal accompaniment.

JARDIM BOTÂNICO

$$$

Olympe – *Rua Custódio Serrão 62.* ☎*21 2539 4542. www.olympe.com.br. Open Mon–Sat.* **French.** Claude Troisgros is the third generation in his family of chefs. His father and uncle were creators of the Nouvelle Cuisine Française. Claude now hosts a TV show where he spices up French recipes with some cheeky Brazilian flavors, a theme that's continued in Olympe. The cherne fillet with caramel bananas and dried-grape sauce, a 1930s recipe passed on from the chef's grandmother, is a surefire hit.

$$

Bar e Restaurante Da Graça – *Rua Pacheco Leão 780.* ☎*21 2249 5484. www.dagraca.com.br. Open Tue–Sun.* **International.** Located up a quiet street, right by the Botanical Gardens, this is an eye-catching little boho place set on a tranquil corner. Creative decor encompasses walls covered in gift wrap and a chandelier made of crepe paper. There are tables outside under the awnings, or you can escape the heat and sit in the shade inside. Menu options range from tapioca pizza with three cheeses and jerk meat to manioc balls and salmon caviar.

Pizzaria Capricciosa – *Rua Maria Angélica 37.* ☎*21 2527 2656. www.capricciosa.com.br. Open daily.* **Italian.** With trendy trimmings, this pizza joint has become a hit with television actors and directors since the Globo TV studios are close by. Will Smith has even popped in for a slice or two. The celebs love the Margherita Gourmet pie, with buffalo, mozzarella, Italian plum tomatoes, parmesan cheese and basil. Or go

pizza-chic with a Tartuffata topped with mozzarella and slices of black truffle.

LAGOA

$$$

Mr Lam – *Rua Maria Angélica 21.* ☎*21 2286 6661. www.mrlam.com.br. Open daily.* **Chinese.** Although the real Mr Lam now lives in New York, this high-end restaurant has three floors dedicated to his sophisticated Chinese cuisine. The top floor is a terrace in which you can eat under the stars and drink in a view of the lake. Opt for the popular sampler combination menu or the famous Peking duck, cooked whole and served with sauce, small pancakes, cucumbers, and spring onions.

$$

Pomodorino – *Av. Epitácio Pessoa 1104.* ☎*21 3813 2622. www.pomodorino.com. br. Open daily.* **Contemporary Italian.** A bi-level restaurant, Pomodoro exudes time-honored class with its chandeliers and white tablecloths. The highlight of the equally classic Italian menu is their handmade pasta, although the cherne fillet with shrimp sauce, Proseco wine and summer squash is so good, patrons always come back for more!

Bar Lagoa – *Av. Epitácio Pessoa 1674, Ipanema.* ☎*21 2523 1135. www. barlagoa.com.br. Open daily.* **German.** Opened in 1934, when a handful of fishermen inhabited this area and Ipanema and Leblon did not yet exist as destinations, Bar Lagoa was first known as Bar Berlim. The Art Deco interior of this listed building is being preserved by the owners. The Kassler, smoked carré with potato salad, is a classic.

WEST ZONE BEACHES

SÃO CONRADO

$$

Nao Hara – *São Conrado Fashion Mall, Estrada da Gávea 899, Shop 304.* ☎*21 3322 2005. Open daily.* **Contemporary Japanese.** On the top floor of the fashion mall, Nao personifies low-key style with its white floors, white chairs and white-clothed tables, overlooking a long row of windows that faces the tropical forest outside. Pull up a wood stool at the chunky wooden bar, where you can sip a saki as you watch the cooks rolling sushi and making pastries behind the glass window. Everything is freshly made on-site, and the much-ordered steamed *bacalhau* (dried cod) teriyaki is typical of Chef/owner Nao Hara's tasty creations.

BARRA DA TIJUCA

$$$

Azzurra – *Rio Design Barra, Av. das Américas 7777, Shop 304. ℘21 3325 0403. www.azzurraristorante. com.br. Open daily.* **Italian.** Tucked inside the Rio Design shopping center, this restaurant has earned its loyal clientele over 19 years. According to owner Sergio Silva, the dish that represents the establishment is King Jorge's original capellini, bathed in a four-cheese and cream sauce with pieces of shrimp and grated parmesan. Zico, Pele and a host of Brazilian celebrities frequent this place.

$$$

Antiquarius Grill – *BarraShopping, Av. das Américas 4666, Shop 160. ℘21 2294 1049. www.antiquarius.com.br. Open daily.* **Portuguese.** This huge and modern space serves up quality Portuguese staples. Think bacalhau (in this case called Never Enough Codfish) and Beef Stew a la Rio and you've got the idea. The latter is a filet mignon stew served with white rice, beans, *farofa* (toasted manioc flour), poached egg and fried plantain.

$$

Benkei – *BarraShopping, Av. das Américas 4666, Shop 1006. ℘21 3089 1238. www.benkei.com.br. Open daily.* **Japanese.** Inside Barra Shopping, Benkei is the ideal food pit-stop

for a break between stores. The very affordable fixed-priced buffet has an excellent spread of sushi, soups, salads and a choice of four hot mains. Although chiefly Japanese, the á la carte menu also lists a number of Vietnamese and Malaysian dishes. The Hot Philadelphia is a keeper.

In House – *Rio Design Barra, Av. das Américas 7777, Shop 344. ℘21 2438 7638. Open daily.* **International.** The owners of this family business care passionately about their food and customers. They offer a vast a la carte menu and an inexpensive fixed-price buffet. Chef/owner Alex Herzog lived in the USA for some time and some of his dishes reflect that sojourn, such as the fish fillet Aloha, a fillet of flounder (aka dourado or San Pierre) on a spinach pancake with seasoned slices of hearts of palm (organic only).

Borsalino – *Av. Armando Lombardi 633. ℘21 2491 4288. www.borsalino. com.br. Open daily (closed Mon lunch).* **Italian.** A large restaurant on a quiet little square framed by coconut trees, Borsalino lies out of the way of Barra da Tijuca's Miami-esque freeways. The a la carte menu is extensive, or you could try a pasta dish, such as the farfalle alla Borsalino (tossed with spinach, gorgonzola, nuts and cream). If you order farfalle Mamma Ilda (with salmon, courgette and tomato sauce), you get to keep the plate as a souvenir.

BARRA DE GUARATIBA

$$

Bira – *Estrada da Vendinha 68A. ℘21 2410 8304. Open Wed–Sun.* **Brazilian Seafood.** Bira is the place the Cariocas head on the weekends after a day at Grumari beach. To eat here is to eat in nature. Decks are suspended on stilts amid the forest. On three sides, you are surrounded by lush, tropical greenery and bromeliads; to the front is a spectacular view of the peninsula of Restinga da Marambaia and the mangroves of Sepetiba Bay. Besides the tasty moquecas (fish stews) that serve two or three people, there's an array of shrimp, fresh fish, seafood risotto, pasta and savory snacks. At sunset it's perfection.

Benkei

Benkei/Cura Comunicação

Point de Grumari – *Estrada do Grumari 710, Grumari.* ☏*21 2410 1434. Open daily 11:30am–6:30pm.* **Brazilian Seafood.** The ideal place to dine after a day out at Grumari beach, this restaurant nestles up in the hills behind the beach, where the panoramic view of the peninsula Restinga da Marambaia, and the ocean is awesome. Manager Claudio recommends the sea bass and sole steaks. Another popular dishes is the bobó de camarão (a prawn stew thickened with mashed cassava). To add to the cozy, rustic setting and decor, there's live music daily (with an optional cover charge). Dine out on the terrace as the sun sinks over the beautiful tropical terrain.

EXCURSIONS

NITERÓI

$$$

Zéfiro – *Estrada General Eurico Gaspar Dutra (no number), Fortaleza de Santa Cruz da Barra, Jurujuba.* ☏*21 3611 0975. www.restaurantezefiro.com.br. Open daily.* **Contemporary**. Set in the grounds of Santa Cruz da Barra Fort, this two-level space—the top floor holds the bar—is 3,000 square metres, built using recycled wood. Chef Bell Melsert recommends Parrilhada, a dish made with shrimp, lobster and calamari over saffron rice. There's a jetty for those who come by boat and an outstanding 360-degree view of Guanabara Bay and Rio.

BÚZIOS

$$$

Sawasdee – *Av. José Bento Ribeiro Dantas 422, Orla Bardot, Praia da Armação.* ☏*22 2623 4644. www.sawasdee. com.br. Open Tue–Sun 6pm–midnight.* **Thai.** Chef Mark Sodré has created a mouth-watering menu of Thai food with a twist of Brazilian flavor. Enticing dishes include Namprik Pla, which is whole fried or steamed fish with a spicy sauce of toasted garlic, coriander and lemon grass. First opened in Búzios in 1997, Sawasdee is so well-loved, that two more have since opened in Rio.

Fried shrimps with garlic, Bira

Y. Kanazawa/Michelin

$$

Bar do Zé – *Orla Bardot 382, Centro.* ☏*22 2623 4986. Open daily.* **International.** The resume of chef/owner Zé includes a stint in Australia, six months on a sailboat, and time in a treehouse in Hawaii. The fare at his beachy bar is as eclectic as his travels. Tropicalia on a plate with a twist describes the likes of tuna marinated in wine; snowy grouper with passion fruit; or beef tenderloin with 4-pepper sauce and sesame rice. Keep with the beach theme, in your cocktail choice, and try a Sex on the Beach.

Café Atlântico – *Casas Brancas Boutique Hotel & Spa, Alto do Humaitá 10, Centro.* ☏*22 2623 1458. www. casasbrancas.com.br. Open daily.* **Mediterranean**. A short and lovely stroll along the Orla Bardot takes you to this beautiful pousada. Occupying one of the terraces, Café Atlântico enjoys the best view in Búzios. Eat in an utterly tranquil and romantic setting with the sound of the waves and quiet music to accompany your meal. The cuisine fuses Brazilian and Mediterranean accents that are as mellow as the ambience. How does prawn brochette with 7-grain rice and cashew nuts sound?

ILHA GRANDE

$$

Restaurant Toscanelli Brasil – *Sag Mini Resort, Praia Brava, Abraão.* ☏*24 3361 5660. www.saguresort.com. Open daily.* **Italian.** Perched on a covered platform and open on the sides, the restaurant's decor is a continuation of the surrounding rain forest. The walk from the village of Abraão is worth it for the natural beauty of the setting. The seafood combination is highly

...hey follow the Slow
...g fresh ingredients
...ishes only once
...ed. No need to rush; have
...er glass of wine while you wait
and enjoy the sounds of the cicadas.

$

Bar e Restaurante Lua e Mar –
Praia do Canto, Abraão. ☎ *24 3361
5113. www.ilhagrande.org/luaemar.
Open Thu–Tue.* **Brazilian Seafood.**
Literally right on the beach, this
restaurant allows you to kick off your
flip-flops and put your feet in the sand
as you sip a cool beer and contemplate
whether to pick moqueca (fish stew)
or the joint's famous, Ilha Grande Fish
with bananas, similar to the fish stew,
but without the coconut milk and palm
oil. For dessert, the banana compote
makes a sweet treat.

Dom Mario – *Rua da Praia 781, Vila
do Abraão.* ☎ *24 3361 5349. Open
Mon–Sat 6pm–10pm.* **International**.
The large dishes served at this upscale
restaurant are for two people. The
house specialty is filet mignon with
gorgonzola sauce. The friendly staff
and rustic surroundings make for a
relaxed and enjoyable meal.

PARATY

$$$

Refúgio – *Praça da Bandeira 4, Shop 1*
☎ *24 3371 2447. Open daily.* **Brazilian.**
This posh charmer sits right by the sea
with a view of same. Indulge in good
eating and local lore when you order
Nick's favorite (named for a pirate who
used to live in the neighborhood):
shrimps in mustard sauce and calamari
in garlic and olive oil.

$$

Margarida Café – *Praça do Chafariz
(no number), Centro Histórico.* ☎ *24 3371
2441. www.margaridacafe.com.br. Open
daily.* **Contemporary**. At the entrance
to the historical center, the cafe's
building dates back to 1829. Chef Paulo
Renato offers a different recommenda-
tion each day. He suggests the seafood
salad of prawns, octopus, mussels,
calamari and fish, or the grilled fish in
a white wine sauce with grapes plated
with risotto made with hearts of palm.

Kontiki Restaurante – *Ilha Duas
Irmãs.* ☎ *24 3371 1666. kontiki@
eco-paraty.com. Open daily summer,
booking essential. Transfer from Paraty
pier available.* **Mediterranean.**
A 10-minute journey by boat from
Paraty, the setting for this restaurant
on a tiny tropical island, with a beach
lapped by clear waters, is unparalleled.

Porção

This is the place for serious eating—Porção literally means big pig. Based on
Brazil's traditional *Churrascaria*, or BBQ restaurants, the original Porção opened
in Rio in 1975. They took the quintessentially Brazilian concept and added some
humour through the name and by little touches such as the card each diner is
given; green on one side for "Yes please, give me meat" and red on the other for
"I'm full."
Each restaurant has an enormous well stocked buffet with fresh salads, cold cuts,
breads, seafood, sushi, and alternative mains for those who don't want meat.
You pay one fixed price, which excludes drinks and dessert, and you can eat like
a king. Rice, potatoes, and bread is brought to your table and immediately the
ever-circulating waiters offer an array of meats on huge skewers. The obligatory
picanha is much in evidence, but there are many other obscure and curious cuts
including chicken hearts, steak-with-cheese-inside, and ostrich. To help tourists,
there is a booklet in English that explains where each cut of meat is from.
*Av. Infante Dom Henrique (no number), Parque do Flamengo, Glória (with a great
Sugar Loaf view); Rua Barão da Torre 218, Ipanema; Av. Armando Lombardi 591,
Barra da Tijuca; Estrada do Galeão (no number), Ilha do Governador; Av. Quintino
Bocaiúva 151, São Francisco, Niterói.* ☎ *21 3389 8989. www.porcao.com.br. All the
restaurants open at noon everyday, but call to check closing times.* **$$.**

$

Restaurante Santa Rita – *Rua Santa Rita 335, Centro.* ✆*24 3371 1206. www.paraty.com.br/santarita/restaurante. Open daily.* **Brazilian.** Paraty's oldest restaurant sits right by Santa Rita church. Generous portions in this family-run place are deliberately sized to serve two. The menu includes a broad choice between meat and fresh seafood dishes, although it's the latter that shine. The freshly squeezed fruit juices here are second to none.

Grão da Terra – *Av. Roberto Silveira 45, Room 975, Centro. Open Mon–Sat (lunch only mid-Mar–mid-Dec).* **Vegetarian.** Food of the earth perfectly describes the delicious vegetarian cuisine and juices served here. The buffet offers a choice of daily specials, quiche, and an array of fresh, crispy salads. Sample the organic nectar-like açai, then finish off your healthy feast with a whole-grain desert. Catering to the cool, this place even has free Wi-Fi.

PETRÓPOLIS

$$

Restaurante Paladar – *Rua Barão do Amazonas, 25, Centro.* ✆*24 2243 1143. Open daily.* **Kilo.** Just at the bottom of the hill from the Santos Dumont House, this charming restaurant has airy terraces and a friendly staff. Tempting offerings on the buffet table include *feijoada*. At the end of the meal you can help yourself to coffee and little pots of caramel that are laid out near the entrance. Afterward, visit the cluster of tourist shops in the same little gated square as the restaurant .

Bordeaux Vinhos & CIA – *Rua Ipiranga, 716, Centro.* ✆*24 22425711. www.bordeauxvinhos.com.br. Open daily.* **International.** In Casa de Petrópolis' former stables, this is a unique place to have lunch or dinner. The *picanha* cooked on a hot stone is the most-ordered dish, perfect with one of the many red wines on the list. The adjacent wine shop has 1,200 labels to choose from. Walk off your meal in the mansion's delightful grounds, or pop into the 1884 fresco-filled house for a fascinating tour.

Restaurante Paladar

Y. Kanazawa/Michelin

Leopoldina – *Av. Koeller 276, Centro.* ✆*24 2103 3000. www.solardoimperio.com.br. Open daily 7.30am–10pm (midnight Fri–Sat).* **Portuguese.** This elegant restaurant in the Solar do Império Hotel (see p 230) serves contemporary, flavorful dishes.

$

Churrascaria Majórica – *Rua do Imperador 754, Centro.* ✆*24 2242 2429. www.majorica.com.br. Open Mon–Sat 8am–8pm.* **Barbeque.** Located in the heart of the historic center, this traditional churrascaria has been attracting locals and tourists alike since it opened in 1961. The welcome is warm and service fantastic.

Palmito

For years Brazilians have enjoyed conserved palm hearts for Sunday lunch as a treat. A vegetable that's harvested from the inner core of certain palm trees, it was simply plucked from the wild. By the 1990s poaching for stems threatened to wipe out entire species. Nowadays there are several sustainable farms in Rio de Janeiro state and many of Rio's restaurants make sure they buy from these legal sources, including **Zuka** who make a vegetarian tagliatelle with shredded palm hearts. **Aquim** serve it raw with rucola and smoked salmon. **Porcão** grill it with herbs and olive oil or serve it as a salad with artichokes, grilled onions and coriander.

ENTERTAINMENT

The city comes alive at night when the residents of Rio de Janeiro turn out in force to sip cold chopp (draft beers) or caipirinhas (cane-liquor cocktails) by the beach or lake, enjoy performing arts, or head to Lapa and Centro to embrace the world-class live music scene.

"What's on" publications include Veja Rio (a supplement that comes with Veja magazine), published on Wednesdays with events for the following weekend. Rio's dailies O Globo and Jornal do Brasil have culture magazines in Friday's papers.

Nightlife

To find the fun without planning, simply head toward, and under, the **Centro** Arco do Teles (Teles Arch) just off Praça XV where you'll find bars aplenty from numbers 2 to 6 on *Travessa do Comércio*. The tiny passageway and surrounding side streets are jam-packed during the week, especially on Friday night when the office workers pile in to unwind at the end of the week. *Avenida Mem de Sá* and *Rua Lavradio* in **Lapa** are where to find all the samba clubs and bars, best on Friday and Saturday nights. Sunday and Monday nights, *Praça Santos Dumont* at Baixo **Gávea** is where the action for twenty-somethings spills out from the bars onto the street. Just around the corner, a more sedate crowd frequents the lakeside bars around the **Lagoa** at the back of **Leblon**. In the same neighborhood, Rua Dias Ferreira and the end of Avenida General San Martin nearby is where the stylish set mingle.

Ipanema hosts the gay scene on Rua Farme de Amoedo. A mixed crowd party between Rua Farme de Amoedo and Rua Vinicius de Moraes. Along the beach road on Avenida Atlântico in **Copacabana,** there are mostly touristy outfits with a few gems between Postos 4 and 6. Up in the hills, the bohemian set gather in **Santa Teresa** around Largo do Guimarães and the surrounding streets.

BARS

HISTORIC CENTER AND SURROUNDS

Amarelinho – *Praça Floriano 55.* ⊙*Daily 7am–3am.* ✆*21 2240 8434. www.amarelinhodacinelandia.com.br.* One of the oldest bars in Rio de Janeiro, Amarelinho (little yellow one) is easily spotted by its bright yellow awnings with waiters in matching vests and tables spilling out onto the pavement. Close to the National Library, this casual concern was

Arco do Teles—thriving nightlife on Travessa do Comércio

©imagestate/Tips Images

founded in 1921 when the area was beginning to gain newfound respect. A full menu is on offer, but it's really a place for a drink along with some *petiscos* (bar snacks).

Bar Luiz – *Rua da Carioca 39.* ◷*Mon–Sat 11am–11pm.* ☎*21 2295 8744. www. barluiz.com.br.*
Founded way back in 1887 (although it has moved location since then), Bar Luiz is one of the oldest bars in Rio, and is firmly recognized as part of its heritage. Photographs of Rio through the ages grace the walls. Some say the best *chopp* in the city is served here; German food is on the menu.

Antigamente – *Rua do Ouvidor 43.* ◷*Mon–Fri 11am–midnight, Sat noon–6pm.* ☎*21 2507 5040.*
One of the many bars in a tiny pedestrian street just off Praça XV, Travessa do Comércio is where Carmen Miranda lived as a child and is where the city of Rio de Janeiro began. An atmospheric and popular spot to enjoy a *cerveja* (bottled beer).

Boteco Casual – *Rua do Ouvidor 33.* ◷*Mon–Fri noon until last customer, Sat noon–5am.* ☎*21 2232 0250. www.casualcheffsantos.com.br.*
This bar in "old Rio," as Cariocas call it, is set among the colonial buildings. If you are there Saturday lunchtime, try the goat; it is the house specialty.

Cosmopolita – *Travessa da Mosqueira 4, Lapa.* ◷*Mon–Thu 11am–midnight, Fri–Sat 11am until last customer.* ☎*21 2224 7820.*
Step inside this old 1906 house and the stained glass windows and "old-timey" vibe will make you feel like you are in a North American saloon. The perfect warm-up to a Lapa night out. House specialty is filet mignon.

Adega Flor de Coimbra – *Rua Teotônio Regadas 34, Lapa.* ◷*Mon–Sat noon until last customer.* ☎*21 2224 4582.*
When you've had enough samba, head to Rio's boho-bar where artists and intellectuals have flocked since it

Bar dos Descasados

Hotel Santa Teresa

opened in 1938. Snack on dried cod balls as you sip Sangria until the early hours.

THE HILLS

Bar dos Descasados – *Hotel Santa Teresa, Rua Felício dos Santos, Santa Teresa.* ◷*Daily 11am–midnight.* ☎*21 3380 0200. www.santateresahotel.com.*
This chic lounge-bar is cheekily called "Bar of the Unmarried" and is located at the bottom of the garden of this newly renovated hotel. Sip a cocktail in bohemian environs under the arches of the restored slave quarters or on the tree-covered terrace. *Caipirinhas* are served with the finest *cachaça* (cane liquor).

Armazém São Thiago – *Rua Áurea 26, Santa Teresa.* ◷*Mon–Sat noon–midnight, Sun noon–8pm.* ☎*21 2232 0822.*
This local institution more commonly known as Bar do Gomez (Gomez's bar) has been going since 1919. Originally functioning as a local food store with bar; the eccentric bar staff and wide range of drinks—including more than 60 kinds of *cachaça*—are the reason most people visit today. This unassuming place evokes atmosphere with original shop fittings and historic black and white photographs.

SOUTH ZONE BESIDE THE BAY

Bar do Adão – *Rua Dona Mariana 81, Botafogo.* ◷*Mon–Sat noon–1am.* ☎*21 2535 4572. www.bardoadao.com.br.*

Baretto Londra

Hotel Fasano

Join the young, hip crowd that hangs out at this colonial venue. A cozy interior with high ceilings, wood floors, tables and chairs, and a massive chandelier; you feel like you're in someone's front room. Nibble from a huge array of bar snacks as you sip your *caipirinha*, *cerveja*, or *chopp*.

Bar Urca – *Rua Cândido Gaffrée, Urca.* ⏰*Daily 11:30am–11pm.* ☎*21 2295 8744. www.barurca.com.br.*
Since 1939, Cariocas have been very fond of this bar. At the very end of Urca right by São João Fort, it's a lovely quiet spot on Guanabara Bay for a drink. Go in good weather because the "chairs" are actually the sea wall on the little road in front of the bar.

Praia Vermelha Restaurante e Bar – *Praça General Tibúrcio, Praia Ver-melha.* ⏰*Daily noon–midnight.* ☎*21 2543 7284.*
On the terraces of the fort at Praia Vermelha, listen to the waves and birds until the live music starts at 7pm *(8pm Fri and Sat).* There's a cover charge, but if you arrive before the music begins you don't pay. Sip a draft beer and watch the colors morph on Sugar Loaf as the sun sets.

SOUTH ZONE BEACHES
Bar d'Hotel – *Marina All Suites, Av. Delfim Moreira 696, Leblon.* ⏰*Daily noon–2am.* ☎*21 2172 1100. www.marinaallsuites.com.br.*
One of the current "in" places to go out *(Thu–Sat book in advance).*

There's a hip yet elegant vibe with fancy mirrors, draped curtains, and chandeliers. Sink into one of the fuscia or orange velvet sofas as you sip the house special, "Royal," a deadly mix of vodka, cointreau, grenadine, lime, ginger, and ice.

Baretto Londra – *Fasano Hotel, Av. Vieira Souto 80, Ipanema.* ⏰*Daily 11:30am–11pm.* ☎*21 3202 4000. www.fasano.com.br.*
This bar is an homage to London, owner Rogerio Fasano's favorite city. The entrance is via a long, curving neon-lit path, framed by theatrical curtains. Once inside, the rock 'n' roll decor is unconventional. Italianized Union Jacks in red, green, and white adorn the brick walls and big, comfy leather armchairs beckon. 1980s vintage vinyl of British bands from Rogerio's personal collection are proudly displayed.

Jobi – *Av. Ataúlfo de Paiva, Leblon.* ⏰*Daily 10am–5am.* ☎*21 2274 0547.*
One of Rio's most famous *botequins*, has excellent beer and *caipirinhas*, very tasty snacks, and a great atmosphere. Friday and Saturday you'll have to jostle for a table and then jostle some more once installed, as the place is tiny. Perfect for a post-party wind down.

Cobal – *Rua Gilberto Cardoso, Leblon.* ⏰*Daily noon–4am.* ☎*21 2239 1549.*
A fruit, vegetable, and flower market by day, the annexed square lined with bars and pizzerias buzzes at night. In spite of the plastic tables and chairs, it is a vibrant setting.

Atlântico – *Av. Atlantica 3880, Copacabana.* ⏰*Daily 7pm–4am.* ☎*21 2235 2947. www.copaclub.com.br.*
Smooth lounge-cool in Copacabana is a rarity. The long steel bar is built for a crowd and the bartenders serve up a sensational *caipirinha* with owner Roberto Peres' specially commis-sioned *cachaça* from Ouro Preto, *Atentapora.* On Mondays this is a gay bar.

Botequim Informal – *Shopping Leblon, Rua Afrânio de Mello Franco 290, 4th floor, Leblon.* ⏰*Daily noon–midnight, weekend noon–1am.* ☎*21 2529 2588.*

A chain of bars that can be found in almost every Rio neighborhood, the Leblon location is always buzzing. They specialize in beer and very tasty bar snacks.

LAKE AND SURROUNDS

Palaphita Kitch – *Av. Epitácio Pessoa (no number), Kiosk 20, Parque do Cantagalo, Lagoa.* ⏰*Daily 6pm until last customer.* ☎*21 2227 0837. www. palaphitakitch.com.br.*

Lounge on heavy wooden sofas as you watch the sunset over the Two Brothers mountains or Christ the Redeemer across the lagoon. A choice of Amazon fruits are served with the *cachaça*, sake, or vodka.

Guimas – *Rua José Roberto Macedo Soares 5, Lagoa.* ⏰*Daily 6pm until last customer.* ☎*21 2529 8300.*

Nice, quiet bistro with mellow sounds. There's a bohemian and classy vibe which is understated and relaxed. The *caipirinhas* are just about the best in town and the bar snacks are excellent. There's a sister branch in Ipanema.

Saturnino – *Rua Saturnino de Brito 50, Jardim Botânico.* ⏰*Daily 6pm until late.* ☎*21 3874 0064. www.saturnino. com.br.*

A good place to choose from a wide range of drinks in a chic and contemporary environment. Try a "Rouge" cocktail: vodka, strawberry, raspberry, and blackberry with lychee syrup and lemongrass. The regular clientele are cool Cariocas dressed in the latest fashions.

Hipódromo – *Praça Santos Dumont 108, Gávea.* ⏰*Daily 9am–1am.* ☎*21 2274 9720. www.hipodromo.com.br.*

A favored spot that caters to diverse clientele and has a casual, laid-back vibe. Cold draft beer is the thing to order and there are plenty of snacks to choose from. Sunday and Monday see the younger crowd turn up to flirt.

Best bars for caipirinha, batida or chopp

Botequim Informal: *Chopp*— lager, pale, and stout (👆*see p 251*).

Jobi: *Chopp*—draft Brahma and Brahma "Black" (👆*see p 250*).

Acadamia da Cachaça: *Caipirinha*—100 different *cachaças* (👆*see p 251*).

Bar do Oswaldo: *Batida*—62 years in the business (👆*see p 250*).

WEST ZONE BEACHES

Academia da Cachaça – *Condomínio Condado dos Cascais, Av. Armando Lombardi 800, Shop 65, Barra da Tijuca.* ⏰*Daily noon until last customer.* ☎*21 2492 1159. www.academia dacachaca.com.br.*

At the start of Barra da Tijuca, this well-established venue in a *shopping* is serious about *cachaça*. The orange and ginger *caipirinha* is divine and there's also every possible kind of tropical fruit on offer besides lime. There's another branch in Leblon.

Bar do Oswaldo – *Estrada do Joá 3896.* ⏰*Daily Tue–Sun noon–1:30am, Mon 5pm–1am.* ☎*21 2493 1840.*

A lovely quirky old bar in Barra da Tijuca that has been going 60 years and is a local institution. Popular since *batidas* (a mix of fresh fruit juice and *cachaça*) were in fashion back in the 1960s and 70s, in the days before the large condominiums appeared in Barra. There's a great selection of *cachaça* and they whip up the best *batida* in town.

NIGHTCLUBS

HISTORIC CENTER AND SURRIUNDS

Passeio Público Dance – *Av. Rio Branco 277.* ⏰*Mon–Fri 6pm until late, Sat 10pm–5am.* ☎*21 2220 1298. www. passeiodance.com.br.*

Monday to Friday you'll find live music that varies from disco to samba and MPB. Saturday nights the DJ plays Brazilian funk, hip-hop, and disco.

Favela Funk Parties

Also known as Funk Balls, they're huge affairs where the bass-heavy funk beats into the early hours. They started in the *favelas* in the 1970s and take place in warehouses, clubs and nightclubs. You can safely join in the party by going with an organized tour with a local company like **Be A Local**, who escort groups of 30 to 100 foreigners to trouble-free, tried-and-tested bashes such as Castelo das Pedras in the Rio das Pedras or Formula do Sol in Curicica. For a reasonable fee, which includes your entrance and access to a VIP area, you are picked up from your hotel in the late evening and dropped off at your door around 4am. *www.bealocal.com. ℘21 9643 0366/21 7816 9581.*

Traditional club with a checkered dance floor, colored lights, and a great atmosphere.

Dito e Feito – *Rua do Mercado 21.* ⏱*Mon–Sat 6pm–1am. ℘21 2222 4016. www.ditoefeito.com.br.*
The fun starts during the week after work, where the downtown crowd relaxes during happy hour. Saturday action starts from 11pm. The music crosses over from MPB to hip-hop, dance, funk, and *axé*.

THE HILLS
Casa Rosa – (*see p 132*)

SOUTH ZONE BESIDE THE BAY
Casa da Matriz – *Rua Henrique de Novais 107, Botafogo.* ⏱*Mon, Wed–Sat 10pm–6am. ℘21 2266 1014. http://matrizonline.oi.com.br/casadamatriz.*
This casual club with a number of intimate rooms on two floors attracts a stylish, alternative crowd. Mostly Brazilian music with electronic, funk, jazz, rock, soul, and indie on any given night. Check before you go.

SOUTH ZONE BEACHES
Clandestino – *Rua Barata Ribeiro 111.* ⏱*Wed–Mon from midnight. ℘21 3209 0348. www.clandestinobar.com.br.*
Down in the basement, this is where the cool locals go to party. Jive to the dulcet tones of funky-house, rock, MPB, hip-hop, soul, reggae, and dance-hall. Friday night is "Black Friday," a chance to get your groove on to an array of black music styles.

Baronneti – *Rua Barão da Torre 354, Ipanema.* ⏱*Mon–Thu 9pm until late, Fri–Sat 10pm until late. ℘21 2247 9100. www.baronneti.com.br.*
With two dance floors and a lounge area, this is a sleek, compact club with a lounge-feel where you can boogie to the sounds of funk-hop, hip-hop, funk, and MPB. The ambience is 1970s high design, with space-age white and dark wood.

Lounge 69 – *Rua Farme de Amoedo 50, Ipanema.* ⏱*Wed–Sat 11pm–5am. ℘21 2522 0627. www.lounge69.com.br.*
Hip locals turn up to practice their smooth moves to the sounds of electro house, electro rock, acid house, rock, funk, and pop. Light projection in acid colors creates a psychedelic vibe. There's a dance area on the ground floor with lounge upstairs strewn with dark sofas.

Melt – *Rua Rita Ludolf 47, Leblon.* ⏱*Daily 8pm–6am. ℘21 2249 9309.*
Start the night at a candlelit table in the dark and cozy lounge bar downstairs with a huge screen showing surfing stunts. Then head upstairs to the large dance floor

Dito & Feito

Dito & Feito

where every style of music (except *axé* and *pagode*) is played. Arrive early to be sure of entry.

The House – *Rua General San Martin 1011, Leblon.* ⏰*Tue–Sat 10pm until late.* ☎*21 2249 2161. www.thehousebar. com.br.*
A chic Japanese restaurant is on the ground floor, the club and dance floor is on the first floor. Well-dressed Zona Sul locals dance to a range of electronica. The decor is contemporary, with an understated mix of wood, brickwork, and marble.

LAKE AND SURROUNDS

Nuth – *Av. Epitácio Pessoa 1244, Lagoa.* ⏰*Daily 7pm until last customer.* ☎*21 3575 6850. www.nuth.com.br.*
Recently opened, Nuth has a club on the first floor with a restaurant on the upstairs. On the top floor you can take a break from the eclectic selection of sounds and enjoy the view of the lake and Christ the Redeemer statue. The decor is modern and funky with shiny white upholstery in the lounge and dance areas. The restaurant has dark wood floors and 1970s-style patterned wallpaper.

Zero Zero (00) – *Av. Padre Leonel Franca 240, Gávea.* ⏰*Thu–Sun 8:30pm until last customer.* ☎*21 2540 8041. www.00site.com.br.*
Slick and chic venue with a small dance floor packed with locals. Outdoors, there is a great space to relax under trees and palms. A stylish food menu and a varied selection of music complete the ambience.

WEST ZONE BEACHES

Apple Mixxx International – *Estrada da Barra da Tijuca 156, Barra da Tijuca.* ⏰*Daily 10pm–late.* ☎*21 2494 9242. www.applemixxx.com.br.*
Brand new, this 1,315sq yd/1,100sq m venue is for serious clubbers. Relax in the Deck Lounge surrounded by waterfalls and tropical greenery before heading back to the reverberating dance floor.

Hard Rock Café – *Shopping Città America, Av. das Américas 700, 3rd floor, Barra da Tijuca.* ⏰*Sun–Thu noon–1am, Fri–Sat noon–4am.* ☎*21 2132 8000. www.hardrock.com.*
Although this is a worldwide chain and the venue is in bland mall-land, Brazilians are the vital ingredient that keep the house jumping and make it a fun-packed night out. Saturdays are a mix of U.S., British, and Brazilian rock.

GAY CLUBS

Le Boy/La Girl – *Rua Raul Pompeia 102, Copacabana.* ⏰*Le Boy Tue–Sun 9pm until late, La Girl Wed–Mon 11pm until late.* ☎*21 2513 4993.*
Going strong since 1992, Le Boy is Rio's four-floor gay club where drag-shows and go-go nights add variety. Thursday's "Connection" night is always busy, as are Fridays and Saturdays. Tuesday night is strip night.

Dama de Ferro – *Rua Vinícius de Moraes 288, Ipanema.* ⏰*Tue–Sat 11pm until late.* ☎*21 2247 2330. www.dama deferro.com.br.*
Concrete bunker open to "beautiful people" at this hardcore electronic and house venue over two floors.

Cine Ideal – *Rua da Carioca 64, Centro.* ⏰*Fri–Sat 11:30pm until late.* ☎*21 2221 1984. www.cineideal.com.br.*
A fine old "belle epoque" building that housed a movie theater, nowadays is pounding to electronic beats and dancing divas. The outdoor terrace offers a cityscape view.

The Week – *R. Sacadura Cabral 150, Saúde, Centro.* ☎*21 2253 1020.* ⏰*Saturday only (midnight). www. theweek.com.br. Taxi to and from the venue is recommended.*
A new club on the scene, located in the Saúde neighborhood, near the port. It has five bars, an enormous dance floor, a huge sound system and even a swimming pool. Electronic, house and tech-house music. Big names sometimes host nights—check their website for information.

Cabaret Casanova – *Av. Mem de Sá 25, Lapa.* 🕐*Fri–Sat 10pm until late, Sun 8pm until late.* 📞*21 2221 6555. www. cabaretcasanova.vai.la.*
An established venue for 70 years, Cabaret Casanova is the Grand Dame of gay clubs with drag queens putting on fantastic performances. In the heart of Lapa and frequented by a mixed crowd.

Live Brazilian Music

SAMBA, CHORINHO, FORRÓ, AND MPB

Most of Rio de Janeiro's live music is a mix of genres (💡*see sidebar p 255*), featuring *chorinho*, *forró*, MPB, and samba. Cariocas are passionate about music and socializing is inextricably linked with music, preferably live. MPB and samba are the most popular genres.

Cidade do Samba – *Rua Rivadavia Correia 60, Gamboa.* 📞*21 2213 2503. www.cidadedosambarj.com.br. (Check their website or call for more details, alternatively call RioTur for up-to-date information;* 📞*21 2542 8080.)*
A vast city of warehouses at Gamboa near Rio de Janeiro's port is where many of the main parade's floats and costumes are constructed (💡*see p 106*). A weekly live show re-captures the spirit of Carnival for tourists who missed it.

Severyna – *Rua Ipiranga 54, Laranjei- ras.* 🕐*Daily 11:30am–1am.* 📞*21 2556 9398. www.severyna.com.br.*
Offering food, drink, and music from Brazil's northeast, this is a unique venue. Friendly and efficient staff wait on customers sitting at simple wooden tables set out over two floors.

☻ A Bit of Advice ☻

Brazilians don't drink without something to eat on the side, whether a meal or bar snack. They enjoy a drink, but rarely get out of control.

Carne de Sol (dried beef) is a menu staple. Live music (samba, *forró*, MPB or Beatles) every night from 8pm.

Teatro Odisséia – *Av. Mem de Sá 66, Lapa.* 🕐*Wed–Sun 9pm until late.* 📞*21 2224 6367. http://matrizonline.oi.com. br/teatroodisseia.*
The first floor has a stage for new bands and singers and upstairs is for exhibitions and plays. Thursday night is *forró* night and Fridays and Saturdays you'll hear samba and MPB.

Rio Scenarium – *Rua do Lavradio 20, Lapa.* 🕐*Tue–Sat 7pm until late.* 📞*21 3147 9000. www.rioscenarium.com.br.*
Probably Rio de Janeiro's most famous samba club, the Scenarium has three floors of 19C and 20C artifacts and furniture that can be hired for TV and film. The main area has a stage with an atrium and two galleries above. The first show begins at 7pm and the second around 10pm. MPB, samba, *choro*, bossa nova, and *forró* are in the schedules. In the annex there is another dance floor where DJs spin MPB, international pop, and electronic music on Friday and Saturday nights. The club is hugely popular and attracts a fun and lively crowd.

Mangue Seco – *Rua do Lavradio 23, Lapa.* 🕐*Daily 11am until late.* 📞*21 3852 1947. www.manguesecoca chacaria.com.br.*
Enjoy samba and MPB as you relax with a drink or meal. An old ware- house with two floors, Mangue Seco has a simple, rustic feel. There's a well- stocked *cachaçaria* where you can choose from an extensive menu of different *cachaças* from Minas Gerais and Paraty. Live music starts from 6pm daily and is free during the week.

Carioca da Gema – *Av. Mem de Sá 79, Lapa.* 🕐*Daily 7pm–3am.* 📞*21 2221 0043. www.barcariocadagema.com.br.*
The bar is one of the most established live music venues on the Lapa strip. They showcase MPB and samba artists. Some of Rio's most famous singers have trodden the da Gema boards, including Tereza Cristina.

Brazilian Music

In case you don't know, *Samba* is Brazil's national music genre. With African and European roots, it is a rhythmic percussion sound that's impossible not to move to. *Chorinho* means "little cry" in Portuguese, but the music often has a fast, happy rhythm and is played with a mandolin and wind instruments and a tambourine. *Forró* is pop music from Brazil's northeast, played on an accordion and percussion instruments. *Pagode* has samba roots, but is slower and sexier, with explicit lyrics. Brazilian *funk*, nothing like the European version, also has explicit lyrics and is a hip-hop derivative. *Axé* music started in Salvador, Bahia, and is a fusion of Afro-Brazilian and Afro-Caribbean styles. MPB is the generic name for Brazilian pop music.

Bar do Semente – *Rua Joaquim Silva 138, Lapa.* ◷*Mon–Sat 10pm until late.* ☏*21 2509 3591.*
A gritty little bar where some of the country's finest chorinho musicians perform. This tiny place has a great atmosphere inside and a view of the Lapa arches outside. Samba and salsa are also in the schedule.

Lapa 40° – *Rua do Riachuelo 97, Lapa.* ◷*Daily 6pm–4am.* ☏*21 3970 1338. www.lapa40graus.com.br.*
The new kid on the block offers live music on the ground floor and pool tables on the second. The top floor is reserved for dancing and the stage is where big Brazilian names like Elba Ramalho, João Bosco, Marcelo D2, Mart'nália and Elza Soares play. From 8pm on Saturdays, pick up some basic gafieira steps to show off later.

Estrela da Lapa – *Av. Mem de Sá 69, Lapa.* ◷*Mon–Sat 6pm until late.* ☏*21 2507 6686. www.estreladalapa.com.br.*
New to the samba-club posse, this night hangout has a fantastic space in a restored 19C mansion. The cathedral-like space has two mezzanine floors from where you can enjoy live music from 9pm, including and an assorted mix of *choro*, blues and hip hop. A DJ follows until the small hours.

Centro Cultural Memórias do Rio – *Avendia Gomes Freire 289, Lapa.* ◷*Tue–Sat 6pm until late.* ☏*21 2222 7380. www.memoriasdorio.com.br.*
Based in a lovely old mansion, this is where you'll find "samba-roots" on Thursdays. Saturdays might be chorinho or MPB; Wednesdays get into bossa nova-mode.

Café Cultural Sacrilégio – *Av. Mem de Sá 81, Lapa.* ◷*Tue–Fri 7pm–2am, Sat 8:30pm–4am.* ☏*21 2222 7345. www.sacrilegio.com.br.*
In an old colonial house on the main Lapa stretch, Sacrilégio is a samba-venue linchpin. Prior to becoming a club, musician João Pernambuco used to organize soirées with big names Pixinguinha, Villa-Lobos and Carmem Miranda. Nowadays it's the likes of Paulinho da Viola, Beth Carvalho and Diogo Nogueira who take to the stage. *Choro*, MPB, and of course samba is played and there is a garden where you can relax with a cold beer.

CinemathequeJam Club – *Rua Voluntários da Pátria 53, Botafogo.* ◷*Tue–Sat 7pm until late.* ☏*21 3239 0488. www.matrizonline.com.br.*
Away from the Lapa scene, this club seeks innovation in Brazilian music where traditional styles including samba, rock, jazz, bossa nova and electronic morph and fuse. The two-story house is in an Art Deco building. Wednesday to Friday is mainly *choro* and jazz and there is no cover charge.

Modern Sound – *Rua Barata Ribeiro 502D, Copacabana.* ◷*Mon–Fri 9am–9pm, Sat 9am–8pm.* ☏*21 2548 5005. www.modernsound.com.br.*
This music store hosts live music daily from 5pm. Twice a week there are live shows with top artists from all Brazilian music genres, including

Summer Festivals

Rio de Janeiro's summer music festivals are hosted in two places, atop Sugar Loaf and at the docks. Both events take place in summer from January to February. "Verão do Morro" includes music shows (samba and Brazilian jazz with artists such as Jorge Ben Jor and Gilberto Gil), cinema, and DJs. The cablecar fee is included in the ticket price. (*Events start 9:30pm and end 4:30am with last cablecar down at 5am. www.veraodomorro.com.br. ✆21 2461 2700.*)
"Noites Cariocas," or "Carioca Nights," takes place at Rio de Janeiro's docks at Pier Maúa, in Centro. They feature mostly Brazilian pop and rock bands such as Skank, Nando Reis, Titãs, and Lulu Santos. (*http://oinoitescariocas.oi.com.br*)

classical and jazz. Maria Rita and Marisa Monte have been past performers when their new releases hit the stores. And they're free! But you need to call the store beforehand to reserve a table.

Espaco BNDES – *Av. República do Chile 100, Centro.* ⏰*Shows start 7pm.* ✆*21 2172 7770. www.bndes.gov.br/cultura*
Catch free MPB, *chorinho* or Brazilian jazz every Thursday night at 7pm. Make sure you pick up a voucher from 5pm to ensure free entry.

GAFIEIRA

Estudantina Musical – *Praça Tiraden-tes 79–81, Centro.* ⏰*Thu 8pm–1am, Fri 8pm–2am, Sat 10pm–4am.* ✆*21 2232 1149. www.estudantinamusical.com.br.*
Atmospheric, but slightly scruffy, dance hall from the early 1920s, this is where expert samba dancers twirl and shake between the old wrought-iron pillars to live samba bands. Maria Bethânia has done the occasional live show. *Samba de Gafieira* (samba ballroom dance) classes are on offer for locals and tourists.

Gafieira Elite – *Rua Frei Caneca 4. Cen-tro.* ⏰*Thu–Sun 10pm–6am.* ✆*21 3902 9364. www.gafieiraelite.com.* 😊*A taxi to and from the venue is recommended.*
Tucked away in an old pink-and-plaster gem of building with arched windows, this club has been going since the 1930s with the likes of Grande Otelo, Pixinguinha and Elza Soares performing. Thursday to Saturdays MPB, samba-groove, and

electro-funk reverberate. The all-important *Samba de Gafieira* is on Sundays.

BOSSA NOVA AND JAZZ

Bar do Tom – *Rua Adalberto Ferreira 32, Leblon.* ⏰*Mon–Sun from 8–10pm depending on show time.* ✆*21 2274 4022. www.plataforma.com.*
A slightly touristy vibe, but a decent ongoing selection of jazz, bossa nova, and samba to choose from seven days a week. Pery Ribeiro and Luciano Bruno have sung here.

Vinicius Piano Bar – *Rua Vinicius de Moraes 39, Ipanema.* ⏰*Live music 9:30pm Mon–Tue, 10:30pm Wed, 11pm Thu–Sun.* ✆*21 2523 4757. www.viniciusbar.com.br.*
Named after Vinicius de Moraes who wrote *Girl from Ipanema*, this establishment is known as the "bossa nova temple" where the bossa elite seduce with their dulcet tones. Live music is featured in the Show Bar, an intimate space with wooden chairs and tables, where you can sample the essence of Brazil with artists like Leni Andrade, Robert Menescal, and Dori Caymmi.

Drink Café – *Parque dos Patins, Av. Borges de Medeiros, Lagoa.* ⏰*Daily shows from 7pm.* ✆*21 2239 4136. www.drinkcafe.com.br.*
Relax in a magical setting at this kiosk-bar-restaurant right by the lake. Bossa nova, jazz, and samba-jazz are usually played, but also *chorinho*, samba, and MPB, so check on the website before turning up.

Esch Café – *Parque dos Patins, Av. Borges de Medeiros, Lagoa.* ⏰*Daily noon–midnight.* ☎*21 2512 5651. www.esch.com.br.*
Relax in cozy but smoky environs to smooth jazz and bossa nova. Live music is on Fridays and Saturdays from 10pm. Cuban cigars are smoked in the especially climate-controlled room as the bands play. Decor is brick and wood with subdued lighting. Waiters in Panama hats add a tropical flavor.

CONCERT VENUES

Circo Voador *(Rua do Arco, Lapa;* ☎*21 2533 0354; www.circovoador.com.br)* is popular with Brazilian rock bands such as Skank and big names like Chico Buarque. **HSBC Arena** *(Av. Embaixador Abelardo Bueno 3401, Barra da Tijuca;* ☎*21 3035 5200; www.hsbcarena.com)* is Rio's largest concert arena where megastars Seal, Ozzy Osbourne, and Andrea Bocelli have entertained.
Canecão *(Av. Venceslau Brás;* ☎*21 2105 2000, Botafogo 2000; www.canecao. com.br)* opened in 1967 and is the best known pop venue in Rio. It is in Botafogo near Tûnel Novo and Shopping Rio Sul. It hosts rock, hip-hop, and MPB artists. **Vivo Rio** *(Av. Infante Dom Henrique 85, Parque do Flamengo;* ☎*21 2272 2907; www. vivorio.com.br)* is a brand new venue music venue especially constructed for acoustic excellence. Good enough for musical elite Joss Stone and Gilberto Gil to strut the boards.
Citybank Hall *(Av. Ayrton Senna 3000, Barra da Tijuca;* ☎*21 4003 1212; www. clarohall.com.br)* is a large venue inside the Via Parque shopping center hosting MPB, rock bands, and the occasional circus/theater piece.
Fundição Progresso *(Rua dos Arcos 24, Lapa;* ☎*21 2220 5070; www. fundicaoprogresso.com.br)* is a medium-sized event space with two stages hosting all genres. Franz Ferdinand, Marilyn Manson, and Nando Reis have hit the spotlight here.

Performing Arts

CLASSICAL MUSIC AND OPERA

Theatro Municipal (⏱*see p 109*)

Sala Cecilia Meireles – *Largo da Lapa 47, Lapa.* ⏰*Box office Mon–Fri 1pm–6pm.* ☎*21 2332 9160. www. salaceciliameireles.com.br.*
Rio de Janeiro's main venue for classical concerts is particularly renowned for chamber music recitals. This concert room is a lovely late 19C building and is named for Brazilian poet Cecília Meireles. Although almost exclusively classical, contemporary music and *MPB* is also performed here.

Escola de Música – *Salão Leopoldo Miguez, Universidade Federal do Rio de Janeiro, Rua do Passeio 98, Lapa.* ⏰*Concerts usually start 6:30pm.* ☎*21 2240 1391. www.musica.ufrj.br.*
Classical concerts organized by Rio de Janeiro's federal university music department. Students, teachers, and visiting international artists perform here. For the schedule see *www. vivamusica.com.br* or purchase the guide "Guia Viva Musica" from any of Rio de Janeiro's cultural centers such as the Bank of Brasil (⏱*see p 103*).

Sala Villa-Lobos – *Av. Pasteur 436, Centro de Letras e Artes, Unirio.* ⏰*Concerts Tue 5:20pm.* ☎*21 2542 3311. www.unirio.br.*
Though a small 80-seat room in the Universidade Federal do Rio de Janeiro, it is nevertheless a popular venue. Up-and-coming talent perform alongside seasoned Brazilian greats such as Eduardo Monteiro, Edino Krieger, and Camerata Quantz.

Centro Cultural Municipal Laurinda Santos Lobo – *Rua Monte Alegre 306, Santa Teresa.* ⏰*Center open Tue–Sun 9am–8pm.* ☎*21 2242 9741. www.rio. rj.gov.br/cultura.*
The Baronesa de Parina's 1907 mansion is the setting for concerts both in the 80-seat music hall and lovely garden outside. Events are free.

Music in churches and museums

Classical music in venues outside of Rio de Janeiro's theaters began in 1997, in churches, museums, cultural centers, and even out of doors... Kill two cultural birds with one stone by having a look around the museum or church before or after recitals. Candelária Church holds regular concerts from December to March.

Schedules are on the websites and many of the concerts are free. www.musicanomuseu.com.br www.musicanasigrejas.com.br

Centro Cultural Municipal Parque das Ruínas – *Rua Murtinho Nobre 169, Santa Teresa.* Center open Tue–Sun 8am–8pm. 21 2252 1039. www.rio. rj.gov.br/cultura.
Enjoy open air concerts at socialite Laurinda Santos Lobo's former home (see p 129). The grand old mansion almost collapsed completely before a restoration in the mid-1990s. Sip a cocktail as you soak up the sounds of artists such as singer/harpist Cristina Braga and soprano Dorina Mendes. There is a fantastic view of Guanabara Bay and Sugar Loaf.

DANCE

Centro Coreográfico da Cidade do Rio de Janeiro – *Rua José Higino 115, Tijuca.* Mon–Sun 9am–8pm. 21 2268 7139. www.rio.rj.gov.br/cultura.
Dedicated to the promotion of dance, this out-of-the-way center is where you can catch a range of dance from samba and ballroom to contemporary dance performances at reasonable prices (or free), every weekend.

THEATER

Teatro do Centro Cultural Banco do Brasil – *Rua Primeiro de Março 66, Centro.* Center open 10am–9pm. 21 3808 2000. www.bb.com.br.
The impressive Cultural Center's theater has hosted some big productions with the nation's thespian elite such as Fernanda Montenegro and Marília Pera. International productions also appear, such as Peter Brook's production *Fragments*. In addition opera, orchestral concerts, and big-name singers such as Tom Jobim and Adriana Calcanhoto take to the stage.

Teatro João Caetano – *Praça Tiradentes, Centro.* Box office Tue–Sat 2pm–6pm, performances from 8–9pm. 21 2332 9166. www.funarj.rj.gov.br.
This theater, opened in 1813, was named after the great dramatic Portuguese actor **João Caetano** (1808–1863). It is considered the first official theater in Rio de Janeiro. Every possible kind of performing art has been staged here from drama to opera and dance to musicals. In 1885–86 both Eleonora Duse and Sarah Bernhardt trod the boards.

Teatro Odisséia – *Av. Mem de Sá 66, Lapa.* Tue–Sat 9pm–3am. 21 2224 6367.
This music, film, theater, and visual arts performance space in a former mansion dating from 1907 is typical of the daring creative independence of Lapa. Democratic and providing a wonderful variety of events (from traditional to cutting edge), it is a cultural melting pot. The entrance floor has a space for new artists and a bar; the mezzanine floor has table seating with food and shows; on the upper floor is an exhibition space, stage, and restaurant.

Teatro Oi Casa Grande – *Rua Afrânio de Melo Franco 290, Leblon.* Box office Tue–Sun 3pm–10pm, shows from 8–9pm. 21 2511 0800. http:// oicasagrande.oi.com.br.
True to the name, it is a large theater housing drama, music, and contemporary and classical dance. It is situated in a space that once had a very important part in Brazilian cultural and political life.

Teatro Municipal Carlos Gomes
– *Praça Tiradentes 19, Centro.* ⓒ*Box office Tue–Sat 2pm–6pm, shows from 8–9pm.* ☏*21 2232 8701. www.rio.rj.gov. br/cultura.*
The building began life in 1868 as the elegant Hotel Richelieu. In 1904 it was converted and given its current name and in 1993, extensive renovations took place. Today, Teatro Carlos Gomes boasts state-of-the-art sound and lighting equipment, a contemporary complement to its exquisite Art Deco interior. Widely acknowledged to be one of the best theaters in the city, courses in music, theater, and dance are all on offer.

Teatro da Casa de Cultura Laura Alvim – *Av Vieira Souto 176, Ipanema.* ⓒ*Box office Tue–Sun 4pm–9pm.* ☏*21 2267 1647. www.funarj.rj.gov.br.*
Overlooking Ipanema Beach, the theater was originally used as rehearsal space by top Brazilian actors. Nowadays there are plays, classical music events, and a cinema (ⓒ*see below*).

Espaço Tom Jobim de Cultura e Meio Ambiente – *Rua Jardim Botânico 1008, Jardim Botânico.* ⓒ*Box office Tue–Sun 3pm–6pm, shows begin 8:30pm.* ☏*21 2274 7012.*
A brand new 500-seat theater in the heart of the Botanical Gardens. Hosting music and plays, it's Brazil's first "eco-theater"—solar powered and built with certified wood. Gilberto Gil, Caetano Veloso, Milton Nascimento, and Tereza Cristina are some of the acclaimed performers who have played here.

CINEMAS

Most films in Rio de Janeiro are shown in their original version and are subtitled in Portuguese and will state "legendado" on the flyers and posters. If it says "dublado" then the film is dubbed, so check carefully before paying. All major shopping malls in Rio have cinemas.

Odeon Petrobras – *Praça Mahatma Gandhi 2, Cinelândia.* ⓒ*Screenings from noon.* ☏*21 2240 1093.*
This is the last of the grand cinemas that dominated the area of *Cinelândia.* Dating back to 1926, there is one vast Art Deco theater that can seat almost 600 people. Now a Carioca institution, independents, documentaries, and main stream films are screened. Movie marathons on the first Friday of every month are also hosted, and on Sundays pre-recorded performances by the Metropolitan Opera are shown.

Roxy – *Av. Nossa Senhora de Copacabana 945, Copacabana.* ⓒ*Screenings from 2pm.* ☏*21 3221 9292.*
Copacabana's only street cinema, the Roxy is a happy remnant of the Art Deco era, when cinemas were huge. Now converted to three comfortable screens, it shows mainstream releases.

Estação Laura Alvim – *Av. Vieira Souto 176, Ipanema.* ⓒ*Screenings from 1pm.* ☏*21 2267 4307. www. estacaovirtual.com.br.*
A lovely cultural center with an appealing vibe in an old building right on Ipanema's beachfront. Three small screens surround a courtyard with a cafe, perfect to meet friends.

Kinoplex Leblon – *Shopping Leblon, top floor, Av. Afrânio de Melo Franco 290, Leblon.* ⓒ*Screenings from 2pm.* ☏*21 2461 2461. www.kinoplex.com.br.*
Comfortable cinema in the shopping mall with great sound and good visibility. A pleasant cafe overlooks the Christ the Redeemer statue. Four screens show the usual mainstream movies on release.

SHOPPING

The shopping scene in Rio de Janeiro incorporates huge air-conditioned malls where Cariocas like to flock on rainy days, eclectic galleries, boutiques, jewelry stores and well-known chains that line the streets particularly in the South Zone, and the colorful stalls of the much-loved open-air markets. Don't forget the museum shops where you can pick up wonderful handicrafts and souvenirs.

Before You Buy

OPENING HOURS

Rio de Janeiro's shopping hours are as eclectic as the stores themselves. The Zona Sul (South Zone) shops are open from 10am–7pm with some businesses staying open until 8pm or 9pm. Saturday they open 10am until 1–2pm with some closing later.

Centro operates from 9am–6pm Monday to Friday; some shops are open Saturday 9am–1pm.

The big malls are open Monday to Saturday 10am–10pm with only the largest ones opening Sundays, from 3pm–9pm, although it's best to check their websites as times vary.

Havaianas on sale

I. Macintyre/Michelin

SHOPPING AREAS

Rather like a bazaar, SAARA Market on and around Rua da Alfândega in **Centro** is the place for cheap and cheerful goods and a colorful vibe. The surrounding streets offer bargains and more recently, designer stores. Rua Lavradio and the surrounding streets in **Lapa** are best for hunting down antiques. The main thoroughfare in **Copacabana**, Avenida Nossa Senhora de Copacabana, is a great shopping strip with an eclectic mix of bargain stores and mid-range high-street chains as well as street vendors; not surprisingly there are also a lot of stores selling beachwear.

Similarly in **Ipanema** is Rua Visconde de Pirajá, where the mix is more refined with popular chains, designer boutiques, and jewelry stores side-by-side. Rua Garcia D'Ávila and Nascimento Silva are where elite brands such as Cartier and Louis Vuitton can be browsed and bought.

Avenida Ataulfo de Paiva in **Leblon** also offers designer goods, bookstores, and a couple of popular high-end malls. Some of the best malls (☞*see opposite*) can be found in **Zona Sul** (South Zone) and **Barra da Tijuca**.

PURCHASING TIPS

Signs like "4x" or "10x" on prices in store windows indicate products that Brazilians can pay for in instalments on credit cards—customers from outside Brazil must pay in full.

Some foreign debit and credit cards arbitrarily don't work seem to work with Brazilian swipe machines, so it's a good idea to have two card options. Staff will reserve a product behind the counter for you until the end of the day if you have any problems paying. In some shops, the assistants work on a commission-only basis and they will write you out a chit for your purchase, which you then take over to the cashier to pay.

DISCOUNTS

It's common in Brazil to get a five to ten percent discount if you can pay in cash, which can make a difference on pricier items. Some larger stores don't offer this, but it's always worth asking. Bartering is also common in smaller stores, particularly if you're paying in cash. It's also worth a try in the more established stores, especially if you're spending larger amounts. If you don't get the price down, you might get some kind of smaller item for free. On the streets it's part of the shopping experience and the vendors expect it, so don't be afraid to be plucky.

RETURNS

The returns policy is 30 days by law although many shops will only offer 15 days in which to return goods. If the item you bought is faulty, they are legally obliged to give you a replacement or credit note to spend. If you simply decide you don't like what you've bought, you aren't entitled to a credit note or a refund. However, out of courtesy some stores might let you exchange the item. Most Brazilian stores don't automatically give you a receipt, so make sure you ask for one.

Where to Buy

MALLS

The *shopping* (mall) has become part of the Cariocas' leisure repertoire as it includes shopping, movie theaters, bars, restaurants, and a crèche or play area for small children—all off the

😊 A Bit of Advice 😊

Many of the shops in these listings are in shopping malls, which means on Sundays they generally open at 3pm (*exceptions to this rule are listed with the contact information*). However, food and leisure outlets in the malls are usually open on Sunday mornings.

street in a safe environment. Although they're all over the city, the best shopping centers are in the South Zone and Barra da Tijuca. Barra has an excellent array because it is a sprawling car-based part of town where drive-in malls fit the bill.

Botafogo Praia Shopping – *Praia de Botafogo. Food and leisure:* ◷*Open Mon–Sun 10am–11pm.* ✆*21 3171 9559. www.botafogo-praia-shopping.com.br.* This shopping mall *(170 shops, mostly clothes and homeware, over eight floors)* is compact compared to the larger malls in the city, which can often overwhelm. There is a multiplex cinema, fast food outlets, and restaurants at the top, where a terrace gives one of the best views in the city of Sugar Loaf.

Shopping Leblon – *Av. Afrânio de Melo Franco 290, Leblon.* ✆*21 3138 8000. www.shoppingleblon.com.br.* A relatively new recruit to Rio de Janeiro's shopping palaces, this is the ultimate shopping experience where part of the fun is to see and be seen. There are around 200 shops, most of which are high-end, international brands although the big Brazilian chains and designers are also in-situ. Check out the top floor which has a multi-screen movie theater plus an array of restaurants, bars, and cafes and a fabulous panoramic view of the lagoon and towering Christ the Redeemer Statue.

Rio Sul – *Rua Lauro Müller 116, Botafogo.* ✆*21 2122 8070. www.riosul. com.br.* In Botafogo, and just the other side of the "New Tunnel" which connects Botafogo to Copacabana, this center is handy if you're staying in Copacabana. Rio Sul is the biggest shopping mall in Rio de Janeiro outside of Barra da Tijuca. Recently renovated, there is a wide range of 400 shops spread over four slick floors. There is also a choice of bars, cafes, and restaurants as well as a multi-screen movie theater and fitness centers.

☺ A Bit of Advice ☺

With increasing bank card fraud across the globe, more businesses are requesting some kind of photo ID when using credit cards, so take some with you for priority buys.

Rio Design Leblon – *Av. Ataulfo de Paiva 270, Leblon. ☎21 3206 9110. www.riodesign.com.br.*
There are around 70 incredibly stylish shops (mostly designer clothes and homeware) across the four floors. Chic restaurants are in the basement and third floor.

Shopping da Gávea – *Rua Marques de São Vicente 52, Gávea. ☎21 2294 1096. www.shoppingdagavea.com.br.*
A stylish mall with more than 200 stores on three floors, with a good range from jewelry to electronics, sports, and opticians. Restaurants are at entry level and a multiplex cinema is on the top floor. It also has four theaters and two children's play areas.

BarraShopping – *Av. das Américas 4666, Barra da Tijuca. ☎21 4003 4131. www.barrashopping.com.br.*
The largest shopping mall in South America; anything you need, you'll find here. With over 500 stores on three floors, you'll probably work up an appetite. Happily there are numerous cafes, restaurants, and bars to restore your energy. If you can't find what you want, there's another mall right next door, the **New York City Center.**

Rio Design Barra – *Av. das Américas 7777, Barra da Tijuca. ⏰Open daily (Open at noon Sun). ☎21 2430 3024. www.riodesign.com.br.*
The sister of Leblon's Rio Design, this is another mega-stylish mall with mostly fashion and homeware stores. On the top *(third)* floor, there's a selection of excellent restaurants. There's also a cinema with three screens.

MARKETS

Markets in Rio de Janeiro are an atmospheric place to buy souvenirs, bric-a-brac, clothing, jewelry, fruits and vegetables… they are not the place to purchase designer goods as they will be fake! Keep your personal items close and to get the best prices barter in a friendly, gentle way.

Feira do Rio Antigo – *Rua do Lavradio, Centro. ⏰Open 10am–7pm first Sat every month. www.polonovorioantigo. com.br.*
On the first Saturday of the month the street of Rua do Lavradio, as well as some of those around it, come alive with people coming to browse and buy antiques, and just as many who want to join in the daytime party atmosphere. Expensive antiques abound, but there is plenty of bric-a-brac too, along with old records, second-hand books, and a fair amount of what can only be described as household junk. Close to 100 stalls are set up for the day and local bars and restaurants fling open their doors. Locals and visitors take it easy and listen to the lively talented musicians who play samba and choro.

Feira de Arte de Ipanema (Hippie Fair) – *Praça General Osório, Ipanema. ⏰Open 7am–5pm Sun. www.feirahippieipanema.com.*
Rio de Janeiro's best-known arts and crafts fair offers some great bargains. Trading since 1968, this vibrant market is not just for hippies. Stalls sell jewelry, bags, homeware, souvenirs, fashion, and arts and crafts. The perfect place to pick up a present to take home.

Feira de Música – *Rua Pedro Lessa, Centro. ⏰Open 9am–5pm Mon–Fri and Sat morning.*
In a small lane right next to the National Library, this is where CDs and albums are bought and sold. If you're a music fan, there are bound to be some gems to discover.

SAARA Market – *Rua da Alfândega and Rua Senhor dos Passos.* ⏰*Open Mon–Fri 9am–6pm, Sat 9am–2pm.* ℘*21 3852 8790. www.saarario.com.br.* Right next to Metrô Uruguaiana is the city's most lively, colorful place. Back-to-back are stores and market stalls selling electronics, kitchen, bedlinen, clothes, gym and sportswear, bikinis, and Carnival outfits for very reasonable prices—especially if you barter well.

Centro de Tradições Nordestina – *Campo de São Cristóvão (no number), São Cristóvão.* ⏰*Open Tue–Thu 10am–4pm, Fri 10am–Sun 10pm (24hrs).* ℘*21 3860 9976. www.feiradesaocristovao. com.br.*
A permanent fair set up initially for the northeastern immigrants in Rio de Janeiro, this is a fascinating outing. A vast group of stalls serve up the food and drinks of the region to the sounds of northeastern *forró*. There are also handicrafts, hammocks, and some clothes for sale.

Feira Avenida Atlântica – *Av. Atlântica near Rua Djalma Ulrich, Copacabana.* ⏰*Open daily 7pm–midnight.* Although an unofficial market, this is so established it's practically official. A shameless tourism spread, it's still got some great bikinis, classic souvenirs, beach wraps, bags, and jewelry plus some paintings. Barter hard as prices are inflated for tourists.

What To Buy

ANTIQUES

Rio de Janeiro is fairly big on antiques and there's two specific parts of town best for browsing; along **Rua Lavradio** and the surrounding streets in Lapa and inside Shopping Copacabana at **Rua Siqueira Campos 143**, Copacabana. You might also be able to catch an auction at one of Rio's most established auction houses, **Century's Arte e Leilões**, at Rua Bartolomeu Mitre 370, Leblon. Or, for a more relaxed time, try the Saturday

SAARA Market
©Uwe Kempa/Flickr.com

morning market under the Viaduto da Perimetral at Praça XV.

Pancotto Antiguidades – *Rua do Senado 43, Centro (Lapa).* ⏰*Open Mon–Sat (closed 3pm Sat).* ℘*21 2221 0927. www.pancottoantiguidades. com.br.*
Owner Julio has some wonderful antiques that are lovingly displayed. From the Baroque period up to the 1950s, he collects all sorts (including a lot of furniture) from Espirito Santo, Minas Gerais, Bahia, and Pernambuco states. Take the spiral staircase up to the mezzanine to rummage for more.

Casa do Brazão – *Rua do Lavradio 60, Centro (Lapa).* ⏰*Open Mon–Sat (closed 3pm Sat).* ℘*21 2232 2670.*
In the business 40 years, Ricardo now works with his son Gustavo. They collect wrist and pocket watches, wall clocks, and jewelry from the 19C to the 1940s. Their main specialty is 1950s and 1960s furniture, including pieces by some of the most famous furniture designers in Brazil, such as Joaquim Tenreiro and Sérgio Rodrigues.

Mercado Moderno – *Rua do Lavradio 130, Centro (Lapa).* ⏰*Open Mon–Sat (closed 3pm Sat).* ℘*21 2508 6083. www.mercadomodernobrasil.com.br.*
This store specializes in vintage design from the 1950s to the 1980s. Two floors of retro furniture, including designers Joaquim Tenreiro,

Zalszupin, Sérgio Rodrigues, Zanini, and Oscar Niemeyer.

Ernani – *Rua São Clemente 385, Botafogo.* ⏰*Open Mon–Sat (closed 2pm Sat).* ✆*21 2539 2637.* *www.ernanileiloeiro.com.br.*
An auction house since 1906, Horácio is now the fifth generation in the business. There are regular collections for sale as well as auctions, but it's best to call before to check times and opening hours. They deal with paintings, sculpture, silver, ironware, and porcelain from the 17C to 19C. Art that has passed through their hands includes Brazilian artists Portinari, Di Cavalcanti, and Cicero Dias.

Onze Dinheiros – *Rua Siqueira Campos 143, Shops 144–146, Copacabana.* ⏰*Open Mon–Sat (closed 3pm Sat).* ✆*21 2256 1552. www.onzedinheiros. com.br.*
A veritable treasure-trove of 18C and 19C Brazilian silver, furniture, and Baccarat crystal tucked away in this corner of Copacabana. The collection also specializes in slave jewelry from the northeastern state of Bahia; a rare antique genre in Brazil.

ART GALLERIES

A Gentil Carioca – (⛱*see p 119)*

Silvia Cintra & box4 – *Rua das Acácias 104, Gávea.* ⏰*Open Mon–Sat (opens noon Sat).* ✆*21 2521 0426.* *www.silviacintra.com.br.*
Representing the very best, Silvia Cintra exhibits Nelson Leirner and photographer Miguel Rio Branco. The gallery has also sold works by Amílcar de Castro, one of Brazil's most famous sculptors. They have a second space, **box4,** which showcases works by young talented artists.

Galeria Laura Marsiaj – *Rua Teixeira de Melo 31c, Ipanema.* ⏰*Open Tue–Sat.* ✆*21 2513 2074. www.lauramarsiaj.com.br.*
In the block nearest the ocean front, you can pop in on your way to or from the beach. The gallery has two spaces for contemporary art. They represent

award-winning artists Carlos Melo and Lucia Laguna as well as a broad spectrum of works by young artists to some of the Brazilian seminals.

Anita Schwartz – *Rua José Roberto Macedo Soares, Gávea.* ⏰*Open Mon–Sat (open noon Sat).* ✆*21 2274 3873.* *www.galeria.anitaschwartz.com.br*
Anita has had a contemporary art gallery for 12 years and recently opened a new three-floor space in Gávea. Her exhibitions change roughly every two months and she represents Gonçalo Ivo, Abraham Palatnik, and Carlos Vilio amongst many others.

Mercedes Viegas – *Rua João Borges 86, Gávea.* ⏰*Open Mon–Fri 1pm–7pm, Sat 4pm–8pm.* ✆*21 2294 4305. www. mercedesviegas.com.br.*
A small space, but nevertheless established in the Rio de Janeiro art world for both contemporary and modern pieces. Mercedes represents eleven artists including Angela Venosa. The gallery also deals with re-sale, including work by Anna Maria Maiolino.

BOOKS

Livraria da Travessa – *Shopping Leblon, Av. Afrânio de Melo Franco 290, Shop 205.* ⏰*Open daily (opens noon Sun).* ✆*21 3138 9600. www.travessa. com.br.*
A large and pleasant bookstore through which to amble. There's a cafe-restaurant to chill out in before or after attending one of the in-store events. A great selection of literature and art/culture books and there are English-language titles available.

Argumento – *Rua Barata Ribeiro 502* ⏰*Open Mon–Sat.* ✆*21 2255 3783.* *www. livrariaargumento.com.br.*
One of a chain of bookstores (also in Leblon and Barra da Tijuca), this store is on one of Copacabana's main street. A decent selection of books includes an English section. Keep your eye on their website for book signings and other events. Perk yourself up at the Café Severino if you're flagging.

Siciliano – *Av. Nossa Senhora de Copacabana 766, Copacabana.* 🕐*Open daily (closed 5pm Sat and 4pm Sun).* 📞*21 2548 2683. www.siciliano.com.br.* Part of a huge nationwide chain, this may not be one of the hippest bookstores in town, but it has a good literature section in English. There are other branches in Botafogo, Centro, Barra da Tijuca, and São Conrado.

Saraiva – *Rua do Ouvidor 98, Centro.* 🕐*Open Mon–Sat (closed 2pm Sat).* 📞*21 2507 3785. www.livrariasaraiva. com.br.* This bookstore chain was founded in 1928 and now also sells CDs and DVDs (👝*see also MUSIC*), stationery, electronics, and computer games. The huge selection of books includes English-language bestsellers and well-known magazines, as well as all the Portuguese-language titles you would expect to find in a mega-bookstore.

CRAFTS AND SOUVENIRS

Brasil & CIA – *Rua Maria Quitéria 27, Ipanema.* 🕐*Open Mon–Sat.* 📞*21 2267 4603. www.brasilecia.com.br.* Just one block from the beach, you can pop in on your way back. Stuffed with wonderful, original arts and crafts that would make fantastic gifts and souvenirs. You'll find mirrors framed by brightly colored rolled-up newspapers, made by a group from the shelter for the homeless in São

Paulo, "Boracea." Also decorating the shelves are the famous tiny painted clay figures from Caruaru, Pernambuco, made by Mestre Vitalino's family in their front room.

Pé de Boi – *Rua Ipiranga 55.* 🕐*Open Mon–Fri 9am–7pm, Sat 9am–1pm.* 📞*21 2285 4395. www.pedeboi.com.br.* Beautifully-crafted artisan pieces made all over the country fill this wonderful shop. Those who appreciate finely made crafts as well as souvenir hunters will find it hard to resist one-off decorated pots, finely woven textiles and hammocks, and pretty basketware. A purchase here means supporting the country's long and rich artisan tradition, as well as taking home a little piece of Brazil.

La Vereda – *Rua Almirante Alexandrino 428, Santa Teresa.* 🕐*Open daily*

Pé de Boi

Y. Kanazawa/Michelin

Lola Atelier Café

Y. Kanazawa/Michelin

National Center of Folklore and Popular Culture (🕰 see p 149)

Lola Atelier Café – *Rua Almirante Alexandrino 342, Santa Teresa.* 🕰*Open daily 10:30am.* 📞*21 2224 7909. www.lolaateliercafe.com.br.*
Filled with brightly colored paintings, notebooks, cup coasters, and tablemats featuring the Christ the Redeemer statue, this wonderful little tourist shop offers some great gift ideas for the journey home.

Produzir – *Rua Real Grandeza 293, Botafogo.* 🕰*Open Mon–Fri.* 📞*21 2332 4901. www.rioartesanato.com.br.*
This store is off the tourist strip in Botafogo, but it's really worth a visit. Artists' and craftsmen's work is rather chaotically displayed in one space that's provided by the local govern-ment and administered by Rio de Janeiro's local crafts association. Check out the wooden crocodiles made by Indians from Paraty and Angra as well as the religious icons made out of newspaper and flowers created from corncob leaves.

10am–9pm (open 1pm Mon). 📞21 2242 9434.
Owner Maria Victoria is passionate about Brazilian crafts and it shows. Santa Teresa's most appealing craft store is stuffed with innovative pieces made by local artists, including jewelry made by members of the group "Ação Communitaria do Brasil" from Rio's Maré favela, as well as individually crafted clothes and delightful Brazilian music CDs. There are plenty of gift and souvenir ideas here and even if you just come away with a classic Santa Teresa postcard or reproduction of a local photograph, you are sure not to leave empty-handed. Every July, the shop participates in Arte de Portas Abertas (Art with Open Doors), which showcases the work of talented local artists.

Artíndia – *Museu do Índio, Rua das Palmeiras 55, Botafogo.* 🕰*Open Tue–Sun (open 1pm Sat and Sun).* 📞*21 3214 8719. www.museudoindio.gov.br.*
Buy something authentic from the "Museum of the Indian" that will remind you of your trip. After each new exhibition, respective artifacts are for sale from the tribe profiled. Masks, bags, brightly decorated pots, and sculptures are some of the items available.

Carnival Costumes

To get into the spirit of Carnival you need to get kitted out, so head straight to SAARA Market (🕰 see p 263) where **Casa Turuna** on Rua Senhor dos Passos 122–124 sells fabrics, jewelry, and costumes and feathers. It's Carnival all year round at **Babado da Folia** on Rua Alfândega 365 where you'll find a selection of masks, ready-made costumes, and haberdashery frippery with their sister-store on Rua Buenos Aires 287–300 selling samba dancing-queen sequin bikinis for the very brave. Buy a ready-made outfit and transform yourself into Fred Flintstone, or a Pharaoh at **Lojas de Bijuterias Silmer Ltda** on Rua Alfândega 171–173 or have customized togs run up by Norma, 35 years in the Carnival business, at **Fantasia da Norma**, Rua Regente Feijó 22. Bon Carnaval!

JEWELRY

Museu H. Stern – (🕐 see p 164).

Amsterdam Sauer – *Rua Garcia D'Ávila 105, Ipanema.* 🕐*Open Mon–Sat.* 🖉*21 2525 0033. www.amsterdamsauer.com*
Step into the world of gems in Amsterdam Sauer's museum. Once upstairs in the international shop it gets more exciting when you see items such as the 188-carat necklace packed with blue topaz, amethyst, and citrine for US$28,000. Mr Sauer famously unearthed Brazil's emerald mine in Bahia in the 1960s, but the store specializes in every possible kind of gemstone.

Antonio Bernardo – *Rua Garcia D'Ávila 121, Ipanema.* 🕐*Open Mon–Sat.* 🖉*21 2512 7204. www.antonio bernardo.com.br.*
Contemporary jewelry that's utterly unique. Have a look at the funky 18-carat gold pendants with a matte finish, hung on a leather thong. Take a peek at one of his display pieces, "Explosion" (made specifically for his "Sex and Romance" show). He also works with diamonds and gems and you are sure to find something inimitably elegant.

Sara – *Rua Garcia D'Ávila 129, Ipanema.* 🕐*Open Mon–Sat (closed 4pm Sat).* 🖉*21 3202 4500. www.sarajoias.com.*
This store has been established for 35 years and it has carved out a solid reputation in Rio de Janeiro. A family business, there are also shops in Leblon and São Conrado. Laja Zilberman is the designer who makes individual pieces with high quality materials (including Brazilian stones) that have attracted the local and international elite over the years. They also sell the big brands such as Rolex and Cartier.

Natan – *Rua Vinicius de Moraes 111, Ipanema.* 🕐*Open Mon–Sat.* 🖉*21 2525 5555. www.natan.com.br.*
Considered one of Rio de Janeiro's top players in the jewelry world, it tends to be relatively traditional design-wise, and known for its high quality materials and stones. They also work with silver, so more affordable items can be tracked down.

CLOTHING

Designers and Boutiques

Isabela Capeto – *Rua Dias Ferreira 217, Leblon.* 🕐*Open Mon–Sat.* 🖉*21 2540 5232. www.isabelacapeto.com.br.*
Each piece is a work of art. Hand-made, it is also very romantic in style with embroidery and vintage lace, sequins, and fabric trims. In Brazil, Capeto is ranked among the top designers.

Contemporâneo – *Rua Visconde de Pirajá 437, Ipanema.* 🕐*Open Mon–Sat.* 🖉*21 2287 6204.*
This is a boutique housing a selection of the latest collections from some of the best Brazilian fashion designers, such as Alexandre Herchcovitch, Fause Haten, and Reinaldo Lourenço. New designers are also given space on the rails. On-site is an art gallery and a cafe.

Andrea Saletto – *Rio Design Leblon, Av. Ataulfo de Paiva 270, Shop 205.* 🕐*Open daily (open noon Sun).* 🖉*21 2274 7713. www.permanenteas.com.br.*
One of Rio de Janeiro's most upmarket womenswear labels; it is understated, low-profile style personified. Classic

Isabela Capeto

Laundry Services

Some laundries provide only service washes, whereby you pay per kilo of clothing. Others have a fixed fee for a fixed number of items. The cheapest way is to load and unload the machine yourself, where you pay per wash load.

Lav e Lev – *Rua Bolivar 21a, Copacabana.* 📞 *21 2549 3996.*

Laundromatt – *Rua Farme de Amoedo 55, Ipanema.* 📞 *21 2267 2377.*

Laundry Service – *Rua Humberto Campos 827 Shop F, Leblon.* 📞 *21 2274 2711.*

cuts using linen, cotton, and silks suit any figure.

Maria Bonita – *São Conrado Fashion Mall, Shop 223, Estrada da Gávea 899.* 📞 *21 3324 5465. www.mariabonita. com.br.*
One of the oldest labels in Rio de Janeiro, Maria Bonita is well known among Cariocas as the place to find impeccably cut, elegant woman's fashion in first-class fabrics. There are also branches in Ipanema, Leblon, and Barra da Tijuca. The brand has an off-the-peg, more reasonably priced sister chain called **Maria Bonita Extra**.

Osklen – *Rua Maria Quitéria 85, Ipanema.* 🕐*Open daily (open 11am Sun).* 📞 *21 2227 2911. www.osklen.com.*
Fun, comfortable, casual clothes that exude understated chic. The design is funky and hip and appeals to active types who want that extra bit of style. Some of the pieces are a little on the avant-garde side. There are both men's and women's collections that include swimwear as well as shoes, bags, hats, and wallets. There are also stores in Leblon, Gávea, Barra da Tijuca, and Botafogo.

Mixed – *Rua Garcia D'Avila, Ipanema.* 🕐*Open Mon–Sat.* 📞 *21 2259 9544. www.mixed.com.br.*
The perfect name for this chic boutique. The people at mixed design

their own collection which is mostly smart day and evening wear, and they have established themselves on the top rung of the Carioca fashion scene. There are also shops in Barra da Tijuca and São Conrado.

Complexo B – *Rua Francisco Otaviano 67, Shop 42, Copacabana.* 📞 *21 2521 7126. www.complexob.com.br.*
This trendy boutique designs and stocks contemporary fashion for the young, hip crowd in Rio. A common theme in their designs is Afro Brazilian religious figures, particularly São Jorge.

Drako – *Rua Francisco Otaviano 55, Copacabana.* 📞 *21 2227 7393.*
Loved by Brazilians and tourists alike, and an established label on the gay scene, this well-known store sells stylish, modern clothing and accessories. In Rio, you're likely to spot men wearing the popular T-Shirts with "Ipanema" or "Carioca" lettering.

Casualwear

Richards – *Shopping Leblon, Av. Afrânio de Melo Franco 290, Shop 208.* 📞 *21 2294 4036. www.richards.com.br.*
Classy casuals for men and women in quality cottons and linens. This is the flagship store, but others are to be found in Ipanema, Botafogo, Barra da Tijuca, Centro, Gávea and there's a second store in Leblon.

Eclectic – *Shopping Leblon, Av. Afrânio de Melo Franco 290, Shop 111.* 📞 *21 2239 3242. www.eclectic.com.br.*
Carioca girls see this shop as a stalwart for their wardrobes. Casual wear with jeans, shorts, T-shirts, jackets, dresses, and skirts that have that fashion-edge. Also to be found in Ipanema, Gávea, Botafogo, Centro, and Barra da Tijuca.

Sandpiper – *Rua Visconde de Pirajá 514, Ipanema.* 🕐*Open Mon–Sat.* 📞 *21 2511 6406. www.sandpiper.com.br.*
Very popular with young Cariocas, Sandpiper has both womenswear and menswear. Casual togs in natural fabrics with some unique designs, this is considered one of Rio's more

affordable brands. The biggest store is in Botafogo and there are also outlets in Barra da Tijuca and Centro.

Wöllner – *Rua Visconde de Pirajá 511, Ipanema.* ◐*Open daily (open 3pm Sun).* ✆*21 2239 3222. www.wollner.com.br.* Casual menswear and womenswear, affordably priced and well-liked by locals. They also have a nice selection of bags and rucksacks. This is the flagship store where there is also a handy internet café. More stores in Botafogo, Gávea, Barra da Tijuca, Centro, and Niterói.

Farm – *Rua Visconde de Pirajá 365 Shops C & D, Ipanema.* ◐*Open daily (open 3pm Sun).* ✆*21 3813 3817. www. farmrio.com.br.* Farm has the "it" factor for Cariocas that even Paulistas want to emulate. With lots of happy colors, the dresses and separates have an after-beach, stylish feel you see out on the streets of Ipanema and Leblon. This is the flagship store, but you can find stores in Barra da Tijuca, Leblon, and Gávea.

Vintage
Eu Amo – *Rua Monte Alegre 374, Santa Teresa.* ◐*Open Mon–Sat.* ✆*21 2221 2855. www.euamovintage.com.br.*

Flavia Monteiro and Deborah Niemeyer are passionate about vintage, so no surprise they called their shop "I love…."
They source and restore authentic 1920s to 1980s menswear and womenswear, as well as accessories.

Anexo Vintage – *Shopping da Gávea, Rua Marques de São Vicente 52.* ◐*Open Mon–Sat.* ✆*21 2529 8253.* Tucked away behind the shopping mall in the annex, this chic store has vintage handbags by the likes of Chanel, Gucci, Cartier, Dior, Lacroix, and Montana. They also stock 1950s and 1960s clothes from time to time.

Beachwear
Blue Man – *Rio Sul, Rua Lauro Muller 116, Shop 201, Botafogo.* ◐*Open Mon–Sat.* ✆*21 2541 6896. www.blueman.com.br.* An established Carioca swimwear store. The women's collection has different ranges where it's possible to mix and match the top and bottom with the style you want, as long as you stick to the same fabric pattern. Some designs are cut more generously across the behind to appeal to European and American tastes and the sizes are also graded larger. There are

---

Buying Musical Instruments

Maracatu Brasil
Y. Kanazawa/Michelin

The art of live music is alive and well in Brazil and there's a host of great musical instrument shops to choose from, especially on **Rua Carioca** in Centro where there has been a generation of specialized stores opening recently.
Acústica at no. 54 is one of these and you can test-drive an instrument in one of their three studios. Another newbie is **Sax de Ouro** at no. 24. **Casa Oliveira** at no. 70 has been established for more than 50 years and Caetano Veloso is said to have popped in to make a purchase. Along the street at no. 43, **Acústica Perfeita** sponsors the likes of samba singer Alcione, while **Sonic Som** at no. 25 has seen Seu Jorge and The Doors cross its threshold. Head to **Maracatu** in Laranjeiras for the very best in percussion (◐see p 132).

men's and children's collections and a range of beach accessories.

Lenny – *Rua Visconde de Pirajá 351 Shop 114, Ipanema.* 🕐*Open Mon–Sat.* 📞*21 2523 3796. www.lenny.com.br.*
A very important Rio de Janeiro chain for chic ladies who like to wear elegant swimwear and after-beach wear that's understated. Lenny designs not only bikinis, but one-piece suits, with love. Join the elite set on Ipanema's Garcia D'Avila for more Lenny, or at Gávea.

Salinas – *Rua Visconde de Pirajá 547 Shop 204–5, Ipanema.* 🕐*Open Mon–Sat.* 📞*21 2274 0644. www. salinas-rio.com.br.*
The truly hip bikini. Made with imagination and a hint of wit, they are regarded by Cariocas as a must-have. In bright colors and trendy styles, you'll stand out at Posto 9, along with everyone else!

Bum Bum – *Shopping Leblon, Av. Afrânio de Melo Franco 290, Shop 108K.* 📞*21 3875 1021. www.bumbum.com.br.*
A cheeky name for some cheeky little designs. You can pick any top you like to go with any bottoms. There is an excellent selection of beach dresses to pull on when you walk back to your hotel as well as beach bags, hats, sarongs, chunky jewelry, and belts. For men, there's a limited choice of lycra trunks. The Leblon store is the biggest, with other branches in Ipanema, Botafogo, and Barra da Tijuca.

ACCESSORIES

MG Bazar – *Rua Figueiredo de Magalhães 414, Copacabana.* 🕐*Open Mon–Sat (closed 4pm Sat).* 📞*21 2548 1664.*
This is the perfect place to stock up on Havaianas, a veritable Aladdin's cave of colored rubber as far as the eye can see, at very reasonable prices.

Fiszpan – *Rua Visconde de Pirajá 580, Ipanema.* 🕐*Open Mon–Sat.* 📞*21 2274 7834. www.fiszpan.com.br.*
Brazilians, especially Cariocas, love accessories. You'll find an ample selection of jewelry including some great wood pieces. There are handbags, scarves, cowboy hats, and chunky bangles. Originally it was a wig shop and you can still buy high quality hairpieces here.

Parceria Carioca – *Rua Visconde de Pirajá 351 Shop 215, Ipanema.* 🕐*Open Mon–Sat (closed 3pm Sat).* 📞*21 2267 3222. www.parceriacarioca.com.br.*
Fantastic, funky costume jewelry as well as colorful bags and sandals. It all started in 1997, when designer Flávia Torres started teaching craft techniques at the Saint Cyprian Project in Rio de Janeiro, which lead to the Jardim Botânico store. There is now also a store in Gávea.

Peach – *Rio Design Leblon, Av. Ataulfo de Paiva 270, Shop 116, Leblon.* 📞*21 2511 8801. www.constancabasto.com.br.*
The younger and more casual version of Constança Basto shoes (as worn by Nicole Kidman and Cameron Diaz), some of this classy and comfy footwear belongs in your cupboard.

Glorinha Paranaguá – *Rua Visconde de Pirajá 365 Shop 2, Ipanema.* 🕐*Open Mon–Sat.* 📞*21 2267 4295. www.glorinhaparanagua.com.br.*
A tropical handbag heaven where bamboo, cloth, leather, and crochet all look stylish. You'll also find purses and costume jewelry.

Jelly – *Rua Visconde de Pirajá 529, Ipanema.* 🕐*Open Mon–Sat.* 📞*21 3813 9328. www.jellyweb.com.br.*
Taking the colorful synthetic shoe much farther than flip flops, Jelly has plastic shoes galore in a kaleidoscope range of hues. Not just the kind you wear to get across a pebbly seashore, but glamorous heels too. Colorful rucksacks, bags, and purses are all for sale as well. Other stores are in Botafogo, Centro, and Barra da Tijuca.

Modern Sound

Y. Kanazawa/Michelin

MUSIC STORES

Modern Sound – *Rua Barata Ribeiro 502D.* ◷*Open Mon–Sat.* ✆*21 2548 5005. www.modernsound.com.br.*
The ultimate music store that is considered one of the best in Rio. The small entrance belies the huge cavernous space behind it, and the staff are friendly and will help you find what you are looking for. All genres of Brazilian music are covered, as well as a great selection of rock, jazz, and classical. There's free live music from 5pm every day and various other live music events. If you're confused as to what to buy, sit at the Allegro bistro for a coffee or meal and contemplate your CD list.

CD Centro Music – *Rua da Quitanda 3, Shop B, Centro.* ◷*Open Mon–Sat (closed noon Sat).* ✆*21 2524 5338.*
A small, well stocked shop where the boss has worked in the music business 40 years. Pelé and Milton Nascimento came to the opening a decade ago. Downstairs there's a pleasant café to seek refuge from the downtown buzz.

FNAC – *BarraShopping, Av. das Américas 4666, Shop B 101–114, Barra da Tijuca.* ✆*21 2109 2000. www.fnac. com.br.*
Part of an international chain selling books, DVDs, and music, this is the only Rio de Janeiro store. There's every kind of genre, although MPB (Música

Popular Brasileira or Brazilian Popular Music) is their strongest section, alongside classical and international pop/rock.

Saraiva – *Rua do Ouvidor 98, Centro.* ◷*Open Mon–Sat (closed 2pm Sat).* ✆*21 2507 3785. www.livrariasaraiva. com.br.*
The large music department upstairs (◷ *see also BOOKS*) boasts extensive MPB and Brazilian rock sections as well as a decent selection of jazz and bossa nova—all available to sample at in-store audio points. A nationwide chain, there are also outlets in Rio Sul shopping center and Barra da Tijuca.

Livraria da Travessa – *Shopping Leblon, Afrânio de Melo Franco 290, Shop 205.* ◷*Open daily (open Sun 2pm).* ✆*21 3138 9600. www.travessa.com.br.*
Inside the bookstore, at the back of the store on a mezzanine level, there's an excellent music department. The best section is jazz and MPB. Branches can also be found at Barra da Tijuca, Ipanema, and Centro.

Plano B – *Rua Francisco Muratori 2A, Lapa.* ◷*Open Mon–Sat (open noon).* ✆*21 2509 3266. www.planob.net.*
A bohemian store where the staff can bail you out if you don't know what samba-funk is. There's a diverse selection of jazz and electronic mixes to rifle through, and plenty of vinyl.

SPECTATOR SPORTS

By far the most popular sport in Rio de Janeiro is futebol (football), which to Cariocas is as essential as samba and Carnival—watching a game at the Maracanã Stadium is a don't miss event. Football, volleyball or Futevôlei (a skilled combination of both) can be watched or played on the spectacular beaches of Copacabana and Ipanema. In June, the picturesque setting of the city also makes for a spectacular marathon route (see Calendar of Events).

Football

With an unmatched five World Cups, Brazil has a strong claim as football's global capital; the dazzling skills of its top players justify Brazilians' reputation as the most stylish exponents of *futebol*—the "beautiful game."

Rio de Janeiro, with the **Maracanã**★, one of the biggest and most famous stadiums in the world, and with four teams in the top division, has a very good case to be considered the Brazilian home of football.

Credit for the introduction of football to Brazil is given to Brazilian-born Englishman Charles Miller, who brought the game to the São Paulo Athletic Club at the end of the 19C. Rio soon picked up on the new craze, thanks to another Anglo-Brazilian, Oscar Cox, who organized the first game at the Rio Cricket and Athletic Association in 1901 and went on to found Fluminense Football Club in 1902.

Fluminense was the first club dedicated only to football but over the next ten years other established sports clubs in the city founded their own teams: Flamengo, Vasco da Gama, and Botafogo; all four teams still dominate today. At first, with its middle-class expatriate origins, football remained the preserve of Rio's white social elite. It was only in the 1930s, once football had become a global sport, with players joining clubs across continents, that the game acquired the mass popularity that it continues to have today.

Since the 1950s, and particularly after Brazil's first World Cup success in 1958, many of the country's best players have played on the hallowed turf of the Maracanã, including current stars Ronaldo, Ronaldinho, Kaká, and Dida. Legendary players seen here also include Garrincha and Nilton Santos for Botafogo; Zico and Romario for Flamengo; Telê Santana and Didi for Fluminense; and Roberto Dinamite, Ademir, and Vavá for Vasco da Gama.

Maracanã Stadium

Y. Kanazawa/Michelin

Rio de Janeiro
FOOTBALL CLUBS

Four teams from Rio de Janeiro: Botafogo, Flamengo, Fluminense, and Vasco da Gama have dominated the region's football leagues over the last hundred years; in fact the last time any other team won the state championship, the Campeonata Carioca, was Bangu in 1966. Flamengo and Fluminense in particular, are supreme rivals, with the leading record of 30 state championships each. Many of Brazil's all-time football stars played their best years in Rio, including Garrincha, Zico, and Roberto Dinamite.

Most big games between Rio de Janeiro's teams are played at the Maracanã, but some teams also have their own stadiums, where other games are played and which they use for training. The city's other major stadium is the Estádio Olímpico João Havelange, also known as Engenhão, which was built for the Pan American Games hosted by Rio in 2007, and is Botafogo's home ground.

The Brazilian football league structure is complex and ever-changing. To cope with the huge size of the country, there are two leagues, one at state and one at national level. The state league—the Campeonata Carioca for teams in Rio de Janeiro state—runs from January/February to April/May; the winners of which go on to compete in the national league, which runs from May to December. There are also annual championships against several clubs in other countries of the continent.

BOTAFOGO
Football Club Founded: 1891 Team created: 1904
Colors: Vertical black-and-white striped shirt
Titles: 18 state championships, national champions 1995
Famous Players: Garrincha, Nilton Santos, Jairzinho
Home Ground: Engenhão
Website: www.botafogo.com

FLAMENGO
Football Club Founded: 1895 Team created: 1911
Colors: Horizontal red-and-black-striped shirt
Titles: 30 state championships; five Brazilian championships
Famous Players: Zico, Romario, Bebeto
Home Ground: Gávea
Website: www.flamengo.com.br

FLUMINENSE
Football Club Founded: 1902
Colors: Vertical claret-green-and-white-striped shirt
Titles: 30 state championships, national champions 1984
Famous Players: Castilho, Telê Santana, Didi
Home Ground: Estádio das Laranjeiras
Website: www.fluminense.com.br

VASCO DA GAMA
Football Club Founded: 1898 Team created: 1915
Colors: White shirts with black diagonal sash
itles: 22 state championships, four times national champions
Famous Players: Bellini, Roberto Dinamite, Vavá
Home Ground: Estádio São Januário
Website: www.crvascodagama.com

TurisRio

Futebol

"The exuberance and happiness of Brazilian fans is part of their football heritage. They are an all-singing, all-dancing mixture of races, sexes, and ages. They are loud, colourful and always up for the party. Brazilians... have taken carnival to the football terraces."

Alex Bellos

from *Futebol: The Brazilian Way of Life*, Bloomsbury, 2003.

Even if you're not an avid fan, you shouldn't miss the opportunity to watch a match at the Maracanã, especially if it's a local derby, such as the annual "Fla–Flu" contest between Flamengo and Fluminense. Never mind the hoped-for silky skills on the pitch, it's the drums, fireworks, and colored flags in the terraces that set the atmosphere alight. Above all, it's the passion of the supporters who one minute heap scorn on the referee, the next explode with ecstasy when their team scores a goal.

Of course, Cariocas' love of futebol is not all about Maracanã and the superstar players, many of whom play full-time for European clubs. For most ordinary residents, it's an everyday game to play in any available space: kicking a can around in a favela backstreet or on the wide flat sands of Copacabana. They have even adapted beach volleyball, creating the fusion game of *Futevôlei* (&see sidebar), which you can also see any day on the beaches of Rio.

ESTÁDIO DO MARACANÃ⋆

Rua Professor Eurico Rabelo and Av. Maracanã, Portão 18. ☞Tickets range from R$20–100. ◐Closed 2010–2013 for renovation. ✆21 2334 1705/2566 7800/2569 3346.

One of the largest football stadiums in the world and arguably the most famous, the Maracanã hosts all Rio's major games and is considered an unmissable attraction for many visitors, whether football fans or not (&see p 120 for details of stadium tour). The stadium was completed for the 1950 World Cup with a capacity of 183,000. The final, which Brazil lost to Uruguay (1-2), saw a record attendance of nearly 200,000.

The sheer size of the stadium means that local games generally don't sell out, and you can buy tickets from the ticket windows up until the game begins. Alternatively, tickets can be purchased at most hotel receptions and through the majority of tour operators in Rio. The price you pay depends on the game and where you choose to sit. There is an area of the stadium reserved for "neutral" fans, where tourists and families tend to go. Be warned—tickets for this more sedate area are pricier *(approx R$40)* than the standard R$25–30.

Beach volleyball on Praia de Ipanema

I. MacIntyre/Michelin

Jockey Club Brasileiro

Jockey Club Brasileiro

Volleyball

Volleyball is played in recreation areas, indoor arenas and on Rio's flat sandy beaches, ideal for the game. After football, it is a Carioca favorite, both for watching and taking part— the women's and men's teams regularly win gold medals at the Olympics. Rio is the spiritual home of beach volleyball, and is the city where the world championships began in 1987. An annual International tournament takes place in Rio at the end of January and early February:

Indoor competitions are held at Estádio Gilberto Cardoso, better known as Maracanãzinho ("little Maracanã"). Situated next to the football stadium, the arena opened in 1954 and was renovated in 2007. It has a capacity of 12,600 and ticket prices depend on the game (world championship tickets are R$100).

Rei and Rainha da Praia
(King and Queen of the Beach)
21 2495 7426/3154 7944
www.reidapraia.com.br

Maracanãzinho
Rua Professor Eurico Rabelo
Complexo Esportivo do Maracanã
21 2299 2917
http://www.suderj.rj.gov.br/
maracananzinho.asp

Horse Racing

The elegant Jockey Club Brasileiro is Rio de Janeiro's only live racing track, beautifully located between the lake and Botanical Gardens. Opened in 1926, the club's grandstand seats 35,000 spectators. *(Races are Mon 6:30pm, Fri 4:30pm, and Sat, Sun 2pm).* Entry is free and visitors are welcome in the members' enclosure area, which has restaurants and bars.

The club's big event of the year is the **Brazilian Grand Prix**, held on the first Sunday of August.

Jockey Club Brasileiro
Praça Santos Dumont 31, Gávea
21 3534 9000
www.jcb.com.br

Futevôlei

When football players practicing on the crowded Copacabana Beach in the 1960s couldn't find space for a game, they moved instead onto the volleyball courts; thus *Futevôlei* was born. Today this exciting sport is played on Copacabana and Ipanema Beaches; the main rule is that players can use any part of the body, except for their hands and arms. Games are usually two-a-side and when top players are on court large crowds gather to watch their aerial ball skills.

HEALTH AND FITNESS

The year-round warm weather, beaches, and mountains of Rio de Janeiro provide the ideal setting for keeping fit outdoors. However, for when the rain comes down, there are many private gyms and leisure clubs offering classes in just about every imaginable form of exercise.

Gyms

With the densely populated south zone neighborhoods squeezed along the coast from Flamengo to Ipanema, residents burst onto the sands to work out, jog, cycle, or just to let off steam. Most Cariocas use their nearest beach as a free open-air gym, complete with work-out stations, jogging tracks, and giant saltwater pool—the Atlantic Ocean. However, there are many fitness clubs in the city, which offer personal trainers and a full range of classes, from boxing to yoga; and the smarter hotels usually have a small gym for guests.

A! Body Tech
www.abodytech.com.br

- Av. N. S. de Copacabana 801
  Copacabana - ℘21 3816 1791

- Rua Visconde de Pirajá 365B
  Ipanema - ℘21 2523 3898/1796

Estação do Corpo
www.www.estacaodocorpo.com.br
R$60,00 per day or R$30,00 after 1pm.
Also has a pool and sauna.

- Av. Borges de Medeiros 1426
  Lagoa - ℘21 2108 3902/2108 3903

Spas

Considering the Cariocas' preoccupation with the body beautiful, the city does not have an abundance of spas. If you want to drop in at one, they can be found at luxury hotels and shopping malls. Outside of Rio it is a different story, with many spas and luxury retreats in the quiet of the surrounding countryside.

Copacabana Palace Hotel
Av. Atlântica 1702
℘21 2548 7070
www.copacabanapalace.com.br

Espaço Nirvana
Jockey Club do Rio de Janeiro
Praça Santos Dumont 31
Gavea
℘21 2187 0100
www.enirvana.com.br

Le Spa
Hotel Santa Teresa
Rua Felício dos Santos
Santa Teresa
℘21 3380 0200
www.santateresahotel.com

Spa Lancome
Hotel Fasano,
Av. Vieira Souto 80
Ipanema
℘21 3202 4000
www.fasano.com.br

Saison Spa
Rua Ministro Armando Alencar 40
Itaipava—Petrópolis
℘24 2222 2380
www.saison.com.br

Spa Posse do Corpo
Avenida Noêmia Alves Rattes 134
Posse—Petrópolis
℘24 2259 3333
www.spapossedocorpo.com.br

Spa Maria Bonita
Rodovia Teresópolis–Friburgo km 56
Nova Friburgo
℘22 2543 1212
www.spamariabonita.com.br

Yoga

Many of the gyms and clubs offer courses in yoga, which is becoming an increasingly popular activity in Rio. There are also yoga centers, which run specialized courses and resources.

Academia Hermógenes de Yoga
Rua Uruguaiana 118
Centro
☎21 2224 9189
www.profhermogenes.com.br

Blyss Yoga
Rua Visconde de Pirajá 318
Ipanema
☎21 3627 0108
www.blyss.com.br

Kailasa Filosofia Yoga Terapias
Travessia Angrense 14/304
Copacabana
☎21 2549 1707
www.tantrayoga.com.br

Cultural Sports

CAPOEIRA

This martial art in the form of dance was originally brought to Brazil by Angolan slaves who then developed the practice.

The twirling, cartwheeling *capoeiristas* perform in pairs inside a circle, or *roda*, of musicians. The main accompaniment is the metallic sound of the *berimbau*, a single-stringed bow-like instrument; as well as rattles, tambourines, clapping, and chants, or *toques*.

The spectacle for spectators is the graceful intertwining of bodies to the hypnotic rhythm of the music; the contestants aren't supposed to make contact.

Although Bahia is the capital of capoeira in Brazil, there are many teachers and clubs in Rio where visitors can take classes or watch *capoeiristas*. Or late on Friday afternoons you can sometimes see informal street performances in the south zone beaches area.

Centro de Capoeira Angola do Rio de Janeiro
Rua do Catete 164
Catete *(opposite Catete Metrô station)*
☎21 9954 3659/2558 8015
http://ccarj.magaweb.com.br

Associão Lagoa Azul Capoeira
Av. Borges de Medeiros
Lagoa
☎21 2539 1809
www.lagoaazulcapoeira.com

Grupo de Capoeira Angola and Centro Cultural Senzala
Clube Copa Leme
Ladeira Ary Barroso 1
Leme
☎21 3209 2518/8232 8745

JIU-JITSU

Many of the more traditional martial art forms are also popular in Rio, including Jiu-jitsu. The best places to go for classes are the gyms and clubs (☝*see other listings on these two pages)*, or some specialists and sports tour operators, including:

Fightzone
Rua Francisco Sá 36
Copacabana *(Posto 6)*
☎21 2287 1423

Academia Brazilian Fight
Rua Rodrigo de Brito 11
Botafogo
☎21 2591 7893/9393 1200

Gracie Barra Rio Sport Center
Av. Ayrton Senna 2541
Barra da Tijuca
☎21 2480 8420/7845 7492

Rio Sports Tours
Rua Buenos Aires 57
Centro
Skype: talkto_francis
www.riosportstour.com

INDEX

INDEX

WHERE TO STAY

WHERE TO EAT

MAPS AND MAP LEGEND

★★★   **Highly recommended**
★★   **Recommended**
★   **Interesting**

Sight symbols

▭●▭▭	Recommended itineraries with departure point		
✝ ♰ ⊠	Church, chapel – Synagogue	▭	Building described
●	Town described	▭	Other building
■ ▲	Other points of interest	�**ı**	Statue - Monument
☆ ⛪	Fort – Mission	🛈	Visitor information
♒	Beach	☀ ⩔	Panorama – View

Other symbols

071	Other route		Major city thoroughfare
═══	Highway, bridge	═══	Major city thoroughfare
═══	Toll highway, interchange	═══	City street with median
═══	Divided highway	◄──	One-way street
═══	Major, minor route	═══	Pedestrian Street
╲ 40 ╱	Distance in miles	≠≡≠	Tunnel
2149 →	Pass, elevation (feet)	✉	Main post office
△ 6288	Mtn. peak, elevation (feet)	✚	Hospital
✈ ✦	Airport – Airfield	🚌	Bus station
⛴	Ferry: Cars and passengers	●	Metrô station
⛴	Ferry: Passengers only	@	Internet Cafe
–··—··—	International boundary	B	Bank
─ ─ ─ ─	State boundary, provincial boundary	⊥⊥	Cemetery
		⟊	Swamp

Recreation

────	Bondinho	⬭ ⚑	Stadium – Golf course

All maps are oriented north, unless otherwise indicated by a directional arrow.